PARENTECTOMY

A Narrative Ethnography of 30 Cases of Parental Alienation and What to Do about It

CHRISTINE GIANCARLO

Parentectomy

Tellwell Talent
www.tellwell.ca

ISBN
978-0-2288-0806-0 (Hardcover)
978-0-2288-0805-3 (Paperback)
978-0-2288-0807-7 (eBook)

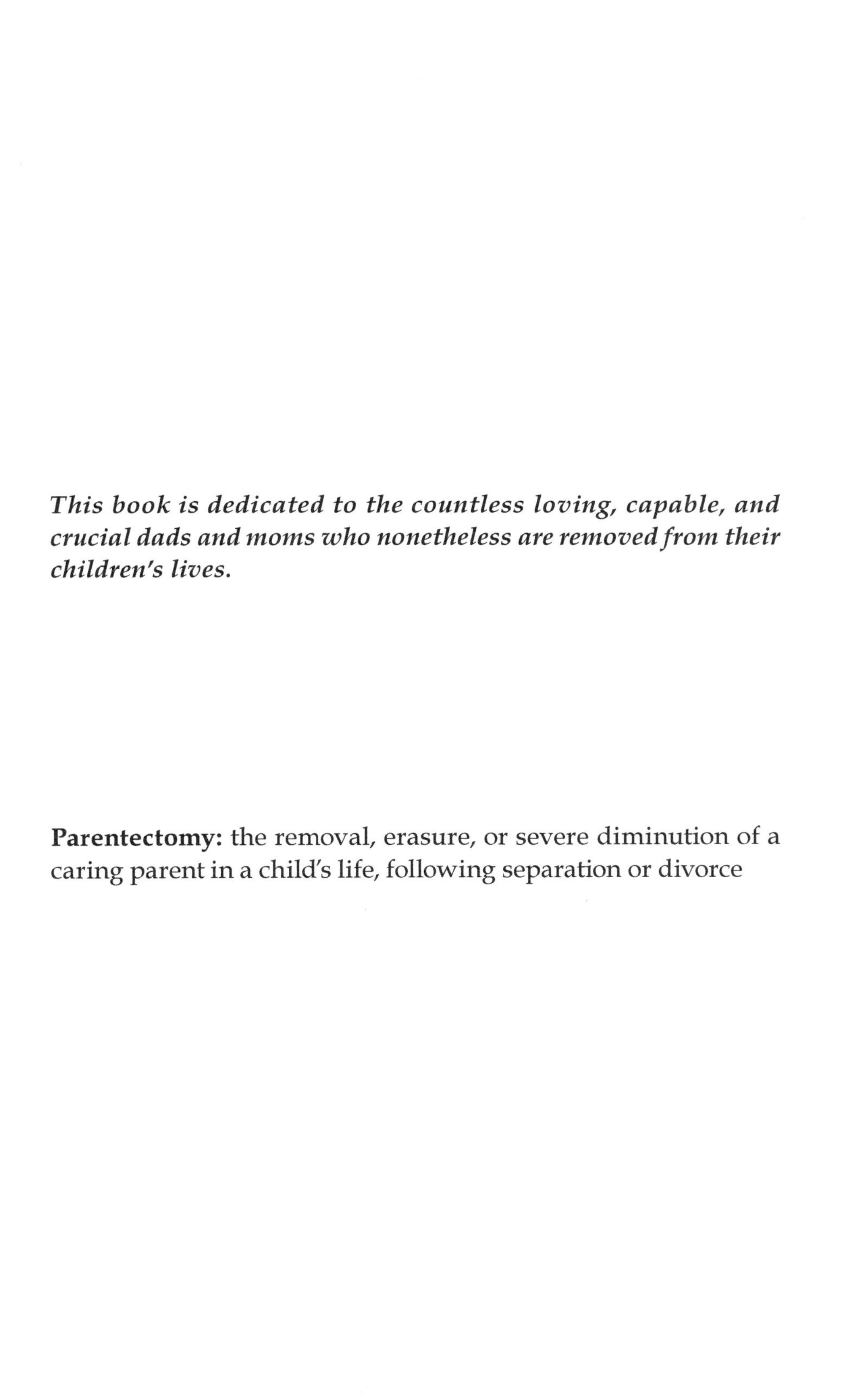

This book is dedicated to the countless loving, capable, and crucial dads and moms who nonetheless are removed from their children's lives.

Parentectomy: the removal, erasure, or severe diminution of a caring parent in a child's life, following separation or divorce

August, 2006

- Suzanne, alienator.
    - *"Stop all legal action immediately or you won't see your children again"*

November 19, 2005

- Emily, 11, in the passenger seat while I was driving her to our house with her sister Madison in the backseat, tearfully blurted out to us:
    - *"I'm just so confused. I really am so confused".*

July 20, 2008

- Emily, 14, one evening as she showed us the bandages on her cut wrists:
    - *"I just do it when I'm stressed out; I can't help it".*

November 18, 2008 10:24 pm

- *"Dad its *Madison* (pseudonym)*. I am still able to come up this weekend"(sic)*

    -then…

November 21, 2008 10:15 am

- *Madison* (pseudonym):

    "I cant go this weekend. Im really distracted and i dont know how much or when the bus is. And im just really stressed. can you understand. (sic)"

Foreword

This book is about a social crisis that, until November of 2004, I had never heard of. I was a 42-year-old divorcee living in Calgary with two happy, productive children and an ex-husband who continued to be an excellent dad and co-parent, following our divorce.

I met Grant, my second husband, on November 14 of 2004 and his three daughters a few months later. In 2015, I decided to write a book based on my years with Grant, and the other 27 stories from our research study, *Kids Come Last: The Effect of Family Law Involvement in Parental Alienation (2015)*, with follow-up in 2017. I have also included 2 more case-stories that are ongoing and still embroiled in the family law quagmire as of late-2018. *Parentectomy* is a narrative ethnography, a compilation of verified empirical accounts, including my own, of parental alienation and a family law system that declares "best interests of the child" in policy but not in practice. Real given names of most participants have been retained on their request. All other involved parties in each story have been given pseudonyms.

Each of the 30 parents, named *"participants"* in my interviews, trusted me with his or her story of parental alienation. Each participant had been systematically removed from their child(ren)'s life through a campaign of denigration launched by their ex-spouse, the *"alienator."* These alienated parents were capable, loving influences on their children, but became erased through the hatred, greed and mental illness of their ex-spouses. As a last resort, each of these targeted parents, mostly dads, sought legal intervention. The Family Law system failed them.

I felt it imperative that our resultant rich database of child abuse, in the form of parental alienation, enabled by our family law system, be made public. My research associate, Kara Rottmann, not only painstakingly reviewed and co-analyzed all participants' transcripts from my recorded interviews , she compiled our literature review and helped in myriad ways to get this book published.

The Introduction describes the background of the phenomenon of parental alienation with a summary to date of its abundant solid, globally documented, evidence-based, peer-reviewed literature. The reasons why and how parents become alienators is explored from a psychiatric and psychological perspective. I discuss the current failure of the Family Law system, in Canada and internationally, as a means of averting and resolving parental alienation.

Chapters 1 and 2 are my story of witnessing parental alienation first-hand through my marriage to Grant. With a heavy heart, I wrote those chapters, immersed again in the love but futility of our desire to be a family, with Grant's daughters first and foremost their mother's and father's children. My son and daughter were doing well; I wanted that for my three stepdaughters as well. But it was not to be.

Chapters 3 through 31 are the other 29 narratives from my voice-recorded face-to-face interviews. Together these cases represent a powerful testament to the need for a Family Law system overhaul and public recognition that children need both parents.

To eradicate parental alienation, a two-pronged approach is needed: Chapter 32 suggests a multifaceted means of preventing the abuse from occurring in the first place, through appropriate legislation, education and mental health initiatives. Where children are already being subjected to this form of child abuse, a model for intervention which actually works, has already been proven to be successful, removes children from the abuse and re-establishes a healthy family dynamic. Above all, Chapter 32 is about love.

Since there is already a multitude of expertise and guidance provided globally by competent mental health experts, support and awareness organizations, we decided to include a Bibliography of helpful literature. There is no lack of empirical evidence that parental alienation is an urgent social issue. We fervently hope that this book will help to illuminate, prevent, and resolve parental alienation in the *Best Interests of the Child*.

Introduction: Anatomy of a Parentectomy

Empirical:

Based on, concerned with, or verifiable by observation or experience rather than theory or pure logic.

> *'they provided considerable empirical evidence to support their argument'*

-Oxford Living Dictionary, 2018

I have heard judges, lawyers, law enforcers, and educators claim that there is no empirical evidence for the existence or diagnosis of parental alienation. This is a book of empirical evidence; 30 cases of it. It is about 30 alienated parents and their 73 biological children, all of whom suffered the loss of a child or a parent, at the hands of the other parent.

What is Parental Alienation?

Parent duos, following separation or divorce, are often mislabeled, especially by the family law systems, as "high-conflict". But they are not. It takes two to tango and in parental alienation, there is only one alienator. The targeted, alienated, parent consistently attempts to placate the other parent, the alienator, in hopes of maintaining their relationship with their children. Parental alienation is a campaign of denigration by one parent, with the children as unwitting and later willing, participants, against the other parent. Its goal is to destroy the relationship between the alienated parent and his or her children[1].

In all cases, parental alienation is unique from more common strained parent-child relationships related to developmental factors such as age, gender preferences, or temporary expected reactions to the parental relationship split. These children of alienation all had positive relationships with their targeted parent prior to the separation of their parents[2]. Cases of parental alienation are separate from justified rejection or realistic estrangement of a parent due to abuse, neglect or significantly compromised parenting[3].

The validity of parental alienation is well established and almost universally accepted by mental health professionals, including psychiatrists, psychologists, social workers and family counselors who assess and treat children of "high-conflict" divorces. Since 2010, well over 100 such academics and practitioners from 30 countries have confirmed the reality of parental alienation and they comprise the *International Council on Shared Parenting.*

Strategies used by alienators usually include the following: withdrawing love if the child indicates affection for the rejected parent, thereby instilling fear in the child and increasing his or her dependency on the alienating parent; noncompliance with court-ordered or agreed-to parenting time and contact; interference with the child's email and phone contacts; seeking restraining and supervised visitation orders, based on unfounded allegations of abuse perpetrated by the targeted parent; failing to pass on to the child phone calls, messages and letters from the targeted parent; interference to access of information regarding the child, such as school, medical or social records and events; limited or

---

1 Bernet, 2010.

2 Kelly & Johnston, 2001.

3 Fidler, Bala & Saini, 2013.

prevented contact with the alienated parent's extended family; and a prohibition from any reference to the other parent[4].

An alienating parent may be of either sex. That said, alienation tends to be perpetrated by the parent with custody or primary care of children and this is usually the mother. If primary care or custody were most often granted to fathers instead, alienators would likely more often be fathers. Canadian data from 1994 show that of 47,667 children about whom there was a custody decision, 33,164 (70%) were placed in sole-custody arrangements with their mother. And half of these children would eventually lose all contact with their fathers[5]. Such dads have been wrongly labeled "deadbeat dads", which suggests they are remiss in their child maintenance payments or are absentee fathers through their own fault. Instead, the vast majority of alienated dads have always paid Child Maintenance as per the Federal Child Support Guidelines, yet these fathers have little or no access to their children[6].

Not much has changed. In 2017, shared parenting (each parent has the child at least 40% of the time) in Canada was negotiated or court-ordered in less than 20% of custody cases. And most of these were mutually agreed upon, not ordered by a judge. Of that 20%, only half were for equal (50/50) parenting time[7]. That means only *10% of children will have equal time with each of their parents following their relationship split.* The current Canadian norm in family law court decisions is known as "joint legal custody" which assigns 21% parenting time to the non-custodial parent[8]. Children who grow up without fathers in their lives are far more likely to experience school drop-out, substance abuse, criminal

4 Vassiliou & Cartwright, 2001; Johnston, Walters & Olesen, 2005b; Baker, 2006; Baker & Darnall, 2006.

5 Kruk, 1998.

6 Braver & O'Connell, 1998.

7 Bala et al, 2007

8 L.L v C.M, 2013

behaviour and be antisocial. Indeed, fatherlessness is an urgent social problem[9].

Why would any parent alienate their children from the other parent?

Children share half of each of their parent's genes. To teach a child to hate a parent is to teach that child to hate one-half of his or her self[10]. A child loves its parents and, from an evolutionary point of view, seeks to maximize for itself each parent's care and attention. This strategy provides its best chance to survive and thrive; the same goes for an adopted child. A parent, in turn, dotes on his or her children out of love but also out of self-interest; to pass on his or her genes. In addition, biological *and* adopted children provide some care giving "insurance" for their aging parents. Children are never the winners in cases of parental alienation. One parent can only provide 50% of possible total parental investment. A parent who is an alienator is not a competent parent, prioritizing his or her needs above those of their child. Alienated parents tend to be competent, loving, and productive. In parental alienation, the child loses a good parent, and is held hostage by a dangerous one.

To date, research shows that alienators do so for one, or a combination, of three main reasons: revenge; money; and most prevalent, perhaps even ubiquitous, their own mental illness in the form of Cluster B Personality Disorders[11]. In cases of revenge, an ex-spouse or partner may be so overwhelmed and devastated by the relationship breakdown that hatred becomes that parent's prime motivator. Such a parent is more fixated on destroying their former partner than on raising a healthy child. All too often, friends and family become unwitting enablers in these revenge campaigns, providing misguided support to the alienator by their

9 Gottlieb, 2012
10 Baker, 2007
11 American Psychiatric Association, 2013

actions and sympathetic comments. Enablers ramp up the campaign of denigration by agreeing with, even adding to, the insults, put-downs and obstacles thrown in the path of the targeted parent. In conversation, an outsider attuned to the tactics used by vengeful alienators will hear "red-flag" words and assertions from the "injured" ex-partner about the other party. Derogatory nicknames, claims of abuse to their children or themselves, and supposed examples of parenting incompetence are common diatribes used against the alienated parent.

Money is a powerful incentive to lie about the other parent, since family law systems, especially Child and Spousal Support and Maintenance programs reward parents who can achieve more parenting time than 40%. A parent who has at least 60% parenting time is entitled to maximum child support by the payor, the other parent (until recently called a "debtor" by the Maintenance and Enforcement Program of Alberta). The custodial parent with 60 (or more) % parenting time is considered to have "Sole Custody" for Child Support calculations. Even if one parent has a tiny parenting-time advantage over the other parent, his or her child support will be greater than if they had equal time[12]. And there is no requirement of accountability for the receiving parent of child support. Though he or she is supposed to use that money to maximize the well being of their children, in reality this money can be used for any purpose the custodial parent so desires. In cases of parental alienation, this monthly income is nothing short of a windfall.

The most dangerous and pervasive reason for parental alienation is mental illness in the form of Cluster B personality disorders[13]. Alienators tend to be Narcissistic or Borderline. In either diagnosis, these alienating parents suffer impairments in personality (self and interpersonal) functioning and pathological personality traits. Their identity and self-esteem are dependent

12 Government of Canada, 2017

13 Bernet, 2010; Childress, 2016; Woodall & Woodall, 2017

on excessive reference to others and they lack emotional regulation. Approval from others is extremely important and they set unreasonably high personal standards in order to perceive themselves as exceptional. Alternatively, though, alienators may set their personal standards very low based on their sense of entitlement. Impairments to interpersonal functioning include a compromised or absence of empathy: instead, they are prone to feel slighted or insulted; a focus on the flaws or vulnerabilities of others; and poor quality, unstable intimate relationships based on mistrust and neediness.

Pathological personality traits include frequent mood changes; emotions that are easily aroused, intense, and often out of proportion reactions to events and circumstances; anxiety, fear around uncertainty or losing control; separation insecurity; depressivity causing feelings of hopelessness, shame and suicidal ideations; impulsivity, impatience and self-harm under emotional distress; risk-taking; and especially, antagonism manifested as hostility and angry outbursts[14]. A model by Dr. Craig Childress of Attachment-Based Parental Alienation (AB-PA), explains a parent engaging in "pathological parenting" as due to his or her own childhood trauma manifested in Cluster B Narcissism or Borderline personality[15]. This model is rapidly gaining ground internationally.

Alienators, intentionally or unintentionally, destroy not only their ex-partner, the other parent, but their children as well. An alienating parent creates a cult-like manipulative power over his or her children, a kind of Stockholm Syndrome[16]. Children who are subjected to the influence of an alienating parent resist at first, aching to see their beloved, but absent, parent but soon learn that the path of least resistance ensures a modicum of peace in the alienator's home. In time, children of parental alienation wholeheartedly turn against their targeted parent.

---

14 American Psychiatric Association, 2013

15 Childress, 2016

16 Merriam-Webster Dictionary, 2018

What are the consequences to children of parental alienation?

In the Mind of the Alienated Child

> *"In the hidden and darkest places of the alienated child's mind lie secrets in waiting.*
>
> *Those hidden and darkest places are unknown to the child but they exist.*
>
> *A diverticulitis of the psyche, passages leading to places inhabited by demons.*
>
> *This is why madness grows in the mind of the child and as they grow bigger the vines and the tangles of things they should not be involved in takes hold.*
>
> *As the mind grows, unconscious of alleyways connecting those things which should be unknown but are not, demons feed from the anxiety created by the packets of poison lying deeply within.*
>
> *Family secrets".*
>
> -Karen Woodall, blog post 15960, April 27, 2018

Parental alienation syndrome (PAS) occurs when one parent in a post-custody separation or divorce arrangement successfully manipulates their child to turn against the other parent. PAS is fostered when the alienating parent portrays the targeted parent as unsafe, unavailable, and unworthy. The alienator also lets the child know that he or she will become less emotionally and physically available to that child if it pursues a positive relationship with its targeted parent. Alienated children show black and white, rigid thinking and are more disturbed overall than other kids in high-conflict divorces. Severely alienated children show flat emotionality but are also likely to behave very inappropriately at times, at least in the presence of the rejected parent. Expressions of oppositional defiance, hatred, rage, rudeness, swearing, hanging up the phone, stealing, lying, keeping secrets from, and spying on, the rejected parent are all commonly reported in PAS children[17].

In the majority of cases, the child's behaviour can indicate a split identity; he or she may show affection to the targeted parent when the alienator is absent, but repulsion or defiance to that same parent when the alienator is present. Such children practice deception to placate the favoured parent. Most damaging, PAS children show temperament, personality and developmental vulnerabilities: They are anxious, fearful, passive, have low self-esteem and lack resiliency[18]. And they are angrier than non-alienated children and more likely to develop substance abuse, eating disorders and sleep problems. These children are often at-risk, truant, and have difficulties forming and keeping meaningful relationships. Adults who were alienated as children often maintain low self-esteem into adulthood[19]. Children who have suffered parental alienation carry the scars for life.

In September of 2014 in Alberta, Canada, 50-year-old Laura Coward murdered her 9-year-old daughter, Amber Lucius. Coward was angry that custody had been awarded to Amber's father. Three days before Amber was drugged and burned by Coward, her parents' divorce was finalized, confirming her father would have full custody. The girl had been visiting her mother on the Labour Day long weekend and was supposed to be returned to her father two days before her body was found. Coward drove with her trusting, unsuspecting daughter to a rural property and there gave her sleeping pills she had stolen from a friend before setting her SUV on fire with Amber inside. The little girl's body was found in the burned-out SUV that had been parked on a rural road near Sundre, about 100 kilometres northwest of Calgary. Justice Scott Brooker, of the Court of Queen's Bench, said, following Coward's 2017 conviction that her life sentence must

17 Gardner, 1992

18 Johnston, Walters & Olesen, 2005c

19 Baker, 2007

reflect "society's disgust and outrage". Duane Lucius, Amber's father, told the media that "As a father, I have had to bury my child and nothing will bring her back. I can only hope that other children are not being used as bargaining chips in a divorce or used to hurt the other parent."[20].

In April of 2018, in Mamaroneck, New York, 2.5-year-old Gabriella Maria Boyd, was stabbed to death by her 28-year-old mother, Cynthia Arce. Sources described Arce as a "troubled" person. Three days before Gabriella's death, her father, Stephen Boyd, was granted temporary physical custody of his daughter. The toddler had been living with her mother and grandmother. Stephen went with the court order and the police to the home where Arce refused to surrender Gabriella. Police took the position that they could not enter the house. The following day, after a 911 call about an injured girl, police again went to Arce's home where she attacked them with a knife. Officers tasered Gabriella's mother, then took both females to hospital where Gabriella died[21].

These chilling events are not isolated[22]. Mothers and fathers who alienate are child abusers; but the manifestation and degree of abuse varies. Two major risk factors related to the occurrence of alienation are the parents' mental health status and the degree of involvement the child has in his or her parents' dispute[23]. Alienators involve their children in their legal battles and romantic relationships, lacking appropriate parental boundaries. The pre-adolescent stage of development is most common for the onset of alienation. Teenagers are more likely to become alienated from a parent than younger children are, perhaps due in part to the adolescent's desire for its own autonomy and its perception of duty to "protect" the alienator[24].

---

20 Grant, 2017

21 CBS, 2018

22 Central Ohio Parental Alienation, 2018

23 Steinberger, 2006a

24 Fidler, Bala & Saini, 2013

What rights do children have?

Almost all countries in the world have ratified the *United Nations Convention on the Rights of the Child* which clearly commits to "the best interests of the child" as its primary consideration, "ensuring the child such protection and care as is necessary for his or her well-being; taking into account the rights and duties of his or her parents, legal guardians, or other individuals legally responsible for him or her, and that those institutions, services and facilities responsible for the care or protection of children conform with the standards established by competent authorities" (Article 3). Then, "... a child whose parents reside in different States shall have the right to maintain on a regular basis, save in exceptional circumstances, personal relations and direct contacts with both parents" (Article 10). "States Parties shall assure to the child who is capable of forming his or her own views the right to express those views freely in all matters affecting the child, the views of the child being given due weight in accordance with the age and maturity of the child" (Article 12). "States Parties shall take all appropriate measures to promote physical and psychological recovery and social reintegration of a child victim of: any form of neglect, exploitation, or abuse; torture or any other form of cruel, inhuman or degrading treatment or punishment; or armed conflicts. Such recovery and reintegration shall take place in an environment which fosters the health, self-respect and dignity of the child" (Article 39)[25].

In 2012, the *Committee on the Rights of the Child* added "The legal reasoning of all judicial and administrative judgments and decisions should also be based on this principle, specifying the criteria used in the individual assessment of the best interests of the child". The United Nations thereby called for a strengthening of efforts so that decisions regarding children must be made in the child's best interests, the child's voice should be freely expressed if/when

25 United Nations Convention on the Rights of the Child, 1990

the child is capable of forming his or her own views, and it has resolved to maintain the parent-child relationships or reunify the child with both his or her parents. Although the Convention does not have the same legal force as legislation or the constitution of a country, it is cited by the courts in many jurisdictions as having persuasive value in interpreting and applying the law[26].

In December of 1998, an exhaustive report commissioned by the Parliament of Canada, entitled *For the Sake of the Children,* was published by the Special Joint Committee on Child Custody and Access. The summary of recommendations for change promoted the overarching mandate of "best interests of the child" and included that the Divorce Act (1985) be amended to add a preamble alluding to: the relevant principles of the United Nations Convention on the Rights of the Child; the principle that divorced parents and their children are entitled to a close and continuous relationship with one another; and that "shared parenting" become the norm in terminology and practice, replacing "custody" and "access"[27]. The 48 recommendations of that report, which included 39 public hearings, 500 witnesses, and 48 recommendations for change were never implemented. The legislative reform pillar of the Strategy was Bill C-22, which would have amended the Divorce Act, the Family Orders and Agreements Enforcement Assistance Act, and the Garnishment, Attachment and Pension Diversion Act, died on the Order Paper in 2003[28].

Currently, Canada's Divorce Act (1985) states the following: "In making an order under this section, the court shall give effect to the principle that a child of the marriage should have as much contact with each spouse as is consistent with the best interests of the child and, for that purpose, shall take into consideration the willingness of the person for whom custody is sought to facilitate such contact".

26 Divorce Law in Canada, 2008

27 Parliament of Canada, 1998

28 Divorce Law in Canada, 2008

In Canada, orders can be registered with a Maintenance Enforcement Program (MEP in Alberta[29]; various provinces and territories each have their own program) by either parent having a Maintenance Order. These programs monitor and enforce court-ordered child and spousal support. In cases of default by the payor, a program has the legislative authority to take steps to enforce the support owed. These collection tools include: registrations at the Land Titles Office and the Personal Property Registry; wage, non-wage and federal support deduction notices; federal license and passport denial; motor vehicle restrictions; and driver's license cancellations. Maintenance Enforcement does not deal with issues relating to parenting time, child access or custody. There is no organization that deals with monitoring and enforcement of parenting time, child access, or custody[30].

The Family Law Act of Alberta clearly states that "In all proceedings under this

Part except proceedings under section 20, the court shall take into consideration only the best interests of the child"[31] And "In determining what is in the best interests of a child, the court shall (a) ensure the greatest possible protection of the child's physical, psychological and emotional safety, and (b) consider all the child's needs and circumstances…"[32]. So, consistent with the United Nations Convention on the Rights of the Child and Canada's Divorce Act, both Alberta's and British Columbia's[33]Family Law Acts confirm that *best interests of the child* are the priority in legislation and in practice when dealing with children's welfare following separation/divorce of the parental relationship. But, there is no legal provision to enforce this priority.

29 Alberta Justice and Solicitor General, 2018

30 Divorce Law in Canada, 2008

31 Family Law Act of Alberta, 2003, 18(1), p.20

32 Family Law Act of Alberta, 2003, 18(2), p.20.

33 Family Law Act of British Columbia, 2011, 4(37).

How does family law involvement affect parental alienation outcomes?

Alienated parents turn to Family Law and the judicial system when they have exhausted other means of intervention and reconciliation to help their children. Legal involvement is a last-ditch effort which undoubtedly carries enormous costs in terms of children's distress, increased alienation tactics by the alienating parent, and emotional and financial hardship, sometimes ruin, for the targeted parent.

The 30 stories of parental alienation in this book are the result of my face-to-face, one-on-one recorded interviews with each of these targeted parents and two grandparents. Our published study, *Kids Come Last*, found that instead of the legal system providing relief and rebuilding for affected families, harm increased. We discovered four major barriers to effective resolution of parental alienation[34]. Here is what we found:

1. *Invoking legal involvement exacerbates the alienation.*

Though these targeted parents sought legal involvement to remedy the parental alienation they were experiencing, none of them succeeded in achieving this goal. Instead, the legal case served as a catalyst to greater levels of alienation. Court action initiated by the targeted parent spurred the alienator on to increase alienation tactics, as a means of "getting revenge" on the other parent. Legal involvement seemed to reinforce the misguided belief in the children that the targeted parent was "out to get" the alienating parent. The fact that each alienated parent had to pursue legal options out of desperation was not communicated to the children. Had the targeted parent informed his or her children that this was the case, the alienator could use the information as ammunition to "prove" the other parent was lying to their children. It was, however, commonplace for the alienator to tell their children

34 Giancarlo & Rottmann, 2015

every detail of the legal case, exaggerating and spinning the truth as needed to justify their contempt for the targeted parent.

A court case is expensive, and since 28 (93%) targeted parents hired lawyers to represent them, financial hardship on the alienated parent was an inevitable result; even the two dads who were self-represented spent a substantial amount on travel, lost work days, court application fees, and court-directed therapy and assessment fees. Due to legal and associated costs, all targeted parents reported a loss in quality of life for themselves and their alienated children. A staggering 24 (79%) lost their homes through: i) being unable to pay the mortgage or rent, ii) having a lien put on their home by a lawyer, iii) paying arrears in child maintenance or due to MEP penalties, or iv) losing his or her job due to stress-related issues or downsizing. The emotional drain on these alienated parents was palpable. The pain of experiencing alienation combined with PAS behaviours in some of the children caused significant emotional damage to the targeted parents. Three of these parents had been diagnosed with post-traumatic stress syndrome (PTSD). Similarly, depression was a common complaint with 22 (73%) alienated parents currently or previously prescribed anti-depressant medications.

2. *Alienating parents are uncooperative in potential resolution initiatives.*

In 5 (17%) of the interviews, mental illness in the form of personality disorders had been diagnosed in the alienating parent. Four of these individuals were diagnosed while the parents were still cohabiting prior to the relationship split. The disorders mentioned were Narcissism, Borderline, and Antisocial. Since these disorders have symptoms that include impairments in personality functioning and the presence of pathological personality traits, it is likely that these alienators have entrenched personality disorders that prevent them from cooperating in any interventions to stop their campaigns of alienation (American Psychiatric Association, 2013). In every case, alienators had already demonstrated their disregard for both the targeted parent and justice system through their noncompliance with parenting orders and other reunification efforts. After all, alienating parents measure success by their ability to sever the other parent from their children's lives.

3. *Legal professionals maximize their profits by prolonging these cases.*

Stalling tactics used by lawyers were reported by 23 (76%) of the alienated parents. Since there is no benefit to lawyers who conclude their cases in a timely fashion, and since they are rewarded for the number of billable hours they contribute to their law firms, it was, and is, in lawyers' best interest to prolong their cases. Various tactics were used by lawyers including: i) stalling and missing deadlines to return documents to the opposing party's lawyer or the case management judge, ii) adding unnecessary and/or inappropriate actions to the case, iii) delaying follow-up court dates and case reviews, iv) suggesting additional counseling with vague expectations of timelines and outcomes, v) initiating inappropriate counseling and counselors for the parents due to lack of competency in managing parental alienation cases, and vi) writing unnecessary or superfluous emails and other communications with clients.

4. *Legal and non-legal, court-directed professionals are ill-equipped to manage alienation clients and cases.*

Many judges and lawyers involved in these parental alienation cases (i) were unprepared for court, (ii) refused to read affidavits, (iii) failed to challenge affidavits, (iv) relied on hearsay evidence from lawyers of the alienating parent, (v) committed perjury, and were noncompliant with their Judicial[35] and/or Legal[36] Codes of Conduct, such as restricting witnesses in the courtroom to only those in support of the alienator.

Although academic and clinical instructional resources on diagnoses, appropriate intervention, and treatment for parental alienation have been readily available since the 1980s, 26 (87%) of

35 Canadian Judicial Council, 2018

36 Alberta Queen's Printer, 2013.

these cases were not argued on the basis of parental alienation. Instead, lawyers acting on behalf of targeted parents presented their cases as due to "high-conflict", "parenting style difference", "child rebellion", or even "jealousy". Almost all the alienated parents, 27 (90%), reported that mental health professionals had been directed by the court to provide counseling or therapy to their children and in some cases, to the parents, either with or without their children. This court-ordered intervention was either too late, too vague, unenforced, or inappropriate. None of these parents were provided with a timeline for the counseling process, nor were they informed of what the process and expected outcomes were. In 15 (50%) cases, psychological assessment of the children was court-ordered yet occurred in only 5 (17%). Twenty (68%) targeted parents reported inappropriate court orders and interventions, given the state of their children's health, ongoing or accelerated parental alienation, or confirmation bias on the part of the judge.

Most often, the nature of the therapy ordered for the children and alienated parent was inappropriate given the entrenched PAS of the children. Five (17%) targeted parents were ordered to, and did, attend counseling sessions, but were instructed by the psychologist or lawyer to remain silent or to "only say positive things" to the children. By all accounts, these sessions appeared to be opportunities for the children to reinforce their professed hatred and disgust for their targeted parent.

Confirmation bias on the part of judges occurred when their decisions about the parents were based on their own preconceived notions. As examples, 24 (80%) fathers reported the judge having used gender-biased, discriminatory language based on an assumption of "deadbeat dad", "Disneyland dad" or "less important parent". Twenty-six (87%) alienated parents had been subjected to penalties imposed by the court as a result of the alienator making false allegations against, or convoluting events about, the targeted parent. These penalties were of four types: Restraining orders in 16 (54%) cases, supervised visits in 9 (30%) cases, police arrest in 6 (20%) cases, and MEP harassment in 17 (57%) cases.

At least two judges presided over each of 25 (83%) cases and there were more than three judges involved in 13 (43%) of them. Each of these participants reported judges showing a lack of background case history or inconsistency with, or ignorance of, decisions made previously by other judges in the same case. In one father's case, during proceedings in one court appearance, the judge told this alienated parent that he was not going to read the affidavits that the father, and mother, had each submitted to the court. This judge stated that the history of the case was irrelevant to his decision. Then, later in the hearing, the same judge said that he would adhere to "status quo".

Though there are many professionals, including legal ones, who *do* understand and want to prevent and resolve parental alienation, most are either unable or unwilling to achieve these goals. The family law system in Canada, and in most countries, remains at best, toothless and at worst, corrupt. In the meantime, this urgent social problem continues to mould children into wounded adults. Targeted parents are hamstrung in their efforts to better their children's lives, suffering mental and physical devastation as a result. Alienators, in desperate need of appropriate psychiatric and psychological treatment, are instead enabled to perpetuate a cycle of abuse at massive socioeconomic cost. These are the stories of 30 targeted parents and their children, told in their own voices through the transcripts of our in-person interviews.

Contents

Foreword v
Introduction: Anatomy of a Parentectomy vii

Chapter 1: Grant 1
Chapter 2: Kids Come Last 61
Chapter 3: Cliff 89
Chapter 4: Russ 103
Chapter 5: Gloria 113
Chapter 6: Larry 133
Chapter 7: Rob 139
Chapter 8: Jimmy 149
Chapter 9: Dave 169
Chapter 10: Ed 185
Chapter 11: David 207
Chapter 12: Arnie 221
Chapter 13: Terry 225
Chapter 14: Mark 231
Chapter 15: Chris 243
Chapter 16: Rene 263
Chapter 17: Carla 273
Chapter 18: Jason 299
Chapter 19: Kath 315
Chapter 20: Greg 327
Chapter 21: Raina 337
Chapter 22: Kier 347
Chapter 23: Sarah 357
Chapter 24: Hailey 365

Chapter 25: Jerry 377
Chapter 26: Craig 393
Chapter 27: John 409
Chapter 28: Orlin 425
Chapter 29: Tom 437
Chapter 30: Jim 467
Chapter 31: Don 499
Chapter 32: Best Interests of the Child 525

Appendix: Families in this book 533
Bibliography 535
Acknowledgements 553

GRANT

CHAPTER 1

GRANT

Grant was a good dad. And he was my husband. I could never have imagined that our life together would be destroyed by parental alienation and the Family Law system in Alberta. This is our story.

2004

I met Grant in 2004. On a cold, dreary November day, we hiked a snow-covered trail in Kananaskis and talked about our histories… how I had divorced but managed to maintain a healthy united alliance with my ex-husband for our two kids… and how Grant tried to maintain a loving, productive relationship with his three young daughters, now 10, 11 and 15, despite an ex-wife with a diagnosed Cluster B personality disorder. Life had been tough through the divorce and since, he told me. Eleven years into his first marriage, he had been blind-sided by arriving home early to find his then-wife, Suzanne, and her male "client" fumbling to re-fasten their clothing as they came down the stairs of the family home in Brooks, Alberta, his three little daughters in the basement watching television. Grant told his wife their marriage was over and she needed to move out.

Several months passed, and Suzanne moved into the trailer of her then-boyfriend, taking all three daughters with her. The eldest, Laura, was nine, Madison was five and Emily had just turned four. The boyfriend was a client of Suzanne's, who was then a social worker. This boyfriend asked Suzanne for permission to go to British Columbia for two weeks alone with Emily, and Suzanne agreed. Her four-year-old daughter was put in the care of a man, unrelated and largely unknown to the family. Grant knew none of this.

Approximately a year after Emily's return from that trip with Suzanne's boyfriend, a teacher in kindergarten reported Emily's preponderance for writing the word *sex* on the classroom blackboard. Grant is unclear about what happened next but was informed by Suzanne many months later that Emily *had issues with a boy from the playground and was acting inappropriately.* In a 2005 conversation Grant had with Suzanne regarding Emily's behaviour, she stated that something "may have gone on" with her boyfriend in Brooks. According to Suzanne, Emily had been interviewed by the Edmonton Police "Zebra Squad" for alleged sexual abuse. The investigation, Suzanne told Grant, had not gone forward due to lack of evidence. She said it was best he not pursue this further as it would continue to upset Emily who was put into counseling.

When the couple split in 1999, Madison was especially distraught as she and her sisters were driven away to Suzanne's boyfriend's home. The five-year-old sensed that family life would never be the same and ached for her father. Over the next year, Grant continued his teaching position at the same school his girls attended and where they could regularly interact with their dad. A few weeks after Suzanne moved to her boyfriend's place, she sent notification to Grant of an impending divorce hearing, to be held that same month in Medicine Hat. Grant immediately called the Shannon Lushner legal firm in Calgary to represent him. He was assigned Barbra Louis as his legal representative, a decision he would forever regret.

After meeting with Barbra, a junior in the law firm, Grant was assured that his bid for joint custody and legal guardianship was looked after. But, when the court date arrived in July of 1999, Barbra Louis did not show. A "desk divorce" was signed nonetheless and Suzanne was granted sole custody of their three little daughters. This was particularly ludicrous because Grant had been the primary caregiver of his kids, since Suzanne had difficulty dealing with the stresses of motherhood and had remained the background parent. Following the divorce, Grant worked to keep his job in Brooks and deal with his impending bankruptcy after Suzanne defaulted on her debt. This debt included a truck she had purchased on credit for her boyfriend. Finally, after covering Suzanne's debt and maintaining a mortgage on the house in Brooks, Grant, declared bankruptcy. The house was reclaimed by the bank, and Grant became a casualty in a system that favoured the defaulter.

Each day, though Grant saw his daughters at school and tried to maintain some semblance of a family life, his influence in his daughters' lives was diminishing. To make things worse, Suzanne was using parental alienation tactics on the girls. By making access and communication difficult between Grant and his daughters, Suzanne was thwarting every attempt Grant made to still be a parent. As in all parental alienation cases, spousal and child support, revenge, and/or mental illness are the causes; in this case, all three were factors. Suzanne needed Grant's continued financial support and resented his leaving the marriage, so she campaigned to destroy his close relationship with their daughters and his extended family.

Within a few months, Suzanne again uprooted the girls, this time moving into Edmonton and subsidized housing. Her relationship to the boyfriend who took Emily to British Columbia collapsed and there was a police investigation into his sexual abuse. The details of that investigation remain unknown since Grant was refused access to Emily's file. This pattern of refusal by authorities to provide information on his daughters' medical, mental health, and educational files contravened the Divorce Order which defined him as an equal legal guardian with generous access. Suzanne had full access to all information at all times. Despite the increased alienation, Grant continued his regular attempts to dialogue with Suzanne, requesting information on the girls and trying to establish a regular visitation schedule with them. Since declaring bankruptcy, Grant had moved to his brother's basement in Calgary as he couldn't afford to live independently and maintain visitation in Edmonton with his daughters. In Calgary, he had managed to secure a job as an assistant school principal.

The three little girls were moved three times in 1999; twice in Brooks, first to live with Suzanne's boyfriend and then elsewhere to live with some of his friends. They were moved a third time to Wetaskiwin where they stayed the next couple years. After this period, Suzanne moved to Edmonton where she changed homes four more times over the next four years. During the second of those years the girls and their mother lived with another of her boyfriends. This fellow Grant had met and thought "quite nice" but by 2004 Suzanne and the girls had been "kicked out" (Suzanne's words to Grant). According to Suzanne, she was given one week to leave, so they subsequently moved into a townhouse in northern Edmonton.

Grant found it increasingly difficult to exercise time with his daughters as Suzanne placed more and more obstacles in his path. Sometimes he drove to Edmonton, only to find that his children were not home and Suzanne was nowhere to be found. He was also subjected to frequent cancellations at the last minute, such as when Madison phoned her dad saying she was not feeling well just two hours after Grant began his drive north to pick up the girls for a visit to Calgary. Grant struggled financially … he had to ask his ex-wife for money to buy gas to return from Edmonton on several occasions. Once, he arrived at Suzanne's to find her seemingly catatonic in a chair while their three little girls rummaged around the house unsupervised. On this occasion, Greg swept broken glass from Emily's room, made a snack for the girls in Suzanne's house and left groceries on the counter for Suzanne before leaving for the weekend with his kids.

Once back to the car after our hike that November day, I asked Grant what happened to his lawyer after the divorce where he lost custody of his daughters. Desperately trying to right the wrong granted in divorce court, Grant contacted Barbra Louie by phone and email; she apologized and agreed to appeal the court's decision within the allowable time period. But this did not happen. Instead, Ms. Louie defaulted once again and the file was closed. By telephone, Grant managed to speak with James Freud, another lawyer from the same firm, who advised him that unless he had substantial funds to fight the decision there was nothing further that could be done. Rendered helpless by the very system that supposedly supports children and allocates justice, Grant withdrew from legal action. But he never gave up on his kids.

In the fall of 1999, Craig Bosch from the Law Society of Alberta phoned Grant, requesting an interview. With renewed hope, Grant recounted all that had transpired with the divorce and Ms. Louis's failure to represent him. Following that interview, during which Mr. Bosch alluded to a number of other complaints against Ms. Louis, Grant believed that his case would be re-opened and corrected. This was not to be. Instead, Mr. Bosch did not follow up at all and Grant never heard from him or the Law Society again. He was not told that Ms. Louis had been disbarred. Finding this out later was cold comfort to a father who lost his daughters through the negligence of his lawyer and the judge, Orville Shats, who ruled in favour of Suzanne after hearing her "testimonial" defaming Grant's character.

For the next several years, Grant tried his best to see his daughters though it was always whenever it suited Suzanne. There was no visitation schedule and due to the ongoing parental alienation, Grant's daughters became increasingly elusive. At the time I met Grant in late 2004, he was still able to phone his girls and did so each morning to get them up for school. If he did not do so, they were often no-shows that day and the school's attendance reminders to Suzanne went unanswered. All three kids struggled at school due to their frequent absences, most of them excused by Suzanne. Madison had over 63 absences from school in just that one year. Though the girls are intelligent and should have had promising lives ahead, their lack of home support and the ongoing alienation from their father hampered success.

Most of the time, Grant's phone messages to his daughters were not returned, his emails were similarly ignored and his cards, gifts, and even cheques from the girls' grandparents were not cashed or even acknowledged. One day in the fall of 2004, Suzanne called Grant saying she could not deal with their kids and needed help. Grant suggested that she move to Calgary where he could help her in the move and they could share parenting. Suzanne seemed enthused by this idea and when Grant hung up the phone, he seemed hopeful that the family's situation might improve. The next day, while Grant and I were walking my dog, his cell phone rang. The call was from Suzanne, who I could hear shouting profanities at Grant about how he didn't care about her and was a useless person. I had only known Grant for a couple months but was dumbfounded by the hostile turn in his ex-wife's behaviour. He calmly tried to settle Suzanne down on the phone, reassuring her of his good intentions for her and their girls but she would hear none of it. Eventually she hung up on him.

I remembered how Grant had told me of Suzanne's struggles with her mental disability, her long-term disability status and her membership in a mental-health day program through a hospital in Edmonton. He told me he was not surprised by the phone call and Suzanne's explosive anger toward him since extreme mood swings and hostility had been a common occurrence since the divorce five years earlier. Suzanne had told Grant the year before that she had been diagnosed by her psychiatrist with *Borderline Personality Disorder*. On that day in 2004, I began to understand how the depth of Suzanne's bitterness and her all-encompassing rage toward Grant fueled her parental alienation. As in all cases of parental alienation, the children, in this case Laura, Madison, and Emily, became victims. During one visit with his girls, Madison told Grant that she was afraid her Mom would hurt herself if she and her sisters were away with their Dad.

2005

In March of 2005, after Grant and I decided we had a solid relationship and wanted to tell our five kids; we were relieved to find that all five were happy about it and enthused about meeting each other. I had not yet met Grant's daughters but did so one Saturday when they were in Calgary for a weekend. Grant had driven up to Edmonton as he always did on the rare occasions Suzanne allowed the girls to visit him. He would pick them up on Friday after school and make the long drive back up again on Sunday afternoon, so the kids could be fresh for school on Monday. They usually did homework in the car on the way to Calgary, with Grant's assistance, which made the drive go by faster and the girls could then enjoy a fun weekend with their dad. Suzanne, though, often allowed the girls to miss school on Monday, blaming their father for their "tiredness". That Saturday, I stopped by Grant's apartment for a few minutes, said hello to the girls and then left. They seemed to be pleasant, friendly, and genuine kids and all three were clearly very close to their dad despite the infrequent visits.

In April of 2005, Suzanne told Grant that she was off work on stress-leave from her job as an intake worker for social assistance. By Easter of that year, the alienation from Grant had worsened and though Grant tried to arrange the weekend for his girls and us in Calgary, Suzanne sent conflicting phone messages and emails about whether the girls would in fact be "available." Up until the last hour, Grant did not know whether his girls were on the bus from Edmonton. He went to the bus station just in case. They did not show. Suzanne informed Grant via email that evening that she and the girls had a "new family tradition" to go for Easter brunch in Edmonton instead. So Grant mailed his daughters the box of Easter gifts and cards from their grandparents and him. He did not receive any acknowledgment that this or any other gift, including cheques, from him or his family had ever reached the girls. Though Laura, Madison and Emily enjoyed visits with their paternal grandparents on the few occasions they were together in Newfoundland, they lost these relationships too as the cancer of alienation spread.

During the 2005-2006 school year, Madison missed over *40 days* of school… and Laura had been absent *40 classes of a single course*. The disturbing trend of increased truancy saw all three girls begin each school year with good attendance, which would soon plummet to infrequent and sporadic. Grant called the school counselor, Ms. Bonnie Newell, and asked that she look into Emily's and Madison's situation. Three weeks and several email and phone requests later, Ms. Newell eventually called Grant back to confirm that she had met with Madison. She would not, however, provide Grant with any details of a plan to help Madison get back on track. Ms. Newell stated that Madison did not want her father involved at that time; this despite the fact that Grant and his ex-wife were both legal guardians of their children. Suzanne was fully informed of all information about her daughters, yet kept it from Grant. Other professionals in the girls' lives also, inexplicably, with-held information from him, including dentists and doctors. Though report cards for the girls should have kept Grant informed, he rarely saw these and when he did, they were hand-delivered by Suzanne long after the school year had finished.

That summer, 2005, we were able to arrange a three-week trip to Newfoundland with all three girls, who had a wonderful time as we did with them and Grant's family. Little did we know that this trip would be one of the last in which Grant would see his three daughters together. After that July, there were very few visits between the girls and Grant and only with one or two of them at a time. In Newfoundland during a walk with us one day, Madison blurted out that "my mother is a psycho-freak". This was seconded by Laura. We did not respond to the comment and as always, maintained our position of never denigrating their mother. Grant and I later talked about our mutual concern for the girls' well being in Edmonton.

A few weeks before Thanksgiving, Grant sent emails and voice-mail to his daughters in hopes that they might visit us over that long weekend. Though Grant had continued his attempts to contact the girls, we had not seen or heard from them since the summer's Newfoundland trip. His calls and emails went unanswered until a week before the holiday. Then Grant received an email from Madison saying they were "too busy" and would not be coming to Calgary for the weekend. There was no further explanation in that cryptic message.

There was a weekend visit that November. Surprisingly, one of Grant's communication attempts was successful and all three of his daughters agreed to come to Calgary. We had a great time, the girls seemed happy to be with us and spent some time with my two teenagers as well. Our five children had seen little of each other but got along well on the few occasions they did. My 16-year-old daughter commented once that Emily "just needs a normal home and she will be okay". Emily was 11-years-old then. On this visit, we arranged a photo session with all the kids and us. We requested that one of the photographs be of just Grant's three girls. Before Christmas in 2005, Grant had two large and framed copies made for Suzanne and her parents. We hoped these would serve as an olive branch to show the girls' mother that we wanted to smooth the relationship for their sakes and those of both families. But no acknowledgment ever came of the photographs being received. Driving home with Madison and Emily from the photographer's studio, Emily asked me, "why did my dad kick us out of our house?" I told her "that's not what happened, Emily, and you will need to have that conversation with your dad one day". She began to cry and muttered "I am SO confused!" In the backseat, Madison was silent the whole way home.

Though Suzanne had never allowed Grant time with his children over Christmas, in 2005 we were able to take them and my daughter to Panorama Ski Resort for five days over New Year's. The trip was not confirmed by Suzanne until December 27th so we crossed our fingers that it would indeed happen and the girls would be allowed to come. Laura, Madison and Emily did show up and we all enjoyed our time together. In fact, Madison even gave Grant and me postcards on which she wrote her thanks and love for us. During that holiday, the girls told us that the two eldest were on anti-depressants, Madison was also on Seroquel (an anti-psychotic) and Emily was being given Adderall for her "ADHD". Since the girls' medical records were withheld from Grant, he had no idea why his daughters were being medicated, especially since their psychiatrist in Edmonton, a Dr. M. Blackmore, had no medical record of Grant's side of the family. Even more concerning, the two drugs Madison was on were, and are, both contraindicated for children under 18 years. They were being prescribed as "off-label", a term used to prevent pharmaceutical companies from being held liable. Madison was taking two powerful drugs meant for adults, for unknown reasons, and… *in combination.*

2006

By early 2006, the parental alienation had effectively removed Grant from his two younger daughters' lives in any meaningful way. He had next to no communication with them as all attempts were thwarted by Suzanne. When he did manage to get them on the phone, they were evasive, often stating they had "plans" so couldn't see him. We did manage to keep some contact with Laura, who was 17 by then. She phoned and texted Grant quite often and even visited alone some weekends when she could. She would never say anything about her sisters except that they "are doing great". One day, however, she told us that it would be easier on her if we stopped trying to keep in contact with her sisters.

In January, Suzanne informed Grant by telephone that she was recommended for a disability pension from Canada Pension, which would come into effect that June or July.

Grant told me that Suzanne and her live-in boyfriend Peter, a person Grant respected and had a good relationship with, had broken up in 2004. Prior to this break-up, Grant could productively communicate with Suzanne and his access to the girls had been strained but workable. Grant said he could usually visit the girls in either city, typically on long weekends and school holidays or some time in summer, as long as it was on Suzanne's terms. But beginning at Suzanne's placement on limited-term disability, that pattern rapidly deteriorated. Grant had written notes on his recent observations of Suzanne seeming "quite lethargic, as if heavily medicated" on several occasions when he picked up the girls or dropped them back at their mother's home.

Grant emailed Suzanne in January asking her which month she wanted for her time with the girls in summer. She said that her parents had booked a cabin on Vancouver Island for August. Grant then requested two weeks with his daughters in July so that we might fly to Ontario for a lake holiday with my parents and my brothers' families. Although Suzanne then asked the girls and reported them to be keen on the idea, she phoned Grant the very next day saying that Madison and Emily could not go… they had apparently now joined an Edmonton marching band. This band was going to Disneyland to perform at that same time in the summer. She stated that the band had no firm itinerary so she could not guarantee that the girls would return in time for our proposed trip. This meant we could only take Laura with us, which we did. Of note, neither Emily nor Madison had any musical background or apparent interest in playing an instrument or joining any kind of band.

Over the Family Day weekend in February, Grant went to watch Emily's band play in Calgary. Suzanne had driven Madison and herself from Edmonton and the girls were to spend the remainder of the weekend with us in Calgary. I did not go as I thought it best not to add fuel to the fire. Suzanne had repeatedly made it clear she resented my being in Grant's life. After Emily's concert, Grant and Suzanne were to exchange the children and move their backpacks into Grant's car. In the parking lot, according to Emily who did come home with us, her mother screamed at Grant, calling him "swears" and accusing him of messing up her life. Madison did not emerge from her mother's car and silently looked at the floor as Suzanne jumped back in her car and drove away to Edmonton. We, nevertheless, did enjoy the zoo and went swimming at the YMCA. Emily seemed sad to leave after the weekend when Grant drove her back north.

In March, Laura confirmed that she wanted to come with us in July to Ontario. There was no further word from either of the other girls or their mother. Just before Easter and out of the blue, Madison emailed and phoned Grant to tell us she wanted to come for the holiday weekend. We were thrilled and began to make plans. But there was no visit. The following day Madison sent a second email, this time informing us that "something has come up". Grant had always spent the Easter weekend with his daughters until that year. A week later, he was able to get Emily by phone and asked her when she could come in May for a special birthday weekend, her 11th. She said she would ask her mom… but he did not hear from, or manage to contact, her again for over two months though he tried over and over again. The birthday came and went. Grant sent a gift which was never acknowledged.

On Mother's Day, Grant received an email message, from Madison's email address, that read, *"Fuck You"* in the subject line. The message content said he would not see his daughters again until he got "some help." And on May 31, 2006, Suzanne emailed Grant that he should *"Stop harassing Children's Mental Health immediately otherwise your ill thought out actions could result in legal action and possible conviction."* I had now observed eighteen months of continued alienation tactics by Suzanne despite Grant's amazingly calm and respectful communication to her. He told me he wished her no ill. He needed help for his girls and Suzanne needed help for herself. Their school's online attendance site showed that both girls were missing *most* days of school and performing poorly. His insurance claim receipts showed the girls were still heavily medicated. And according to Laura, Emily spent many weeknights at "sleepovers." Emily herself told us that her mom had instructed that the girls "keep our family secrets".

In May of 2006, we drove to Edmonton and accessed Emily's school file for review. We hoped to get to the bottom of what had happened to Emily and what was being done to help her now. In a psychological report in that school file, Suzanne claimed that the perpetrator in the abuse of Emily was a 6-year-old boy in a Wetaskiwin school yard. We discovered that Emily had a history of resource support in school –having been coded "severe behavioural exceptionality."

After much consideration, Grant and I found a lawyer, Alice Harvis, who agreed to help us help the girls and develop a parenting plan that included a monthly parenting schedule. I believed, wrongly as it turned out, that by pooling our resources, Grant and I could use legal means as a last-ditch effort to resolve the ongoing parental alienation that was destroying the lives of his kids and our families. Grant was uncertain; he said that recruiting a lawyer was a "lose -lose proposition". I didn't, and will likely never, understand what he meant by that comment. We both knew his children had little hope of a healthy life given the level of neglect, deception and hatred they were living with. By May, Laura, at 16, had already moved out of her mother's home with a boyfriend. We embarked on a six-year legal journey that led us ever further from any positive outcome. Of note, Suzanne continued to receive Child Support payments for three children after Laura had moved out. Several months later, with Laura's written statement, we were able to have Laura's portion sent directly to Laura, no longer to her mother.

Father's Day was ignored. Grant had not seen either Madison or Emily for five months. In the third week of June, Grant wrote Suzanne, requesting to have Emily visit the first two weeks in July. Though he phoned and emailed her several more times, all attempts failed. On July 2, Emily unexpectedly and finally phoned her dad, telling him that she has been "over at the neighbours, feeding their cats until now." She said she was now "home for supper" and was coming to Calgary tomorrow for two weeks. Grant was taken aback but happy and asked if Emily could please put her mom on the phone to talk about details. Emily said her mom was in bed… it was six o'clock in the evening. Nonetheless, Suzanne did come to the phone and Grant put it on speaker so I could witness the dialogue. Suzanne agreed to put Emily on the bus to Calgary the next day. Grant said he would phone her in the morning to clarify the arrival time of whichever bus worked best for them.

Meanwhile, Grant sent Madison $100 to spend on her marching band's trip to Disneyland. Next morning as promised, Grant called Suzanne on speaker phone. She asked why Grant "is so mean" to her and then stated that maybe Emily would not be coming to Calgary after all. The barrage of verbal assaults on Grant continued until he hung up the phone. He tried to call back but got only Suzanne's voicemail. Later that day, he emailed all three girls and Suzanne asking that they have a conversation with him to sort out everyone's plans for the summer. There came no reply. And Madison left for Disneyland without any communication between her or her dad. On July 4, Grant managed to contact Suzanne by phone on the first try. He asked politely to speak to Emily, but Suzanne said "there's no one here who wants to speak to you -your email will be reviewed." She then hung up the phone. We would not see Emily until November of 2006, nine months since the previous visit.

On July 5, Grant's family doctor noted that his blood pressure remained dangerously high, despite Grant's being on prescribed medications to deal with his ongoing stress. He had been divorced for seven years then, yet the hostility emanating from his ex-wife had continued, even accelerated, over those years. Grant was a targeted parent, but his children were victims too. Grant's blood pressure was 170/110 despite his medications and regular physical activity including hockey, soccer and running. He was then 44 years old. The doctor prescribed, in addition, a mild tranquilizer to ease his chronic anxiety level. I was worried for his health, both mental and physical. I wondered how he could go on for this long without some relief; he wanted…and needed… to be a parent to his kids. In turn, his children desperately needed his love and to be free of their dire home-life.

Grant's parents came for a visit from Newfoundland to Calgary later that July. Grant's dad was very ill with terminal cancer, so they hoped to see all their children and grandchildren living in the west. Though Grant repeatedly tried to reach his daughters, all communication attempts remained fruitless. He wanted his girls to have a chance to visit their grandparents. Using the marching band's itinerary over the summer, Grant was able to find a date on which Madison would be playing at a nearby amusement park west of the city. On July 15, Grant's mom, he and I went there and watched from the sidelines as the band paraded through the park. Grant's dad was not well enough to come along. Along came

Madison, stone-faced and staring straight ahead. For a second, she glanced our way and a very brief smile came to her lips. I knew she was glad to see us. She then looked away and did not make further eye contact. Following the parade, the band members immediately returned to their tour bus, waiting in the parking lot. The three of us approached casually, Grant asking a chaperone nearby whether Madison was now on the bus. The woman looked away and said she didn't know. At the same time an imposing-looking man approached so Grant asked him to let Madison know we were there in case she would like to come see us. He got on the bus and one minute later returned stating that "we asked and she doesn't want to see you." Grant, crest-fallen, replied "ok, thanks" and we left. None of the girls saw their grandparents that trip and six months later, in January of 2007, their "Poppy"was dead.

One night in August, Madison phoned Grant on her cellphone from Vancouver to apologize. She was then visiting her maternal grandparents with her sisters and Suzanne. Each year, the girls spent much time with these grandparents who must have wondered why the kids spent more time with them than they ever did with their father. During this phone call, Madison said she was sorry for what had happened at Calaway Park and that she missed Grant. I heard her words, since we were in Grant's car on Bluetooth. Madison said she wanted to make up for her behaviour. She and her dad had a positive, loving conversation and Grant suggested Madison write to Nannie (his mother) and to me about her feelings. He told her it would start to rebuild relationships in our family. She enthusiastically agreed and did follow through. She and I spoke by phone in September and talked about her friends, school and other normal interests.

In early September, Grant phoned Laura and was able to also speak with Madison who was with her. Madison asked if she could visit us for Thanksgiving from Friday to Monday. We readily agreed. She informed us she would be on the bus that Friday arriving in Calgary at 7:20. During that month, Madison called us three more times to confirm her reservation on that bus. One day, Grant phoned Edmonton and connected with Emily, who was home alone. She informed us that she had flown to Ottawa by herself last summer, on the exact date she was supposed to fly to Calgary for her holiday with us. She had not gone on the band trip and in fact had altogether quit the band before summer. When Grant asked her if she remembered she had made plans with us, she said, "I don't remember any of that". We were very concerned. We had seen Emily from a distance at her school back in May and now she was sounding emotionally flat. She did not look or sound well. We suspected she was being heavily medicated.

On October 3, Grant emailed Laura, Madison, and Emily, and copied Suzanne, inviting the girls for the weekend of our wedding that November. He said that it would be just family and held outdoors so they should be sure to bring warm clothes. We only heard back from 17-year-old Laura. She congratulated us, said she would be there and was looking forward to it.

Madison did arrive for Thanksgiving but only on the third bus to arrive past the one she told us she would be on. We had no idea why she was not on that 7:20 bus. No one had informed us of this change and we were very worried. Regardless, Grant made sure Madison phoned Suzanne right away after we picked her up safely. That weekend was very troubling. We had not seen Madison in ten months. Although she said she was glad to be with us and my teenagers, she seemed preoccupied and lethargic. At dinner, my son asked about our wedding plans. We had tried exhaustively for months to let Grant's girls know but all communication attempts by Grant had failed. Madison inquired of her dad why he had not told her; he explained that he had tried his best. That night, Madison came into our bedroom and silently sat on the edge of the bed for a few minutes, eyes downcast and seemingly agitated. She showed us some "pills" prescribed to her by Dr. Blackmore, the Edmonton psychiatrist we knew the girls and their mother had been seeing. Madison was 13 then. She also shared that her sisters were also on pills prescribed them by this physician.

The following evening Madison again came into our bedroom, this time lying down between us as she sometimes did while we all took turns reading. She asked us why "lawyers are threatening my mom". We had a long conversation about telling the truth and unconditional love. Madison, that night, told us things we could never have imagined about her life with mom…secrets that she had been made to promise never to share with us or even her sisters.

These secrets included:

- Suzanne warned Madison last summer that while in her marching band at Calaway Park, she was not to acknowledge us or she would be in trouble.
- Dr. Blackmore told Madison "don't talk to your father as that makes you anxious".
- A social worker, "who was a bitch"(Madison's words) used to come to their house every weekday morning to get Madison and her sisters up for school.
- Last Thursday, Madison "did not take my pills and I felt shaky and my heart was racing all day" as a result.
- Suzanne's "old boyfriend" went to jail for what he did to Emily. When we asked what he did, Madison said she did not know.
- Suzanne has no money because "her boyfriend took a whole bunch to pay for his truck and never paid it back".
- Suzanne says Madison's dad is mentally ill.
- Suzanne has a mental illness caused by stress; Madison's dad and the three girls cause it. Suzanne can only "get well" if she and the girls don't contact Grant in any way…ever.

I glanced over at Grant whose eyes were brimming with tears. I asked Madison whether she thought her life would be better if we stopped our legal case; she said "no". She said she needed "things to change" and she understood why we had a lawyer. Madison also let us know that her life was bad in Edmonton, but she was worried about her mom. She said she tries to defend Grant when her mom speaks badly of him. Grant, in a soft voice, reminded Madison that there should be no need to defend anybody.

The following day, we took Madison to the YMCA and then met my son and daughter for breakfast. Madison was chatty and enthusiastic. Her "boyfriend" as she referred to him, called on Grant's cell phone and talked with her for a few minutes. He later called again to tell Madison that he was *over at Suzanne's having dinner.* The unspoken message to Madison was clear; her mom and her boyfriend were together and she was missing out since she had chosen to visit us.

On Thanksgiving Monday, we took Madison to the zoo and later to the bus station for her trip back to Edmonton. Grant had Madison phone her mom to let her know what time the bus would arrive; Mom was in bed at 3:30 p.m. Emily answered the phone and went to rouse her mother. Grant asked Madison to phone us when she arrived home and she promised to do so. As we all hugged and said our good-byes, Grant gave two hand-written cards to Madison, asking that she give them to her sisters. The cards invited the girls for the weekend of our upcoming November wedding. We did not hear from Madison that evening. Grant phoned Suzanne's house but was only able to leave voicemail. He politely asked Suzanne to confirm that Madison had, indeed, arrived home safely. There was no response.

At 8:20 the following morning, Madison called her dad from Edmonton, apologizing for not phoning when she got home the night before. That day, Grant sent an email to all three girls and copied to Suzanne, again inviting them for the Remembrance Day weekend for our wedding. He reminded them to bring warm clothes. A few days after, Grant got an email from Suzanne with this message, *"Cease all legal action immediately if you want to see your kids again".*

On Friday, November 10th, we picked up Laura and Emily at the bus station. They had come from Edmonton for the weekend but Madison had not. The two girls told Grant their sister had "too much homework" to come to our wedding the next day. On a cold, snowy day, we were married in a Calgary park with two of Grant's daughters and my children in attendance. We missed Madison but were glad to at least have Laura and Emily with us. On Sunday, the girls reported that "we have to go home early because Mom is cooking a roast." To avoid any stress on his daughters, Grant and I were able to get them on the early bus and Grant left a voice-mail with Suzanne to let her know they would be arriving in Edmonton at 5:30 p.m. At about 4:00 p.m., Madison phoned Grant from north of Edmonton, saying "we are out of town visiting mom's friend." He let her know her sisters were on the bus and their expected arrival time. Madison asked Grant a lot of questions about the wedding and said she was sorry she missed it but would see us soon.

We did not see or hear again from the two younger girls for several months. Christmas came and went as did New Year's and though Grant tried to contact the girls by phone and sent emails, he received no response from them. Laura visited us for a few days before school started up again in January and as always, we enjoyed our time together.

2007

Grant's dad died in late January after a long struggle with cancer. His granddaughters had been prevented, by their mother, from seeing their "Poppy" last summer, when he and their "Nan" visited Alberta. There was no acknowledgement at all from the girls when Grant left messages with this sad news. All three girls had enjoyed much time with their paternal grandparents in their younger years and their Poppy was dearly loved.

We did not hear from nor see Madison or Emily until July, but Laura came to Calgary for a couple weekends. It was almost as if she tried to make up for the absence of her sisters. Though she suffered from depression and told us she was on anti-depressant medication, she appeared to be otherwise holding her own. From the start of our legal intervention in 2006, Grant and I stuck by our decision to keep that action away from the girls and not to discuss the details should they ask. Laura, however, seemed to know much about it and asked us what we hoped to achieve. She agreed that her mother needed help and her sisters needed support but she said, "You are wasting your time." She informed us the lawyers would make her mother "ramp things up and make her (Laura's) life worse".

Although we began legal proceedings about parenting and access last May, we waited a *full thirteen months* before our case was finally brought to court. In the interim, *over a hundred emails went* back and forth between our lawyer, Alice Harvis, and Suzanne's lawyer, Wayne Shymlo, and between Ms. Harvis and Grant. The legal fees mounted while nothing got done to help the girls or their father. Suzanne continued her alienation tactics, including preventing the girls from visiting us. We did not see Madison or Emily until the day we went to court in July. Since Laura was close to turning 18 and would then be a legal adult, our lawyer completely excluded her from Grant's legal application.

Grant had agreed that the case be heard in Edmonton, not Calgary, to reduce any disruption to the girls' lives. So finally one day in early July, we drove to Edmonton. Once there, we met with Laura for a few minutes and surprisingly, her two sisters were standing on the sidewalk waiting for us as well. We were thrilled to see all of them but sad that it was under such difficult circumstances. Hugs went all round, but soon we had to leave in order to make our court appearance.

In the courtroom, Judge Hilyard began by saying "Oh my goodness, this has gone on so long", referring to the length of time since the parents' divorce. He did not seem to know that the time elapsed before legal action commenced was due to two main factors: Grant's persistent attempts to build some sort of co-parenting schedule with Suzanne; and his resultant bankruptcy following divorce when Suzanne's unpaid debts were piled onto him. It was clear from this first comment that Judge Hilyard was ill prepared for our case. He did not allow either of the parents to speak but said he was relying on affidavits that had been written by each of them. He also listened to the statements made by each lawyer.

Though Grant's affidavit was thorough and all information was proven with attached documentation, Suzanne's was a barrage of accusations against Grant without evidence. Some of her claims included that Grant was "verbally abusive", was "mean" to her and the girls, wrote "nasty" emails, and did not try to see his daughters. We had read her rebuttal affidavit ahead of time when it was sent via Mr. Shymlo as per required court process. Judge Hilyard stated that he did not "like the sound of" Mr. R's (Grant) emails" to Suzanne. To what emails was he referring, we wondered, since Grant was always respectful to Suzanne in his emails and verbally, at least in the years I had known him. There was not a shred of evidence to support this judge's remark. Ms. Harvis explained to the court how Grant was seeking a parenting schedule with regular access to, and communication with, his daughters. He also sought academic and home supports for them since they were doing poorly in school and apparently suffering from the stress of their home life, since they were all being heavily medicated by psychiatrist Dr. Blackmore.

Judge Hilyard listened to Mr. Shymlo's hearsay claiming that Madison did not want her father involved in her life. She had told us otherwise, many months before, and even that day before court began. Suzanne's lawyer continued, saying that Emily might want to see her father but Mr. Shymlo wasn't sure about that. He reiterated the so-called inappropriate emails from Grant, *emails that Mr. Shymlo could not produce*. Throughout his testimony, I saw Mr. Shymlo regularly engage in what looked like nervous twitching behaviours. He would jerk his head sideways and shrug his right shoulder repeatedly. Judge Hilyard did not question *any* of Mr. Shymlo's claims and accepted Suzanne's affidavit as fact. After a couple hours, the total time allocated for this case involving two children and eight years of neglect and abuse by their mother, this judge directed that the parents go into a backroom together with their lawyers to hammer out a "parenting plan". They did so. There were no other directives of any consequence and Judge Hilyard effectively removed himself from having to advise on the welfare of Grant and Suzanne's two younger daughters. According to Grant, the "discussion" in the backroom involved Suzanne's shouting and standing up in anger, at which point Mr. Shymlo told her to sit down and be quiet. After approximately thirty minutes, the four returned to court and Mr. Shymlo announced to Judge Hilyard that they now had a parenting plan draft. Suzanne's lawyer agreed to subsequently and in timely fashion have it typed and sent to Ms. Harvis for approval and signing.

We all left the courtroom. While standing in the hall waiting for Grant, I was approached by Suzanne who was walking out with Mr. Shymlo. She hugged me and said "I hope this works. My girls *so* need a good influence in their lives". I was dumbfounded and wary. As it turned out, for very good reason. That court hearing in the summer of 2007 was not only a sham, but it ramped up the alienation beyond any means we could have imagined.

Starting on July 27th, Madison, Emily, my daughter, Grant and I had planned a three-day horseback pack-trip into the mountains from a Kananaskis ranch. Though this was a lot of money for us at the time, we looked so forward to having the girls together for a few days. Unfortunately, Laura had to work so could not join us. We had only seen the girls once since November of last year, for a few minutes on our way to court. Grant sent emails and voice-mails to Suzanne in early June so she would have lots of notice of our upcoming trip; to no response. Then, on July 23, Grant received an email from her demanding that since Emily wanted to come to Calgary for a week starting July 25, we would need to make sure she visited a dentist as she had a cracked tooth. Grant agreed via email and we picked up 12-year-old Emily from the bus as planned. Madison, though, was not with her. She had told us she wanted to come on the pack trip. We had no idea what was going on. Grant wrote Suzanne again, as Emily told us that Madison, for some reason, was now in Ottawa. He asked Suzanne whether it would be better to have Madison fly directly from Ottawa to Calgary so she wouldn't miss the pack-trip. Grant did not ask why Madison was in Ottawa at all and without his knowledge. Suzanne wrote back that since the pack-trip was to end on July 29th, she wanted both Laura and Emily on the bus back to Edmonton arriving that same night. On July 26th, the day before our pack-trip, Laura arrived saying that she was going to fill in for Madison who was not coming.

Grant had made arrangements several weeks earlier to drive the girls back to Edmonton on July 31st following our pack-trip. Suzanne was well aware of this. Yet she decided it was instead appropriate for Grant to send their daughters on the bus from Calgary to Edmonton on the *same day* they were returning to Calgary after three days in the mountains. Once again, Grant wrote Suzanne a respectful and patient email asking that they keep the original arrangement so he could drive the girls back to Edmonton after they had a day of rest in Calgary. Suzanne did not reply so Grant drove the girls home on the 31st. It had been seven months since Grant had had time with Emily, yet Suzanne tried her best to thwart even this visit. It was already more than eight months since he had had any time with Madison. We had a wonderful horseback trip with beautiful weather, campfires and cowboys who told us stories of the wilderness. Emily seemed happy and calm, a very different girl from her mother's reports of her "bad behaviour" at home and school. She told us she was "not taking any drugs from Dr. Blackmore" any more. Prior to our trip, we had taken Emily canoeing, swimming and on several long dog-walks, all of which she seemed to thoroughly enjoy. She especially seemed sad to go the day Grant drove Laura and her back to Edmonton. We assured her we would look forward to arranging another visit very soon.

The draft Parenting Order was now in its fourth amended version, thanks to Mr. Shymlo who watered down the original further each time, rendering it virtually toothless. There was a court directive to start a journal that the parents would each write in for the other's benefit, reporting achievements and necessary information about Emily's schedule and health. Grant and Emily shopped for and bought such a journal, and Grant explained to his daughter how this would help communication between her parents. She was keen to use it. When she returned to Edmonton and gave her journal to her mom, we never saw it again. Although Grant emailed and left voice-mail with Suzanne asking her to return the journal on the next visit, she did not reply and never did so.

That summer, I sold my half-duplex and together Grant and I bought a modest bungalow in a nice neighbourhood with a great yard and enough bedrooms for the kids. My son was now an adult and had moved downtown, but my daughter lived with us half time and we hoped to have Grant's girls with us more often. Grant and Emily bought her chosen paint, bright blue, and together they painted her new room. She was settling in and excited with her "second home." But Emily was never allowed to come back to see us again. She was always "too busy" or at "sleep-overs" that fall. We had a couple more visits from Laura that year.

Grant had set Madison and Emily up with an online school tutoring program that they could sign in to whenever they wished. He showed them how it worked and they seemed eager to give it a try. Though he paid for the service monthly for the next several years, the girls never did sign in again from Edmonton. When school began, the two youngest girls continued their now-consistent pattern of truancy that worsened as the academic year progressed. Emily was in Grade 7; Madison in 9. Emily could not yet tell time and thought she was "too dumb to do math." Madison rarely passed any tests and missed taking most of them. Yet both girls are of normal intelligence.

One Saturday, Grant and I drove up to Edmonton since Emily had emailed Grant that she was to play soccer that afternoon. We arrived before the game started, but there was no sign of her on the field. A few minutes into the game, however, Emily, showed up walking slowly and wearing garish face make-up, appropriate for only for a costume party or a red-light district. Her mother followed behind. We noticed Emily sat separately from her team-members and we were reminded she had told us of being bullied at school. She had, previously that year, arrived at the bus station for a weekend with us wearing a black mini-skirt, torn black seamed stockings and a low-cut, tight sweater; she was then 12-years-old. After the soccer game, we waited for Emily so we could give her a hug and perhaps even take her for supper. But Suzanne whisked her away without even a good-bye as soon as she saw us talking to her.

Judge Hilyard had suggested family counseling. Suzanne emailed Grant asking that he attend "parents' counseling" instead which was not what the court had recommended. Grant knew there was no point in this type of therapy since one parent was an alienator, intent only on the goal of removing her daughters from their dad's life. No counseling occurred though Grant was agreeable to the court's directive and offered to attend all family-counseling sessions in Edmonton. He contacted Emily's school and talked with a counselor there, Ms. Philamena, who expressed much concern about Emily's behaviour and lack of motivation. Emily was apparently now enrolled, Grant was told, at the Children's Mental Health Centre.

Many emails were exchanged between Grant and Suzanne that fall, as Grant tried to schedule visits with his girls, in either city. Though initially Suzanne would comply, she would cancel at the last minute or the girls would email Grant with various excuses for why they couldn't see him. These included: too busy, too much homework, I'm sick, I have to feed my neighbours' dog and I'm going to a birthday party. There had been no mention of any of these *plans* prior to a day or so before the next scheduled visit. One time, Grant was *one hour away* from Edmonton after driving up to have a supper visit with Emily when she called and told him she was "too busy" to see him. In every emailed request, Grant was flexible about time spent with the girls and asked Suzanne what would work best for her. Even during the Christmas break from school, Grant asked which week Suzanne preferred since the court and draft Parenting Order stated that these parents were to equally share school vacation time. Suzanne did write about money she wanted for "trips and music activities" though Grant knew nothing about what these events were. Suzanne also asked for money to cover drugs, dentists and orthodontists above the agreed-upon proportion consistent with federal Child Support and Maintenance guidelines and Section 7 extraordinary expenses.

We did not see the two younger girls during the Christmas school break. We did have a nice visit with Laura, who continued to try her best to make up for the absence of her sisters. She did not talk about her mother, her sisters, or life in Edmonton. She did let us know that Madison had not come to our wedding a year ago because she was *"afraid mom will hurt herself"*. Madison told us the same thing a couple years later, though we had not asked her and she didn't know we were already aware of this.

Suzanne had now recruited another public counselor to "help" the girls with their stress. These counselors were chosen only by Suzanne and the version they were told about Grant and the family's situation is unknown. It is certainly one-sided. We have no idea what narrative was concocted by Suzanne to support her alienation tactics, but she was never challenged for her outrageous claims.

2008

The start of a new year did not help matters. The first week back at school, Emily missed several classes. Madison, too, was showing truancy according to the online attendance record available for parents. Grant's emailed query to Suzanne went unanswered for a week and then she wrote him that Emily "was absent due to personal comfort and support to others in various situations. The vice prinicple (sic) has discussed options with Emily (sic) so she is not accounted for in class, such as discussing with her teacher what is going on before she leaves class." We did not even understand Suzanne's response and remained baffled about both girls' frequent school absences. When Grant would phone or write the school administrators asking for information, they did not return his queries. The few times one did respond, he or she simply stated that Grant should ask the custodial parent for that information.

Toward the end of January, Grant requested of Suzanne that she give permission for Dr. Blackmore, the psychiatrist "treating" the girls, to release their medical record to him. Suzanne already had the girls' information and since Grant was their equal legal guardian, he should have been accorded equal knowledge about his daughters' health. Suzanne refused. When Grant directly asked for release of their records to him, Dr. Blackmore's office responded by email that Madison was a "mature minor" and as such, could grant or refuse permission of her parent(s) to her own medical records. So Madison, at age 14, brainwashed and drugged, refused access by her father to her health, and any other, record. Suzanne wrote Grant that since he had asked for access to Madison's psychiatric record, Madison would "likely never want to speak to you (Grant) again". Grant was sent, by this psychiatrist, a lengthy typed "report" of Madison's mental health status; all but her basic information such as birth date and age was blacked out. Grant subsequently wrote up a formal complaint again Dr. Blackmore. It was dismissed in its entirety by the Alberta College of Physicians and Surgeons, even upon appeal, and Dr. Blackmore was never investigated. He continues to practice as of the writing of this book.

Grant also requested of Suzanne that he have the girls for the Easter weekend in March, thus giving her ample notice. His mom would be in town from Newfoundland and was anxious to see her granddaughters. Adding confusion to the already tenuous communication between these parents, Suzanne, who had asked Grant that all requests to see the girls go through her first, now responded that she had "no control over whether the girls choose to visit you or not." Several emails later over the next few weeks, Grant heard from both Laura and Madison that they would like to visit on the Easter weekend. He heard nothing more from Suzanne and nothing at all from Emily. On March 19, Grant sent voice-mail and email reminders to the girls and their mother that he would leave Calgary at about 1:00 p.m. the next day. He would drive to Edmonton to pick up all three daughters for the long weekend. At 2:00 p.m. on March 20, Grant was sent an email from Suzanne stating that Emily would not be seeing her father this weekend and "I'll leave it up to her to explain to you when she is able". This same email also confirmed that Emily did want to go to Newfoundland in the summer with us and her sisters, as we had requested, so we should go ahead and buy a ticket for her.

Laura and Madison did join us that Easter and we spent a lovely time with the girls' Nan, aunt and uncle in Calgary. We loved our new house and were eager to make it a real home. To date, Emily had not been back since the summer before when she painted her room with Grant. We maintained hope that with legal intervention, perhaps the parenting plan would come to fruition and we would finally have all our kids with us on a regular basis. Again, Grant's mom was not able to see Emily. This despite the fact that Suzanne's mother had died recently and the girls were pulled out of school for a week to visit their maternal grandfather in Vancouver.

As spring arrived, Emily's absences became the norm. She missed a full consecutive week and Madison was doing scarcely better. When Grant continued to try and find out from Suzanne and the school what was going on, both told him she had ADD/ADHD and was frequently sick. He asked the nature of her sickness, but Suzanne did not reply. Suzanne would only tell Grant that Emily was going for an ultrasound to investigate a stomach complaint. Then she had strep; then a viral infection; then asthma testing. Then she was taken out of her school and placed somewhere else, but Suzanne would not give details of why or where she was now enrolled. On May 1st, Grant phoned and emailed Suzanne saying he wanted to go to Edmonton to visit with Emily on Saturday. Suzanne's reply via email was "I am sorry but Emily (sic) does not wish to visit at this time."

Grant, respectfully as always, mentioned his confusion to Suzanne who had asked that visits be arranged through her but now said Emily did not want to visit and Grant should contact her himself. He could not do so anyway because, as he found out later through his daughters, his phone was blocked by Suzanne and their emails to him were infrequent and evasive. He stated his concern for Emily's overall health and her withdrawal from school. He asked for clarification on her situation. In an email ten days later, Suzanne wrote that "there is no apparent medical reason for Emily's (sic) physical symptoms." That was the entire message.

After making an arrangement to meet with Emily's school principal Jack Batton, vice-principal Greg Dannel, and guidance counselor, Bonnie Nowlen, Grant left work early on May 9th and drove to Edmonton and the school. Only Mr. Batton showed up for what turned out to be a fifteen-minute meeting, making excuses for the absences of the other two staff. This principal provided Grant with Emily's recent report card and attendance record, nothing else. Mr. Batton said he would email Grant on May 12th with the answers to Grant's questions that he could not provide at the May 9th meeting, "due to FOIP". Nevertheless, Mr. Batton neglected to follow through. On May 15th, Grant emailed Mr. Batton, again asking for the answers to these questions:

1. What has your school done to support my daughter, Emily (sic) over the past few years, given her high absenteeism and poor achievement? (resource support? home support?)
2. What is your school doing presently to intervene given my daughter has not attended school over the past five-consecutive weeks?
3. What is your school planning on doing to support my daughter in the future?

On June 2nd, Grant finally got a cursory email response from Mr. Batton, in which he stated that he had contacted Emily's mother with ideas for support. No one had ever contacted Grant with any information on the status of his daughters. Though he was an equal legal guardian of his children, the school withheld their information for years. Now extremely worried, Grant called Alberta Children's Services and told them of his concern regarding Emily. The social worker he spoke with promised to find out what was going on. As it turned out, this worker called Emily's cell phone (how she got the number, we do not know) and told her that her father was worried about her. This call angered Emily who claimed she was fine and her dad should stop following up on her. On June 3rd, Suzanne sent Grant an angry email stating that she had been told about his phoning Social Services asking them "to investigate me (Suzanne)". She wrote "our youngest daughter has voluntarily agreed to meet with AADAC (Alberta Alcohol and Drug Abuse Commission). She has specifically stated she does not want you (Grant) involved at this time. I will continue to keep you informed with her progress so that we may all celebrate her successes together." She signed off this message with "Kind regards".

In the meantime, Emily had written a short email to Grant in April, stating that she *did* want to come to Newfoundland in the summer. She had also written several emails to her cousins in Newfoundland and Ontario, saying she would be visiting soon with her dad and me and was looking forward to seeing them.

Finally, the Parenting Order was signed after *nine months* of pointless drafts going between lawyers. It was now a watered-down version of Judge Hilyard's decision from July 2007 and was without any enforcement clause or penalty for noncompliance. The Order was summarily ignored by Suzanne. Although it stated that Grant was to be kept fully informed and was an equal decision-maker in his children's lives, this never happened. On June 6th, Suzanne wrote Grant that Emily would not be going to Newfoundland after all. She copied Mr. Shymlo on this message. We had bought her an airplane ticket as per the emailed confirmation from Suzanne in March. By this time, Emily had been out of school since early April, for reasons unknown, and was apparently now a client at a drug-addiction facility. We had no idea what had transpired. Our worst nightmares were soon to be confirmed.

On June 23rd, Grant received a rather jumbled email from Emily saying that she did want to come to Newfoundland. Grant confirmed this, along with an itinerary and contact numbers, with Suzanne and picked up Laura, Madison and Emily in Edmonton on June 25th. All five of us were to fly to St. John's on the 27th. That evening and the next day, both Grant and I noticed the same lethargy in Madison and major social withdrawal in Emily. Suzanne, in Edmonton, continually phoned and texted the younger girls, especially Emily. At one point on June 26th, I took Madison and Emily for a walk with our dog in a nearby Calgary park and counted six texts that Emily read and answered from and to her mother over the course of ninety minutes. When we got home, the barrage from their mother continued.

I left home when Grant got there as I had to teach an evening class on the 26th. When I arrived back home after 9:00 p.m., I found Madison and Emily curled up on opposite ends of our couch and Grant was sitting in a nearby chair. Both girls had been crying. No one said anything. In a quiet voice, Grant said to me "Could you please come in and sit down? Emily has something she wants to say to you". She held out her arms to me, inner wrists exposed, and I saw the unmistakable, partially healed cut-marks across each one. I felt faint; I asked her what had happened. I will never forget what she said: "I am so stressed; I do it to help me be less stressed". These marks, of which there were between 30 and 50, clearly showed many attempts to injure herself over at least several months. Emily told us she was, and had been, using the street-drug, Ecstasy, as well as marijuana. Over the next two hours, both girls told us about their confusion, their secrets, their need to protect their mother, and their fear that Suzanne would hurt herself in their absence.

Finally, we were all somewhat settled down and exhausted. We went to bed, but Grant and I could still hear Emily texting in the next room. Within three hours, at approximately 2:30 a.m., Grant heard Emily crying and went to her room. Emily said she did not feel "safe" with us and wasn't "well enough" to go to Newfoundland. Suzanne had texted Emily that she was, right then, driving down to Calgary to save her and that she would arrive within the hour. Grant tried in vain to talk to Emily, but by then she was completely closed off from any communication with him. She just sat on her bed and despondently looked at the floor. Sure enough, the doorbell rang soon. By the time Grant got to the door, Suzanne had gotten back into her van at the curb. Emily ran for the door and through it. She jumped into her mother's vehicle where there sat a male teenager, Emily's "dealer", according to Madison. They drove off. *This was the last time we would see Emily for six years.*

Grant and I had a desperate argument that night after Emily left. I believed he should have stopped her from leaving. I knew she had been manipulated by her mother and was afraid to say "no" to her. She was a 13-year-old drug addict and school drop-out, also on "medications" prescribed by Dr. Blackmore. She suffered from Parental Alienation Syndrome, very similar in its symptomology to Stockholm Syndrome in which the captive sides with his or her captor. Grant believed that had he intervened to prevent Emily from returning to her mother, he would have been arrested and thrown in jail, since he was the noncustodial parent. But this was his allocated and Court-Ordered parenting time. We knew the Family Law system ignored the pleas of children and their targeted parents. Grant was effectively hamstrung in any effort to help Emily. That night was a turning point for Grant, perhaps for us both. The next day we flew to Newfoundland, without Emily.

Our trip was bittersweet. We had three weeks with family we loved and Grant's two older girls enjoyed their vacation with us and their extended family. It was wonderful for Grant's mom to finally have time with at least two of her granddaughters. Grant was quiet and preoccupied; I felt agitated and had trouble sleeping. I worried constantly about Emily back in Edmonton. I can't imagine how Grant managed to maintain his composure, but he was undoubtedly stressed. We noticed that Madison was taking at least two different "medications", remained lethargic and was sometimes confused. Grant wrote Ms. Harvis while we were in Newfoundland imploring her to do something to help Emily.

That August, after many attempts to contact Suzanne for an update on his 13-year-old daughter, Grant got from her a short message that Emily had been placed in a program called Transitions at the Y, a junior high-school outreach program, to take effect on September 2nd. By September 23rd, a teacher at the Y school, Roxanne Eyre, wrote Grant that she would be happy to send him weekly updates on Emily's progress. She did so consistently, for which we were extremely grateful. The first update showed her marks as 31% in Math, 10% in Language Arts and 0% in Social. Ms. Eyre told us that Emily was often absent already, had trouble focusing, seemed tired and was often belligerent. Two weeks later, she was unable to stay awake at school and had missed most of the week, despite Ms. Eyre having met with Suzanne more than once, asking for her support in helping Emily. Grant informed Ms. Eyre of a new software program that might help Emily with her math. The school could not afford to purchase it so Grant offered to cover that cost. He did so with Ms. Eyre's blessing… but Emily never used it.

By the end of October, Ms. Eyre informed Grant that Emily was now being "home-schooled by Suzanne and her boyfriend" (someone who Grant knew nothing about). Ms. Eyre said that Suzanne was "planning on getting medical help" for Emily. A week later, Ms. Eyre wrote Grant that Emily was now in AADAC full time due to "personal issues" and that Grant could only get further information from Suzanne directly. Though he tried consistently, Grant received no communication at all from Suzanne.

Madison, meanwhile was also sporadically attending school. As early as mid-September, she had missed a staggering number of classes. She was in Grade 9. Of note, Suzanne wrote Grant on October 30th that she had received notification from our lawyer, Ms. Harvis, that there was to be a return to court on a Contempt Order application. It would deal with Suzanne's total noncompliance of the Parenting Order. Suzanne wrote that she was unable to pay for more court costs and asked Grant to delay any court action until June 2009. In the same email, Suzanne stated that she, Laura, Madison, and Emily, had "received a gift to fly to Disneyworld at Christmas break".

In the same October 30 email, Suzanne wrote that "all three girls have chosen to go to Disneyworld" with her from December 20 -January 2. Despite the parents' Court Order stating that Grant was to have his daughters for half this Christmas vacation, Suzanne was effectively removing any hope he had of seeing the girls during the school break. She asked that Grant write her a letter of support for this trip so that she could use it to get the girls across the United States' border. Grant wrote her that he would agree to Suzanne taking the girls for one of their two weeks of holiday but not for both. He said either week was fine with him.

Four days later, on November 3, Suzanne wrote Grant that since he would not write a letter of permission for a two week trip to Disneyworld, he was welcome to contact her when he changed his mind. And later that day, Grant received another message from Suzanne: "Until further notice Emily (sic) will be voluntarily attending the AADAC day program not Transitions (sic) at the Y. Transitions at the Y will be holding her spot. You can go to the AADAC web site for further information."

On November 6, on the 12th, and again December 2nd, having still received no communication at all from Suzanne, Grant wrote her asking for information about Emily's health and school status. He was sick with worry about his youngest daughter who was now apparently in an addictions day program at AADAC. There still was no response from Suzanne. Then on December 10th, Suzanne, three consecutive times, phoned the school where Grant was principal. She left the same message with the school's administrative assistant each time: Suzanne said she wanted to pass on a message from Ms. Eyre at the Y program which Emily had attended previously; and she wanted to know if Grant had changed his mind about writing the letter of permission for Disneyworld. Grant responded when he could that day, again asking Suzanne via email for information on Emily. Of note, due to Grant's own negative experiences in trying to talk with Suzanne and on the advice of his lawyer, he now communicated to Suzanne only through email. Grant had also tried his best to get information on Emily's situation from the AADAC program and from the psychiatrist, Dr. Blackmore, but to no avail. Even after her three phone calls to his work that day, Suzanne did not answer Grant's email.

Laura, Madison and Emily were taken to Florida for both weeks anyway… with their mother and her male partner (we did not find out Suzanne had remarried until four years later in a 2011 Judicial Dispute Resolution hearing) who had paid for the trip. There were Facebook photos of the girls and their mother in a limousine on the way to the airport and in Disneyworld. *They apparently had no issue with Customs getting over the border despite there being no permission letter from the equal guardian and father of these children.*

2009

To date, we had spent over $70,000 in legal and professional "counseling" fees, and though the 2007 Court Order stated that

Grant was to be kept apprised of his daughters' medical and academic records, none had been provided by Suzanne nor any family physician (Grant did not even know which family doctor Suzanne took the girls to), psychiatrist, counselor or psychologist involved. The girls' mother continued to completely ignore the Court Order, even taking them into the United States without their father's permission and during his court-ordered parenting time. Ms. Harvis, our lawyer, continued to write long emails that achieved nothing while costing us thousands of dollars. There had been no help for the girls since we began legal proceedings in June of 2006.

On January 19th Ms. Harvis wrote a long email to Grant stating that she had just finished a 20- minute teleconference with Mr. Shymlo and Zella Harmon, a lawyer now appointed to legally represent Madison and Emily. Ms. Harvis wrote that this children's lawyer had met with both girls, found Emily to be "on the right track" and now enrolled in yet another school, this one named Guardian Angel, as of that day. We had no idea why Emily did not return to the Transitions at the Y school. Our lawyer also asked whether Grant had completed the court-ordered High Conflict Parenting after Separation course…he had… and to provide proof of completion to Ms. Harmon. Suzanne, however, as we discovered later, did not attend this course. The email also said that Madison was asking for counseling, felt "caught in the middle and depressed", and Ms. Harmon wanted to recruit another psychologist, Marshall Whet, to counsel Madison. Ms. Harmon said she could access Legal Aid to pay the counseling fee up front until the legal fee responsibilities were decided by the court in future. The Court Order had directed there to be a psychological assessment of the girls but this, as yet, had not occurred. We hoped that now it finally would.

Grant agreed to Madison's counseling with Mr. Whet, though we were dismayed that Emily was not included in this initiative. The latest email from Ms. Harvis was assurance at least that Emily was still alive; we had heard nothing earlier. Grant also wrote in surprise that his permission was being requested since this was the first time he had been considered relevant in decisions about his daughters. He reminded Ms. Harvis to please let Ms. Harmon know that Madison was still on anti-psychotics and anti-depressants simultaneously since at least a year before, both drugs contraindicated in children. He worried that the longer the children were exposed to their mentally-ill mother without intervention, the worse off they were becoming and he feared for their welfare.

We don't know whether any actual meetings occurred between Mr. Whet and either girl. He did write a one-page summary to Judge Hilyard supposedly following a meeting with Madison but it was vague and seemingly inaccurate. Ms. Harmon, too, wrote a one-paragraph email "summary" of her interactions with both girls. Again, this "report" seemed unprofessional and read more like hearsay rather than fact. It appeared that the counseling by Mr. Whet was a tactic by the opposing lawyer, Mr. Shymlo, to stall contempt proceedings against Suzanne. It worked. Grant had asked Ms. Harvis to return to court to have an enforcement clause attached to the 2007 Court Order finally filed on May 22, 2008. There was a court date set for February 2009, but it was now cancelled due to the children's new lawyer coming on board.

In February, I had Reading Week off work and spent the five days organizing all the paper, emails, and texts sent and received by all parties in this convoluted legal case. I laid out piles of documents on our living-room floor and slowly put them in order. Grant and I wrote and re-wrote letters and developed new ideas to move forward. We researched everything we could find on Family Law, parental alienation cases, and child welfare. Grant and I talked about nothing but the court case and his three daughters. We were at a loss as to why the legal system was not intervening when the documented evidence was so clear that the girls needed immediate help.

By spring, Grant was showing extreme fatigue and it was increasingly hard for us to enjoy the normal, good things in life. My children were astounded that Grant's girls, who so clearly loved and wanted to be with their dad, were not able to see him.

Emails from Laura and Madison were scarce and always evasive. We didn't know what was going on with any of the girls but we knew they were keeping secrets as coached by their mother. Ms. Harvis seemed to do little except send more emails between herself, Mr. Shymlo, and Ms. Harmon for no apparent purpose. Legal bills were amounting to $4000 a month on average with no end in sight. Grant was terrified of losing our house and being rendered bankrupt, for a second time. My work has always been contract so we were financially and emotionally teetering on the brink. Through this time, Grant continued his fruitless attempts to see Madison and Emily. Laura occasionally came for a visit but was always careful to stay away from any talk about her sisters. It seemed from what she told us that she rarely saw them since moving out with her boyfriend a couple years earlier. We did know from Madison that she had been given permission by her mother to fly to Arizona to meet with a "boy who is in the military". She had sent us pictures of him and said she was interested in spending time with him sometime this year. She was 15-years-old yet her mother encouraged her to go unsupervised. Grant asked Laura whether Madison had indeed flown to Arizona, but Laura shrugged and said she didn't know.

Grant and I submitted formal letters, complete with verified documentation, to authority figures we hoped would intervene in our case and in others also needing help for their alienated children. We wrote a letter of complaint to the Judicial Council of Canada. The response letter we received stated that judges have autonomy and can direct whatever they wish in court. Then we wrote to Alison Redfall, then Minister of Justice and Attorney General, and were told in her curt response letter that family law was outside the jurisdiction of the attorney general's office.

We also tried to put in a complaint with Alberta's Ombudsman but discovered that this office does not deal with issues about the courts or lawyers. We wrote to the College of Alberta Psychologists, since Mr. Whet had not followed through on the court's directive that he counsel and assess both Madison and Emily. The only work it seemed he had done was the vague summary he had written to the judge regarding his supposed meeting with Madison. This complaint was finally, but positively, responded to by the College in 2011. That organization ruled that Mr. Whet return $750 he had kept "in trust" for counseling of Emily that had not occurred. He was also made to write a letter of apology to Grant for his negligence and he was to be monitored for a period of approximately six months by a Randall Spalliscy of The College. We received the apology letter within a few weeks but Grant had to follow up with Whet's office to remind him to repay our $750 held by his office. This penalty represented a slap on the wrist for Mr. Whet, and Grant's children remained in dire straits. This was nonetheless the closest we ever came to obtaining any sort of help for Madison or Emily.

Finally, after much soul-searching and the blatant conclusion that our lawyer, Ms. Harvis, was interested in maximizing her billable hours (she has her own practice) but could or would not provide any relief to our ongoing dire situation, we paid her final bill and fired her. This lawyer had represented our case since May of 2006 but had achieved only a non-enforced and toothless Court Order that took a whole year to file, and in no way represented the scope of support the girls, Grant, and even Suzanne needed. Our relationship with Ms. Harvis had cost us dearly, for we had hired her as the expert to take control and direct us all to a reasonable and progressive resolution. She did not even speak on our behalf in court, did not cross-examine any of the far-fetched and undocumented claims of Mr. Shymlo, and wrote copious emails that put us on the brink of poverty as we struggled increasingly to pay her exorbitant bills.

Each of the complaints we wrote were between 5 and 20 pages of text, complete with attached evidence in the form of emails, texts, and letters from the girls, Suzanne, schools, the psychiatrist, psychologist, and lawyers. These took hundreds of hours to compile. Grant was a school principal who specialized in learning disabilities in children. I was, and am, a lecturer and researcher at a university. These tasks were overwhelming, especially coupled with the emotional toll of constantly worrying about Grant's three daughters and our need to retain our united parenting model for my kids, who were doing well. Even my ex-husband Lorne was incredibly supportive of our situation and the juggling we were forced into while we each held a full-time job. We spent all our "downtime" engaged in the second job of maintaining our legal struggle.

I remember one evening when we began to sort, and chronologically order, all the emails and texts from just Suzanne and the girls over the years. We did not stop that night until we finished the task at 6:00 a.m. next morning. Then Grant, without sleep, showered, put on a suit and tie, and drove off to his school. I similarly headed off to teach my lectures.

Then one day a car stopped outside our house. A bailiff came to the door with court documents initiated by Suzanne through Mr. Shymlo, asking Grant for more Child Maintenance dollars. This even though he had always paid more than he was required to by the federal Child Maintenance Guidelines and had made sure to apprise the Maintenance Enforcement Program (i.e., MEP) in Edmonton of any raises and promotions he earned. This notification by MEP stated that Grant was required to submit his tax returns and mine (of note, I did so but Suzanne and her husband, unbeknownst to the court, did not) over the last several years. We did so. This paperwork named Grant only as *"The Debtor"*, not as father, parent, co-parent, equal guardian or any other critical part of his daughters' lives. The terminology clearly reflected the dismissal of Grant as anything but a portable bank.

By November, our third anniversary, we were both highly stressed and had little time together. We both were working extra time and I had taken on an extra contract to help us pay our legal bills. Though Ms. Harvis was now removed from our file, we were still paying off our account with her. We had also initiated "taxation" against her, meaning we filed a claim stating that she overcharged us, given her lack of initiative and results. Some months later, we would meet with a court-mandated mediator and Ms. Harvis would subsequently repay us a minimal sum of approximately $4200. The decision was based on her charging us full fees for all activities on our behalf, rather than downloading some of these costs onto a junior lawyer or administrative assistant.

One Saturday, Grant and I stopped by a Rona hardware store to get a replacement stopper for our bathtub. This was about the extent of our "leisure" time by now. We bought one for $3.24. When I got home, I submitted our numbered cash receipt to an online contest with 75,000 Air Miles as a prize. This purchase resulted in a beacon of hope for us. We won! The Air Miles were applied to my account and Grant and I decided to use some of these to take a trip over the Christmas holidays. Though we continued to try to contact Madison and Emily, there was no response… ever… by now. It seemed we would not see any of the girls over the break. Laura had to work but, to our delight, did visit us over New Year's. Grant had not had any of his daughters with him over Christmas since his marriage breakdown back in 1999. He did not argue this point with Suzanne and was resigned that it was never to be. So on Christmas Day of 2009, Grant and I flew to Jamaica for a wonderful week that likely, in hindsight, saved our marriage for the time being. We returned home to Laura's visit and my children; the three got along well together and enjoyed each other's company. We could have felt like a real family, finally, had we not been consumed by worry about Madison and Emily.

2010

Laura had been reinstated at University of Alberta, after leaving for a year to "sort herself out." We were proud of her and how she was managing to stay afloat despite the ongoing dysfunction of her family. She had done well since moving away from her mother's house and was mature and capable. Sometimes, while visiting us, she would silently sit close to either Grant or me and stare at the floor. She frequently seemed preoccupied and on guard, though she was affectionate and eager to please. One day she said to me, "Do you know what my worst fear is? That I'll become my mother". We talked about how she is her own person and how proud of her we are.

After no contact and only a couple of cryptic emails from Madison in over two years, Grant got a voicemail from Suzanne one afternoon saying that she had some "bad news" about Madison and "how are you going to pay for the body cast that she needs?" Grant called me on my cell, terrified about what had happened to his daughter. He had tried calling Suzanne back many times to no avail. Her phone just rang and rang. This was *two days* after an accident in which Madison had apparently fallen 6 meters off a school roof. Finally Grant got through to Suzanne by phone. She told him that Madison had been "on the roof one night with a couple friends when it happened. She slipped and fell when they thought the janitor was coming to chase them or something." She gave no further information except which hospital Madison was now in.

Grant left immediately for Edmonton and went to the hospital to see his now-estranged daughter. He told me how happy Madison was to see him and how relieved he was to find out she was not paralyzed. At the hospital, a staff member stayed in the room with Madison, telling Grant they were "advised by mom" (i.e., Suzanne) that Grant was not allowed to be unsupervised with Madison. There never was, however, such an Order from the Court or any other entity. She was kept in hospital about a week and was then discharged in a corset-like body cast, which she would need to wear for many weeks.

Many months later, after missing weeks and weeks of school, Madison attended some physiotherapy and finally wrote an email to Grant updating him on her recovery. She then phoned him to talk. She said she had not been drunk when she climbed on the roof but was just "being stupid because I'm super mad." He was, as always, loving and supportive though they did discuss making good choices. Being a school principal with a specialty in special education, Grant was particularly gifted with positive communication skills, and I was in awe of this and his unfaltering patience. Madison had grown up, as had her sisters, with very little parenting, much less appropriate parenting and she spent most of her time alone in her room with earbuds in. She remembered foraging for her own meals at home or wherever she could from a very young age. She told us she didn't have a bus pass and couldn't get up for school. She believed herself to be "almost an adult" and told Grant she knew what she was doing. She was now 16. Grant learned that Suzanne would take the girls to fancy brunches and heap awards such as Disneyworld on them when they were supposed to be spending time with us in Calgary. Throughout this conversation with Madison, Grant maintained his composure.

In April of 2010, my dad passed away suddenly. Our home phone rang at 4:30 a.m. one morning… it was my mom giving me the news. I had been close with my dad who was and will always be a major positive influence on my life. Grant was supportive, but this event added to our ongoing stress of the lawsuit and our dwindling finances due to regular, huge legal bills. We both slept poorly, but were managing our household as best we could, trying to hang on to a semblance of normal life as a family. Grant had always been connected and involved with my two, now adult, children. He often drove my daughter to basketball and talked guitars with my son, who also played. This latest event was tough on us all.

Several months later, during which there was still no visit from either Madison or Emily (who Grant had last seen two years before), Madison called Grant to ask if she could come for a visit. We were thrilled though wary, since she had asked many times before and then cancelled at the last minute. Madison is a creative soul and had a special interest in music and theatre. Some years, Madison did come to Calgary in late July as she enjoyed, along with us, volunteering at Calgary's annual Folk Festival. This year she wanted to come and made arrangements to do so. Grant drove to Edmonton to pick her up, hoping he just might be able to see the now 15-year-old Emily and 20-year-old Laura. But there was no sign of Emily and Grant returned home with Madison, who was still recovering from her back injury.

Grant's mom had arrived from Newfoundland and joined us at the Folk Festival for a weekend of fun and time with at least some of her grandchildren. Grant's brother from British Columbia also came with his wife and three young children; they camped in our backyard. Grant's brother in Calgary also spent time together with us all. Madison seemed to be in good spirits and enjoyed the visit with her extended family. It was a relatively happy weekend, one we so needed. But even then, Suzanne called and texted Madison incessantly. She could not leave her in peace for even a short time. We did notice, though, that sometimes Madison would look at her phone but not respond. It seemed like she was beginning to pull away from her mother's all-encompassing spider-web.

There was a hiccup when I told Madison I could not drive her anywhere in my car. I explained she would need to go with her dad when we needed two cars. I feared that if anything happened on the road with my fragile step-daughter in my car, Suzanne would jump at the chance to go after me. She had alluded many times to Grant's "little girlfriend" and the girls told us their mother resented my being part of the family. By this time, I had been with Grant for almost six years.

We saw Madison again for a weekend later that summer. She told us she had been raped by her boss at the restaurant where she worked. According to her story to Grant, she had been working there to earn credits for high school upgrading. She had recently altogether stopped attending school and had been working for a couple months but now abruptly quit. Her employment was arranged as a work placement through the Edmonton Public School Board. After the rape supposedly happened, Madison did not go to the police, but she did tell her mother. Suzanne suggested counseling. Madison made her dad promise not to go to the police. Grant kept calm somehow as Madison relayed her story, but he was furious when he told me later. He was shaking and crying and obviously distraught. Though I asked Grant how he knew she was telling the truth, he said he believed her because he knew his daughter and her demeanor was authentic. I couldn't help, but I wanted to more than I've ever wanted to do anything. I wondered how much more strain a person could take before he would implode.

Grant did not break his daughter's trust. He decided to abide by Madison's wishes that he refrain from reporting to the police. He was so afraid that he would lose this daughter too. I disagreed and was frustrated by Grant's choice. He did, however, report the restaurant and owner to Madison's school principal and counselor. His complaint fell on deaf ears. We don't even know if this work placement was removed since Grant was, as usual, prevented from accessing any information about the incident. The school said they could not release information due to Alberta's FOIP legislation.

Now without a lawyer, Grant and I were stymied about how to help the girls. We had fired Ms. Harvis in 2009 so now had no legal representation. At that time, there were few resources available to which targeted parents could turn for guidance. In fact, we only knew through hearsay amongst our work and social circles that we were not alone; others had experienced or were experiencing parental alienation too. We didn't even know the name of this phenomenon. One night after perusing the internet for information, using various keywords to describe our situation with Grant's daughters, I came upon someone professing to be a "parental alienation consultant" named John Goldburn. I emailed him and he soon responded, asking for a telephone conversation to gather history on our case. He was in Florida at that time but spent much of his year in Ontario. I spoke with him first, giving him the background including that our finances were seriously depleted and we were at the end of our rope. I let John know that Grant was depressed and felt there was no hope for support from so-called professionals. I, too, was wavering in terms of my overall faith in justice.

There was a second phone call; this time between John and Grant. It lasted almost 45 minutes. I could hear Grant's voice quavering as he related his story. When he got off the phone, Grant sobbed with his head in his hands for a long while. I believe he felt both fear for the new load of debt that would undoubtedly now push us toward financial ruin (i.e., another bankruptcy for Grant and thereby, me), and relief in finding someone who could finally help us and the girls. John, he told me later, seemed to know how to help us and knew which professionals we needed to recruit to get our case sorted out… in essence to do damage-control following the botched legal attempt by Ms. Harvis. We sent John $3000 which we could barely afford, his fee to sort through our file and make the necessary referrals for us. The following weekend I went to my workplace and spent most of the day there, copying our entire case file, which amounted to a full banker's box of documents. This, too, I shipped to Mr. Goldburn. Two weeks later, I received an email that he had read through our file and knew what we needed to do. Over the telephone and electronically, John gave us contact information including that for a lawyer, Ron Faulter Q.C.; a psychologist, Tara Taylan; and three other psychologists who lived outside our Alberta, one of them American. According to Mr. Goldburn, these people could and would help us but it would be expensive.

Though we could certainly not afford to hire out-of-province experts, we did hire Mr. Faulter, the lawyer, and Ms. Taylen, the recommended psychologist, both in Calgary. Both of these people asked, during the first visit, for "retainers" to formally make us clients: Mr. Faulter, in the amount of $8000 plus an ongoing $1000/month agreement; and Ms. Taylen, $3000 up front. So before the first half of 2010 was up, we had again begun to see our finances cratering, after the short hiatus between lawyers. In June of 2010 alone, we paid Mr. Faulter a total of $28,790. I cashed in $10,000 of my RRSP to pay him over Grant's pleas not to do so; I was, as a result, gouged in taxes for "capital gains" the following spring.

We first met with Ron Faulter, who told us our case "is a 9 out of 10 on the scale of parental alienation and you have a six-week window to get an intervention". He told us his hourly rate was $500; within six months he raised his fee to $700 per hour. Grant only met with Tara Taylen once; she had no information or expertise beyond what any person could easily find on the internet in short order. As a result, Grant sent a complaint letter and was reimbursed $2100 of the original retainer. His one-hour, pointless appointment with her had cost us $900.

There was another "court hearing", which was in fact a teleconference, on June 30. This one included our lawyer Ron Faulter, the Justice Hilyard, Wayne Shymlo (counsel for Suzanne) and Geoffrey Kelly, who had apparently replaced Ms. Harmon as the children's lawyer. Justice Hilyard began by stating that he had never "been formally seized to the file" and was therefore not the Case Manager. He did mention that he had presided over the original court hearing in July of 2007 and again in October 2009. Now he stated that he felt he "should step down from the file" since we (Grant and I) had reported, to the Judicial Council of Canada, his inaction and incompetent acceptance of hearsay for his decisions. Nevertheless, the lawyers for these parties now agreed to make Justice Hilyard the Case Manager and he accepted.

As a result of the July 30 "court hearing", Mr. Faulter phoned and sent a court memo to update us, stating that "the most important thing is to try to save these girls, we'll worry about the rest later". He said "There will be a psychological assessment done of these girls (Madison and Emily) by Dr. Steven Carton in Edmonton and sent to Case Manager Justice Hilyard by the end of August". In fact, all that occurred was that Zella Harmon was removed as the children's lawyer (perhaps our complaint to the Law Society about her inaction had caused her removal; we don't know) and was replaced by another, the equally unmotivated Geoffrey Kelly. Ron Faulter contacted us to report this change in the children's lawyer as if it was his doing. This replacement in no way helped our, or the girls', situation and it was Ms. Harmon who briefed Mr. Kelly on the girls. He did not meet with the girls in person that we know of until many months later in 2011, though in the "court hearing" he had said he would do so in the next week and report back to the Justice.

That summer, counseling did commence between Grant and Madison at the request of Dr. Carton, the psychologist in Edmonton. Grant paid a retainer of $8500 to his office, as per the court's direction, and met with Dr. Carton and Madison. Each one-hour appointment required Grant to take a day off work to drive up to and back from Edmonton. Suzanne would drive Madison to the appointments, but except for the first one, Suzanne was not included in the counseling sessions. Dr. Carton began by telling Grant that Madison was uncomfortable with him and he should refrain from any contribution to the ensuing conversation. He was only to sit quietly and observe. Though Grant had repeatedly asked that Emily be included in the counseling either together with Madison or separately, Suzanne, according to Dr. Carton, told him Emily simply "couldn't make it". There was no dispute about this and Mr. Faulter did not even attempt to have Emily brought into the initiative. Emily had been completely severed from Grant's life, yet the legal system did nothing to intervene, provide supports for, or reunify this girl with her father.

At the same time that spring and summer, Grant received notice from the Alberta Maintenance Enforcement Program (MEP) that he was required to pay an increase in Child Maintenance. This was rather baffling since Laura had not lived at home in three years and Madison had also now moved in with a boyfriend and away from mom. And Grant had voluntarily increased his monthly payments to Suzanne every time he got a promotion. This MEP notice stated that Suzanne was claiming Maintenance for three children, plus retro-payments for years when Grant had paid less than the amount now tallied as owing. Of note, Grant's gross income was approximately three times mine yet due to Child Maintenance and legal bills, he netted less than I did each month from 2006 on. Our legal bills and counseling fees were paid by our combined contributions as household expenditures, so we were financially tanking. These costs were intended to get help for the girls, including court-ordered mental health assessments, Social Services intervention where necessary (i.e., this had already been in place before we even began our legal proceedings in 2006 but terminated at Suzanne's request), learning supports for school, and an enforced Parenting Schedule. There was no help and our money continued its hemorrhage. Maintenance is in no way tied to access so alienators, almost always the custodial parent, receive maximum Child Maintenance with zero accountability.

Grant contacted Ron Faulter immediately after being hit with the MEP request for retroactive and increased payments as well as penalties for failing to pay in a timely fashion. Suzanne was lying and MEP was openly supporting her agenda. We believed Mr. Faulter would take action to correct this mistake; we depended on his doing so and quickly. He said he would apply for a "Stay" in our legal case until Justice Hilyard could make a decision on what to do going forward with this outrageous MEP demand. But our lawyer failed to do so. He later told us he forgot.

A few days later, one Friday evening after work, Grant and I met at Safeway to buy our next week's groceries. We were under the impression that Mr. Faulter had done his job so for once, we weren't completely consumed by fear of another legally-sanctioned financial assault. We were at the cashier with a line of other people waiting behind us. Grant inserted his debit card and it was declined. He was confused since he had been paid that day. He then tried his credit card; declined. Unsure what to do and trying not to hold up the line of customers, I used my debit and credit cards...both were declined. Now we were both panicky about what to do and what had happened. I decided to phone my then 20-year-old daughter for help. She drove straight over and used her money to pay our grocery bill... and saved the day.

That was how we found out Mr. Faulter failed to file our Stay of legal proceedings. As a result, MEP took immediate action and seized not only Grant's bank accounts but mine too, as well as his Driver's License and Passport. He was rendered unable to drive to his workplace, which was an hour from Calgary. Grant's words to me, upon reflection in 2012, were "I couldn't even get groceries because this idiot hasn't done his ___ing job! I have massive arrears and you talk about stress load. I am trying to manage my work, I am worried that my kids don't go to school, they use drugs, are fed drugs, and I have a friggin' lawyer who doesn't even bother to keep my head out of the noose...".

By September little had changed and we were still trying to get some legal relief for the grievous error Mr. Faulter had made. MEP did unlock our bank accounts a week later once the Stay was signed as an emergency action by Case Manager Hilyard. Then it would be another year until Mr. Faulter finally succeeded in putting together a Judicial Dispute Resolution meeting. Justice Hilyard, however, had determined this the best course of action. It would include him, the three lawyers Faulter, Shymlo and Kelly. Suzanne would be present as well. We already knew this would be a waste of time, since Suzanne had created the alienation and as such, failed to co-operate on any level to enhance Grant's ability to parent.

There was no word at all from Emily; and little from Madison outside of the few "counseling sessions" at which Grant sat silently. At these appointments, Madison recounted all the hatred and false realities she had been brainwashed with by her mother over the years. Dr. Carton allowed Madison free rein to speak without asking her for detail or elaboration on her claims about Grant, such as "he doesn't pay Child Support" and "he is too demanding". She told Dr. Carton how *her family* (i.e., which included her mother, sisters, and maternal grandparents, but apparently not Grant or his immediate or extended family) had secrets which were no business of Grant's or mine.

Through the crushing load of worry and fear that we endured, we still tried to find some good things in life. I love my children dearly and I believe Grant was fond of them as well. They were, and are, bright spots in our lives and their humour kept us going. We were aware that they worried about us and were confused by the failure of our legal case. They would see Laura once in a while when she visited Calgary, but none of them spoke about the elephant in the room; the welfare of Madison and Emily.

At a "Meet the Teacher" evening at Grant's school, one of the rural dads mentioned to Grant that his dog had recently had puppies. He wondered whether we might be interested in taking one. Grant told me about this when he got home and the next day, emailed me photos of the litter. They were the product of a collie mother and sired by an unknown, perhaps neighbour's, dog. It so happened that we had lost our dog that previous November and missed her very much. I went with my 90-year-old aunt to have a look, and, on the second visit, Grant came along. We brought Gavin, our new puppy, home on my birthday. This was a happy, precious event that lifted our spirits and those of our children. Grant wrote to his daughters about our new addition and even Emily wrote a short email back, saying she was excited to visit and see the puppy. But this was not to be. Laura did come for a weekend soon after, but both younger girls were "too busy", according to Suzanne.

Since Mr. Faulter's failure to file the Stay of Proceedings back in September, we received 17 so-called Case Conference email messages, letters, and Notices of Motion that flew between lawyers Shymlo, Faulter, and Kelly, two psychologists, Judge Hilyard, and Grant before the year was over. Still, Suzanne's court application to increase Grant's Child Maintenance went unresolved. There was absolutely no attention given to the issue of my step-daughters' deteriorating health and welfare, despite Grant's continued pleas for intervention on their behalf.

Christmas and New Year's came and went with no word at all from any of the three girls. Grant was resigned to the situation by now. We held no expectations to see any of the girls but we worried continually for their safety. One day Grant said to me that "every time the phone rings, I wonder if it's about one of my girls being found dead on the street somewhere".

2011

By this time, I always slept poorly and had frequent nightmares that included Grant dying, his girls being run over, and my kids and our dog being abducted. I knew this was interfering with my ability to do my job and though I was, and still am, physically healthy and active, I was often so tired I struggled to make the three flights of stairs to my office. Grant, an excellent hockey and soccer player who regularly met me for after-work runs, was similarly finding difficulty in staying focused and energized. He often woke in the night with what he called *flashbacks* to negative events he and/or we had experienced about his daughters.

Despite our increasingly tenuous circumstances, especially with our finances, I loved this man more completely than ever. I had one wish and that was to find a way to help him…and all of us. I remember watching him leave for work in the mornings in his suit and tie and I thought how no one except me knew the hell he lived with all day every day. He managed to smile when he came home after work and we always hugged and said we loved each other. He called me "my refuge". Sometimes he drew little pictures of us doing happy things such as hiking and left them on the counter for me. He brought me flowers some days. And each morning he poured my orange juice and left it for me on the counter. Those are simple memories etched deep in my heart.

On February 17th, Grant received a copy of the original letter to Justice Hilyard confirming a "Case Management meeting" to be held on April 6th. On February 24th, three letters came to Grant from Alberta Justice: One restricting Grant's access to Alberta Registry Services; another requesting Grant's statement of finances, and a third which threatened to deny Grant's driver's license renewal. The next day, on the 25th, came another letter from Alberta Justice asking Grant to fill out the enclosed "Personal Property Writ". On the 26th, yet another letter from Alberta Justice enclosed a notice of pending penalties against Grant from the Department of Justice Canada. Several days later, on March 4th and in response to his request for MEP to Stay penalties until his upcoming Case Management meeting, Grant was emailed a request to send all his financial records since March of 2010 to the opposing lawyers Shymlo and Kelly. He did so. This was the third time Grant had sent this information to all three lawyers in our case. The two representing Suzanne and "the children" denied ever having received them earlier, though we had email proof of their being sent. This was only the beginning of a harassment campaign targeting Grant about his status with MEP.

On March 5th and 11th respectively, we received two more letters from Alberta Justice: The first stated that Grant's drivers' license had been revoked and his "arrears status" filed at the credit bureau; the second was a notice that Grant's statement of finances was now overdue. And on March 11th, a letter from the executive director of MEP warned of penalties now imposed: on the 24th all Grant's bank accounts were frozen by a MEP Court Order. We believe that the entirety of this action by Alberta Justice and MEP was due to Ron Faulter's failure to file the Stay of Proceedings. *This lawyer has, nevertheless, a Queen's Court (QC) designation and is still practicing law. He markets himself as a parental alienation expert.*

The April 6th Case Management meeting did occur, resulting in a Court Order with all Child Maintenance arrears regarding Grant's eldest daughter vacated immediately. Justice Hilyard also ordered, for the third time, that Laura was no longer a child of the marriage under the Divorce Act, reaffirming his decision from 2007. This Stay of Enforcement was nonetheless conditional upon Grant's continued payment of Child Maintenance to MEP in the amount of $1,200.00 per month. Directions were to be put into Consent Order form and filed immediately. A copy of the Order was to be sent to MEP as soon as it was filed.

But it was twelve days later when Notice of the new Order was finally processed by MEP and Grant was given a partial reinstatement of his Registry privileges. There remained a pending court application for a final judgment on Child Maintenance scheduled for May 18th; this was later postponed until July 27th. No reason was given though Mr. Shymlo made the request, and it was granted.

On the 21st of April, Grant's tax refund was inexplicably seized by the Court. The assessment notice showed that $3027.51 was transferred, without Grant's knowledge or any explanation, from the Canada Revenue Agency to MEP.

This latest assault on Grant was very difficult for both of us. One evening he came home with a gift and beautiful letter of gratitude from his boss at the School Board. Finally, a good thing had happened, and I was so proud of my husband. But arriving in the mail that same day was another invoice from our lawyer, to whom we now apparently owed over $46,000, despite our previously paid retainer and ongoing monthly instalments. I noticed how Grant was fixated on the bill, rather than his work accomplishment. He and I were completely obsessed by the deterioration of his daughters and the state of our finances. We even tried counselling, and when the psychologist asked us how stressed we felt, we answered almost in unison that "our house is flooding right now and we've come to this appointment while Carmen (my daughter) is bailing to keep the water at bay. This doesn't even faze us in the least. It is nothing compared to our everyday lives".

I decided to take a one-month Spanish immersion opportunity in Mexico sponsored by my employer. For several years I had thought about going but hoped that one year, both Grant and I could take advantage of this excellent program. So in early July, Grant drove me to the airport where I, with a heavy heart, left him, thinking it would be beneficial for us to spend some time apart. It increasingly seemed that my husband just wanted to be left alone. We emailed when we could, but I could tell Grant was terrified of what the upcoming "Judicial Dispute Resolution" (JDR) would mean for his daughters and us.

On July 27th, Mr. Faulter attended this JDR in Edmonton with Grant, Suzanne and Mr. Shymlo, Mr. Kelly, and Justice Hilyard. Faulter invoiced us soon after in the amount of *$8,000 for one day*; $2400 for his travel to and from Edmonton and the other $5600 to attend the JDR.

Interestingly, though Suzanne had claimed Child Maintenance for all three girls to get more money from Grant, her lawyer now retracted that claim and stated there were only two eligible daughters. Though Laura was, by this time, 22 years old and a graduate from the University of Alberta, Grant continued to voluntarily supplement her income directly as he had done since she was 18. The JDR meeting lasted a couple hours during which, as Grant told me via phone conversation later, Mr. Shymlo had to twice tell his client, Suzanne, to sit down and be quiet. The entire meeting was about Grant's Child Maintenance and supposed arrears, penalties, and future payments to Suzanne. Of note, not a word was spoken about the welfare of Grant and Suzanne's daughters, nor the wretched life they were living despite Grant's ongoing and reliable Child Maintenance payments to Suzanne over 12 years! No one discussed the failure of the court-ordered "counselling" with Stephen Carton and Madison. No one mentioned Emily at all. The JDR was nothing more than a cash grab for Suzanne, three lawyers, and the judge.

I returned to Calgary late in July. My four weeks away had been therapeutic as I was somewhat distracted from the ongoing hellish situation at home. Despite all this, I had missed and worried about Grant so much. When I saw him at the airport, my heart melted. How could we resolve this and move on to a happy life? He smiled when he saw me, but there was little conversation as we returned home.

As a result of the JDR, yet another Court Order, the sixth, was filed on August 11th, confirming a reinstatement of Grant's credit and reputation. It also ordered that he continue to pay for 16-year-old Emily's Child Maintenance, though we suspected she had lived on the streets for years by this time. The last grade she had successfully completed was 6. Grant was to pay Madison's share of Child Maintenance directly to her until she turned 22. Grant had lobbied hard for this change, but Mr. Faulter took ownership of this "huge breakthrough" in our case.

Ron Faulter was charging us $632.97 per hour of his time and he had four other junior lawyers working on our case as well. From the invoices, it appeared that the lion's share of these exorbitant fees went to his reading of emails. To date, our case had involved at least seven lawyers, two judges, a psychiatrist, six psychologists, five school principals as well as Child Services, the Alberta Alcohol and Drug Abuse Commission (AADAC) and countless legal and mental health "professionals". Mr. Faulter's signed August 9th invoice to us stated that "we have clearly gone beyond our projection of fees" and quoted our outstanding balance to date as $46,102.14. This number excluded the retainer and monthly instalments we had already paid since hiring him in 2010.

Finally, on October 11, a full thirteen months after MEP had begun their harassment campaign against Grant, this Court Order with amended Child Maintenance payment terms was put into action. We fired Ron Faulter the same month. On November 7, the Notice of Withdrawal of Lawyer was filed at Court of Queen's bench, signed by Faulter. We were again without a lawyer. Grant's girls were now 22, 18 and 16. It was clear that there would be no help from any legal avenue and our attempts to do so had been an extremely costly failure.

Since Madison had moved out from her mother's home two years earlier, we had begun to reconnect regularly with her. She could now contact us freely and Grant could call or email her and get a timely reply. Madison was living with her boyfriend and had been since she left Suzanne's, but we were thrilled she was getting her life on track. Sometimes Grant even felt like a parent, since the two older girls would visit and we could talk openly with them about their plans and goals for the future. As always, it was clear to me that they loved their dad. He was a good listener and could help them work through the complications imposed on their lives due to years of alienation. Laura was now working full-time, and Madison had enrolled in a theatre productions certificate program. We were so proud of their resilience in the face of adversity. Maybe we could all, one day, get our lives back and be a real family.

That fall, Grant spent some time online searching out parental alienation and came across a website of the Equitable Child Maintenance and Access Society (ECMAS). Those posting on the ECMAS site were targeted parents of both sexes, grandparents and concerned family members. About the same time Grant found this organization, he and I began to talk about my work as a researcher at the university and whether we could conduct a peer-reviewed study on parental alienation. These discussions gave us some hope that we could find some good in our terrible experience by helping expose this widespread, but misunderstood, child abuse phenomenon. I subsequently applied for support from my university and obtained clearance from its Ethics Board. I then recruited 28 participants living in Alberta or British Columbia, all alienated parents or grandparents, from a total of forty-nine candidates who contacted me about being part of the study.

By phone conversation and legal documentation, I was able to ascertain who the most reliable participants were; that is, those who had iron-clad histories of being excellent, involved parents prior to the relationship split from the other parent. These targeted parents, mostly dads, signed consent forms and committed to be interviewed in person by me within the next year. Grant seemed interested in pursuing this goal; in fact, we had discussed doing research together years ago before the lawsuit took over our life.

By year's end, we were in financial distress but were still trying to hold on to our relationship, our home and our five kids. It was 3.5 years since we had heard from or seen Emily. Her sisters told us nothing about her. They felt they were betraying their mother if they divulged any information about their sister. They rarely spoke to each other, and we weren't sure whether they actually even knew where or how Emily was. The holidays came and went and as usual, we made the best of our time with my grown children and the few days we had with Laura in Calgary.

2012

We realized the strategy of all involved lawyers was to stall our case until all three children were legal adults; at that point, the case would be dismissed in its entirety. There was no point in hiring another lawyer because of the girls' ages and because lawyers thus far had only worsened our family's situation.

On January 3, we sent letters to the Alberta Minister of Justice/ Attorney General Alison Redfall (for the second time; the first letter to her was in 2009 and was also dismissed) and the Manager of Complaints for the Alberta Law Society, Maurice Dupont. In these, we requested action to intervene in the unethical practices of Family Law and in our case specifically. In both cases, responses were received, but our queries were blown off and dismissed. In the case of Ms. Redfall, her office responded that our concerns were *out of her jurisdiction*.

In the meantime, we compiled substantial documented evidence against our former lawyer, Ron Faulter, and on January 31, mailed Grant's formal complaint. We had paid Faulter an enormous amount of money, yet there had been no respite from the hell Grant's daughters and we continued to endure, largely due to legal incompetence in this severe case of parental alienation. Nevertheless, on April 17th, Grant received a response from Jim Oakley, Complaints Resolution Officer for the Law Society, dismissing our complaint in its entirety. Grant appealed the decision but in a hearing that summer, of the Law Society, Ron Faulter and Grant, the Law Society upheld its decision.

Grant's and my conversations began to change gear. They were once about hope for the future and ways to help Laura, Madison, and Emily, to have a "blended family" and to find a way to manage our relationship with the girls' mother, Suzanne. But Laura was now 22, Madison 18 and Emily 16; we knew there was nothing more we could try other than to let them know, as always, that we loved them and were always there if, and when, they wanted to contact us. We had no idea where Emily was or how she was doing. We began to discuss ways to raise awareness about parental alienation. My research into this phenomenon became increasingly important, since we now knew there were thousands of families dealing with this and the Family Law system was feeding off the vulnerability of targeted parents and their children.

During Easter weekend, since Grant was on a break from work, he decided to build a pergola in our backyard. He recruited his friend, Kevin, and worked over three days to get it built. I came home one day to find it finished: The project had cost $3000… money we didn't have. There had been no discussion about this. Grant wanted to do it, but I was disappointed he hadn't shared this decision with me. In hindsight, this was another turning point in our relationship. We were both in survival mode; I was bent on doing this research project on parental alienation while Grant was bent on escaping the reality of our dire financial situation. We were equally damaged by the corruption inherent in our legal system and our futile desire to help his children.

By April our house was for sale. I felt that we had to sell; in this way we could pay off the outstanding balance apparently due to Ron Faulter. He had a lien on our house so we had to pay him first before so much as a leaky tap could be fixed. So we sold.

The Calgary market was teetering before an economic crash so we felt we did well to break even on the sale. The proceeds paid off Ron Faulter and he was thankfully gone for good. Since I had provided, by the sale of my duplex in Silver Springs, the down payment on our co-owned house in the inner-city neighbourhood, I now banked this money in hopes of purchasing another house in the near future.

The new owners took possession of our house in June. I believe Grant was never the same after that. He had struggled throughout his life to become financially secure. His career trajectory had continued upward through hard work and perseverance despite his divorce and subsequent alienation from his most cherished relationships; those with his children. But we couldn't make ends meet.

We rented a main floor of a bungalow in Killarney, an inner-city neighbourhood close to my work but an hour away from Grant's. I was feeling somewhat encouraged; since we had reconciled the legal debt, we could now save for a new start on the future. But Grant was too sad to notice. He remained depressed and afraid since our finances were still marginal and our landlords greedy; they were two RCMP officers looking to invest in a real estate "flip" for profit. They didn't care about the decrepit state of the house or the drug-addicted tenant in the basement. This was near the end of an economic boom in Calgary so rental suites were still hard to find.

KIDS COME LAST

CHAPTER 2

KIDS COME LAST

We were in the process of selling our home in June when I began interviews with targeted parents. I used a voice recorder signed out from my university to record each of my face-to-face interviews with the participants. Each interview was between 2 and 4.5 hours in length and was emotionally exhausting for the participant and for me. In a semi-structured format, I asked about the background of parent-child relationship prior to the parents' split. In every case, each participant was a loving, positive influence on his or her child(ren)'s life and the decision to end the parents' relationship was heart-wrenching but necessary, even inevitable. The ensuing campaign of parental alienation was, and is, the most painful experience each participant could imagine. Each was devastated by the loss of his or her child(ren) as the partial loss of one's self.

Feeling somewhat nervous for the first interview, armed with voice recorder and lap-top at the ready, I called on Cliff who met me at his partner Gail's home one afternoon. I was immediately taken by the cosy, friendly atmosphere of their house and their warmth towards me. Cliff thanked me for taking on this project and voiced the need for parental alienation to become publicly recognized and resolved for the sake of families everywhere. He has two children, a daughter, 20 and a son, 16. Cliff, Gail and I sat over coffee at the kitchen table while Cliff's story unfolded (Chapter 3).

I had booked three more interviews a week after Cliff's, in Edmonton this time. Grant and I were in the midst of moving after managing to sell our house. I took a couple days off from packing boxes and left Grant at home while I drove to Edmonton. The first meeting was with Russ in a hotel lobby at the city's south end.

Russ was well educated in the issue of parental alienation, much more so than I was at the time. He was an alienated dad with a 12-year-old daughter and a 10-year-old son. Along with trying to help his own children, Russ also spent, and still spends, much of his *free* time helping other alienated parents prepare their own legal cases (Chapter 4).

I called Gloria to confirm our interview for the next day. She suggested we meet at a nearby mall at a quiet diner, easy for me to find. Gloria's tragic story was much different from Cliff's and Russ' since she is a grandmother of her son's two young children, her 16-year-old grandson and a granddaughter, then 12. Gloria's son, David, took his own life at the age of 37 (Chapter 5).

After our interview, Gloria invited me to dinner that evening in her lovely, modest home. She said she wanted me to meet someone also named Chris who was then-president of the ECMAS (Equitable Child Maintenance and Access Society) chapter in Edmonton. Before that dinner, however, I had booked another interview. She and I agreed to reconnect in a few hours and I drove off to meet Larry in a small suburban coffee shop at the other end of town (Chapter 6).

Larry is a grandfather of two girls, aged 11 and 13. He and his son, the father of these girls, were alienated from them. His case involved a bizarre allocation of custody to the other set of grandparents, instead of the children's father. After our interview concluded, I promised to keep Larry informed of my progress with the study and added him to my fast-growing list of legitimately alienated parents and grandparents.

It was late in the day, and I was tired but gratified. Four people thus far, each living with parental alienation, had opened their hearts, their very souls, to share with me their stories. They did so, they told me, because I suffered too. I was, and am, humbled by their trust in me. I phoned Grant who encouraged me and said he loved me. We could make a difference; maybe my husband and I could contribute to the resolution of parental alienation and raise awareness toward prevention of this devastating social crisis. With clarity and higher spirits than I had felt in months, perhaps years, I now concerned myself with finding Gloria's house for dinner.

Upon arrival, I met Chris, once an alienated dad himself, who had since remarried and now had a young baby. He told me he had decided to stay involved with ECMAS and another organization, the Parental Alienation Awareness Network, as he was so profoundly affected by the alienation experience he and his children had endured. Desperate for an intervention, he had finally hired a lawyer and for many years thereafter was embroiled in a lawsuit to obtain a parenting agreement with teeth; one with real penalties for the alienator and enforcement of access to his children. He did achieve such a court order, but his ex-wife simply ignored all terms. His case was chillingly similar to those of the 4 participants I had recently interviewed. Another alienated dad, Greg J, who was having a hard time making ends meet and living in Gloria's basement, also joined us for dinner. Both men and Gloria illuminated for me the recurrent pattern of parental alienation which ramps up with legal involvement, causing deeper and deeper damage to the children *and* the targeted parent.

Driving home from Edmonton that night, I had several hours to process all the information gathered in these three interviews plus Cliff's thus far. Each had been exhausting as the participant recounted his or her personal struggle to parent and to help his or her children. It was clearly very difficult for each person to talk about. There were halting sentences, fidgeting, even tears as each brave parent laid out his or her story while being recorded. There was, and is, so much love for these children from each participant. They sought only to give their children a good and productive life, but each was hamstrung by an alienator… and a legal system that aids and abets in the continued abuse. I couldn't wait to get home to my husband, my kids and our dog. I needed a hug, to feel loved and to love those in my Calgary family. I wanted reassurance that our terrible situation would have a happy ending and especially, I wanted Emily and her sisters to somehow be okay.

The next couple weeks were sad and busy as we made the move out of our northwest Calgary home to the rental house in the southwest part of town. On the day before the moving van arrived, we had a storage box dropped in our alley. We packed it with furniture and such that we would be unable to fit into the little rented house we were going to. At a cost of $300/month, we stored this box for the next six months while trying to get on our feet again. I mowed the lawns one last time while Grant was at work. The following day the movers took our necessities to the rental house.

Grant waited at the rental house while I finished up dropping keys and doing a final clean-sweep through the first house we had bought together and lived in for 5 years. It was hard to leave but I felt the weight of our financial debt to Ron Faulter taken off my shoulders as I locked the door one last time. The yard looked beautiful; the trees and flowers were in full bloom and the purple clematis that climbed the back wall was splendid. We had replaced the back fence so it too enhanced the look of the yard. Even Grant's pergola and the deck he had also built with his own hands reminded me of the dream that we had tried to realize.

By the end of June, I had been able to book six more interviews, this time in Victoria, British Columbia. Though I had no research funding, I used my annual $500 professional development stipend to help pay for my flight. Grant and I talked about how he could accompany me for a few days to temporarily escape reminders of the house sale and current problems at the rental house. We had enough Air Miles to pay for his flight and a couple nights at a hotel by using them. After a short flight over the Georgia Strait on a Friday afternoon, we arrived in lovely Victoria and took the airport shuttle to our hotel. I always find that Victoria smells like flowers and this was certainly a welcome beginning to our three days there. We checked into our accommodations and I left Grant to explore downtown. I had two interviews scheduled late that afternoon.

First, I grabbed a taxi, which took me to a funky little coffee shop where I met Rob in its upstairs loft. It was a bustling place downtown, convenient to his workplace and easy for me to find.

Rob seemed a little shy to begin with but said he was glad to share his story. He said there were few people he talked to about his family situation because he didn't "want to sound like a complainer. Besides, no one understands what this is like unless they have gone through it." Rob was struggling since his split from the mothers of his three children, girls twelve and eight and a six-year-old son. The interview took about two hours. I had to watch the time in order to make my next one right after. It was hard to say good-bye, since I already felt Rob was a friend and wasn't sure whether I would be back or when. As with the other participants thus far, Rob made no demands of me and thanked me for taking the time to listen to his story. He was so gracious and kind (Chapter 7).

A short cab ride later, I was in another coffee shop, this time to meet with Jimmy. A father with a small son, Jimmy was especially concerned by his son's apparent abuse by his mother, in the form of "Munchausen-by-Proxy" (MSBP) syndrome. I was immediately taken by Jimmy's straight forward, no nonsense communication style and obvious devotion to his 8-year-old little boy. Three hours later, we completed the interview and I turned off my voice recorder. Jimmy and I agreed to stay in touch and he restated his commitment to helping keep Kellan and other children from being manipulated by a parent (Chapter 8).

By the time I got back to our hotel, it was late evening. The next day started with breakfast by the ocean and some welcome downtime with Grant. Later, we wandered around town and ended up back at the hotel for my first interview of the day. Grant had brought work to do so while I headed to the lobby, he went back to our room for the afternoon. In short order, a tall, fit man in a bike helmet walked in. This was Dave, the participant I had arranged to meet next. He smiled and warmly shook my hand as we settled into a couple of armchairs where it was relatively quiet. This unassuming, confident dad told me how he stayed mentally strong by cycling as much as possible and through his regular yoga practice. His story unfolded over the next few hours (Chapter 9).

Following the interview with Dave, I jumped in a taxi and gave the driver Ed's address. Arriving in front of a quaint little wooden bungalow with a welcoming front porch, I made my way to the front door and rang the bell. I was soon welcomed into the house by another fit looking, wavy-haired man in bare feet. He introduced me to his partner in life, Mary. She was busy in the kitchen making supper for her two boys and one of Ed's two sons. Ed and I decided to talk in his office where it was quieter. So looking out on his well-kept and spacious backyard, complete with a trampoline, I listened while Ed recounted his long struggle as an alienated dad (Chapter 10).

Ed's house smelled of wonderful home cooking as I left that evening to meet my last participant of the day, David. He had suggested we meet at a trendy eatery frequented mostly by locals. The outdoor patio overhung the ocean and it being such a beautiful evening, we decided to sit outside. It was Friday but there were still a couple picnic tables available so we grabbed one. Thus began the interview. David is an avid cyclist and told me he rode everywhere, rarely needing to use his little car. Over several hours during which David poured out his story, I was enchanted by his joy over his daughter's successes and his earnest, sometimes, teary recall of minute details of their life together (Chapter 11).

On Saturday, I had no interviews booked so Grant and I rented bikes and spent the day cycling around the seawall and on the local bike-path system. We were fortunate again to have perfect warm and sunny weather and the day did wonders for my spirits. I actually felt happy from time to time until the demons would creep in and I'd return to thoughts of parental alienation and the state of Grant's daughters. But I noticed Grant was rather quiet and irritable, lost in his own thoughts and worries. Increasingly, there were times when I felt a terrible distance between us, a chasm that I could not bridge. I didn't understand it. I so needed my husband and believed that since we had shared and told each other everything for almost 8 years, this recent gap in our communication would be temporary. We just had to remind ourselves that we were, above all, there for each other.

At dinner that night, Grant seemed somewhat more animated and I saw glimmers of his old, fun and loving, self. He had always been supportive and affectionate toward me, so his dark times were the more unsettling. My husband told me as we walked back to our hotel that he often re-lived the day when Suzanne had driven away with their daughters and he saw Madison's little tear-streaked face in her mother's rear window, staring back at him standing in the road. He said he had other dreams, all of them scary, that involved bad things happening to the girls or to me. He still worried that Emily would be found dead on the street somewhere. Grant was increasingly haunted.

On Sunday we walked hand in hand for several hours, just exploring and enjoying our time together. We would be flying home that evening. But during our walk, Grant got a phone call on his cell and it was Suzanne. Within a couple minutes into that call, during which Grant was calm and polite as always, Suzanne began to yell and I could hear every word. She was angry because money Grant was putting into a trust fund for his daughters was not accessible to her. He had successfully petitioned the court to administer the trust as such for his girls' direct benefit. After that phone call, we were subdued and sad again.

Later, Grant returned to the hotel to pack while I met Arnie at Tim Horton's, a few blocks away. He is a distinguished-looking man in his sixties who has 4 children from two marriages. The first words to me out of Arnie's mouth were, "Hi! I should tell you right off that I wasn't a very good husband sometimes". I shook his hand and asked what kind of father he was. He immediately teared up and in a halting voice said, "My kids have always been my life". Arnie recalled his years with each of his two wives and the turmoil that followed both divorces. Arnie was, and is, clearly an excellent and capable father who tried his best to navigate a tumultuous home life for his children's sake more than his own (Chapter 12).

After Victoria, I made more interview appointments in Alberta, where the rest of the participants in this study lived. In mid-July, I made another road trip north to Edmonton. My first interview there was with Terry, a dad with three older teenagers. He lived in a lovely house where his children had grown up, and which he had been able to hold on to following his divorce. One of his daughters was currently living there with him. Terry had made muffins and coffee, which he now served us at his kitchen table. We began the interview. About half -way through, a battery in my voice-recorder died so there was an unfortunate interruption in Terry's narrative while I switched out the battery and we continued. Terry understands young adults well, as he is also a college instructor. We discussed the trials and tribulations of letting one's children become independent while managing a hostile post-divorce relationship with their other parent. Terry wanted his children to be productive, good citizens and he was constantly placating their mother's attempts to thwart his fatherly influence (Chapter 13).

I emerged from Terry's house to a sudden downpour. Terry loaned me an umbrella so I could keep dry as I navigated puddles to my car. Promising to stay in touch, I pulled onto the Anthony Henday ring-road, driving further north to a satellite community 30 minutes drive from Edmonton. There, in his office in a busy suburban plaza, Mark met me on that rainy summer's afternoon. Mark was a friendly, well dressed professional who nonetheless seemed stressed and sad. He recounted his years of trying to keep a relationship with his two young sons while their mother discouraged contact with him, their dad. His story was all too familiar, including bankruptcy, harassment by MEP, one-sided disclosure of finances and an ongoing campaign by the alienator to manipulate Mark for monetary gain (Chapter 14).

Following my meeting with Mark, I stayed in Edmonton that night. Early the next day, I used GPS to navigate my way on a remote country road to find an old house now rented by my next participant, Chris. Unable to find a doorbell, I knocked hesitantly, hoping this was the right place. Soon a smiling but weary-looking man answered the door and welcomed me into his little farmhouse kitchen. Chris showed me a couple of short home videos of his daughter playing with him and her grandmother at his house. One was when she was only a toddler and the second was as a pre-teen several years ago. Chris was so appreciative that I was interested in watching this footage of his family in happier times. His house was rather dated and needed renovating, but it was what Chris could afford and had a nice, big bedroom for his now 18-year-old daughter. His relationship with her was fragile due to years of alienation. She had rebelled against him a few times, even refusing to see him at all. Now Chris was hopeful of rebuilding their relationship, as his daughter had reached 18 recently and was going away to another province for post-secondary schooling (Chapter 15).

After leaving Chris' house, I drove back into Edmonton and found my next participant's tiny basement suite, which he rented with the little money he had from his disability cheque and doing odd jobs. Rene had had a tough life but was a fascinating and talented intellectual and musician. He showed me some of the instruments he played and recounted his gigs around town and his network of interesting people. While dealing with his own demons, Rene had learned to face into his past and resolve the negative influences. He is a strong but gentle person, leery of those such as me, who had entered his life wanting things from him but never giving back. He wondered whether my interviewing alienated parents was just a way for me to build my resume, or whether I really cared about this social crisis. I appreciated his honesty and reassured him as best I could. Since I, too, was dealing with my own family's experience with parental alienation through Grant, I believe I gained Rene's confidence and am very grateful for his accepting me (Chapter 16).

I felt sad leaving Rene's place, having seen the toll taken on another loving father ravaged by the court system and its enabling of parental alienation. Though Rene was a talented guitarist and obvious bookworm, the loss of his daughter was unbearable.

Still, he had tried his best to keep humour and lightness in our conversation.

Calling Grant from my hotel room, I filled him in on my day and my thoughts. He said he was fine and missed me. Whenever I was away from Grant, I felt rather adrift and was looking forward to returning home the following day. I had months ago given up asking him whether he had heard from any of his children that day. The answer was always the same, excepting Laura with whom he communicated every week or two.

Next morning I met with Carla in a busy suburban Starbucks on the south end of Edmonton. She is an entrepreneur who has built a career of helping people with similar experiences to her own with cult behaviour and Stockholm Syndrome. Carla waved me over to her table. She is a charismatic, outgoing and accomplished mom of 7 children. Her history was shocking. The fact that she had been so completely alienated from her children by their father reinforced the literature and my own personal belief that *parental alienation is not a gendered issue,* but one that can equally make either parent the target (Chapter 17).

I left Carla with the assurance that she would continue her vital work in deprogramming cult victims, reuniting families and educating the public about parental alienation and other forms of mind control.

After picking up more batteries for my voice recorder, I proceeded to a townhouse complex where Jason lived with his life-partner and moral support, Deirdre. Jason had an older daughter from a first marriage, with whose mother he amicably shared custody. This daughter was doing very well in school, had nice friends, and got along well with Deirdre. The three were almost a complete family unit. But Jason's second daughter was the result of his relationship with an alienating mother. This little girl was tormented, did poorly in school and rarely, and more recently never, was allowed to see or contact her father. Jason and Dierdre were heart-broken by the absence and deterioration of this other daughter (Chapter 18).

I had three more interviews to do before driving back to Calgary that evening. First, I found Kath's house on a lovely tree-lined street where she lived with the memories of her once-intact family who lived in that home for many years. Her son and daughter were now legal adults and though Kath, a teacher by profession, had been a stay-at-home mom for much of their lives, both kids were now completely estranged from her. Kath and I settled with tea in her cosy living room and she began her tearful story (Chapter 19).

Leaving Kath's house I made my way back to Gloria's place where Greg lived downstairs. He had some time that afternoon to share with me his story of alienation and the rebuilding of his relationship with two now-teenaged kids. Although this was the only interview with a somewhat happy ending, Greg had nevertheless worked tirelessly to engage with his children who finally realized they needed their dad (Chapter 20).

I popped into Gloria's suite upstairs to say hello on my way out, after concluding my interview with Greg. She was about to pick up her grandsons from school and babysit until their mother came to pick them up sometime that evening.

It was almost 8:00 p.m. by then and I was still to meet Raina and her partner in a restaurant for our interview. Following this ninth interview of my second Edmonton trip, I would finally make my way later that night back to Calgary and my family. The rain had begun to fall heavily so I parked and made a dash for the door where we were to meet. Inside, I glanced around and saw a nicely dressed couple waving from the far corner. This must be Raina and Mike. Shaking hands warmly, we ordered food before Raina commenced her story (Chapter 21).

I stopped for coffee on my way home and called Grant to let him know I was on the way. He said he was worried about the roads as it was raining hard and to take my time as he needed me home safe. It was well past midnight when I arrived at the rental house but the front door light was left on and the door unlocked. Grant was fast asleep as I slid into bed and moulded my body around his. He was my solid foundation; I was, he said, his refuge. Nothing could separate us.

A few days later Madison came with her boyfriend to stay with us over the Calgary Folk Festival weekend. This was an event both Grant and I enjoyed and he had been involved with for over ten years. We loved the music, rekindling acquaintances and enjoying the perks of volunteering. Laura usually came for the weekend and my kids even joined us there a few times. This year Grant's mom also came from Newfoundland, so along with his two closest brothers and their families, Madison enjoyed some precious time with her relatives and little cousins. One evening there, even my ex-husband and his girlfriend showed up at the beer tent and we smuggled them into the volunteers' after-hours party. It seemed as though we were getting our lives back slowly and despite the wreckage of parental alienation and its exacerbation by the legal system. But there was no Emily and no word of her at all, from anyone.

Madison told us she had enrolled in post-secondary at Grant MacEwan University for the fall term. We were thrilled! Despite all she had endured, she was now making good choices for herself. It was not lost on us that since she had escaped the pattern of alienation and guilt instilled in her by Suzanne, she was flourishing.

Living at the rental house was difficult, since the tenant downstairs often hosted weekday parties in the backyard that began at 2:00 a.m. When the bar where she worked closed for the night, her partying began. Finally, one night Grant asked her to keep it down outside, and her friend retorted with "It would be a shame for something to happen to your dog". It was 4:00 a.m. on a Tuesday morning.

A week after my trip to Edmonton, I had two more interviews booked there, so I made a third trip for a day. This time I met Kier, a father of two little boys, whom he clearly loved dearly but was now alienated from. He had been targeted by his ex-wife immediately following their separation. Fortunately, the coffee shop where we met was quiet that morning (Chapter 22).

Now 1:00 p.m, I said good-bye to Kier and drove a few minutes away to yet another local java joint. There were a few people in the restaurant, but Sarah and her friend had taken a small table in a sunny, quiet corner. As it turned out, the noise was of little concern as Sarah is deaf. I listened while Sarah spoke carefully and sometimes signed to her friend. Sarah was also amazingly adept at lip-reading and was able to catch most of what I asked without help. She had written a book about her tragic experience with her own daughter. But Sarah's was also a landmark case of both parental alienation and blatant gender discrimination by the Family Law system in Alberta (Chapter 23).

I drove home on a beautiful, late summer afternoon. The latest interviews underscored the troubling pattern I was witnessing over and over again. In just four weeks, I had heard, first-hand, 21 cases of widespread child abuse in the form of parental alienation. Just as shocking, in every case it was enabled by professionals entrusted to care and intervene for the well being of our children. Twenty-one cases thus far. And I was living our own case every day since 2004; Grant had been since 1999.

The following week I drove two and a half hours south to Lethbridge where I met with Hailey, married to Karl. They had a new baby together and Hailey was also step mother to Karl's 4-year-old daughter. Hailey runs a day-home and struck me as an excellent mother and caregiver. We talked for almost three hours in a coffee shop along the bustling main drag of the city. This one-day trip was another eye-opening interview; this time from the perspective of a step-parent. I could readily empathize with Hailey, being both mother and step-mother myself (Chapter 24).

Several days later I met two more participants living around the city of Red Deer, approximately ninety minutes north of Calgary. The first was Gerry, along with his wife, Tara, who welcomed me into their delightful home for snacks and tea. Tara had a teenaged son who was doing very well and lived with them half time when not with his own father. Tara had an immense store of knowledge about parental alienation. I found this trait common to the step-parents in our study, who were trying their very best to help resolve the alienation of their current spouse from his or her children (Chapter 25).

Each of the seven step-parents I met, over the course of my interviews with all participants, also had his or her own children from a prior relationship, usually marriage, but *these* children were all healthy, achieving and compassionate people with close ties to both biological parents. Each also had a loving, supportive relationship with his or her step-parent, a participant and alienated parent in this study.

From Gerry and Tara's house, I drove west into rolling hills and lake country to a thriving tourist town where Craig had a job teaching at a private school. I waited outside until the bell rang. Craig came to find me a few minutes later. We talked in his colourful, upbeat classroom where he unpacked for me his long and sad story. There were pauses during which he needed to compose himself for, like the others, Craig's narrative was heart wrenching. He had three small children, all of whom he had become systematically alienated from (Chapter 26).

After almost three hours with Craig, I switched off my recorder and we said good-bye. As had become usual by then, we agreed to keep in touch and I promised to use his story to help raise awareness to end parental alienation. When I got back to Calgary late that evening, Grant was already asleep. I got into bed and just watched his beautiful face for a long while. He looked peaceful, and I wished with all my heart that he could, that we both could, keep that peace when he woke up.

It was now September and my third month of interviewing participants. As I listened to more and more personal experiences with parental alienation, I was flabbergasted by the similarity of the behaviour pattern of each alienator, from the time the couple was together to the present time. Each alienating parent indicated an intelligent, manipulative personality with an overwhelming desire to control all behaviour of his or her children. These children did not see, talk to, or otherwise interact with their targeted parent without negative consequences for doing so from their alienating parent. The phenomenon of parental alienation with its close parallel to cult behaviour and Stockholm Syndrome was not lost on me.

Back home, Grant and I were talking about trying to buy another house since the outstanding lawyer fees and the lien on our previous home were now reconciled. One day in October, Grant sent me a link to a listing he had found online for a house in the same neighbourhood we loved and had lived in before. It was perhaps a five-minute drive from our old house and just as close to parks and amenities. Maybe this house would have no basement flooding issues either. Paying rent had helped us reduce our outstanding debts and this house would be a great investment. We went to see it that evening.

On a beautiful fall evening, we finalized the deal and found ourselves homeowners again. I was thrilled and couldn't wait to get out of the rental house and back into our own space. The downstairs tenant where we were living had been evicted but did not leave quietly. Though she was given proper notice and reasons by the landlords, she took her case to court and I had to speak with a judge on two occasions before the decision was made to oust her. Grant, though, did not want to act and said he could not take any more stress. At the time, I felt we needed to resolve that awful living situation, since we didn't know how long we might have to stay renting that house.

A couple days after we bought our new home, I interviewed John, an alienated dad with four children, all of whom lived in Calgary. John is from the east coast and he, too, exuded that warmth and authenticity that so attracted me from the start to Grant. As it turned out, John's eldest daughter was a student at the university where I teach, though I have never encountered her. As I write this, I believe she is graduating next month or did so last spring. I hope that is the case. And I hope that her dad will be, or was, there to share in her joy and accomplishment (Chapter 27).

There were three more interviews to conduct following John's and then I planned to have all 28 transcribed for analysis. I had found an experienced transcriber through the University of Calgary who believed in the importance of this study. Amanda had never heard of parental alienation when I hired her. But after listening to 28 audio-recorded interviews, she told me how each made her realize how fortunate she was to have a loving, intact relationship with her husband and their two preschool-aged children.

I met Orlin one Wednesday evening in a church lobby within a few blocks of the suite he rented. He was an avid cyclist and rode his bike over for our interview. Orlin, as the others, was articulate, kind and hopeful that telling his story would help change legislation and heighten awareness of parental alienation. He had immigrated to Canada several years earlier with his wife and small son (Chapter 28).

My realization of the staggering enormity of parental alienation was overwhelming. We knew there was little more Grant and I could do with respect to trying to help his girls. Our legal attempts had made theirs and Grant's plight even worse and each daughter was nearing legal adulthood. Each time I asked Grant to give me his time preference to be officially interviewed by me, he was evasive. I let him know that I could finish the study without his input if it was too difficult for him to relay his story yet again. But he remained firm that he wanted to be included in our study. One Sunday afternoon he announced that this was a good time, and so I set up to record his story. In just two weeks we were to move into our new house. It should have been, I thought, an easier time for him to talk since we were digging ourselves out of the emotional and financial abyss our family had endured for so long (Chapters 1 and 2).

Grant's story is my story, too, from the beginning of this book. But for him the alienation from his children began in 1999 and never ended. He was strong, loving and wise, but his children did not receive the benefit of those strengths. After his divorce from Suzanne, Grant was relegated to the sidelines, first by Suzanne and Judge Shats who gave her sole custody, and then by all legal and mental health "professionals" involved in his case. Grant spent the next 15 years as little more than a parent-in-name-only. Though he tried with all his energy to be their dad, Grant's three daughters rarely saw him, the youngest not at all for over six years. Laura kept a loose connection to him but suffered the resultant wrath of her mother for doing so. Madison tried to see us when she could but finally, for a few years, gave up like Emily had, drugged into submission by an unethical psychiatrist in Edmonton. As adults, Grant's three daughters became lifelong victims of parental alienation with all its negative repercussions on their quality of life.

Following my interview with Grant, he left the house, banging the door behind him. He was visibly anxious, shaky and sad. I did not know then how severe the emotional damage had become. When he returned later that night, I was in bed and pretended to be asleep. We never spoke of that night again. My hope remained that once we were moved into our new home, our life and relationship could recover.

We moved, leaving behind six months in the decrepit old rental house. My daughter was still living at home and her help, as always, was a huge support through sheer muscle-power and organization… but equally with humour and optimism. She was then 22 and just two years away from finishing a double degree with distinction at the University of Lethbridge. She was, and is, my rock and reality-check. My son, who had lived on his own by then for several years, also helped see us through the many years of frustration and devastation. They knew, and had experienced, our hell from the moment the lawsuit began in 2006. They loved and respected Grant and could not fathom why he had been severed from his own children's lives.

Over the Christmas season, we had a visit from Laura and then a week later, Madison. The last time we had seen all three girls together in Calgary was in 2005. They rarely interacted, even in Edmonton, as Suzanne discouraged them from spending time together unless she was present. Eventually, they had little in common and Laura resented the extra stress her sisters, with their needs, put on her. The girls had been taught early on to fend for themselves.

One evening we had a dinner party, which included my mom, my ex-husband and his girlfriend, her daughter, my kids, my brother, Grant's brother and family, and Madison. It seemed that Madison enjoyed being with all those people who cared about her. I hoped she would also see that although we had split many years before, my ex-husband and I were able to maintain an amicable relationship for everyone's sake. He, like Grant then, was an honourable man.

2013

Five weeks after moving into our new house, in the wee hours of a Thursday morning, we were awakened by flashing lights and several emergency vehicles clustering on the street. The house across from us was on fire, flames licking around the foundation and the eaves. That day, a woman living in that house died, but the rest of her family managed to escape. This event seemed minor to Grant and me. I began to wonder about how the past years had affected both our states of mental health. We were emotionally flat or angry most of the time. But there were bright spots such as when we spent time gardening in our yard. After one such afternoon in June, Grant said "Babe, this was a good day. Finally, a good day".

My final interview of the study occurred after a morning at work. I met near the campus with Tom, who told me one of the most bizarre narratives yet. He and the mother of his three children had lived in Thailand, where they owned a bike shop. Tom also did some teaching in Business in a post-secondary institution there. At the time of our interview, he was working at the university where I teach. His family had moved to Calgary a few years earlier (Chapter 29).

After four hours interviewing Tom on record, I sent all 28 audio-files to Amanda for transcription and I enlisted Kara, a former student and cracker-jack technical writer and data-miner, to help with finding resources and building a reference list for our resultant peer-reviewed article entitled *Kids Come Last: The Effect of Family Law Involvement in Parental Alienation (2015).* Kara painstakingly did a review of all academic literature to date on parental alienation. Though I had researched the topic a year before, there were ever-increasing numbers of publications on the subject; no doubt due to its global ubiquity. Since I was a contract employee at Mount Royal University, I had no research funding with which to pay Kara. She worked for free over hundreds of hours in getting the article and this book published.

By mid-June, it became clear to me that Grant's and my relationship was beyond strained. Neither of us could sleep well: he told me he often suffered flashbacks to the trauma of losing his kids and before then. We both struggled to manage our professional lives as best we could. We began to see a counselor in hopes that he could help Grant and me back to our good place, the place we had always wanted to live in our hearts. But by fall, Grant was still preoccupied, detached and angry. The counselor noted that he was not doing well, and our doctor prescribed anti-depressants for him. These he took begrudgingly, as he had no faith in drug "therapy", having seen it so misused on his daughters by Dr. Blackmore. As the dosage increased, Grant became more distraught and lethargic. Finally, he, overnight, quit the regimen altogether.

We had, in 2010, planned to hike the Chilkoot Trail in Alaska, the Klondike gold-rush route. But due to our dwindling finances and ongoing stress, Grant and I postponed that adventure. We lived for the outdoors and physical exercise; it was our solace, our reconnection time and our positive grounding with the real world. So here we were in 2013, in our new house, rebuilding a positive future, or so I hoped, and we began to again plan for this long-awaited trip. It was a dream I held onto, and Grant said he still wanted to do it with me. It would entail five days back-packing on our own. I thought it might be just what we needed. We were both seasoned in the back country.

On my own, I visited our counselor and asked whether he thought it a good idea. We both knew Grant was in poor health physically and mentally, but my husband insisted he wanted to take this challenge. Sidney, our counselor, thought it would be cathartic for Grant. He encouraged me to be supportive and embrace this opportunity to get back to our healthy selves; I agreed.

During the afternoon of June 20, steady rain began in Calgary and it continued unabated for the next couple days. This was to become the famous Calgary Flood of 2013. That day, I finished writing the article for academic publication based on my twenty-eight interviews of parental alienation. Kara and I had been sending drafts of the paper back and forth until finally, there were no further edits needed. I sent the final version by email out to all participants in the study. Kara and I wanted to be sure everyone involved was agreeable to my submitting the article for publication. With a few hours, I began to receive responses. All were positive and encouraging. Participants had waited patiently to have their stories made public. They wanted lay persons to understand parental alienation and they were, and are, warriors for legislative change to give children both their parents. I did not, however, get any acknowledgment from Grant, nor did he return home that night.

We left for Alaska by car in early August. Grant and I had spent many hours organizing our gear for this backpacking adventure. The weather was perfect and remained so for the entirety of the two weeks we were away. On the second day of hiking, I knew Grant was having trouble keeping up. This was highly unusual for my former athlete of a husband who could skate, run, hike and climb circles around me. On a rest break one 30-degree, cloudless day in the most breathtakingly beautiful scenery of my life, Grant told me he couldn't believe how he had let himself go. I could only answer that sometimes we all need a jolt to scare us into moving in a healthy direction. He said he needed this trip and he knew what he needed to do to get back to his "good self".

I was encouraged after we got home. Although the trip had been physically tough and emotionally difficult, I knew I still loved this man and would do whatever was needed to get our life back. But Grant did not get healthy. He continued to struggle and said he had no faith in "professionals" when I suggested he seek help.

It was now over five years since he had seen his little girl. *Five years*! He missed Emily so much he no longer cared if he lived. Only his other two daughters, he told me, gave him any reason to. Each day was a case of "putting one foot in front of the other" (his words) and he told me on several occasions that "I'm worth more to you dead than alive so what do you care?" These seemingly bizarre, and hurtful, statements came more and more frequently.

There were occasional visits from Laura or Madison, but Grant seemed to look forward to these less and less. He didn't talk much and was very unlike the man I thought I knew when we married. Sometimes he slept in the spare bedroom instead of with me. Usually he was still on his laptop when I went to bed. I rarely got or offered a hug. I was losing my husband. But at the time, I put that terrible possibility out of my mind.

Over Christmas 2013, we didn't socialize with our friends. We didn't have anyone over for dinner. We both retreated further into our respective dark places. The irony was that as our finances stabilized, we saw more of Grant's girls, and he was again promoted at work, but my husband deteriorated further. One night I dreamed that Grant had fallen into a deep, dark mountain sinkhole. I stood on the lip frantically trying to grasp his hand and finally succeeded. But the more I pulled, the looser the grip became. He then started to shake his hand to free it from mine. Then I woke up.

2014

There was little change in the first few months of the year. My grown children were doing okay but were worried about our strained relationship. So was Laura. She asked me if I thought her dad was alright. I could only say that I didn't know.

One evening a family lawyer phoned me at home, saying he had a client who found my contact information online. He wondered whether I might agree to be a court witness in a case on behalf of this alienated mom. I was interested and told him so. This could be a way to start the process of changing biased judicial decisions that currently favour the custodial parent, often an alienator. When I recounted this phone conversation to Grant, he told me I was "selling your (my) soul". But, I assured him, I wouldn't even be paid for this job. I wanted to do it; to become familiar with how parental alienation cases fester and stall in the courts and why most judicial decisions are so badly skewed.

In March I received notice that I had been successful in obtaining funding to present Kara's and my *Kids Come Last* paper at both the University of Western Ontario and University of British Columbia, in May and June respectively. I immediately texted Grant the good news. He wrote back quickly with "Congratulations, Babe! Way to make a difference in the world". But, twelve days later my world was shattered.

Grant's birthday was in early April. The couple of weeks prior to that day he was especially out of sorts, saying little and spending most of his leisure time alone. He told me that every day he was just trying to put one foot in front of the other. It made no sense to me. We could be rebuilding our lives in a positive direction but instead, we were unravelling. On his birthday, Grant and I walked over to a local pub for supper. We didn't talk much and I felt like this person across from me was almost a stranger. On the way home, Grant thanked me for taking him for a birthday supper. I found this a curious statement, given that I was his wife.

On Saturday, April 5th, I was busy marking student papers while Grant went off to the park with our dog. When he returned, I asked him how their walk was. He came upstairs, looking rather nervous and said something that will stay with me forever: "I need to be on my own". I asked him what that meant and he proceeded to tell me he needed to "peel back my (his) layers" and that he "can't do this to you (me) anymore". I asked him what he needed to get well and how could I help. He just replied with little emotion that he needed to find a place to live on his own.

A week later, Easter weekend, we had listed the house for sale and Grant was repainting the garage trim. This baffled me since he was using a very different shade of blue than the existing colour on the house and garage. He had demonstrated little energy to do anything beyond going to work prior to his announcement to leave me. But here he was expending much time and effort in cleaning out and painting the garage and packing his belongings.

On Sunday, he didn't emerge from the spare bedroom all day. By mid-afternoon, I was so worried that I knocked on the door and asked if I could go in. He said okay. He was still lying in bed.

I sat on the edge and asked him as calmly as I could whether he was going to kill himself. His words were: "If I was going to kill myself, I'd have done it years ago." Through tears, I told him I didn't want to give up on him. And he responded with "What if I've given up on myself?" I slowly and sadly left the room, closing the door behind me. So began our separation and a year later, divorce.

He was moved out entirely by Mother's Day. I closed up the house and moved away from our futile hope of a future together. Grant stayed away. He did not try to contact me, nor did he visit our dog or recognize my daughter's university graduation. She, like Grant, had become a teacher. My daughter had always been living with us, so she lost her step-father too. So did my son.

Two weeks after Grant left, I did present our paper at the University of Western Ontario. I flew to Toronto with my daughter and we stayed a few days afterward with my brother, Stu, and his family. He is a dad with two daughters in his life but also has an alienated teenaged son who lived then with their mother, in the same small town Stu does. This young man had seen but not spoken to his father since soon after Stu and his wife separated in 2005. A couple times, Stu's son was lifting weights on a bench beside the one being used by his dad, but although Stu said hello, there was no response at all from his son. The two even look alike. Of note, as I write this book, Stu, an excellent father with a formerly close relationship with his son, has still not been able to contact his now-adult son *in almost 13 years*.

In June, I presented in Vancouver at the University of British Columbia. Both presentations were grueling for me, since my split from Grant had been so recent and my hope for reconciliation was so profound. Every day I thought of little else but Grant. Was he doing okay, getting the help he so needed, still working? And most of all, I wondered if he thought of me and wanted to someday rekindle a life together. I realize now that my hopes were unrealistic but without closure, I still had, and have, so many questions unanswered.

The rest of 2014 was rather a blur as I recall it now. I bought a small house and renovated the basement to accommodate a rental suite. Kara and I were busy making minor edits on our paper before it went to press. It had received peer-reviewed approval and was to be published in early 2015. I undertook a thorough analysis for the lawyer who had requested my help. My subsequent report concluded that parental alienation was indeed the underlying cause of his client's alienation from her two daughters, aged seven and nine years. Coincidentally, a couple weeks after Grant left, I was asked to do an interview on the local news and was also contacted by Alberta Health Services to be interviewed for an article, both events focusing on parental alienation. I also had my regular teaching responsibilities at the university and these distractions gave me direction through the confusion and grief. Friends and family were amazing supports for me through those dark days… dark years. I can never adequately express my gratitude.

2015

In January I sent a hand-written letter to Grant at the address where I believed he was living. I wrote it in the wee hours one morning but waited to mail it for five days, until I was sure I wanted to. I had no idea what the response from him, if any, would be. The letter was a query about his state of mind, whether he wanted to meet for a conversation, and I let him know that despite all we had been through I still hoped we could find a way to a good place. He never responded. So, after one year since our separation, I filed for divorce.

Around this time, I met another alienated dad who lives in Lethbridge, Alberta. He had found me on the internet and was hoping to find some direction for his legal case. Jim was alienated from all four of his children. The eldest, a son, had been out of communication for years and Jim did not even know what region he lived in. There were allegations of abuse made against him yet, similar to some other cases I had researched, there was no evidence. The youngest of Jim's children is special-needs and nonverbal. He was, and is, particularly concerned about her welfare since he has seen her regressing as he has become increasingly alienated from her. He clearly loves his kids and has to energy to keep trying to overturn the disaster his legal case has become. I decided to include Jim's story in this book, based on his interview with me, all court documents, affidavits and reports by involved parties such as social and family support-workers, therapists and parenting supervisors (Chapter 30).

Kara's and my academic paper was finally published in May. I was also an expert witness in another parental alienation case, this time for a dad who was a firefighter and father of two alienated little girls. This dad also had a new baby and a healthy relationship with her mother. Though his court case had been grueling and the alienator unrelenting in her efforts to remove him from the older girls' lives, the judge determined that dad was important and directed a Shared Parenting Order (Chapter 31). This case boosted my spirits a little. I began to think about how I could use my own experience with Grant and his daughters to work toward the eradication of parental alienation through education and changed legislation.

I heard from Madison once and we met for lunch when she was in Calgary. She was doing well, had graduated from her theatre program and had some work lined up in that field. I was thrilled for her. She told me she had not seen Laura in a while but thought she was doing alright too. Her dad, she said, was not doing well, but she didn't elaborate. She told me she was conflicted: On the one hand, she felt like she should move in with him to "look after him" but on the other, she didn't want to see him at all. Surprisingly, she also mentioned that Emily had resurfaced in early 2014 and that she had been texting with Grant off and on since then. I knew he had never given up on Emily and continued trying to connect with her even after six years of estrangement. Now, according to Madison, her little sister, now 19, had graduated from high school and had moved in with Grant.

Although I was pleased that Emily had reconnected with Grant, Madison told me that the co-habitation had not gone well. After three months, Emily had moved out and went back to Edmonton.

After so many years of trying desperately to be a dad, Grant was again relegated to the sidelines. This time, when his girls came back, Grant was no longer able to be a healthy father for them.

Our divorce was finalized in November, 2015. There had been no conversation between us, only a signing of impersonal documents at the courthouse. Then the relationship was over forever. It was, and will remain, irrevocably tragic. As my elderly and wise mom said to me, "You two never had a chance. I guess Suzanne *won*". My three step-daughters, who from early childhood, we had sought to help, were instead subjected to ongoing neglect and abuse, manipulation from and fear of their mother, Suzanne, and her threats to harm herself if they abandoned her. Our efforts to obtain supports for the girls and their mentally ill mother, a shared and enforced parenting plan, and fair Child Maintenance, all failed. The federal and especially provincial, family law systems were enablers, even facilitators, in the deterioration of these children's welfare and severance from their targeted parent, a loving, capable and necessary father.

CLIFF

CHAPTER 3

CLIFF

I have two children: a daughter, now 20 and a son who's 16. My wife and I separated in 2003 after many unhappy years trying to make our marriage work. We were able to sort our finances rather quickly, but I can't say it was ever amicable. We also made a verbal shared-parenting agreement. The kids would spend one week with their mom and the next with me and so on. I bought a house only a block away from my ex-wife in order to make the logistics easier on our kids. For the first three or four months, the kids did go back and forth as we had agreed. But "mom" made it clear to the kids and me that she was the primary caregiver and could change the terms of parenting as she "thought necessary". She proceeded to make co-parenting as difficult as possible.

Sometimes she would deny my daughter her thyroid medication by "forgetting" to put the pills in our daughter's suitcase. When I would call mom to ask about them, she would say it was up to me to come get the pills. In a couple of instances mom was out of town and had not sent along my daughter's meds. I had to go to the drugstore and beg the pharmacist for a couple of pills to get her through the weekend. Mom told the kids that clothes and toys at her house stayed at her house, so they were not allowed to bring things to my house. She would insist that my daughter go back to her (mom's) place in the morning and dress there for school. So the things that were important to my children she made difficult; it was unreal. My daughter was then eleven and my son eight. After these early months, I got a letter saying that I was being taken to court to resolve the custody issue.

Legal involvement started with my receiving notice that I was to attend a DRO (Dispute Resolution Office) meeting, which was apparently a pilot project. I was told my ex and I had been selected to attend to see if we could resolve our issues there. I agreed, thinking we certainly needed some help to smooth the co-parenting situation. We had not even been involved with lawyers yet, so it was unclear to me how we were chosen to participate in the DRO. The officer was "snarky" and no help at all. She suggested we hire (we each paid half the cost) a mediator named Larry Fung and were told he was one of the best. He supposedly also travels all over to train mediators.

Well it was a bad idea; at our meeting Fung frequently rolled his eyes and looked bored whenever I tried to make a suggestion about our settlement terms. The meeting resolved absolutely nothing and neither of us signed off on any terms of agreement.

So a court date was set for September 2004. I hired my first lawyer. We parted ways a month before the court date when I refused to negotiate my kids away. My second lawyer usually did wills and estates while family cases comprised about a quarter of his load. I did a lot of research prior to our hearing, which I think helped my lawyer a lot. I stayed up nights reading judgments and found one made in Edmonton from just a few weeks earlier. That case was almost identical to mine and my lawyer used it in court. I think it helped an awful lot since the judge interrupted my lawyer and said "I'm very familiar with that case." I've kept a hundred pounds of paper in a container which has all the details of my case.

A month before the court date, we were told to attend another DRO meeting. My ex's lawyer joked with mine beforehand about what a waste of time this second DRO would be. Sure enough, the Plaintiff (mom) broke down saying she couldn't afford her 50% of parenting responsibility and the DRO suggested I pay mom more. We had equivalent salaries although I also paid for a before-school caregiver. I would drop the kids there on my way to work as she lived only a few doors down from the school. When I refused to increase my payments to mom, the DRO slammed her book shut after ten minutes and walked out of our meeting. This same DRO, Kate was her name, had taught the Parenting after Separation course, which I had taken. There, she had stated repeatedly how important a dad's influence is on positive child-rearing. What a hypocrite. Interestingly, the day prior my ex testified at the deposition hearing that I was a good dad and could be counted on by my kids.

At our court hearing in the Calgary Court of Queen's Bench, a visiting Justice from Edmonton ruled against the Plaintiff, opting for joint, equal custody and suggesting the children should be free to go back and forth between houses. The Court Order did not include a Corollary Relief. I have been told years later that this was a mistake as there were no ground rules set out in court for our family.

But over the next couple years, my interactions with my daughter became increasingly difficult. She was angry with me and just got plain miserable. When she was 13 my daughter left my place and then I didn't communicate with her in any meaningful way for almost five years. We'd have the odd good conversation at my house… but 15 minutes after my daughter returned to mom's my girl would call and scream at me. It seemed to me that mom expected that behaviour from her. My ex moved across town so we no longer lived a block apart. But Okotoks is a small town. We should have been able to co-parent just fine. I saw my daughter on Father's Day, my birthday and maybe a day at Christmas but the interaction was nasty. One particular Father's Day my daughter showed up, dropped a gift off, and then drove away.

Both kids were not allowed by their mother to talk to me about anything to do with their lives. I didn't know what they did most of the time or who their friends were. Mostly they just came to my place if my parents were going to be there. For a time, my daughter was very angry with her grandmother and told her off on the phone a couple times.

My ex was a teacher in the Catholic Board… she would keep report cards and info from me and I was not welcome at my kids' school. My complaints, even to the Board superintendent, fell on deaf ears. My daughter excelled at school. By Grade 7 she had a part-time job teaching music lessons and taking them. "Look how well you are doing with dad out of your life," was probably the message she heard. She was very driven in everything. She became very religious for a time and looked down on everyone else. My ex had that history and eventually my daughter was carrying around a Bible everywhere.

My kids changed doctors, dentists, houses, schools and everything after their mom and I separated. All these people refused to share my kids' records with me, their co-parent. And when we went to court, my ex had people at the school write support letters on her behalf. Stuff about what a wonderful mother she was.

One day my son, who was in elementary school, went to the high school where his mom teaches and just happened to run into a counselor there. This counselor interviewed him for some reason and "discovered just how sad this boy is". She wrote a letter signed as a Registered Social Worker and my ex-wife had it filed as a formal complaint about me. She wasn't even working at my son's school or assigned to our family in any way. There were all kinds of inconsistencies in her story, the dates on the letter, the date the "interview" happened and such. I reported her, as she had no business in our case, yet she had formed an opinion and reported it. This just made matters even worse.

In March of 2006, after two years of 50/50 parenting time, my daughter was taken by her mother on the day of her 13th birthday, never to return. There was no contact with my daughter or her mother for weeks. She was hostile towards me for most of the next 4-5 years. My lawyer recommended we see a local specialist in parental alienation. The plaintiff refused to attend with me. This psychologist advised me that legal action to enforce access and parenting arrangements would do more harm than good. This counselor educated my daughter separately on her "rights as a 13-year-old" and the two of them, during this "counseling session" rehearsed my daughter's announcement to me that she would never return to my house. There was never a psychological assessment done on either of my children. This organization facilitated the breakup of my family.

A third DRO meeting was scheduled for a few months later. This DRO entered the room, apologizing for being some 20 minutes late, and suggested that we aim to achieve just one success in the remaining ten minutes. This suggestion was that our family consult a parenting expert. We were to interview practitioners and come to an agreement on who to work with.

I interviewed a handful of practitioners by phone. The Plaintiff and her counsel then switched direction by making it mandatory that this be a Practice Note 7 Intervention, which resulted in the exclusion of all of the practitioners that I had consulted, as no one would perform this particular service. I agreed to Nicola Sheltin, as suggested to me by the Plaintiff, by means of a Consent Order. This psychologist suggested that my lawyer knew nothing about a Practice Note 7 Intervention and my lawyer suggested that Sheltin knew nothing about the same thing, so here we had a group of players who knew nothing about the process they were nevertheless pushing us into.

In the meantime, I had to hire a third lawyer when my second one stated that the situation had escalated beyond his abilities. Lawyer 3 couldn't wait to take my matters to court. A Practice Note 7 Intervention was granted by a Court of Queen's Bench Justice by means of a consent order. Its stated goals were:

1. To assess concerns of each party with respect to parenting arrangements
2. To assess the needs of the family
3. To determine steps either party should take in order to foster more effective communication
4. To determine what services or programs would be beneficial
5. To prepare a report for the court and counsel

After months had gone by, I was asked to meet with a more senior lawyer in the firm just a week before the court date, who suggested that being drawn into another court ruling would be a mistake and all should be addressed by means of a Consent Order. The Plaintiff's lawyer had bundled our family law issues along with outstanding issues in our property agreement, issues that the Plaintiff refused to resolve.

Sheltin had grandiose expectations for our family. She expected us to all celebrate the following Christmas together and all sit together in church. I questioned how she could view herself as a change agent when her role was to simply assess our situation. I lodged an official complaint about this psychologist and the process. By definition, there are two types of Practice Note 7's -Interventions and Assessments. Our Order stipulated an assessment as shown in the five points above. The psychologist performed what is referred to as "dual roles". She would state that we were to fix our problems right there and then, or she would send us back to court. She created conflict within her process, addressing hot-button issues such as finances, and then reported on the conflict.

She failed to follow her own process with respect to the number of, and transportation of the kids to and from, appointments with her. She noted tensions with both kids, but refused to discuss that their mother had 1) moved them into four houses within four years; 2) one steady male companion after another, the first appearing on the scene just days after I moved out of our matrimonial home; and 3) exhibited endless examples of parental alienation, some even harmful to the kids' physical health. Mom was even flying in and out of Calgary and I was never informed of my kids' whereabouts. *Of course my children were troubled*!!

According to Sheltin's "report", my children's problems were all due to their relationship with me, their dad. She suggested we needed "parenting coordination" and more counseling. I had volunteered to pay an additional $2500/year for additional expenses, but I refused to open a joint bank account with the Plaintiff, due to past experiences. But wasn't the process simply an assessment? Before the process was to finish, because we could not come to consensus on certain financial issues the psychologist slammed her book shut and "fired herself" from the process prematurely. While there was a report written, I was not allowed a copy. Instead, I was forced to sit outside the Justice's office in the courthouse and was not allowed a pencil or paper while studying the report.

Just weeks after the psychologist's final report, my ex asked if I would switch weekends with her so she and her new partner could take our 11-year-old son for the long weekend to a lake. I complied, but mom failed to return him as scheduled. It was weeks before I was able to reach him on the phone. It was almost two months before I saw my son again, despite my living just across town. He was abducted and nobody cared. In the last four years, I have not had him for weekends and there is no first right of refusal when his mother is not available. He sleeps over just a few nights a year. I haven't spent a day with him in either of the last two summer holidays. My ex eventually told me he is afraid of me. I went from having my kids half time to zero time just like that, overnight.

My son was throwing up frequently for a while and had stomach problems. But his mom refused to seek any counseling or medical help for him. My church parish has a support program for kids going through divorce but my ex would not hear of his attending. Finally my son was so sick she agreed to his seeing a psychologist. This therapy seemed to help but then, at the age of 11, mom refused further appointments. I was completely powerless to help my own son.

So in September of 2008 I had to hire a fourth lawyer, Geoff Wyser, who charged $450 an hour and said he was one of the Top 5 in Calgary. I attended this lawyer's office to prepare an affidavit. After repeated calls to his office early in 2009, I finally reached his assistant who said she didn't know who I was or why I was phoning.

This matter finally went before the same Court of Queen's Bench Justice in May 2009. In a letter to my lawyer #4, the Plaintiff's lawyer questioned why this application had been sworn and filed the previous November, but not served. Lawyer 4 made it very clear his hatred for opposing council, referring to her in terms that can't be repeated and mentioning that their war of words was shared with all of his partners in a meeting, who prompted him to reduce the harshness of his wording.

The Justice ordered us to Parent Coordination. She also directed that I see my son two nights a week while he had basketball practice, and he could stay over at my house then if he felt like it. But basketball was over in two months. When I asked for clarification and whether this constituted a relationship and real parenting, I was told by the judge to sit down and shut up. We were assigned to James Bender, a parenting coordinator. After a few stalling tactics by my ex, we met with Bender a couple times. But then he discovered that the court order directing him to do his job had not yet been written! The two opposing lawyers, mine and the Plaintiff's, fought over the wording of that court order for *363 days!* At one point I wrote to the judge, asking whether it was what she had in mind that it would take almost a year for me to see my son. She finally signed the Order in May of 2010.

It had been a year after the court date, two years after my son was abducted, that we started parent coordination. We were told it was optional for my ex to attend, participate, comply, or align with any of the parenting coordinator's recommendations. Bender suggested that my son attend with me to rebuild our relationship and my ex agreed to bring him. She never did. To Bender's credit, he wrote a nasty email to the Plaintiff in March of 2011 saying he had done precious little coordinating and was very frustrated with the "process". All that we achieved through parenting coordination was how we would pay for our daughter's university education. There was absolutely no addressing of access.

We were instructed to see a psychologist…again… from the same firm which had facilitated the break-up of the relationship between my daughter and me. The psychologist was to see both kids, I would drive them to these appointments, and then we were to discuss each session afterward. None of this ever happened.

One noon hour I met again with the parenting coordinator at which time I asked why he had only written a page of documentation after witnessing much poor parenting behaviour by my kids' mother. He left me a phone message later saying that his lawyer had advised him not to write more about our family, so he couldn't write a real report.

Lawyer 4, Wyser, was very disorganized and appeared at hearings twice on my behalf but without my knowledge. For instances, in October 2009, Wyser contacted me at 1:30 p.m. one afternoon saying that I needed to be at another (*the fourth*!) DRO meeting at 3:00 the same day! So everyone attended but me. The lawyer gave me a lack of notice "courtesy discount". I have no idea to this day what was discussed. And on October 14th, the Plaintiff's lawyer sent me a Consent Order regarding our court hearing scheduled for the very next day. I tried to contact Wyser that next morning only to find he was already in court! So I missed that court date too. Again I got a "discount". These things should have never happened. Wyser hated opposing counsel…it was totally dysfunctional. Wyser is still my official lawyer, but there is nothing left to fight over; my kids are too old and the damage is done.

In 2012, this spring, I called Alberta Justice and asked how I could lodge a complaint about the lack of due process in my case. I talked with one gal who then put me onto her boss and then *her* boss so they basically passed me around on the phone. One suggestion I heard was that I should go to court again and get a Court Order to force my ex to comply with the Parenting Order. Seriously? After more than seven years of trying, spending all my money and getting several toothless court orders already? Finally, one boss quite high up asked me why I wanted to complain and I said "It is my belief that there isn't another guy in this country who should have to go through what I have been through just to be a father to my kids". So she invited me to come and discuss in person and I did. We had a good 2.5 hour conversation which brought her to tears at one point. She told me I should have gone through Provincial Court as I would have been treated better. But I found out it's as bad there as in Court of Queen's Bench. This same senior manager in Alberta Justice told me to just be patient with my kids. I should just be there for them and they would come back to me.

There was no plan, no navigation through the system, no timeline, nobody to say that these kids need both parents. There was nobody to look back and determine whether any of the steps taken generated any positive results. So many psychologists, "parenting experts" and trained professionals refused to acknowledge what was plain as day. Nobody would acknowledge that I had virtually no access to my children for years, while my children showed many textbook signs of suffering from parental alienation. I believe they were simply pawns in a system designed for the financial benefit of lawyers and related-professionals.

How much harm, including physical harm, such as denying children treatment or refusing access to vital medication, is done to children before practitioners are willing to acknowledge and consider the impacts? Our family's experience proved that our institutions are ill equipped to deal with family breakup. Policies and biases faced at Blue Cross, our local school and our local doctor's office added to conflict and even put our children's health at risk. I told the woman at Alberta Justice that *you are either on the side of the legal industry or you are on the side of children and you need to decide.*

So in eight years, nothing had been achieved and I didn't see either of my children. I began to pay child support, and still do, when my son was abducted. Until that time, our agreement had been equal time with both parents. My ex continues to fight for more child support from me, even now. I pay child support directly to my adult daughter and my ex wants it. She is threatening to take me back to court this summer to get more money from me. We were never registered with MEP (Maintenance Enforcement) as I've always paid voluntarily. Every month I write a cheque to my ex for our son. We still have joint RESPs too, as my ex refuses to separate them.

Just before my daughter turned 20, she contacted me. This was after five years of no contact or communication with her. She wrote me a long letter telling me how controlling her mother is. She wrote that her mom and mom's new husband had taken $15,000 from my daughter to help buy a house for themselves. She said she was in total conflict with her mother and this new husband and wanted to move in with me.

Recently, I called my son hoping he might want to join us in visiting his grandparents. I had to leave a voicemail so called again the next day as we hadn't back heard from him. He picked up, but the conversation involved mom's new husband yelling at my son that he should not go with me. I could hear every word this man said.

And so it continues. I have been on medication for panic attacks, I sleep poorly, and my relationship with my girlfriend has been pretty much on hold for ten years. She has two children from her first marriage, and they are doing well with a smooth co-parenting arrangement. We have not tried to blend our families as mine is in such turmoil. She is such a patient partner.

It seems that professionals drive wedges into your relationships and then bankrupt you and it all makes no sense. My ex stressed all along that I was a good dad. I love my kids, they love me, and we are active together, but for years and years and years, I had to go on defending just that.

2016

I could not be happier with the relationship that has developed between my young adult children and myself given the many years that we spent apart and the years of conflict in the court system. Studies have shown that harmful impacts of parental alienation can last into an adult's forties, although some of the psychologists I have seen suggested that my kids would figure it out and come back and they were right, while it happened much earlier than expected.

My daughter is now 22 and has completed her first degree and is on to a Master's level program in the United States. She grew up very quickly having moved out-of-province during her under-graduate years, the best thing that could have happened. Not only has our relationship grown stronger but also her relationship with her aunt (my sister), her grandmother (my mother) and my partner have too, relationships which at one time were considerably strained.

It is sad to see that my daughter is facing many of the same conflicts with her mother that I did during my marriage and through the divorce process. She was forced to send a nightly text to her mother through her university years to indicate that she was home safely, while told that financial support from her mother (ordered by the courts) was tied to her willingness to do so. Other issues include her mother meddling in her relationships, as well as joint investments which were used to exert control.

At the end of her 3rd year of university, my daughter chose to spend the summer months at my house and in fact had little to do with her mother who lived in the same community. My son is 18 now and a wonderful relationship between us has also developed. He faces the same controlling behaviour from his mother and while on a trip to Asia, was forced to text daily in exchange for his mother supplying the phone. There's always a catch, and my kids are very conscious of this. I was not allowed to partner with my children in the purchase of their first vehicle; instead, the vehicle was purchased by their mother, and there were numerous strings attached.

After my son turned 18, I found out that he suffers from bulimia, an eating disorder. I was advised by my daughter that my children's' wishes were that their mother was not to know, even though he still lives with her. While little may be known about how this disease comes about, it may not be a stretch to conclude the emotional roller-coaster that my children have been dragged through, such as living in multiple homes, having friends ripped from their life and having multiple father-figures thrust into their life, while having been alienated from a loving and caring father, has had a negative impact on their emotional well-being.

I made a point of telling psychologists forced on our family throughout the court process that my children lived in an emotionally harmful environment having been taken from me by their mother and perhaps this is the result. My son was recently sent to emergency for hours of intravenous for a related potassium-deficiency and is facing a long hard road to recovery.

RUSS

CHAPTER 4

RUSS

I have two children: one adopted daughter who was six months old (now 12 years) when I met my second wife and our biological son (now 10 years). I have no children from my first marriage. Let me start at the beginning of my nightmare. My girlfriend (who would become my second ex-wife) and I moved in together in 2000 after a six-month relationship and I bought a house. As soon as I did so, she quit her 4th year of university, stopped taking the Pill without my knowledge, and we became pregnant. I now believe this was a set-up.

We married in 2002 but it only lasted ten months. She would pick fights with me so she could build an arsenal to use against me. Each time I tried to walk away from the marriage she threatened police action, said she would go to the women's shelter and I would never see my children again.

Early on she encouraged me to get a job overseas so we could move there to save money and then move back to Canada. When our son was born in January 2002, I had just started a job in Abu Dhabi. I was to do my first tour of two months and then come back to get her and the kids. We talked by phone every day while I was away. She packed up the house in the meantime but unbeknownst to me separated her stuff from mine. When I got home for a month, we all went camping and took some nice family photos, spent some time together in the U.S. and then came back home a few days before I was due back at work in the U.A.E.

I thought we were moving there as a family. But my ex had other ideas. She was extremely insecure and had a lawyer friend whose husband had been awarded custody upon their divorce. At our baby shower, I overheard this woman telling my wife that all men are cheaters and instructing my wife on how long she needed to stay in our house before she was entitled to the sole ownership of it.

We had a third bad argument over nothing, and I chose to sleep on the couch. Every time it should have been a five-minute conversation but turned into a six-hour yelling match. On this occasion the police got involved and so did my mother. My ex walked out of our house with a bag, which appeared to have been pre-packed. The police said they wouldn't arrest me as there were no grounds and I agreed to go stay at a friend's. Our kids went to my parents' house so they were safe. But my ex told the police she was going to the women's shelter. They asked her why since I was already leaving. She just said she wanted to. By now it was about 5:00 in the morning. The police reported that the whole mess was about money… it was!

My ex was mentally abusive, made me throw away all photos from my first marriage, cash in my RSP investments, then racked up all our credit cards. One time she bought me an expensive watch on our Ben Moss card, but then sold it at a pawn shop and bought herself a bracelet. She sold our furniture. She hadn't paid any bills, not even the mortgage, while I had been away. I was broke! All this came out at our trial.

We separated with joint custody, my ex-wife got primary care, and she registered with MEP (Maintenance Enforcement Program). Very few staff there were knowledgeable about the MEP or knew what they were even supposed to do. I was ordered to continue working overseas so I could pay Child Support based on a salary of $120k even though I was making $75k. I wasn't allowed to come back to Canada for work to be a real parent. Even when I legally had primary care of our kids, MEP was still pursuing me for Child Support. It doesn't even recognize court orders!

So I hired a lawyer and all of a sudden my ex wanted back in my life. I guess she knew if I was thrown in jail her gravy-train would end. The next day my wife called me at my parents' house, came over, and even drove me to the airport. I hoped we could reconcile and for the next two months, it looked possible. But then I got a call from her that she was leaving me, just after the adoption papers were filed and my step-daughter became my daughter. I am thrilled to have my daughter, but it was more than coincidence that I signed those adoption papers only two months before my wife told me she wanted a divorce.

On my way back to Canada, my ex called me and said she would have me arrested when I arrived home. I didn't know whether to get on that plane or not. I didn't know what the hell was happening. I called my lawyer who assured me I was okay, but my ex had filed a restraining (emergency protection) order (EPO) application. For an entire month, my lawyer tried by email and phone to reach the Plaintiff's lawyer and I was never served the court documents. The judge gave my ex the restraining order, primary care of our children, sole possession of the house, child and spousal support. I was then paying support, legal fees, the mortgage, utilities and her vehicle but was unable to see my kids.

I represented myself in court a couple times after to save money, but the judge told me to get a lawyer "for my own protection". We were then assigned to Case Management in 2005. Justice Tressle was a good judge, but then she retired and we were assigned to a useless judge who sat on our case for another year. He figured I should have time with the kids over Christmas. My lawyer, however, reminded him I wouldn't even be in Canada, since I still had to work overseas.

In 2008, the school realized why my kids were not going to school. Their mother was not taking them. I was already banned from the school as the staff thought I was a monster. That's what my ex had told them. But the school phoned me one day while I was in transit in Asia, saying the staff could not find my ex. They had phoned and phoned, but she didn't answer and her voicemail box was full. A school bus driver had my daughter but didn't want to drop her at mom's house since nobody knew where she was. Then the daycare called about my son. Apparently it wanted to close for the day, but mom had not shown up. So I got a relative to pick up my kids. I felt so helpless being so far away. Soon after, while I was in Papua, New Guinea, a business manager for the school called me and said my kids needed help and the situation was unacceptable. *I told them this was what I had been dealing with for years!*

We were assigned to a new case management judge in the spring of 2008. She overturned the earlier ruling and gave me primary custody of the kids. My ex didn't even show up for the meeting. Her lawyer had tried to reach her to no avail. So the judge said "I don't think you should be working overseas because you now have the kids. Try and find yourself a job here (Edmonton) and we will sort everything out in court in two weeks". But as usual, we didn't get into court until September so I took a leave of absence from my job overseas. As it turned out, my ex stated at the trial that she had moved and left the kids at the Children's Cottage. This is a 24-hour respite shelter for kids, but my ex abandoned them there for five days. My children were six and eight years old then.

The judge ordered that my kids reside in Edmonton and not be moved out of the city. He also granted that when I was out of the country, my parents would care for our children. I got a court order stating that at the age of five years I could get my kids passports so I could take them on holiday to the U.S. But my ex will not sign her consent and when we have gone back to court to get that clause enforced, she adds a bunch of other issues to deflect my request.

After that court appearance my ex's lawyer quit. I kept mine. Her name was Sylvia Thernsold. She was very good and could see through all the crap being thrown at me. I went back to court many times, I think 50 times by now. My ex never followed the court orders and was always trying to get me arrested. I still have a restraining order against me. There were three instances where my ex failed to show up in court and I was therefore finally granted a police enforcement clause to make her comply. At this point, the judge told my children's mother that if she refused access as per the court order, she would be held in contempt and she would go to jail. Of course, this penalty never happened. What a waste of time.

One time she wrote in her affidavit that she should be given sole custody because we are always in conflict and have been to court so many times. She also asked that I only be allowed supervised access to my kids. She's the one causing the conflict though. Fortunately that judge realized mom's deceit and instructed that I be given custody because "he is more reasonable than the mother and facilitates access." If I had followed that court order to a T, my ex would not have had time with our children until December 27th. My adopted daughter's birthday is the 17th

so I decided in good faith to give mom access that day.

That Christmas Eve of 2008 was my first with the kids since they were infants. We put out milk and cookies for Santa and it was great. But mom then claimed I was denying her access to the kids and wrecking her Christmas. Next thing I knew she had me back in court on this claim, yet I had followed the court order and given her extra time. My ex had both kids Christmas morning through Boxing Day but that, apparently, was not enough.

There were times when I could not pick up my kids from daycare because mom had told the staff I was not allowed to. They believed her. And sometimes I'd be home during my month off and my ex would keep the kids from me for the entire time except maybe one day. I would spend the month trying to get action from the court and police to enforce my court-ordered parenting access.

Then I had to start paying fees to criminal lawyers, because my ex kept trying to have me arrested every time I came home to Canada. She said I was stalking her, vandalizing the house, not paying daycare fees, etcetera. In fact, she was to pay for the daycare up front and provide me with receipts. My legal fees were spiralling out of control. MEP was still coming after me. My court order had still not been filed, because the lawyer assigned to me after Sylvia was Geoffrey Kelvie who later went over to Legal Aid.

He couldn't care less about kids and knew how to stall the process for his own benefit.

In 2010 my ex went through Child and Family Services to get at me. I was remarried by then. They recommended I take a parenting course, which I did, and placed a social worker in our home to look for areas of concern. There were no concerns but the social workers stated that my ex tried to persuade them to lie and say there were. Again, she suffered no penalty. We did notice how my children would be quite poorly-behaved after being at mom's but would settle down within a day or so of being back with us. Even the social workers witnessed that.

I still have my kids most of the time. They go to mom's Wednesday nights and three weekends per month but the struggle continues. It is always difficult to communicate in any way with my ex but she has discovered that if she does so, things are smoother. She doesn't want to go back to court as her affidavit was proven to be riddled with lies.

I have become somewhat of an expert on the MEP organization though I wish I'd never had to deal with it. It still harasses me. I met with the former MEP director when he attended International Children's Day and gave a speech. He told me to write him a letter of complaint. I let him know I had already sent several complaints to him. Two days later, someone else from MEP phoned me announcing that all actions against me had ceased. Interesting timing, wasn't it? It was Justice Dane Li who chastised MEP about my case. He is a decent judge and regularly reins in MEP for its unwarranted harassment of payors.

I paid way over a $100,000 in legal fees in the first six years and for what? I've had to use so many lawyers. And MEP has been on my case for years, even when I have primary custody of my kids. One time my dad paid MEP for me when I was away, and he was treated so poorly by MEP staff that he told me he would never go there again. This could have all been avoided. My kids just need their parents. Now I'm poor and have a crappy vehicle and still work overseas a lot to pay our debts off.

The reason I try to help other alienated and harassed parents wade through the MEP disaster is because I understand what they are enduring. I know they are stressed to the max, just trying to make ends meet, make their child and spousal support payments, deal with vengeful exes, and somehow still be a meaningful part of their children's lives.

GLORIA

CHAPTER 5

GLORIA

I had two sons. David was born in 1971 and was a nice boy and good student. His father and I divorced and I moved to Edmonton when David was four. I tried to encourage a relationship between the boys and their father, but because of the distance, it was very difficult. Their dad lived in New Brunswick. My ex paid child support and I did shift work so we made it work, although money was tight. David's brother died tragically in 1990 when he was only 24. This loss was extremely hard on David and me. Their father died from cancer a few years later.

David began to date a girl named April while he was attending NAIT (Northern Alberta Institute of Technology). He wanted to be a firefighter. I was concerned about this relationship as Alice seemed very possessive, even controlling where and when David would go. David was seeing his friends less and less. I was surprised when they announced their engagement in 1995 after an on-again off-again relationship. Alice's father paid for their extravagant wedding and they began to renovate a condo near David's in-laws.

In 1996, their first child was born and David had quit NAIT to work for better money on the oil rigs. David was close to his father-in-law and the two of them decided to buy a bakery as a family business. This way David could work close to home instead of being up north on the rigs for weeks at a time. Alice continued her tendency to control and insisted on looking after their financial affairs.

In 2000, David found out he was bankrupt. Their RRSPs were cashed out, jewelry had been pawned, and David's truck was sold. It became apparent that Alice had a gambling addiction and had squandered $80,000 of their savings. Alice was fired from her job at a bank and now unemployed, but David managed to pay off the outstanding debt by working extra hours. But both parents were abusing substances and this added to their volatile relationship. David successfully completed a rehabilitation program and I hoped the family could rebuild as a healthy unit.

The bakery never materialized as Alice's father, too, died of cancer in 2001. On a brighter note, David and Alice's daughter was born in March that same year. In August, Alice asked me to co-sign a loan so they could buy a house. I declined as I was in no financial position and had my own mortgage. Soon after, they sold their condo and moved to a resort community south of Edmonton.

David was proud of their new house and worked on completing the basement on his days off. Their new home was full of expensive furniture, televisions and computers. If the dishes did not match the décor, Alice would throw them out and purchase new ones. I did not visit very often as I respected Alice's wishes that David spend his precious few days off with her and their children.

By 2003, David was again working the oil rigs to make enough money to finance their costly lifestyle. They needed the money, but Alice resented David's long absences. Once Alice called David to ask that he come home immediately because the cat had died.

By the end of that year, Alice asked David to move out. He did so and spent a few days over the holidays at my home. Their two children spent a day with David and me. In an Ex Parte Order (one party is not present) granted (though David's location was known, he was not made aware of Alice's court action) by Justice Faster in January 2004, Alice claimed as her only evidence, a year-old letter from the rehabilitation facility. It stated that David had enrolled and was successful in his sobriety program. This letter had been confidentially sent to David's employer, but Alice convinced the boss to release it to her. Alice claimed expenses without evidence and excused the family's hardship by alleging that David squandered his paycheques to support a drug habit. None of this was substantiated evidence, but the court awarded Alice interim sole custody, possession of the matrimonial home, child support of $1,167 plus extra child expenses of an additional $593 and spousal support of $1000 per month, and $2000 for Alice's court costs. This award was in fact $500 more than Alice had requested in her claim. David's pension funds were frozen by the Maintenance Enforcement Program, and he was given thirty days to file a Statement of Defense.

The court also ordered that both parents take the required "Parenting after Separation" course, which must be filed with the Clerk of the Court before any notice of interim relief can be filed. David did; Alice did not. Yet Alice's court applications were nonetheless accepted and filed.

In the court transcript I obtained from that day, Alice's lawyer said "Sir, I also have an Ex Parte application for you, if you will humour me, Sir". There had been no legitimate reason for an Ex Parte hearing, since this was no emergency, yet Judge Faster ruled anyway. He even said "I expect that will get him in here", apparently meaning that the decision would spur David to defend his rights. But David was not informed that this court hearing had even transpired.

The award was crippling to David, who moved into a shared basement suite near his ex-wife, wanting to stay close to his two little children. He also knew that Alice could otherwise file a claim stating she did not know where he resided. The family car, a sub-compact Neon, was in David's name, but Alice retained its use with David's approval. She racked up parking tickets, but did not pay them. David, however, did. She eventually got the truck, which was co-owned by both Alice and David. David had consistently over time been paying down its loan. She slandered David's name to anyone who would listen to her tales, including David's employer. She even called the police claiming she feared that her ex-husband would take things from their home.

One day when I visited my 5-year-old grandson to walk him home from school, he told me he was mad at his dad. He said he and his mom (Alice) would spy on his dad at home through the basement suite's windows and she told him that all the boxes in dad's home were filled with drugs. Keeping afloat financially amidst the enormous payments to Alice each month was very difficult, so David soon moved in with me to save money.

In 2005, a Notice to Disclose, filed by David's lawyer to expose Alice's finances, was mysteriously adjourned, then canceled completely. The matrimonial house was sold without David's permission though mortgage payments came directly from David's bank account. His lawyer, Mr. Wenless, failed to file a Statement of Defense to challenge the gross financial award Judge Faster had given to Alice.

Mr. Wenless had instructed David to sign a Consent Order. He was behind in his monthly payments to Alice and this lawyer advised that David could go to jail if he did not pay in full. He believed, as the court had, that David made $89,000 per year. This was the claim made by Alice despite David's single year at that salary due to an oil boom. His regular income was approximately $50,000. David agreed to give Alice his RRSP and pension in order to lower his spousal payments and he released all claim to both vehicles. The Order was mute on household contents. My son trusted his lawyer. Ordinary people know little about the complexities of the law. Lawyers are paid a lot of money to know them and to advise and protect their clients.

David tried his best to pay his arrears. MEP requires much documentation of earnings, assets, and employment. David gathered and submitted all these things, all the while never knowing how long he would be in town before his next job on a rig. At one point, after the Consent Order was signed, David did not make his payments on time. As a result, MEP garnished a large portion of his salary to make up the regular payment due plus part of his arrears. This monthly amount of $2500 was to remain in effect for five years.

When he was in the field, David had a hard time reaching his children by phone. When at home with me, he was a long way from the town where his children lived. He saw them as often as he could, but Alice made it difficult and had a boyfriend now living with them. After some months, Alice began allowing the children to spend every second weekend with us.

After Alice moved to Edmonton, there were happy times when my grandchildren and their dad could spend time together. They played croquet, rode horses at our friends' acreage, and played board games… they never wanted to leave. But Alice would phone constantly when the children were with us asking if they were okay. She insulted David on many occasions in the presence of the kids. I kept quiet, as I did not want to jeopardize these visits. On one such occasion, my grandson took some money from my purse and when I confronted him, he said innocently "Grandma, it's ok, Mom says you have a lot more money than we do".

One day while the kids were at my house with my son, Alice phoned David to tell him she now had been granted a second Ex Parte Order, this one giving her permission to take the children out of the country without David's permission. This was 2006. David demanded of his lawyer a copy of this Order and found it dated September 7, 2005, issued by a Justice D.A. Searrs. From the transcript I later obtained, this Order was signed without question and included all Alice's lawyer's terms. Justice Searrs simply rubber-stamped it.

Alice's affidavit claimed she did not know where David was and asked that all future legal documents be sent to my home, and by regular, not even registered, mail. Justice Searrs approved this outrageous request making it impossible to prove whether or not Mr. Molder, Alice's lawyer, ever mailed any documentation at all. And in Alice's written request, she misspelled my address. This was the supposed reason that David never received the Order. He found out by searching the internet at the end of 2005 that a court hearing had occurred on October 19th with Justice Gerard granting their divorce. My son was unknowingly divorced. Alice was granted permanent sole custody and guardianship of my grandchildren; David was erased.

This affidavit alleged that David "has not played a significant role in the lives of our children for the last several years" and "has not even called the children on the telephone". She wrote that "I will continue to parent our children on my own, without any assistance from the Respondent". The truth about David's relationship with his children is a very different picture. He tried so hard to be with them, he moved close to them, he took them skating on the outdoor rink by my home, but the constant hostility from Alice made it difficult even to talk to his kids by phone.

Alice lied under oath at the 2005 divorce hearing as I found out reading the court transcript years later in 2010. She had quit work, sold the matrimonial home and David's truck, and kept all proceeds. Yet she told the judge and her lawyer, Mr. Molder, in her affidavit six weeks earlier that she was working very hard to support her kids and take them on holiday to the U.S. Alice began to mention her gambling debts, but was interrupted and stopped by Mr. Molder as she spoke to the judge. In less than a year, MEP statements showed that David had paid Alice $11,585.44 but when Alice was questioned in court by her lawyer about this, she did not disclose this information. She also failed to disclose the thousands of dollars David had voluntarily given her prior to the Consent Order.

Subsequent to the "desk divorce", David struggled emotionally through 2006. He told me he had trouble focusing and felt "scattered". When he saw his kids, they would ask him when he was going to get his own place. David continued to live with me to save money. In March, he endured a recurrence of an old back injury that required hospitalization. Physiotherapy was prescribed but without medical coverage, David instead treated himself with only ice-packs. He could not work, and his employment insurance ran out.

Later that year, David found retail work outside the oil patch, but these jobs never paid enough for his court-ordered support payments. He rode his bike to work to save money. But over time, he was falling farther and father behind in his payments through MEP. In 2006, David was required to pay $20,004, yet his total income was $11,000. MEP garnished $8,378.17 that year.

Finally, after much red tape, David successfully obtained a lawyer through Legal Aid. His intention was to have support payments made more realistic for his earnings. The appointed lawyer, Gerry Kerowak, filed David's affidavit and a Notice of Motion to let Alice know he was going to challenge his required payments to MEP. Mr. Kerowak told David he hoped to cancel the arrears altogether. Documented evidence was included that disputed the allegations made by Alice in court. He included tax returns, receipts, bank account statements, everything that showed his contributions and assets since their separation. When Alice was hospitalized for a surgical procedure in the summer of 2006, David looked after his children with the agreement that Alice would resume their parenting schedule once she was recovered and back to work. But Alice did not return to work and six months after David's affidavit was filed, she went on welfare.

David's court hearing finally occurred after 18 months following his filing the affidavit. All that time, dates were scheduled and then canceled by the opposing lawyer. It is my opinion that Mr. Kerowak did not press the issue, even though David's finances were in dire straits.

Mr. Kerowak led my son to believe that all financial examinations by MEP were on hold until their upcoming court hearing. This was not the case. In January of 2007, David received a Notice to Attend a MEP Examination of Finances on March 1 and he was to fill in a Statement of Finances. He had provided all this information to MEP long before and his situation had not changed. In response, David went, with his paycheque receipts in hand, to the MEP office in Edmonton and successfully had his garnished wages reduced to $631 per month from the current $1000. This bought him the time necessary to legally vary his Order in court. But David understood that this temporary arrangement recused him from attending the MEP Examination of Finances. So he went back to work on the rigs before shutdown in spring, desperately needing the money after missing February. That month he had lost work time in order to attend a court hearing… one that Mr. Kerowak failed to notify him had been cancelled.

Failing to show at MEP's Financial Examination resulted in its Senior Financial Examiner, Kevin Noolan, requesting a court Order to Compel Attendance. David was to bring all documentation, as before, to this redundant meeting. Mr. Noolan was remiss in his failure to state David's earlier submission to MEP of all this documentation. Mr. Noolan also wrote that David was in arrears in the amount of $44, 475.66; he neglected to note David's earlier payments to MEP; he did not state the special payment reduction made with MEP recently; he left out David's 2006 court application showing David's exorbitant payments far exceeding his income level (e.g., his tax forms for 2004 and 2005 showed he earned $46, 272 and $45, 668, respectively); and he omitted the huge property value David had lost to Alice. So David appeared to be a deadbeat dad.

Justice W.E.Wellison granted this Order to Compel and David was to attend the MEP Examination now scheduled for June 26, 2007. Prior to this date, a Ms. McMillan working as legal counsel for MEP wrote the court that David owed the Crown (i.e., Social Assistance) $4,121.12 and another $350 owed the Director of MEP as a default penalty. She also opposed in writing any reduction in David's support payments, claiming that David was capable of an income of $89,000 and she falsely stated that he had "not provided any information with respect to his income for 2006". This letter supported the impression that David was avoiding his responsibilities and legal obligations.

At his court hearing on June 6th, 2007, David was left outside the courtroom while Alice and the two lawyers convened with Justice Versaille presiding. I do not know why David was not allowed into the courtroom; this is very unusual. David was not aggressive or prone to outbursts; in fact, he was extremely passive and that likely made him an easier target for the injustice he suffered. Since I was unable to attend the hearing, I cannot know whether David's lawyer represented him well and honestly. Alice was still not required to produce her financial statements nor substantiate claims such as her costs of $800-$1000 a month incurred for having her own mother (the children's grandmother) babysit. And the maternal grandmother was not taking time off work to babysit. Mr. Kerowak failed to cross-examine Alice on this point or any others, such as why Alice remained on welfare.

David's cash payments thus far amounted to $29,568.04 (MEP claimed he owed a total of $35,488) and he had received none of his rightful half of the RRSP and pension. If he had, he would, after-taxes, have had more than $6000 and could have paid off the rest of his arrears. This calculation does not even include what should have been his half of the matrimonial house sale. Perhaps most shocking, David's own lawyer Mr. Kerowak, asked the judge for a $25,000 penalty to be invoked on David should he miss another payment. But MEP already has stringent penalties for noncompliance with court orders. In addition, Mr. Kerowak knew that David did not have regular paycheques, so there was likelihood that he might miss a payment, depending on when he could find contracts. In effect, the court signed my son's death warrant when it created that Order.

Justice Versaille asked that Mr. Kerowak file the Order as soon as possible. But Alice was granted permission to approve it before the filing occurred. In the following few months, David repeatedly called MEP and Mr. Kerowak asking for a copy of the Order. All this time, MEP continued to take monthly payments from David's account in the original amount. The new court Order was to reduce his payments immediately. In August 2007, MEP ceased David's driver's license due to his outstanding arrears. He was able to regain it by paying Motor Vehicles $65. But MEP again took his license two weeks later. I'm not sure if he ever got his license back that fall.

The new Order was finally filed on September 18th, 3.5 months after the court hearing. David picked it up from Mr. Kerowak's office, but noticed his lawyer, who had been instructed to write it up, nevertheless had not signed it. There was just a signature of someone from MEP. Should David's lawyer not have signed this? I read the Order and told David this was not in his best interest. He said dejectedly that it was over and nothing could be done about it.

Three weeks later, Mr. Kerowak filed with the court a Notice of Ceasing to Act for David. I am unaware why he suddenly quit David's file. Since this was Legal Aid, there were no fees outstanding on David's account. It was six months after the court hearing when MEP finally wrote to tell David it had received and processed the "new" court Order. Their own lawyer had been present when the Order was created, so the delay was inexcusable. MEP later told me it is normal for a new Order to take 14 days to be processed. There was no information in MEP's letter about whether David's payments were now reduced or what was to be done with his outstanding arrears. Years later, MEP told me David could have looked for that information on its website.

David, since the court hearing, became increasingly despondent. He was often sitting by my backyard fire-pit, just staring into space, when I'd get home from work. Other than his children's occasional visits, he looked forward to nothing. On Christmas Eve, 2007, my grandchildren called David to tell him they were not allowed to visit over Christmas unless he gave their mom more money. Parents are not allowed by the courts to prevent court-ordered parenting time, yet this behaviour by Alice, and scores of other mothers as I have since discovered, was never penalized.

I took our presents to Alice's brother's house and asked that he give them to Alice and David's children. This was to be David's last Christmas. On January 16th, 2008, I returned home from work and David wasn't there. There was no note, which was unusual for him. The next morning he phoned me with the news that he had been arrested the night before because apparently he had not paid MEP enough. My son had never been in jail before. I told David to talk to Duty Counsel and I would try to get him a lawyer immediately. I knew from working at the Law Court building that David was unlikely to get representation in Family Court, since it is grossly over-loaded with cases. But on a criminal charge, a judge will require that the accused have legal counsel to enter a plea. In that case, David would be given bail or released on his own recognizance unless he was a threat to society or a flight risk.

As it turned out, Mr. Noolan of MEP had applied to the court for a warrant to have David arrested due to his failure to appear at the Financial Examination back on June 26th. The date of Noolan's application was just after David had received Mr. Kerowak's Ceasing to Act for David letter. In this application, Kevin Noolan grossly misstated that David was in arrears of $54,416.60 as of October 22, 2007. Again, there was no mention of David's cooperation with, and payments to, MEP over the years. And there was no mention that MEP continued to garnish David's wages.

The police station record showed that David, upon arrest, had been cooperative and sober. There was also a background criminal check record him, which showed only minor misdemeanors and the fines paid as consequence. This information, though useful for me, was supposed to be held "in confidence" by MEP according to Section 15(1) of the Maintenance Enforcement Act.

On January 18, 2008, David was arraigned before Justice Gecko. I obtained, in 2009, the court transcript, which told what happened in court that day. The court charges $1 per page to provide a copy of court proceedings, perhaps as a deterrent to those members of the public who have a right to know what has transpired.

David entered the court in hand cuffs, prison uniform and without counsel. MEP's acting lawyer, a Mr. Callow, painted a bleak picture of a deadbeat dad. Now the amount of David's arrears was stated as $29,901.14, an amount consistent with the new court Order filed in September, 2007. Mr. Callow further stated that David's last "voluntary payment" had been made in December 2006. MEP's lawyer made a case that David was unwilling, rather than unable, to pay off his arrears in full. There was certainly no mention, at all, of the outrageous penalty of $25,000 which now accounted for almost all the arrears.

Mr. Callow requested that David be held in custody until January 31st, so that MEP could conduct a financial examination of him while in jail. He asked that for a Default Hearing on that date. In court, when asked about employment, David told the judge he was now working as a well tester since his previous employer had had no work for him in months. Though being held in custody would certainly cause David to lose this job too, Justice Gecko nevertheless directed that he be "remanded in custody". Her words did not specify how long he was to be held there. She advised him to get a lawyer before the January 31st hearing.

David was frantic when he called me. I told him to immediately apply for legal counsel and I would do everything possible for him from my end. I first called Mr. Noolan, who said "If you pay $5000 or give me some assets, I will get your son released so he can work". Then I called Mr. F. Lendy in the Solicitor General's office. I was told he doesn't deal with MEP Orders. And I found the Ombudsman's office similarly does not investigate contested court orders. The Human Rights Commission does not deal with Family Court; and the police, according to the 28 -year veteran constable I spoke with, begrudgingly pick up MEP violators all the time, mostly fathers. I also phoned Justice Minister Alison Redpath's office, but her staff member dismissed my request for intervention in David's case, saying "It is obvious he did not pay and it is surprising how much money people can come up with to get their child (i.e., debtor) out of jail. People thank us for collecting money for the children".

One lawyer I phoned in hopes of obtaining counsel for my son said he would not represent David who was "one of these guys who makes the big money in the oil patch and then throws their (sic) money away. They come here and expect me to get them out of trouble". I called politicians; one MLA's assistant called MEP on my behalf. It did no good, however, as I found out she was transferred to another office shortly after my call. Her replacement would not tell me where she had been sent.

David's financial exam by MEP occurred on January 23, 2008, inexplicably moved up from the 31st. The interrogation was of a personal and financial nature and questions included whether David drank, belonged to a union, received any inheritance, or had a parent who could pay off his debts. The two examiners, Mr. Noolan and Ms. Philip, even asked how much David had paid his previous lawyer, Mr. Kerowak. My son explained that he had sixty-four cents in the bank, no assets, and a silver chain he once received as a Christmas present. Everything else had been given to, or taken by, his ex-wife. Mr. Noolan expressed surprise that David had a history, prior to the separation, of owning a home and paying off his bills fully and on time. This examiner also said he found it sketchy that David had experienced such a decrease in salary while remaining employed in the oil patch. David responded that there had been little available work recently due to the global economic downturn.

David told Mr. Noolan how he had recently been hired into a new job as a well tester's assistant and that he hoped he could work his way up into a supervisory position for better pay. In response, MEP's investigator said that effective immediately then, MEP would begin to garnish 40% of David's wages from this new job. And then he asked David what he was willing to pay immediately to encourage Mr. Noolan to recommend David's release from custody. David reiterated that he had no money as yet, having just started this new job and being regularly garnished beyond his means. Ms. Philip then asked if in the meantime David could borrow funds from someone.

I called David's new employer who was sympathetic, having dealt with MEP himself in the past. His co-worker sent me $417.59, the entire amount David had earned to date. The company also wrote a letter on David's behalf, confirming he was employed and reminding MEP that as long as he was kept in jail, the longer David was prevented from earning a paycheque. I sent Mr. Kerowak all David's paperwork including his tax returns, T4 slips, and a letter from Manulife insurance confirming that Alice had received David's RRSP. David was released on his court appearance date of January 31st, 2008, after spending two weeks behind bars. I remain unclear as to why David was kept in jail a full eight days after his MEP examination.

At the January hearing, Mr. Noolan presented himself to the judge and asked to speak to David outside the courtroom. This was allowed. This MEP examiner help up a piece of paper and said

"I am increasing your monthly payments by $1000. You sign this or you go back to jail for another 60 days". David, under duress, signed. He was not given a copy of that document. When Mr. Noolan went back into court, he told the judge that David had agreed to the revised terms.

I worked as an officer for Corrections for 29 years. I know that jail is a dangerous place. David told me that a stabbing had occurred while he was there. Mr. Noolan suggested to me just before David's court hearing that David had an easy time in jail because I worked there. In truth, the opposite could well have been the case. If inmates found out I worked there, David could have been in much danger in jail. I gave Mr. Noolan the money David had earned from his new job. Yet two months later, on April 8th, at a continuation of MEP's financial examination, Mr. Noolan would state that David made no voluntary attempts to contribute to his outstanding arrears.

At the Family Law Centre, I begged for help finding a lawyer to represent my son. Ms. Skelter was assigned his case and I gave her Mr. Kerowak's file on David. The follow-up MEP examination happened April 8th, though the court had ordered it for March 14th. Mr. Noolan and Ms. Philip were again present along with the addition of Ms. Kooperstay, then Manager of Examinations and Investigations for southern Alberta. David's lawyer, Ms. Skelter, was also in attendance. Ms. Kooperstay opened with a warning that she would decide who would speak and for how long, any abusive language or action would render David in contempt of court and criminal charges would be laid. Ms. Skelter asked to Ms. Kooperstay, "Are you trying to terrorize him? I need him to be calm when he's answering your questions".

Mr. Noolan claimed he did not yet have all the documents needed from David's file, and Ms. Skelter would not proceed without them, so Ms. Kooperstay adjourned the examination until April 24th. She would also ask the court to postpone David's Default Hearing until after that date. On April 10th, the court adjourned its hearing until June 12th but did issue a warrant for

David's arrest to be activated June 12th, pending David's upcoming MEP examination.

In court on June 12th, Justice Wackolos adjourned the Default Hearing further to September 11, 2008. And the warrant for David's arrest issued on April 10th was vacated. Ms. Skelter seemed to want to act in David's best interest, but a whole year after David's release from jail, he was still waiting for justice and his day in court. The continuation of MEP's financial exam had still not happened. This was a massive amount of ongoing stress with no relief in sight.

In late August of 2008, David wrote another affidavit in yet another effort to get his arrears lowered to a manageable level. For reasons unknown, there was no final version of this document and Ms. Skelter did not file it with the court. Part of David's original version stated "In giving the Plaintiff and extra $54,207 in property, I received nothing in return other than persecution by the Plaintiff and MEP for Orders that were wrong and draconian in their penalty provisions. I was unaware that I had other options. I was never able to get on my feet after giving the Plaintiff al the matrimonial property, a total of $113,114.38. I don't believe her need was proven through tax returns or budgets, as in this entire time I have never seen a tax return from her proving her income."

As far as I know, my son had not seen his children since the Christmas phone call demanding more money in return for their pending visit. David looked old; he was half-hearted about everything he did and though he readily went to work, it was sporadically available. Without his children, he said he had little to live for. His entanglement with Alice had begun when David was just 32 and now, five years later, he wondered if his Old Age and Canada pensions would go to MEP as well.

I, as a mother, felt sick. I saw a counselor through my workplace and told her I needed to find help for my son. She advised me to go out for a nice supper and get my hair done. I guess I looked too thin and my hair was a mess, but I understood she knew I needed to look after myself. I called the Suicide Hotline and they asked me if I was going to kill myself.

When David had signed the agreement outside court for Mr. Noolan, the one that increased his monthly payments by $1000, David's driver's license was reinstated for one year from February 8, 2008. But on October 17, 2008, he received a MEP notice that his license was now cancelled outright. Another notice dated the same day, also from MEP, said his license would be cancelled in 21 days. Of note, MEP can also put restrictions on vehicle registrations without prior notice. So a person's vehicle can be towed and he or she fined $2000 should that person be unaware of his or her license having been revoked. The justice system gives more leeway to impaired drivers…and people on house arrest are sometimes allowed their license to drive to work.

On September 18 with a follow-up on October 3, letters came for David from MEP again requesting a Statement of Finances. This despite Ms. Skelter's obtaining a delay for the continuation of his financial examination. Both letters contained strong language warning David of "serious consequences" should he not provide the requested information. This year alone, MEP had collected $8000 from David, more than enough for reasonable child support but not enough to pay down the unjust $30,000 in supposed arrears.

David went back to the drilling rigs. He bought an older car and asked me to register it since he could not, due to the MEP restriction. I told him he was not thinking clearly, as MEP would again pull his license. Then he told me he was going to work doing renovations and would find a place to live with a buddy. He did move to a basement suite with a guy he knew years earlier, and he started working on a home nearby. He came to pick up his mail every day from my place. There were frequent letters from MEP. David said he had made an appointment to see Ms. Skelter, knowing he needed to get back into court or he would be in big trouble.

Then in November, David became more worrisome. He asked my niece to bring him to my house one evening, then changed his mind. He similarly called me and asked to come home but then cancelled. On November 22, I left him a phone message.

There was no call back from him. On the 23rd the police came to my home. They told me *they had found David hanging in a stranger's garage on the 22nd*.

Two months after David's death, I received a notice from MEP expressing their condolences. The letter stated that "we will not be proceeding with collection action" but that MEP would collect David's amount owing from his estate. This letter was not signed.

April 15, 2009: A letter came addressed to my son from the Department of Justice Canada. It stated "Take notice that on April 11, 2009, the government of Canada was served with a garnishee summons. This summons was served by the following court, provincial or territorial entity: Maintenance Enforcement Alberta (MEP). David was to pay $30,272.09 on May 19, 2009; plus there would be a $190.00 fee charged to him for this action. *My son had been dead four months.*

MEP ceased the phone calls and letters after I requested my MP Mr. Rathenberger to do something. Apparently he did. Regardless, MEP still took David's 2008 tax return refund of $1767.75 from his total income of $15, 681.13 in the last year of his life.

My granddaughter and my grandson were at their dad's funeral; they were nine and twelve years old. They paid the ultimate price and lost a dad who loved them. Someday they will read his story and know the truth. I am haunted by my son's last words to me, "Quit fighting, mom, nobody cares".

LARRY

CHAPTER 6

LARRY

I am a grandfather of two girls now aged 11 and 13. Their father, Kelly, is my son. When my granddaughters were 3 and almost 5, their mother died of cancer. The girls went immediately to their maternal grandfather's. I'm not sure why. Kelly was staying with me so each morning he would go the couple blocks to his father-in-law's house and stay with the girls all day until they went to bed. The reason the kids had been staying there was so that Kelly could be at the hospital with his wife.

On the day of his wife's funeral, Kelly went to get his daughters but was told by his father-in-law that they were going to stay with him because Kelly was "unfit". Kelly's father-in-law had five lawsuits on the go for a while. It's almost like he does that for a living; he sues. His brother is a lawyer. He sued his own wife while she was dying, and he sued when his daughter got in a car accident. When Kelly's wife was dying and no longer lucid, during last rites with 30 people in the room, he wrote out a will on her behalf and had a lawyer sign it.

We hired the best lawyer we knew of, Randy St. Pere, to contest the will, since Kelly's wife had not had her faculties when it was signed. We needed a statement from the doctor who cared for Kelly's wife at the end. He put a caveat on while he took *10 months* to get this statement. He blamed the doctors for the delay, saying he couldn't get in to see them for a signature.

In the meantime, Kelly's father-in-law took custody of my grandchildren. *He is actually listed as the children's mother,* can you believe it? He got an interim Order from Justice Versaille and Kelly had a green lawyer named Byron Poyet assigned to his case. It was called a Justice Special hearing. Turns out that Byron did a good job but as a result, as I found out later, he quit Family Law afterward and went back to an honest job that he had done earlier in life. This judge ordered that Kelly could only have supervised visits with his own children. The father-in-law wanted Kelly's wages garnished as he claimed Kelly needed to pay him more child support.

Soon after this Order was made, we went to court a couple times to try to get the kids back to their father. No other judge would overturn Versaille's decision, so Kelly's case went to Special Chambers. It took three months to get there; March 24. Justice Morey ordered our case to trial immediately and said he would give us a Court Order to make that happen. I didn't know at the time that a Court Order without an Enforcement clause is totally useless.

By July we still didn't have a trial date, and we hadn't received the Court Order from Judge Morey either. The lawyers did a good job of holding it all up. Kelly gave up on the lawyers and wrote a letter directly to the judge. He said the lawyers couldn't agree on the terms of the Order and he needed intervention by Justice Morey. The next day we were informed that Justice Gecko had been assigned as our case manager.

That seemed okay but it turned out Justice Gecko just put us in our place. *We have been in front of her, I think, 67 times now!* Never have these court appearances done one bit of good. In case you don't know, it was Ms. Gecko who basically caused Gloria's son (author's note: refer to Chapter 5) to kill himself. That judge also sent David to jail and slapped the $25,000 penalty on him.

The last time Kelly was in Court of Queens Bench, Justice Gecko had three armed guards in the courtroom and she used intimidation tactics, making him give them his keys and wallet upon entering. The whole time in court, those guards sat staring at Kelly and me. My cousin was there as a witness so he saw the whole charade too. I later asked the court staff whether this was at all irregular and they assured me it certainly was. Then one staff guy told me the guards were in court because Kelly had written a "threatening" letter to the judge. Threatening? He just asked for help since the Order he had been promised was still undone, against the stated need by that court for expediency.

Justice Gecko is still the case manager. Kelly had supervised visits for a while. Then he had the kids one week on, one week off. He was ordered by Karen Challer to get a psychological assessment. He did that, and it showed he was fine mentally. But he is angry now after years and years of stress, not the same Kelly he once was. We have had five different lawyers and at least three judges involved in our case. Ms. Gecko keeps this thing from going to trial. At one point Kelly was told by Joy Muller, a psychologist, that he should have obeyed his lawyer. She then told him that he should have stepped in and disagreed with his lawyer. That blew me out of the water. He was in a no-win from the start.

We complained about our lawyer, Debbie Mulder, but the Law Society of Alberta dismissed our complaint. Specifically, it was Kathryn Whitley who relied only on affidavit evidence from Ms. Mulder, so let her off the hook. We appealed the decision, but of course that was dismissed too. They all (i.e., lawyers) protect each other.

I have exhausted my RRSPs and stuff like that, all for nothing. It didn't help the kids. It didn't help my son. No one cares about targeted parents. For me, it is a fulltime job just to keep my family together. We've been fighting a corrupt system since 2004 and now it's eight years later.

ROB

CHAPTER 7

ROB

I have two daughters, Laila, twelve, and Ella, eight, and my son Tyson is six. Laila's mother, Laura, was my first wife and the other two were born in a subsequent relationship with Joy. Laila's mom and I separated when she was just two years old. I was already in another relationship so I think that's the reason Laila's mom decided to hate me. She was really upset about it. Next thing I knew, Laura told me she was keeping Laila, our home, and everything else and I was going to pay, pay, pay.

Being new to this stuff, I thought I had better get a lawyer. I hired Mick Cruise and the weird thing was, I didn't despise my ex then but Mick liked to called her "the wifey". He also encouraged me to "look broke, drive a crappy car, that's how you play the game". I was not of that mindset; I just wanted to do the separation fairly.

Mick was brutal; his hourly billing rate was middle of the road but he charged me for every single little thing. Sometimes I would get invoices when I thought we were in a quiet period so I couldn't imagine what he was charging me for. I asked and his response was something like he had met another lawyer in the hall and they talked about my case for a while. I let him know I didn't want him acting unless I gave him permission to do so or something significant needed attending to. It was a "silly bugger" game; he asked if he should read any emails or faxes then. After I had to ask him a third time to stop charging me thousands of dollars for nothing beyond "make work" emails and phone calls, he quit my case. I had paid him about $15,000 by then, for absolutely no progress.

Right after separation, I had an Interim Order which amounted to my parenting Laila about 30% of the time. It was every other weekend but included Friday and Monday. It wasn't too bad. I hoped for 50% but figured at least this was decent. Soon, though, Laura would put conditions on my parenting time. For example, she said that if my girlfriend was going to be there with me, then Laila was not coming. Laura even demanded that I give her written notice or a phone call to confirm whether my girlfriend (Joy, who later became my second wife) would be around when Laila was with me. I realize that I should not have jumped into another relationship, my rebound, right away, but that was not the point.

In fact, I was living in my friend's basement after we separated. Laura was in the marital home and stayed there for a few years. She wouldn't sell it; wouldn't accept any reasonable price for it even when we got two good offers. Laura had no costs since she wasn't working and I was paying for everything so why should she sell? That left me with about $200 a month to live on so it was an immensely stressful time in my life. My job was as the go-to technical guy in a large consulting firm and I made good money, yet I was cratering financially.

I had to hire another lawyer when Laura decided to file for sole custody. This lawyer, Michelle something, did a lousy job and as a result, the judge gave Laura much more parenting time while I was shuffled off to the sidelines. The judge, some old guy who seemed bored or disinterested, said we should take a break and go sort things out between us. He believed he "should not rule your lives and you should be mature and solve your problems yourselves". These judges have no idea about parental alienation and just assume mom is the only worthy parent. This judge thought it takes two to tango but the fact is that it takes only one when that person has a revenge agenda at your child's expense. We took that break as instructed but of course Laura was not about to negotiate anything.

Michelle told me I would have to appeal that decision and had 30 days from the date of the Writ Order. I agreed and a couple weeks passed. I heard nothing from her office so I phoned her, asking when we were going to submit our appeal application. Michelle told me I had lots of time because she had not yet even seen an Order.

A few days after that conversation, Michelle's assistant called me asking that I stop in over the lunch hour. Michelle needed to discuss something urgent. When I got to her office, a senior partner at that law firm joined us and said there had been a mistake. Michelle had missed the appeal date. The deadline was actually 30 days from when the judge spoke the terms of the Order. Michelle was in tears and I was shell-shocked. She told me I would have to wait until there was "a significant change in circumstances" before I would be allowed to go back to court. I don't even know what that means and I don't think they knew either. A "significant change" was, apparently, not moving homes in the same city, nor changing jobs, but perhaps losing my left arm would count.

That legal firm repaid my legal fees but that only amounted to a couple thousand dollars so far. I basically lost my daughter for a year and a half by that point, and now I had to get a new lawyer and start the whole process over again.

The Order only gave me six days with Laila over the summer and I had a trip planned. I represented myself and went to court which turned out to be a complete waste of time. There was a different judge who agreed with me that six days was insufficient for parenting time. On the other hand, she said there had been no significant change in my circumstances since the Divorce Order several years earlier. Her ruling was to change nothing, so I could not take Laila to my grandmother's 90th birthday party.

My next lawyer was Stephanie Bride-Pouceur. This woman knew her stuff and didn't rip me off. Sadly though, she was still defined by the terrible Family Law system, even though she had a great memory and argued well for me. She worked out of her home so avoided the law firm competition between lawyers to maximize billable hours. We filed for more parenting time and we succeeded. Stephanie argued a change in circumstances by suggesting a custody assessment. Laura took Laila in to see a psychologist, then I took her in to see that same psychologist and I think the whole assessment took 15 hours. It cost a lot of money but it worked.

The custody assessment read that it was in Laila's best interest to have more time with her dad. I got 5 days with her out of every 14 and that's 36% of the time. But if you then add in 50% of two summer holidays and 50% of the Christmas holiday, the math shows I actually got 38.9%. It's rather curious that at just under 40% custody the non-custodial payor's child support decreases by a huge amount. No doubt Laura's lawyers made sure she would retain her maximum.

I have three children and I am single. I pay $2,500 a month after taxes in child support. I have a four-bedroom house so each of my kids has one. I have a friend who lives with me Monday through Thursday which helps a bit. Both my exes now have double-income homes. I also paid Laura spousal support for two years but thankfully that ended.

Joy, my second ex, has two other ex-husbands and two of us pay her child support. She works minimally and says she would prefer not to work at all. At one time, she worked for the same firm as I did. I know that if she went back to a decent job like that one was, she would easily make $60,000 to $70,000 a year but she doesn't want to. Joy has told me that she tried a couple business ideas but "they didn't work out" and claims she now makes $8,000 a year. I have provided, several times, my financial statements upon lawyers' requests but I have never seen any of Joy's financials. I feel like I've been trapped because I have been honest. Since I made a fair salary last year, I am now in trouble because MEP will recalculate my child support based on that unusual year.

I am already in debt to the tune of about $500,000. The court made me pay $50,000 to MEP right away. Who has that kind of cash? And I am accruing arrears when I can't come up with the total amount owing each month. I am so afraid MEP will take my house, car, passport, driver's licence and throw me in jail.

For a while I supported the former Alberta Party and there was a meeting of its members about policy, divorce and child support. I got up and spoke to the audience about my situation and you know what happened? More than a few members laughed at me. They thought it funny that I got divorced and was now complaining that my ex-wives were destroying me.

In 2009 Joy and I went to court for the first time. It was about parenting time and again, the court gave me just under 40%t custody of Ella and Tyson, who were then 5 and 3 years old. At that time, I was doing contract work and was between contracts. I didn't know when the next one would come along. Fortunately, I did find work fairly soon after the Order was made but I was without income for about six weeks between those contracts. MEP didn't care so my debt to them skyrocketed. MEP had averaged my wages at $80,000 a year, but soon Joy was asking for a huge increase in child support. She claimed that I did not pay any child support for five months, even though I had the cancelled cheques in hand. Since the cheques did not show they were for child support, Joy said the money was *for other things I owed her.*

I asked for a meeting with MEP and the result was that I was to pay a smaller amount until my case got into court. Then the new terms would determine how, and how much, I would have to pay right away and going forward. I decided to up my payments by $200 a month to make sure I wasn't going to be penalized.

We went to court and the judge ordered new terms in about 20 seconds. Of course then the lawyers took that judgment and turned it into a 10-page Order, very lucrative in billable hours. The judge excused herself, saying she had an appointment at 4:30 p.m. so the court appearance was very brief. There was no time for the custody issue, the real problem of my not seeing my kids. But the money was dealt with, as it always is. This judge wanted me to pay about $150,000 to MEP. She had not even considered the amount I had already paid. When my lawyer brought up this point, the judge did not understand the relevance of what dads have already paid before they get to court. Hence, my big debt-load and ongoing financial struggle.

In the intervening years since our settlement, Laura has settled down and seems to actually understand the benefit of my being a big part of Laila's life. At first though, when she heard Joy and I had separated, Laura pulled me aside and demanded an increase of $200 a month or she would drag me back into court. I told her this was extremely bad timing and asked if we could discuss it at a later date. My lawyer instructed me to just pay up rather than end up in court, where I would have two simultaneous legal cases. Laura's demand of me was extortion but I cooperated anyway.

Today, Laura is usually quite amiable, as long as I pay for everything to do with Laila's activities. The problem is that sometimes she will change in a heartbeat so I don't know what to expect when we communicate. Laila is doing very well, I am happy to say. My two kids with Joy are not as lucky. She does weird things; for instance, when I send our kids back to her with new clothes, she keeps these clothes and next time I pick up Ella and Tyson, they are back in rags. Joy has two sons from an earlier relationship and the older one is a strange fellow, verging on sociopathic. He likes to bully and my children are uncomfortable when they are all at Joy's home. I worry about them. Joy, too, cooperates with me as long as I pay for all activities for Ella and Tyson. Needless to say, my finances remain very sparse but at least I have my children in my life.

I have submitted an application for equal custody with Joy. She hates me so there is no way we can negotiate outside court. Laura has reason to hate me but Joy was caught having an affair with our neighbour so I'm not sure why she is out to get me. Joy is a risk-taker, can't focus and has trouble keeping commitments, such as a work schedule. I am concerned that my children may get hurt physically due to her bizarre activities. Maybe she has Attention Deficit Hyperactive Disorder (ADHD) but in any case, she has not been diagnosed so her issues are unresolved.

Laura and Joy are both decent mothers but their desires outweigh those of my children. Laura is an overly-protective mother, enmeshed with our daughter to the point that Laila gets whatever she wants. Joy is neglectful and sees our kids as a way to make money, lots of money. I don't think either mother has my kids' best interest above her own.

I have spent way too much time, heartache and money in trying to smooth my relationships with my two exes, for the sake of my kids. They are doing okay, despite the turmoil that has become normalized in their lives. If I am successful in getting 50/50 custody of Ella and Tyson, we will be more of a family and Laila will be in their lives more. I will keep being the best dad I can be and hope that someday dads will mean something to society beyond a source of money.

JIMMY

CHAPTER 8

JIMMY

I have a son named Kellan who turned 8 recently. After his mom and I separated in 2004, we had joint (i.e., shared) custody. Kellan's mom has always been kind of unstable. We split up only two months after our son was born.

Jerilyn and I met in a bar. She told me she had three foster children so I figured she must be a good and responsible person. The next weekend we met again and ended up at her place. In hindsight, I thought it strange that her foster kids were home when I was there. She told me she had been divorced only three months earlier. She also said she had a miscarriage a week before she met me.

Things got weirder as I found out more about Jerilyn. She often bragged that she could stay in bed all day if she wanted and she would still get $4,000 a month from the government. Often, she went out to bars and left her own kids for the foster children to babysit. She told me she had five children, each with a different man. She had had a bad childhood, full of abuse and her mother was a prostitute. She got pregnant the first time we had sex. I thought we should try to make our relationship work since we were going to have a baby.

A week after Kellan was born, Jerilyn wanted us to escape to Jasper for a few days and leave the kids behind, even our new baby. *Who does that*? She went back to the bar scene right away.

She asked me if we could have another baby. I couldn't take her bizarre behaviour. We broke up soon after and immediately after I left her, Jerilyn had Kellan at the doctor saying he was lactose intolerant. As a result, Kellan was raised on only baby formula for the first two years. She never breast-fed or tried to.

From the start, in 2004, Jerilyn made it difficult for me to have time with Kellan. That first Christmas, when Kellan was only a few months old, I called Jerilyn every day asking if we could set up a schedule but she would not agree. When I did see him, we had fun but those times were difficult to arrange. Sometimes I would work out a plan with Jerilyn but then I'd go to pick up my son and there would be a sign on her door that she was away. Often, she would not answer her phone. She wanted more and more money from me but it was getting increasingly difficult for me to see Kellan. On the other hand, when she wanted a babysitter she made sure to get hold of me and I always was happy to oblige. Finally, I'd had enough so I hired a lawyer, Lauren Branger and asked her to get a parenting plan in place.

Jerilyn took Kellan to the doctor so many times. When he was a toddler, she took him to request that he be circumcised because she didn't want to clean his penis. She told the doctor she had been sexually abused when she was a teenager so she just couldn't do that job.

The most important part of my situation is that Kellan is a healthy little boy. When he's with me, everything is great and we do a lot of outdoor things together. But when he goes to his mother's, Jerilyn reports that Kellan has every illness under the sun. Even when he was on baby formula, I knew he could tolerate regular milk because he had that *and* normal baby food at my place and did very well on those foods. He was tested by a Dr. Robe and found not to be lactose intolerant. Nevertheless, Jerilyn went to court and got a judge to declare me responsible for 83% of Kellan's baby formula. As a result, for the next 21 months, I had to pay her a lot of money so she could feed our baby an unnecessary and unnatural food.

After 21 months, Jerilyn was still feeding Kellan only baby formula. I made us a mediation appointment to deal with the feeding issue but of course, Jerilyn failed to attend. She instead put the phone beside Kellan and let him cry for 55 minutes while the mediator and I listened. Her story was that Kellan was crying because he was a very sick baby. I got a court hearing in which the judge ordered a mini-assessment through Social Services on Kellan. The assessor chosen was a 21-year-old social worker who was clearly inexperienced. She told me I should give up all access to my son, which at that time was only one day a week. I had not seen this "assessment report" but Jerilyn and the court had.

My lawyer then was Chris Johannson who phoned to tell me that my access was still one day a week but there would be no sleep-overs anymore. I fired him. The next day he appeared at my door demanding $700 to close my file and give me the report. I paid him and got the 32 page "assessment". It was all bullshit, including how I supposedly had no car seat for Kellan, beat my kids, was having a sexual relationship with my 15 year old daughter and so on. There was no evidence, just hearsay from mom (Jerilyn). The report also stated how Jerilyn spent much time away from home at the bars and frequently had different men sleeping at her house, where the children were! The court allowed this, so no action was taken to support my kids.

At this time, I was making $40,000 a year. I lived in a little basement suite, paid $400 a month for child support, $400 more for baby formula, and $300 for babysitting. I obviously fell behind in my payments as I could not afford them. I called Maintenance Enforcement (MEP) and asked, to no avail, for a break. Since Jerilyn was registered with that corrupt organization, MEP decided to garnish my wages. When I saw my next paycheque, MEP took it all except $250. That happened again, and I was in big trouble with arrears continuing to accrue.

Then I hired Grant Breen, a lawyer in Edmonton, who was a really good guy. He was also a professor and was very concerned about Kellan and the discrimination against dads rampant in family courts. He would do up my affidavits at night with me at his house, sometimes until almost midnight. I was only charged $100 an hour and he worked so hard for me. He went to court for me a year later stating that the allegations made in the so-called "assessment report" were unsubstantiated. Grant got the "Zebra Patrol" (now called Zebra Child Protection Service) in Edmonton involved and it questioned my 15-year-old son to see if any of the allegations against me were true. That son was 11 when his mom and I separated and we have had an amicable parenting plan working ever since. There was no legal involvement in that relationship, thank God.

In the meantime, I would drive out to Fort Saskatchewan, 52 kilometres away, to see my little son and would stay there all day, since it was too far to drive back and forth. Kellan was about nine months old. When I would arrive to get Kellan, he would still be sleeping, in wet diapers, so I would get him up and take him outside; often we went swimming when it was nice enough. Sometimes at the last minute, Jerilyn would change the location where I was supposed to pick up Kellan. On several occasions, when I took Kellan back to his mother's, only the foster children were there, not Jerilyn. Both those kids had been sexually abused earlier in life, yet Jerilyn found it appropriate to go out to the bar and leave my toddler alone with them.

The Zebra Patrol determined that the allegations against me were false. We went back to court and this time, Jerilyn denied ever having accused me at all. Before our court appearance, however, Jerilyn called the police and accused me of stalking and harassing her. Interesting since that whole year, she had been attending family outings with my family, we were in counseling, yet I was stalking her? I think she knew I would get back more access and sleep-overs with Kellan, so she was trying to make sure that didn't happen. Grant was doing a good job; he actually cared and knew what he was doing.

I had to serve Jerilyn the court documents at a bar, since I couldn't find her at home for several days. Grant knew it was imperative that I get the necessary documents into her hands as per the timelines of the court. Four days later, I was taking Kellan back to Jerilyn's and as I drove up, I saw a police car in the driveway. The officers told me I was being charged with stalking and harassing my ex. Although I let them know we were about to go to trial, they arrested me anyway and took me to their detachment.

Grant advised me to get a criminal lawyer in Fort Saskatchewan, which I did. She threw me under the bus at the trial, making me agree to a peace bond that said Jerilyn was afraid of me. If I didn't agree, this lawyer said she would quit my case. She reasoned that with the peace bond, both Jerilyn and I would be equally culpable if we breached its terms. That bond stated that I could not pick up Kellan at his mother's home, or even in her town! So from that point, my sister began to pick up Kellan two hours away from our city, I would wait at a nearby gas station, and then my sister would transfer Kellan to me for the day. It was insane! For a year we had to juggle Kellan that way, and often Jerilyn would not release him to my sister. The police would have to be called.

After that year we got into court and Grant represented me. He tried to get all 300 pages of Jerilyn's Family Services records but of course Jerilyn lied and said they didn't exist. I knew about her huge file because I had seen it, and it was also in the social worker's report. At least we got about 100 pages of it. Some of its content showed that Jerilyn slapped her children and gave one a bleeding nose. Kellan was four years old by then, living in absolute chaos with a mentally-ill mother. Grant did a great job so I was sure the court would see the pattern of inconsistencies and lies that were continuous in Jerilyn's testimony. But even then, the judge gave Jerilyn sole custody of Kellan and all decision-making authority. What did work for me was that I would get Kellan every weekend and holiday.

Jerilyn had shown up at the trial with who she said was her fiancé. That meant, according to the judge, they were now a stable family. They had gotten engaged just before the trial and she said they were going to buy a house together. At least I got a driving allowance and the judge discontinued my Section 7 responsibilities. That meant I no longer had to pay for things like baby formula.

That first year after the trial, I had Kellan a total of 135 sleepovers so that was great. Basically, I lost all rights to my son but then I had more time with him. Bizarre, right? I had him 38% of the time, not quite 40, so Mom still cleaned up on her child support payments from me. Jerilyn got married a few months later in August. She just emailed me that I needed to keep Kellan with me as she was going to a family wedding and if I couldn't swing it, I would have to pay for a babysitter. She didn't even take Kellan to her own wedding! And by the next January, she and her new husband got divorced.

Jerilyn got Kellan assessed and he was diagnosed with speech problems so he was enrolled in a special preschool. Only a couple months after he started there, however, she decided not to take him anymore. She told me the teachers there had noticed him behaving inappropriately, kissing Barbies for instance. On the 20th of May, 2008, which was Kellan's birthday weekend, I got an email from Jerilyn's lawyer. It read that I was not allowed to see Kellan and I was being charged with sexual abuse. Since he was behaving inappropriately, I must be abusing him at home. *This was their logic*!

That birthday weekend, Jerilyn instead took Kellan somewhere in the mountains with her new boyfriend. My lawyer at the time, Jordan Kroeger, was really good and got me before a judge in three days following the charges against me. Judge Grassly got it… truly. He said there would be no denial of access and he wanted an investigation into my case. The Zebra Patrol did another interview with Kellan and decided the allegations were false. Jerilyn was penalized, sort of; she had to behave or else she would be in legal trouble. The judge did say that even though she had made false allegations against me, Jerilyn was likely a caring mother nonetheless. I couldn't believe the bias against me. Would a caring mother make false allegations of sexual abuse against their child's other parent?

Following preschool and that court decision, things did not get better for Kellan. His mother put him in kindergarten five blocks away from her house but after December, he didn't attend any longer. That year was a bust, so he started Grade One in 2010 without any good foundation for education. Transferring Kellan between parents only happened in the police station parking lot as per the Court Order by Judge Grassly.

In first grade alone, Kellan missed 130 half-days of school! I kept calling the school to find out what was going on. None of the staff seemed to know. He was usually only with me during weekends at that time, so I couldn't do much to change this pattern. I had a Court Order from 2007 stating that Jerilyn was not obligated to tell me about Kellan's school performance. I *was* allowed, however, to contact the school myself. I was also allowed to talk to any of my son's healthcare providers. I always got information that way. By calling doctors and teachers, that's the only way I could get any information about what was going on with my son.

Even with a Court Order giving me access to information about my son, Kellan's school principal denied my volunteering there. I wrote a letter of complaint and the Board Superintendent reversed that decision. Still, I continued to be denied as a volunteer for a "multitude of reasons". I am sure the staff got an earful from Jerilyn about what a bad person I was and am.

I was even blocked from phone access to Kellan for a while. I would call Jerilyn's house and whomever answered the phone would tell me Kellan was unavailable, in the bath, doing homework, playing a video game, at the park, and so on. The agreement between us was that I could phone every Tuesday at 6:00 p.m. but that was denied to me. I would rush home from work to talk to Kellan, but either Jerilyn's cellphone would go dead within a couple minutes, or she would email me to say Kellan didn't feel like talking to me. I had to go to court just to get that phone access back. The judge reprimanded Jerilyn, but made no effort to resolve the impasse in communication.

I began to make court applications to get custody of my son when Kellan told me his mom thought he was always sick and shouldn't go to school. If you are a mother in Alberta, no one cares if you keep your kid out of school but can you imagine if a dad tried that? The mother has full control; they don't even bother talking with dads. Finally, one school principal said he was concerned about the ongoing absences and repeatedly phoned Jerilyn. The school was five blocks away from her house and she didn't even have a job. She is a foster mother. Jerilyn invented an illness that prevented Kellan from showing up for school; she said he needed his tonsils out. Kellan had never even had tonsillitis. I found that out when I came across a prescription for him and contacted the doctor's office. Jerilyn had not told me about this apparent tonsil problem.

The doctor agreed to meet with me where I told her that Kellan slept well, didn't snore, and seemed happy when he was with me. Jerilyn had reported him as having sleeping issues and needing medication for that too. She told more than one doctor that Kellan had a sleeping disorder and inflamed tonsils. She reported that he slept better at her house than mine. Her house was safer but mine wasn't, according to Jerilyn. This doctor gave me the contact information of the ear-nose-throat specialist that Jerilyn had taken Kellan to. She suggested I tell him what I had told her.

I live in Edmonton but the specialist worked in a different town. This was nothing new. One year, in 2005, Jerilyn took Kellan to *32 different doctors*! My son's mother was trying to make him sick. She gave him melatonin every night. I asked her not to, but she continued.

I did see the specialist who told me he had booked Kellan for a tonsillectomy. He didn't do any testing before diagnosing, just relied on Jerilyn's claims and the dark circles under Kellan's eyes. Well, Kellan has always had those dark patches, still does, but in the summer if he's outside a lot, they aren't visible. We go swimming, camping, he sleeps great, so if he had tonsil problems, wouldn't he have some symptoms? Swimming, even underwater, is no problem for Kellan and he loves it...we love it!

I had no say; Jerilyn got an emergency Court Order to have a tonsillectomy done. I was pissed. The judge had me on speakerphone and I asked him how this surgery could possibly be approved. Jerilyn and I were already scheduled for another case management meeting in two weeks. I had a lawyer at that time but there was no chance of consulting with him as it all happened so fast.

That same afternoon, the specialist called me and said he was going to postpone the surgery until he could meet together with Jerilyn and me. I emailed Jerilyn and set up an appointment at a time that worked for both of us. The day of the appointment that specialist would be working in yet another town, two hours away from Edmonton. I didn't care; I wanted to talk with this doctor and Kellan's mom. I had nothing against surgery that was necessary but for the life of me, I saw no hint of Kellan's needing a tonsillectomy.

I took a half-day off work and drove to the specialist's clinic in the town of Barrhead. I brought a voice recorder in case I would need a record of that conversation. After waiting a bit, I was ushered into the specialist's office but Jerilyn was not there. She had agreed to our meeting and been sent a phone reminder from that office. Half an hour before the appointment, though, Jerilyn apparently had called the office saying she was not going to be there because "I am afraid of Jim." The specialist told me he was finished with this case. He cancelled the surgery and wanted nothing more to do with Jerilyn.

After that, I went back to court and told the judge the whole story about the tonsils. The judge said he would make an Order stipulating that surgery could only happen with my consent. That was a huge relief. But mom just continued keeping Kellan away from school claiming he was always sick. She took Kellan to another specialist at the Stollery Children's Hospital without my knowledge. I found out that Jerilyn *and* her boyfriend, whom she claimed was the boy's step-father, had taken Kellan. They would have appeared to be an intact family that way. The following Monday both Jerilyn and I went to an appointment there.

I must have looked clueless when the doctor asked whether I agreed to Kellan's surgery. I had been under the impression that that issue was resolved. At least the doctor acknowledged that Kellan's missing 130 days of school was "due to bad parenting" no matter how bad his tonsils might be. The Stollery has an excellent reputation as a children's hospital so I agreed to have the surgery done. When I went in his room after he came out of anaesthetic, Kellan was in the company of his 14-year-old half-sister; Jerilyn had gone home. I would have thought a mom would want to spend the night with her little boy following surgery.

The next weekend Kellan was doing well but his throat was still sore. Once he was back with his mother though, Jerilyn took him to a walk-in clinic, not even to the doctor who performed the surgery. She convinced that doctor that Kellan had an infection, so he wrote Kellan an antibiotic prescription for four days. I called the surgeon's office for confirmation, but the surgeon said Kellan was fine and did not need medication.

I tried to hire another lawyer in August as my trial date was set for one day, December 12th. I had been representing myself, but ran into a young lawyer, Daniel Maul, in the courthouse who said he sympathised with dads because "they always get shafted". Soon after, I paid him a retainer of $1,500 to be my representative. After that, I heard nothing from his office until mid-November when I phoned to find out what was going on. Then I got an email from Daniel saying that he couldn't make the trial!

He said he would write the judge and cancel the date. But what about my trial? I had been waiting so long and now there was no plan at all. I went to Mr. Maul's office and asked what would happen now and he told me the judge was "out of town". It was now mid-January. So, I began writing the judge and all of a sudden, I was told that that my son needed his own lawyer. Off I went to Legal Aid to find one.

Kellan's appointed lawyer, as of July 2011, was Geoffrey Kelly. He turned out to be the worst of the worst. He didn't care about Kellan; he didn't do his homework re our case; and he was preoccupied with his own chronic illness. Why was he practicing then?

Geoff Kelly wanted to talk with the judge about our case. My lawyer, Daniel, who was still supposedly representing me, didn't want to do so and didn't want to go to court. We finally got to court after a very long time and Jerilyn, after months of requests from us to her lawyer, finally signed a Consent Order for Kellan to have a counselor. I guess it made her look good to sign at court, as if she is a cooperative person.

Mr. Kelly decided Kellan needed a psychiatrist. Nobody was looking at Kellan's mother, nobody. Kelly made an appointment for Kellan to see Mason Whyte, a counselor in Edmonton. As I found out later, Kelly always used Whyte for his clients. Whyte had a bad reputation as an incompetent, uncaring therapist. I'd heard that from two other alienated dads whose kids were sent to Whyte, and it was a disaster. In fact, there were sanctions against Whyte at the same time as a result of a complaint made by a Calgary father over Whyte's so-called "report" of that dad's daughters (*Author's note: Grant lodged that complaint about Whyte).* I called Whyte and asked for his plan for Kellan. He told me he planned to meet with Jerilyn again the next Friday and then he would write a report. I don't know how he thought he was informed enough to write anything about Kellan's welfare.

We also had another therapist, Brian Hindman, who cost $8,000 to tell me I should "just get over it". He was no help whatsoever and I don't think he read any of the background documentation I provided him with. On the ECMAS (Equitable Child Maintenance and Access Society) website, other parents had posted their disappointment in Hindman too, so I knew mine was not an isolated case.

You know, I obtained nine Court Orders in all and Jerilyn ignored every one. She never did disclose her financials either, despite a court directive to do so. Meanwhile, I had always disclosed my financials and the court was requiring my girlfriend also do the same. But not Kellan's mother. How does that work?!

Daniel asked for $7,000 more to do the work he should have done a year before. I paid him as I was desperate to get help for Kellan. All of a sudden, we had a court date, just a couple months ago in fact. The day before court, I got a call from Daniel at 3:30 p.m. saying that again, he wouldn't be able to attend. It was I who had to call the court clerk to let her know Daniel would not be in court the next day. I actually had to borrow a phone from one of my company's customers because I didn't have a cell and was on the road as a courier.

Both Jerilyn and I were then self-represented in court. I didn't get her affidavit because she sent it to me on a USB stick, not in paper form. When I tried to open it, all 20 pages were blank. When we went to court, Justice Grassly asked again for Jerilyn's financials which she said she didn't have. She claimed that she did her taxes online and couldn't print out a copy. She also got off without penalty for sending me a blank affidavit on a USB stick. Justice Grassly asked me, "Well, what do you want me to do about this? Your ex says she lost the documents". He is the judge! He had been our case manager for almost five years, since 2008, but he didn't know what to do. Unbelievable!

Justice Grassly's assistant often gave Jerilyn advice, but the agreement was that any legal correspondence was to go to both parents, her and me. I was kept in the dark most of the time, however. When Jerilyn got that Emergency Protection Order against me, Justice Grassly wasn't even in the country. Instead, his court clerk told her how to get the Order, and no one informed me until I was in court. No one holds case managers accountable and the Judicial Council of Canada says that judges have the autonomy to make whatever decisions they feel are the best ones. So there is no one higher up to complain to when your judge isn't making good, or even informed, decisions about your family.

My second-last lawyer told me she had never, in 17 years of practicing law, been unable to get hold of a judge when necessary. But Grassly didn't respond to her letters or phone calls. This lawyer told me I had three options, but the best one was to let Jerilyn have custody and forget about it. Another of my lawyers, Mr. Smith, took my money, I gave him my file, and then I heard nothing from him. As the court date approached, I was frantic and left him a voicemail asking whether he intended to represent me in court. I had called him eight times before, to no avail. It turned out that Smith also used Hindman, so he certainly did not want to be adversarial in court against Hindman's position.

I have been seeing a counselor myself, since 2007. His advice to me is always the same: "You see Kellan three weekends a month, so why are you stressing over him?" What I tell all these professionals who advise me to give up on my child is that Kellan is not safe with his mother.

Since 2004, I have been in the court system trying to get supports and appropriate interventions in place for my son. In these eight years, I have spent over $100,000. I have had six judges and got nine court orders. I have had 10 lawyers represent me, and I can tell you that none of them gave a shit. Grant Breen tried, but didn't get far in our disgusting family law system. Lawyers are predators; they are making huge money at the expense of vulnerable parents.

Every day I am afraid to read my mail and email. I can't live a normal life or have a normal relationship. My girlfriend is so patient, but this nonstop stress is so difficult. I can't walk away from my child, because he needs me. Even if I did, then I would be labelled a deadbeat and I'm sure MEP would come after me in a heartbeat. Recently, I received a $2,600 bill from Jerilyn for babysitting! I'm paying for Kellan to be babysat by 11-year-olds when Jerilyn is at the bar instead of parenting our child.

Kellan asked that I not question him because he doesn't want his mom to know we talk about stuff. One night one of Jerilyn's daughters dropped a candle and set the bathroom on fire. Even then, Jerilyn didn't go home to her kids. Instead, her latest boyfriend showed up and took the kids to his house. My son knows who his capable parent is; he just can't say it for fear of betraying his mother.

2017

I have sole custody of Kellan and he is doing very well. Since you interviewed me in 2012, Kellan's mother has continued her quest to make my life as miserable as possible, at Kellan's expense.

On May 27th of 2016, Geoff Kelly, still involved with our case since 2011, sent Justice Grassly, Jerilyn, and me a confirmation letter for an upcoming Case Management meeting that was held

June 10th of last year. Both of us were then self-represented. Jerilyn had requested the meeting be adjourned "yet again" but Kelly went ahead filing his letter in case Justice Grassly refused the adjournment. In that letter Mr. Kelly stated that Kellan had "grown weary" of the whole court matter and wished it resolved. Well, no kidding! I wanted it resolved for good years ago. Kelly enclosed his report on Kellan's state of mind and asked that we refrain from showing its contents to Kellan.

Then on June 6th, Jerilyn wrote Justice Grassly, "withdrawing my Application for the week/week parenting schedule as that is not Kellan's desire." She said she had been approved for Legal Aid and was waiting to be assigned a lawyer. In response, a court clerk informed us that Justice Grassly had refused Jerilyn's adjournment request, so the meeting was going ahead June 10th. That was a huge relief to me.

The outcome of that meeting is as follows: time with each parent was assigned, and Jerilyn asked for late-June through mid-July.

Then, on January 2nd of this year, I filed my affidavit, Grant Breen again helping me write it. I painstakingly laid out Kellan's health and education status and explained in detail how he had improved since I became his primary parent in September of 2012. Kellan has been an honours student the last four consecutive years, is no longer depressed, and has many good friends. He talks about going to the University of Alberta to study Political Science. He has missed only seven days of school since 2012 and his Grade 7 marks show high A grades in all core subjects. The only issue with school is that when he stays at Jerilyn's home some weekends, his homework is neglected and unfinished by the time he comes back to me. Kellan's mother failed to attend his sixth-grade graduation and continues to be frequently absent when Kellan stays at her home.

Kellan is requesting that he be allowed to stay with me when his mother is working out of town. He does not wish to be cared for by a stranger, nor does he want to go with Jerilyn to her work "events" which start in the evenings and end in the early hours of the next morning. He finds the music too loud, there is drinking by the patrons, and he is left unattended there for hours.

I was able to have Mr. Kelly removed as Kellan's lawyer and since then, there has been a happy, open line of communication between my son and me.

Jerilyn was absent the entire three weeks of parenting time she had asked for at the case management meeting June 10th of 2016. Kellan told me he was not allowed to go outside at all and just played video games the whole time he was at his mom's house. Since Kellan was left on his own during that time, it became apparent to Justice Grassly, finally, that Jerilyn is an unfit parent. Justice Grassly even said "Maybe I made a mistake. We all make mistakes" in reference to his earlier decisions regarding Kellan's custody with Jerilyn.

In fact, Kellan saw his mother once on September 2nd; that's it. She did, however, collect a travel allowance from me which was supposed to help her commute back and forth between our homes to see Kellan. Our workplace buildings are adjacent to each other so basically, Jerilyn got a travel allowance to go back and forth for work.

There have been 18 case management meetings since Justice Grassly became our case manager in May, 2008. Twice Jerilyn charged me with allegations of sexual misconduct, both of which were subsequently dismissed. In January of 2009, she was found in contempt of court. There have been 13 court orders for Jerilyn's financial disclosure and all 13 have been breached. Back in 2011, Jerilyn claimed that her annual income was $14,723 but her tax statement showed $24,753. And this amount did not include her other sources of income.

I obtained primary custody of Keegan in September 2012, but an initial child support order was not granted until five months later, and it was not made retroactive. It took over four years to get an Order dealing with child support for September 2012 to February 2013. That February, Kellan's child support was based on Jerilyn's approximated income of $20,000 though this amount has never been substantiated and is likely much higher. She was not required to pay retroactive child support at any time. She lied about who was living with her and did not include the foster children under her roof, who, according to her, were not "official" but instead "private arrangements". In 2015, Jerilyn finally supplied her tax return which was significantly higher than what she had claimed, and she had been earning that higher amount since at least 2013. Justice Grassly has admitted that in his opinion, Jerilyn is also chronically underemployed – her lifestyle choice. He said that he was "highly suspicious" that Jerilyn could live on the amount of income she was declaring. He believed she had other sources of undeclared income.

I need adequate child support from Kellan's mother, but Jerilyn's underpayments to me have not been rectified. The Court Order from 2016 states that MEP may not penalize Jerilyn by seizing her driver's licence. This runs contrary to MEP's enforcement policies. Can you imagine a father being similarly given a break by MEP? No way! It would never happen. Grassly knew that Jerilyn's declared income for 2015 was over $53,000, but in 2016, he nevertheless based her child support on her previous approximated income of $20,000.

She has a business licence obtained in November 2016 for a dance school among other undeclared income sources. In May of this year, the special needs child living with Jerilyn stole a car. Consequently, she was given a Probation Order which states in part, "Remain in your home for 24 hours each day unless accompanied by a responsible adult designated by your Support Worker Jerilyn". Jerilyn is clearly earning income as a support worker as well.

On April 18th, we went back to court. Justice Grassly directed a new Order with the following provisions, based on his stated recognition that Jerilyn had not complied with his 2016 Order and deliberately misled the court. Her child support was raised, but only to an annual income level of $40,000, much less than Jerilyn was actually earning. There was no retroactive payment owing. She continued to get a travel allowance, which she could deduct from the monthly child support payment to MEP. There would be no provision for counseling, since Kellan appeared to be doing well without it.

On May 25th, 2017, Justice Grassly supposedly sent Jerilyn and me a letter. There was no attachment on the email, so I contacted his court clerk. Her response was that their "email system has been plagued with problems this week" and she re-sent it with the letter attached. Grassly's letter stated first that he suggested Kellan have more counseling for a resultant Voice of the Child Report. Grassly had changed his mind from one month before! Kellan has already endured three separate Voice of the Child assessments of his mental health.

It has now been 13 years since we became involved with the family law system. I am happy that Kellan is doing so well, despite the volatile and unstable childhood he was burdened with. I can only hope that his mother will stop her lifelong vendetta against me to give us all some peace. Kellan deserves a good life and I will continue to be the best dad for him that I can.

DAVE

CHAPTER 9

DAVE

My daughter, Sally, and I have always been close. She is an amazing kid and she's 12 now. She is close to my whole family and I have six siblings. What's happened between us since my divorce from her mother is tragic.

Recently, I was told by the court to refrain from posting anything about/to Sally or my ex on Facebook. My ex, Marnie, got that Court Order. So now I have to write in the third person if I write anything at all. For example, I write things like "I know a person in Victoria who has a daughter he doesn't get to see and it is shameful" but it is all factual. Even then I've had police call me a couple times to warn me not to post that kind of thing. I just tell them that I'm not naming anyone, so am not doing anything wrong. Then they leave me alone for a while.

I've spoken with my MLA (Member of the Legislative Assembly) at least a half-dozen times in the last few years but that effort has gone nowhere. I asked her about the *For the Sake of the Children* report. She was aware of it but did not question why its recommendations were summarily ignored. I asked her what she was doing in our province of BC to help fathers and kids stay connected; she didn't answer.

Anyway, to go back many years to the root of the problem, my wife and I cohabited for seven years and then got married two years before Sally was born. It was Marnie's 3rd marriage. We had an okay relationship, but had lots of trouble trying to get pregnant. My wife lost three pregnancies and that was really hard on her... on us. Then Sally came along two months early, weighing in at only two pounds thirteen ounces. She was healthy though, and came home after only a month in hospital. Sally was, and is, my pride and joy; a beautiful child. Her mother and I split up when she was four years old.

Here's what happened: We moved to Whistler because I got a very good job there. Marnie, my wife then, wanted to open her own business so we signed a lease and got a business plan together. We got settled in our new community and were there about a year when all hell broke loose. Marnie had been going back to Victoria every few weeks to visit her mom who was ill. She told me she needed to sell her mom's condo and move her to a smaller place. As I found out later, though, Marnie had been having an affair with the realtor for about three months. There had been affairs twice before in our relationship; boy, was I stupid to trust her again.

One morning we took Sally to her daycare and then spent a nice morning together before work. But late that same afternoon, Marnie picked up Sally, went to Victoria and never came back. She and Sally were gone for a week before I got a phone call from her. During that week, I was frantic. I called her cell phone, but it was turned off. I called her friends, but nobody answered my calls or phoned me back.

After that week, Marnie called me at my desk on a Monday morning to say that she was never coming back to Whistler and was done with our marriage. I immediately flew to Victoria, but it took me a couple days to find her and see my daughter. We got a divorce a couple months later; she got the paperwork done quickly. I was okay with that since she had made it clear she was now with the realtor guy.

I got a lawyer, a good one so I thought, because I wanted to make sure I got 50/50 custody of Sally. I had no idea how the family justice system worked as far as custody and access were concerned. My lawyer was Christa Buchanan. She was my lawyer for the next three years... then I fired her. All she did was cause me a lot of pain, emotionally and financially, and I am still paying off my debt to her company. I lost everything and it was humiliating. I had to move back in with my parents; can you believe it?

After Marnie told me she wanted a divorce, I went home to Whistler and started sorting our things. Amongst her papers, I found a receipt for the anti-pregnancy drug, Plan B. This was particularly strange since after Sally was born, I had had a vasectomy. We had decided not to have more children, as we didn't want Marnie to be put through all that again. She had already been through four pregnancies by the time we had our daughter. The date on the prescription was two weeks before Marnie left with Sally.

Marnie had it all planned. When she took off to Victoria with our 4-year-old, she drained our bank accounts, took the car, and froze everything else. It was a complete shock to me. We had just finished getting the name approved for her new business and had been working for five or so months to get it off the ground.

I started to do some research, thinking there must be a reason for her strange behaviour. I know there are two sides to every story, but Marnie was doing really weird stuff. I wondered whether she was bipolar because she couldn't stick to one thing at a time, kept moving job to job, residence to residence, even man to man. I was her third husband and she has recently become engaged *again*. She showed her latest engagement ring to my mom, whom she has continued to try to manipulate into her vortex. The pattern of her behaviour seems to be quite predictable.

When Marnie has no man in her life, she reverts to being nice and cooperative with me. So when she broke up with realtor Bob, she invited me over for dinner. I was happy to go as I just wanted things to be smooth for Sally. It was an uncomfortable evening as Marnie was clearly coming on to me. Our relationship was over, and I just wanted to be a good dad. Marnie called me "honey" that night as she used to when we were married.

Shortly after then, I found out Marnie had a new man, Geoff, and the parenting door was again shut on me. Marnie didn't want me going to Sally's school, made it difficult for me to see her, and basically tried to remove me altogether from Sally's life. I was always very involved with my daughter's School Council and as a regular volunteer. But once Geoff was in the picture, Marnie told the principal she was afraid of me and I should not be allowed on the school grounds. I heard from the school staff that Marnie told them I have a history of abuse. In truth, I had a strict upbringing that taught me to respect others, especially the women in my life. I have never raised a hand to any woman.

My lawyer, Christa, said the best parenting schedule she could get me was every other weekend and each Wednesday evening. I didn't know what to do, but I didn't appreciate my time with my daughter being called "visitation". In court, Marnie's lawyer succeeded in getting her full, interim custody of Sally with its reward of maximum child support. We have always been equal guardians, but as you know, that is a meaningless term. Marnie was instructed to share Sally's education and health records with me, but she never did. Altogether, Christa got three court orders, none of which Marnie cooperated with, and which cost me over $40,000. The third order was initiated by me so that I could go to Sally's school. Marnie got her lawyer to ask the judge for a "No Contact Order" so that I would now have to pick up Sally at a "neutral" location such as Starbucks or the police station, every interaction involving a third party. There were some nasty emails that transpired between Marnie and me due to my frustration over being unable to spend time with my daughter, prohibited from her school, and prevented from accessing her educational and medical records. I guess that got her the desired No Contact Order.

Marnie has had three lawyers and her most recent one took me aside and said "You are doing a good job and I can see what you are trying to do. It seems like you are a good dad and Marnie needs to get over her anger". I have never heard a lawyer talk like that, when supposedly representing the other side, but in any case, Marnie's lawyer then sent me a letter stating that she was no longer representing Marnie. I have been self-representing for the past couple of years.

After firing Christa, I only used lawyers to get advice from time to time. One told me that I was doing all the right things, but would have no success in the legal system because it doesn't act in favour of the alienated parent or the children. Instead, he advised me to try and keep the peace and somehow stay in contact with my child. If your annual income is less than about $35,000, you can access free legal advice at the Family Law Society, but if you make more than that, forget it. And, if that week's assigned advice lawyer is also representing you or your ex, you are out of luck. Sometimes I've needed advice right away, but had to wait until a different lawyer took over.

Marnie made sure to register with FMEP (British Columbia's Family Maintenance Enforcement Program) and asked the court for Spousal, as well as Child, Support. Fortunately, she didn't succeed with spousal since there was no reason at all why she couldn't get a job. The Family Law Society and FMEP don't care that your net income is super-low. I pay so I am called the debtor; my ex is the creditor. Twice I have been late with my child support payments because I had to scrape up enough money to send FMEP. The second time I was charged a $400 penalty and that happened again over the eight years I have been paying. If you are late the interest accumulates too. When I was late, my wages were garnished, and my driver's licence and passport were revoked. FMEP does not care why you are late. I am also a part-time ski coach so, to do that work, I need my passport.

Going back in time, Sally was a colicky baby for the first few months of her life. We didn't get much sleep then, but fortunately that stage didn't last long. Once Sally could sleep through the night, my sister came to visit for a bit. One evening, we decided to get a babysitter so the three of us could go out for dinner. We all enjoyed ourselves. After dinner, Marnie insisted my sister and I stay for a while but she wanted to get back to Sally. My sister and I hadn't seen each other for a long time so we stayed an hour or two longer, then walked home. As we came through the front door, Marnie came running toward us, stark naked, and holding the baby. She was screaming and crying, "Where the hell were you? I needed you!" My sister was shocked but I had seen Marnie's bizarre freak-outs three or four times a year. They are scary. This time she had the baby in her arms, so I was really concerned. I grabbed a robe and got it on Marnie. I took Sally from her while my sister calmed her down.

I took Sally to our bedroom and soon my daughter fell asleep on my chest. Sally usually slept in our bed when she was little. A few minutes later, Marnie came into the bedroom, screaming that I was drunk (I wasn't) and would roll onto the baby. Then she started hitting me. I had one arm up to protect Sally and somehow Marnie's shoulder or some other body part hit my elbow. She immediately called the police who came and arrested me. My sister witnessed the whole event. I was put in handcuffs and thrown in jail that night.

I need to pause here and tell you a bit of background about the first time I saw Marnie freak out. She had been estranged (or alienated?) from her dad for many years, but then reunited with him as he was dying of cancer. Marnie is an only child. Her mother had always painted him as a bad man, abusive and such. He seemed, to me, like a really nice, gentle man. When I asked Marnie how she knew all those awful things about her dad, she said her mother had told her. Interestingly, Marnie had also told me how her own first husband was a bad, abusive philanderer. I know that Marnie's first husband remarried later on, had children with his second wife, and they are still married after 25 years. Marnie also told me that she had been raped as a 13-year-old, but the circumstances seemed dubious to me. I have a hard time believing anything she tells me.

The next morning after my arrest, the police told me that whenever they are called to a "domestic situation", they have to arrest the man since he is a lot bigger than the woman is. One officer mentioned how he often gets these calls but is "just doing my job". I was released and walked home, thinking that I would get an apology when I saw Marnie. It didn't happen. In fact, Marnie had her mom come over and both of them now tore a strip off me. I became so wary of my wife, but I still wanted to make the marriage work for our daughter's sake. Sally was about ten months old then.

Marnie's first boyfriend that I know of was the realtor, Bob. He was a bully, an abuser, a real ass. Whenever our paths crossed, he would do his best to harass me. On Sally's sixth birthday, Bob, almost killed me.

I had taken Sally out for a special afternoon and dinner, bought her a new dress, and my mom came along with us. At this point, Marnie and I were trying to make co-parenting work but Bob was still in the picture. I think Bob was angry that Marnie and I were trying to work together. When I took Sally back to her mom's at 8:00 p.m., as Marnie had asked me to, she actually invited me in. We were having a nice conversation about our day and Sally was so happy we were getting along. But then the house-phone rang and Marnie ignored it; then her cell phone rang and she ignored that too… this sequence continued a few more times.

I got worried and suggested to Marnie she answer her phone and I would leave her house. I was pretty sure it was Bob calling her. After a hug and kiss for my daughter, I left and immediately saw a light flash in the driveway. It was Bob in his truck and there was no escape. The narrow driveway had a wall on one side and trees on both. As I walked onto the driveway, Bob hit the gas and drove toward me as if to pin me between Marnie's vehicle and his. Then he backed up and drove forward three more times, scaring the hell out of me. The fourth time I ran between the cars, got away, and called the police. I walked toward my car but as I turned around, I saw Bob coming at me with a two-by-four! I didn't duck in time and got bashed in my temple and fell. My head opened up and I was rushed to hospital to get stitched and checked out. I remember that Bob kept hitting my head into the pavement while the 9-1-1 operator was still on the line. She was saying she could hear me and help was on its way. Three police cars and an ambulance showed up and Bob was arrested and taken away.

The next morning, as I lay in that hospital bed with a stitched head, eyes swollen shut, and a fractured orbital bone, Marnie came to visit me. She sat on my bed and cried while saying over and over how sorry she was. She promised to get rid of Bob forever. It took a while until I was healed enough to see Sally. I didn't want to scare her, as I looked pretty bad. Finally, Marnie and I got together with Sally and told her that problems are not solved with violence and Bob was gone for good.

Well, Bob was gone for *one week.* A few days after I got out of hospital, Marnie suddenly stopped answering my calls, and I knew he was back with her. I think she felt guilty about telling me but nevertheless, they decided to move in together and started looking for a house. About four months later, they found a place, changed the phone number and put their "family greeting" on voicemail. Two days passed and all of a sudden they split up and Marnie took Sally elsewhere. I was so very relieved.

It wasn't long before Marnie had Geoff as the next boyfriend. He lasted about 18 months and we had no run-ins, just kept to ourselves. There was talk of their getting engaged. He had grown-up kids of his own, two grandchildren, and was about ten years older than Marnie. He was not threatening and seemed nice, even gentle. Geoff volunteered as a crossing guard at Sally's school and when I saw him while picking up Sally, he would wave to me. I think he understood children and was just being helpful. He and I eventually became friends and we still are.

One day while he was at the crosswalk, working, he motioned me over and started asking me questions about Sally and Marnie. A week later, he phoned me and said he had been asking around and realized Marnie had told him information that was inconsistent with others' recounts. He let me know he thought I was a good dad and that he had broken up with Marnie. Once he was out of the picture, Marnie invited me over for dinner as I have recalled earlier in my story.

My family really doesn't know what I am going through. Two of my brothers have custody of their kids, so they can't see why I am struggling to see my daughter. My mom is starting to understand, but it took a while. I just saw her the other night and she asked what Sally and I were doing that next Wednesday, as per our supposed parenting schedule. I let her know that actually, I had no idea where Sally was. And mom said "Again? That is happening again?" Sally had also seemingly "disappeared" the month before. That time, Marnie took her out of school for two weeks in the middle of May. Even with her grades dropping markedly, Marnie took her out of school and didn't even tell me. I went to the school one Monday morning to drop off Sally's homework. She had been with me the Wednesday before, and I later found she had forgotten to take her homework back to school. I found it in her bedroom and knew it was due Friday so she had missed that deadline. She had been missing a lot of deadlines by then, and I was worried. Sally was not telling me when she missed assignments; this was very unlike her. I went to the school and it was an excuse to see my daughter. Marnie was making it so difficult to see her by this time. I looked into her classroom, but Sally was not there. My hope was that she was just late arriving, since this tardiness had become commonplace. Sally's report card showed 18 absences and 39 late days so far that year. Anyway, her teacher told me that Sally would be absent all that week and she apologized to me since I clearly did not know.

Marnie had taken, without my knowledge, Sally to the U.S. for the whole week. I was finally able to reach my daughter by phone once she came home and told her I was very worried as I didn't know where she had been. I reminded her that I got her the phone so we could communicate and I did say, point-blank to her, that her mother did not keep me informed. Sally then told me that she doesn't get my messages because her mom ignores, deletes, and turns off calls when she sees they are from my number.

Earlier, I had been banned from Sally's elementary school, due to Marnie's slandering me, and had to go back to court to reinstate that privilege. Now, this middle school seemed to understand my concerns and actually communicated openly with me. It wasn't easy though; Marnie badmouthed me to that school's staff as well, so I had to show court orders to prove I was legally allowed to see my child. Marnie even brought an old, expired court order to show the school, hoping I would be banned from this one too. She committed fraud. Next year, I've heard that the current principal may be going to another school. I am worried I will have to go through the whole process again to maintain my access to the school and my daughter.

One day I was helping Sally's school by cooking hamburgers for its "Cops for Cancer" fundraising event. Marnie showed up to volunteer as well and sure enough, she freaked out when she saw me. The vice-principal came running out with a radio, telling me I had to leave. I did so because I knew what Marnie is capable of. She once, in 2006, charged me with sexually touching my daughter. Marnie is a Child and Youth Counselor so she knows well how to play her twisted game.

When she was little, I used to bathe my daughter and put her to bed. One night she got soap in her privates and it stung so she cried. Marnie used that incident to concoct a story of my being sexually inappropriate to Sally and a month later, the police were at my door wanting to interview me. I was taken down to the station, but not handcuffed, and interviewed by the lead investigator for about 90 minutes. I saw the 30-page-long file on me. That report was blacked out in a ton of places so I don't know what all was said against me. Apparently, weeks earlier, the police interviewed Sally and Marnie for about four hours. I felt sick… so sick. All the investigators and police had already determined no sign of inappropriate behaviour by me at all, yet they still dragged me down to the station and humiliated me.

Just last July, I got a phone call from Marnie's lawyer asking if I would meet with her and Marnie to discuss how to sort out the parenting mess and make life better for Sally. I was happy to do this and felt somewhat optimistic. Marnie's lawyer, Brooke Maclean, agreed with my suggestion that we get a "Views of the Child" report done so that Sally could voice her opinion. Brooke put that agreement in writing, so I *will* make it happen. I have initiated that proceeding. I am going to interview and get contact information for three different counselors who can do a Views of the Child report and then I'll let Marnie choose whomever she prefers for Sally. I'll have to make another court application and pay another $80 to file it but the paperwork is easy and I don't mind if it means we are moving forward.

I also met with BC Families in Transition to get some free advice. Since I am self-representing, I really need help and they have a program for parents who "can't get their shit together" called "Caught in the Middle". Next Wednesday I am going there for an intake meeting to talk about who I am, why my family needs help, and what sort of help. Then they will talk with Marnie separately and then finally, at another appointment, Sally. Sally, at 12, recognizes that her mother is trying to control her every move. But she is afraid to disobey her mom. She has told me that, and it is so hard on her. I want to find the right counselor to talk with Sally, someone who is not damaged and can actually be unbiased and professional.

Earlier, I got sucked in because my head was in the clouds and I didn't know the system. I am an educated, smart person, but I was manipulated, beaten down to the point where I couldn't make decisions. I trusted people to do their jobs and thought I would get quality treatment in an honest system. But I woke up at some point and realized that the Christa Buchanans of the world just work the system to their own advantage.

Nothing is planned for summer because vacation time was excluded from our parenting schedule in 2006. Then Marnie and I went to mediation and it looked like we made a fair, almost 50/50-time, parenting agreement for Sally over school vacations. That cost $6,000, but it never got filed with the Court. I put that mediation agreement in my short, succinct and evidence-based affidavit, but the judge ignored it. The judge took the alienator's affidavit seriously, without any evidence and full of hypocrisy, but the alienated parent was dismissed.

So every time I want to have some vacation time with my daughter, I have to file another application in court, every time. And every time I am successful Marnie walks out of the courtroom, seething. I also make sure to put a police enforcement clause into each application. If Marnie prevents my access to Sally, I use that clause. It doesn't work, though, because the police just want to avoid having to charge a mother.

I have been involved in the family justice system for 8 years now, obtained 10 court orders, had a case management judge, and the situation now is worse than ever. Frequently over the years, Sally asked her mom for more time with me but Marnie would not acquiesce. My little girl did/does not understand why she can't spend time with her dad since we have always been so close. I just tell her I am trying to make things better but it has been so long, I doubt she believes me anymore.

The terrible treatment I have endured by the Family Law System has taken a huge toll on my life. I have tried on my own to figure out my best course of action because lawyers are so expensive and mine was useless. I am upset, depressed and I don't want to keep having to deal with this nightmare. I find myself in the dark with the blinds closed in my house, I don't want to talk to people, and I have no interest in pursuing another love relationship. I know I have to take care of myself so I go to the gym, to work, and I'm not a drinker, thank God. That would be so easy to fall into as an escape but I won't do that.

2017

August 2014 was the last time I saw my daughter until this year. I missed out on four Christmases and birthdays with her. I missed most of her teenage years. Four years is so much time. December 26, 2014 was the last time I spoke with my daughter.

Prior to the 2015 election, I reached out to many MPs (Members of Parliament) in the Vancouver area. I hoped to inform them about parental alienation and the need for change in family laws and the judicial system itself. Most were "keen" to hear me but nothing really happened beyond a meeting or two with each of them.

I was hopeful that 2016 would be a turnaround year. However, I was aware that it was in my best interest not to rely too heavily on *hope*. To do so would bring me down if I expected things to change.

That year, Marnie moved with her boyfriend and Sally to California. Again, I was not told. Following that move, I heard nothing from Sally despite my regular efforts to find and communicate with her. In early 2017, Marnie moved back to British Columbia. On a positive note, since she arrived back in Canada, Sally and I are able to connect again though it has been infrequent and only via Twitter.

Finally, this spring, I got together with Sally in person four times. Each time was wonderful because it seemed like we had never been apart. Sally was affectionate and my heart was bursting. We were the same old goofy dad and daughter, had fun, and the feelings were not lost between us. But if I tried to talk to her about anything deeper, any tough issues, she avoided me and went "underground" for a week or two. I don't blame her; she has been through too much.

Sally just graduated from high school. A few weeks before that happy event, the Parents Advisory Committee at her school hosted a Block Party for the grads and families. The kids looked great all dressed in their gowns and suits. They were all being bussed to a local hotel for a dinner/dance. I did my best to communicate to Sally that I intended to go to the block party. But when I saw her there with Marnie, both looked shocked to see me. I felt crushed and out of place. It is one thing to be rejected by your ex, but this was a terrible thing to be rejected by my own daughter.

At least Sally and I were able to talk a little during that block party. There were, unfortunately, some tears, and she said she was upset because I was there. I think she was really upset that her mom and dad were in the same place at the same time because, as she told me, "my parents hate each other". I reassured her that I don't hate her mother but I didn't agree with her decisions that kept us apart and sad. I told my daughter that I love her, I am here anytime she needs me, and I just want to be her dad. Then I walked home alone.

ED

CHAPTER 10

ED

My two biological boys are Jared, 13, and Carson, 8. Their mom and I married in 1992 and we are both respiratory therapists. We met while we were both working at a hospital in the Maritimes.

In the beginning, we were kindred spirits. Shelby, originally from Alberta, and I hit it off on our first date and all our friends knew we were very close. We were together three years before we married. Our plan was to work in the United States as her step-dad was a doctor there but we couldn't get our Green Cards. Instead, we found work via a head-hunter and moved to Saudi Arabia.

We arrived in Saudi in1992 with jobs waiting for us at an Armed Forces hospital. Although we planned to stay for two years, it became three since we met nice people and loved our jobs there. The reason we came back to Canada was that Shelby was experiencing PTSD (Post-Traumatic Stress Disorder) symptoms related to sexual abuse she suffered in childhood. We spoke to a Canadian physician who felt the resources in Saudi Arabia were insufficient for treatment of PTSD.

I knew Shelby was the victim of sexual abuse at the hands of her stepfather. She had told me that on one of our early dates. Shelby's parents divorced when Shelby was about two and she lost all contact with her biological dad, David. Shelby's mother soon remarried, this time to the abusive stepfather. He was her stepfather from a very young age until Shelby was in her early twenties. Supposedly, her mother didn't know about the abuse but Shelby recalls how her step-father's knees were "squeaky".

Shelby was about 25 and I was 30 years old when we married. I would ask her how she was doing, but we talked very little about her history with her parents. Then in Saudi Arabia, something must have triggered Shelby's traumatic memories. Culturally, women are very repressed in Saudi and no doubt that was a huge contributor. A few years after we arrived there, Shelby started writing stuff and she told me she was having flashbacks to her childhood abuse incidents. We returned to the Maritimes, where my family originated, and stayed there a year while Shelby sought counseling. Fortunately we had good savings from our overseas work and Shelby went to a good counselor, Louise McFarlen, in our little community.

In 1996, we travelled to Vancouver Island, where my uncle owned a tourism business. We both loved it there and being a small town boy, I was thrilled for the chance to experience more of Canada. We stopped for a while in Calgary, but I had a medical scare there. Shelby reconnected with her biological dad, David, in Calgary and found out some pretty upsetting things from him about her mother. David seemed like a great guy and he took us sailing into Sooke Harbour on the Island. That was September and while sailing, we got a call from a healthcare company that offered us both jobs. That's how we came to live here. My asthma cleared up on the Island and I began running and playing hockey. Shelby, too, began playing hockey quite competitively as she had in the Maritimes. We had a good core group of friends, sang in our United Church choir and life was good.

In 1999, we had Jared. I left my job with the small company and returned to acute care in a hospital. That paid much better, but we had agreed to avoid the stress of Intensive Care and Emergency work. I only stayed a couple weeks and then was lucky enough to get into another homecare company. Eventually, Shelby got a job there too. We had been blessed with Jared and waffled about having another child. One day, an elderly patient advised us to have another, saying he had been an only child and always wished for a sibling. That man made us decide to try for another baby, but we had a miscarriage.

Prior to then, we had thought about going overseas again, but decided travelling was too hard. So instead, we brought the world to our home and began boarding international students from time to time. We renovated our single garage into a bachelor suite. Shelby stayed home while I continued at my homecare job. Our basement was rentable, so we got a tenant in October of 2003. And in December of that year, when Jared was four, we were blessed with Carson.

It was only a month or so later when the police showed up at our door, asking for the tenant. Apparently, $5,000 had gone missing from the courier company she worked for. Shelby thought it would be prudent to evict this tenant, but I thought we should keep her on. I had found our tenant a job at a local organization for developmentally-delayed people and she was cycling to that job and becoming part of our family.

I assured Shelby that things would be fine so Tamara Demin stayed living with us. Tamara did tell us that she had sued a former employer, Purolator, for sexual harassment or something like that, and was awarded approximately $8,500. There was, she said, a gag Order on that action, so I didn't find out details. Tamara was a couple years older than Shelby and a couple years younger than I am. When Carson was born, Tamara gave us a bouquet of flowers with a card that read "Welcome to Our Family". I found that a little strange, kind of presumptuous.

Seven weeks after Carson was born, Black Monday I call that day, Shelby dropped my friend and me off for our hockey game, kissed me, and said, "Make sure you phone before you come home". I thought that was really weird; no, cryptic. Usually, Lloyd, my friend, just came to my house for a hot tub after our games, but on this particular night, I decided to go home alone.

I always kept a journal since we got married because I wanted to remember our special events and I had recently added Carson to our joys. Even after our break-up I kept journaling, but unfortunately now, when I read back to that day, it horrifies me. Anyway,

I went home alone and found my wife in bed with our tenant! I didn't say or do anything; I was kind of shell-shocked. I remember thinking that this was a dream. I slept beside Jared that night with my heart in my throat the whole time.

She had to know I had come home. Our 70s-era bungalow creaked and groaned when we walked and the baby was in the other room. The next day, a Saturday, I emerged from Jared's room and right away, Shelby said to me, "You knew what I was, didn't you?" Well, no, I did not know she was a lesbian. Then she made me a nice breakfast and went to work.

The next day, Sunday, when we had a chance to talk and even made love, I let her know that I realized she was dealing with a lot of things; we had just had a second child, for example. I thought she might be dealing with post-partum depression. When Tamara got home from work, I hugged her and thanked her for being there for my wife. I really thought this would be a temporary glitch. At that moment, Tamara took Shelby by the hand and they disappeared into her section of the house, closing the door behind them. I went out and bought some relationship books, still thinking I could fix myself so she would want me.

On Monday, February 23rd, I went to work with an uneasy feeling and when I returned, both Shelby and Tamara were gone. They left with all the baby stuff and both of our children. I was panicking, began driving around looking for them, and was in a state of shock. Jared was then 4 years old and Carson 3 months old.

Eventually Shelby called me and said she was staying with Tamara at a bed and breakfast owned by some good friends of ours. She admitted to having an affair with Tamara and came home just to get some items from our house. From that point, I could only see my children at my lawyer friend and his counselor wife's house. Shelby and Tamara would leave the kids there, and I would drive over to spend a bit of time with Carson and Jared.

As I found out three years later, Shelby had concocted a story for our friends that I had pulled out an axe we kept under our bed and threatened her and Tamara while Shelby was breastfeeding. We did, in fact, have a camping axe under our bed since some drunken idiots were one-night partying out on our front lawn. I thought I'd better have a way to defend my family if needed. There was also a hockey stick under there, but I guess the axe made a better story.

I got some legal advice and my lawyer advised that I stay in the house and not move out, since it was my wife who left me. Soon I received a one-month notice letter from Tamara that she was going to vacate our home. I was so glad, but after that month, instead of returning with our children, both Shelby and Tamara moved back in on April 1st, Shelby's birthday. I moved out and got my own place. I took with me my journals, our wedding videos, family photos, my musical instruments and my personal belongings. I left all the boys' stuff.

For a while I wrote Shelby letters, letting her know I was there for her and wanted us to be an intact family again. Her responses to me were complaints about my personality and that she thought I was a terrible husband. Several months later, she mentioned divorce. I was carrying expenses for two homes; Shelby was still on maternity leave.

I was a bit of a mess by this time. I was seeing a counselor through an Employee Assistance program in order to deal with my stress and depression. I took six weeks off work on stress-leave. When I went back to work our colleagues were asking whether Shelby was a lesbian so yes, it was very difficult. My friends talked to Shelby and convinced her I needed time with the boys and there was no need for supervised "visits". Finally, she relented and Carson could come to my apartment sometimes.

I decided to take the Co-parenting After Divorce program that BC offers. I jumped right into their free services, used their Single Parent Resource Centre, took courses such as How to Talk So Kids Will Listen: How to Listen So Kids Will Talk and what is now called BC Families in Transition. I also enrolled in their Evolutions program in April of that year, 2004, to help me deal with my grief and that was great support once a week.

At that time, I was seeing my kids about twice a week. I contacted a Dr. Sally Wiegand in town to try and find ways I could spend quality time with my boys. I knew these were the formative years for Carson and I wanted to touch him, bathe him, and he needed to be able to touch me. When I told Shelby this was my hope, she said that Dr. Wiegand would never agree once she heard about my sordid past and what I am like. What sordid past and what am I like? I didn't know about her invented narrative about me.

In September, I wrote Shelby telling her that I planned to move into a house, as it would be better for the boys. I needed to get some things for them from our marital home. The email response was actually from her and Tamara's new joint address. Jared had been telling me for a few months that Tamara was their new "stepmom". When I was with my boys and we would pass Tamara on the street, she glared at me. When she moved back into our house, my wife's and my house, she brought a very expensive bike (perhaps bought with the missing money belonging to her employer?) and did not ask permission to enter the premises. She told me then that I would never get my family back.

Jared started school and I wanted so much to go with him. But it was Shelby and Tamara who took him that day. I volunteered as often as I could at the school. By January of 2005, Shelby wanted to go back to her job. While she was absent, I had done both our jobs for a year, was the therapist and the sales guy out drumming up business from doctors. Our company gave me a $6,500 bonus as a result. Then the manager decided they only needed one of us. I was scared that if I got the job, as I have a science degree and more experience, Shelby would freak out and punish me. My boss realized the predicament I was in and gave me some time off work. There had been another of their employees, a fellow whose wife had recently left him, who hanged himself in the backyard. So they did not want a repeat and were keeping an eye on me. I quit the job and went on unemployment insurance for the next year.

Shelby got the job at our former company, but it meant I got time with Carson. I provided daycare, which meant that until 2006 I saw him every day and we started implementing overnights too. We also started to see a child psychologist who helped us formulate a parenting plan. I wanted to proceed with the least resistance possible. But nothing got signed… our parenting agreement was tenuous, but it seemed to be working. I got a fulltime job and we divorced in April of 2006 with joint custody after two years of dealing with lawyers.

The Divorce Order did not specify parenting time, so it was left up to the parents to work out a mutually acceptable schedule. If there was any disagreement we were to contact a counselor to help resolve the terms. For a while this arrangement seemed okay and we could transition the boys between the parents fairly smoothly. Sometimes I would take the kids back to Shelby, and she would chat with me out on the lawn. There was reason to be hopeful.

My house was about a mile up the hill from our matrimonial home where Shelby and Tamara still live. It is always hard to pick up the boys there and see Tamara coming out of our bedroom, which is by the front door. But the arrangement then meant we were all close to the boys' school and our respective workplaces.

Eventually I found a girlfriend, and we bought a house in the town of Langford. She was also divorced and had two boys. I suppose this was, in 2007, my rebound relationship, but we wanted to make it work. I was working at the company I am still with. My girlfriend and I took courses on step-parenting and blended families to try to arm ourselves with skills to manage our family dynamics. We knew the statistics on second marriages and their high failure rates, especially when kids are part of the picture.

In May we invited Shelby, Tamara and the boys, along with some friends, out to our new house for a big birthday party. We were hoping this blended family could work. I was keeping the boys a couple days a week and every other weekend. But Shelby then proposed that I have my boys only every second weekend, citing my 30-minute drive from their school as the reason. Truthfully, the drive was a bit tiresome since some days I was driving in and out of town three times. To solve this problem, I quit my job and found part-time work so I could pick up the kids right at 3:00 p.m. when school ended.

The problem was that my girlfriend's sons were involved in school activities in Langford where we lived and their dad lived in that same town. She and I, amicably but sadly, decided to end our relationship, as I needed to go back to Victoria. I thought Shelby would then leave alone her idea to reduce my parenting time. A year after I left to rent a home in Victoria, my ex-girlfriend and I finally sold the Langford house. But that was during the real estate crash.

My boss, Gerry, an angel of a man who had six kids of his own, appreciated my situation and allowed me flexible hours during my parenting time. The 50/50 parenting agreement was working. I had a babysitter and daycare provider as needed, but this was very expensive. I purchased another house with the idea to be a care-home provider for Community Living Victoria, helping brain-injured people. I could care for a client in my home and had connections through friends to obtain that job. I had experience in a neuro-intensive care unit and a reputation as an upstanding community citizen. I was also a Block Watch captain. I was assessed and approved for that work, which would have allowed me to stay home and look after my boys.

I was still paying lawyers from my divorce and had lost money on the sale of the Langford house. Then funding for the brain-injury rehabilitation program dried up, but I fortunately found other work. In mid-2009 I met Mona, and she has two girls almost the same ages as my boys. That October, I helped Jared's school raise $1,000 by putting together a team to run the Victoria Marathon's kids' run. We had the most participants, so were awarded that big cheque for the school.

On Friday, a week later, I got a phone call from the "Ministry" while out visiting one of my patients. There were allegations of child abuse being levelled against me! I almost passed out. That whole weekend I could not reach anyone to tell me what this was all about. By late Sunday night, I was so devastated that I went to Mona's house. I thought if I stayed alone "I was going to have the big one". Mona was there for me and then my brother flew out from New York, where he teaches, to help too. The next day a senior constable from the local police department called me, saying, "Listen, you have probably been going through hell all weekend. I was off, but am involved with your file and have interviewed both Jared and Carson."

I knew nothing prior to this information from the officer. He told me I had nothing to worry about since my boys love me, but he would have to come over to my place and interview me for the file. Apparently, so he said, the abuse charge stemmed from an alleged incident in which I pushed Jared, he fell in the kitchen and hit his head on the stove. I asked when that even supposedly happened. The officer heard that Carson and Jared were fighting over the TV remote during a televised hockey game. It turned out that Shelby and Tamara had engaged the boys' school and their on-site counselor with this story.

Interestingly, Tamara had, sometime earlier, obtained a job at my kids' school as a playground supervisor. She told her lie at recess to the administration so allegations against me were due to the school's fiduciary responsibility to follow up. Anyway, the charges were cleared but the police officer I dealt with said, "This is off the record, but I want you to know these women (i.e., Shelby and Tamara) are out to get you". Apparently, these women had gone so far as to level a complaint against the police department following their investigation of me. He even added that in his opinion, Tamara was the aggressive one, so I should give her an "especially wide berth". And then I got a call from a retired RCMP officer and now UPS security officer who recommended that Tamara be kept away from my ex-wife and children. If only Shelby and I had conducted reference checks on this woman before she became our tenant.

After that fiasco over several days, our shared parenting continued as if nothing had happened. To the boys, there wasn't even a disruption of our usual schedule. Basically, one day I was an axe-wielding child abuser and the next I was a great dad.

In December of 2009, Shelby again emailed me that she wanted to change the parenting schedule. This time she said that Jared sometimes seemed confused about which of his parents' homes he was to go to on a given day. He was playing the cello, had a newspaper route, and was, according to Shelby, too stressed. So, her solution was to reduce my parenting time to every second weekend, the same plan she had proposed two years back. I didn't address her request until after Christmas because this was the first year since 2004 I would have my children for Christmas.

At New Year's I got an email from Shelby that since I had not responded, she and Tamara were going to implement the "new schedule". They were not going to return the boys as previously discussed and were now going to keep them until the next weekend. I wrote back that I hoped we could discuss this and come to a solution. I had bought Jared a cellphone for Christmas so he could contact us at any time. He was being bullied at school. Shelby suggested I go to his school during lunchtimes since she had done this the year before. She said this would make up for my lost time with the boys since her "new schedule" was implemented.

I went to pick up the boys after school as per usual standard schedule, but this time they were not there. The school staff told me that the boys had been taken out of class "to protect them from your anger". I had to get a lawyer, Gary Cole, involved then. I had been without one, thankfully, since our divorce was finalized in 2006. The lawyer who did up my divorce was Nichola Reed and she got the job done. I wanted to hire her again, but she was unavailable. Now it was 2010 and I had to start paying legal fees again. In an email to me, Tamara wrote that I should accept the new schedule, "as any sensible and caring father would. Your actions are based on your own self-interest".

Tamara's email read that she hoped my boss, Gerry, knew I took my boys with me sometimes to see clients. Well, yes, Gerry did know that and in fact, Shelby also took them to see clients. Their presence was always much appreciated by our clients who are elderly, suffering lung disease, and are lonely. Tamara also wrote that "during other periods of your (my) unemployment, it has been left up to us to provide the major portion of expenses. Jeopardizing your employment is not in the best interests of our children." The email was not copied to Shelby, who seemingly remained out of the loop.

There had been a few earlier incidents involving Tamara's directly intercepting my parenting time. One of these was in January of 2010 when I went to Jared's school to talk to him about finalizing plans for my birthday. I asked him if I could pick him up early, as it was my usual day to retrieve him after school. As we talked, Tamara suddenly showed up with her orange supervisor's vest on. In front of him and some of his friends who had just re-entered after recess, Tamara called me a "woman abuser" and a "child abuser". She said I needed to leave the school and asked me whether Shelby knew I was there. Tamara, Ms. Demin, even admitted to this incident in her affidavit later when we went to court.

Mr. Cole, recommended by Mona's good lawyer, got our former parenting schedule back. The negotiation involved Shelby's and my agreement to have a custody and access assessment done. We agreed to find a qualified professional to do the assessment with a future parenting schedule to be contingent on its outcome. I went out and interviewed a few psychologists and they recommended that I use Margaret Ny, who is a retired lawyer. Supposedly she had done a good job with these kinds of assessments and only cost about $2,000.

In February 2010, Mona's and my kids were all together for a sleepover at my house, and we planned to watch the Olympics. But Jared was watching Star Wars and he would not let us change the channel. So the rest of us went to the bedroom to watch the opening ceremony on the little TV. I told Jared he was being uncooperative and his behaviour was inappropriate, but he pushed me away. I had never seen this attitude shift in Jared before and it worried me. He was almost 11 years old then. On his cellphone Jared, unbeknownst to us, texted Shelby and Tamara.

Mona and her girls left for home a few hours later. Within several minutes, there came a knock on my door. It was Shelby and Tamara. They said that Jared was afraid and wanted to go to their house. I assured them all was fine, but Jared was already dressed and out the door. They then demanded to take Carson as well and did so. They went into his room, woke him up and left. The next day I phoned Shelby and apologized for Jared's being upset, but I explained the situation to her. Shelby said the boys were not comfortable with me and did not feel safe. I called my lawyer, Gary, who did nothing to help.

I let the assessor, Ms. Ny, know what had happened and that we were enrolled in a program in BC called Caught in the Middle. It was an eight-week program and the boys and I attended. They would go into one room, I into another, each with a therapist. Shelby and Tamara did not attend.

By this time, I was often being excluded from doctors' and dentists' appointments for the boys. One time I was with Carson who seemed to have a little hernia or something so he asked me to go with him and his "moms" to see a doctor. We all attended, Tamara too, and it was there that Carson shared with the doctor that his moms were getting married. I hid my surprise and said, "Hey, that's great you two are getting married!" Jared had been ring-bearer for my brother's wedding so I asked Carson what his role would be in this one. That evening the boys and I attended our weekly session of Caught in the Middle.

A few hours later I got an email to my work address from Shelby that read "How dare you call me a "homo" to Carter? She alleged that I had called her a homo or "hobo" or something like that while we were at Caught in the Middle. I wrote her back that I never said anything of the sort and I thought it a good idea for us both to talk to Carter about his choice of words. My response was positive but she just wanted to attack me. She accused me of years of verbal and emotional abuse and said she believed Carson, not me.

I had to report this incident to the school of Carson's misuse of words. I told his teacher what had transpired and the misunderstanding about what I had said of my ex-wife and her fiance. Next thing I knew, I got another email, this time from Tamara, who stated that she had a list of people working at the boys' school who were all aware of the abuse my boys had suffered and were suffering at my hands.

I had spoken to Jared's class about the dangers of bullying, whether from an adult or another child. It was part of an anti-bullying program at the school. Here was Tamara, with no formal education or experience with kids, defaming my character. She wrote me that it is a tell tale sign of fathers who are doing wrong to show up at their kids' school to appear a perfect dad. So, if a dad wants to appear innocent, he should refrain from overcompensating. She said she was "trying to help you because you are making such a fool of yourself". I shared that email with the principal, my lawyer, Gary, and some of my friends. The principal reprimanded Tamara and my friends advised me to sue the school board.

There was no point in pursuing my claim of defamation. I didn't want to rock the boat and I didn't want to pay more legal fees. I just wanted to be a good parent. You know what? Tamara still works at the school as a yard supervisor. Weirdly enough, I felt that Shelby was fortunate to have a partner in her life and I hoped our co-parenting would smooth out after their wedding. It could have worked out okay.

I would have lived on the street if I thought it would make my boys have a good life. Shelby had told me she supports my relationship with my kids, but that's not the experience I have had. Eight years after our split, I need to give up hope that co-parenting can work. That idea was based on who I am and who I thought Shelby was. Maybe Shelby was being bullied by Tamara, who knows? But Shelby, not Tamara, is the mother of our children, and I felt she had to be responsible for her actions and their effect on our boys.

Each July, I used to take my kids to the Maritimes for the lobster festival. That year, 2010, we couldn't go because the psychological assessment was being done. Also, Shelby and Tamara chose their wedding date to coincide with my big homecoming weekend in Pictou, Nova Scotia. I could perhaps have gotten a court order to allow the boys to accompany me home, but it would look bad on me. I'd be seen as the uncooperative father who is also, apparently, a bigot.

Due to that complication, I went to Nova Scotia with Mona and her daughters to meet my family. Our assessment was released in June. Ms. Ny proposed a parenting schedule, but it would move the boys on Saturday evenings at 9:00 p.m. between their parents' homes. Nevertheless, I agreed to it for the sake of resolution and that schedule remained through the summer and up until May of 2011. It was not court-ordered, so I tried to negotiate with Shelby to let the boys have a whole weekend at one parent's house, instead of moving on Saturdays. I wanted to take my kids to church as we used to, and then we could have Sunday dinner together. Shelby refused.

Keep in mind that Shelby and Tamara's strategy was to paint me as an abusive dad with "anger issues". My son has a t-shirt of a band called The Killers which shows a guy with an axe and blood dripping from it. I really wonder who bought him that shirt! I found an online assessment for anger issues and took it. It was a questionnaire called, I think, the "Novaco Anger Management Assessment Tool" with scores attached to one's answers. The outcome was that I scored in the very bottom percentage for *provocation*, so it looked very unlikely that I had trouble dealing with anger.

I also consulted with a Dr. Richard Heiler in Victoria. He and I had a couple of counseling sessions and his synopsis of me was that I have no anger issues. He said the only person angry right then was him because I had been put in that situation of false-allegations. Dr. Heiler advised to fight fire with fire. He wanted to go to the school and confront the principal about why no action against Tamara was taken when allegations of abuse were made. He wanted to investigate Tamara's former employers to find out her history. Dr. Heiler asked how I managed to stay cool when I found my wife in bed with someone else. I asked my lawyer, Gary Cole, about this and he said not to proceed. Since I had a parenting plan in place, he felt any investigation would jeopardize that and we would have to go to court. To deter me, he told me how much money that would cost.

I presented my counseling report to Ms. Ny to analyze for her assessment, but instead she included all kinds of information about how I needed to go for anger management training. I showed the report to Dr. Heiler who said it was one of the shoddiest reports he had ever seen. He couldn't believe I had spent $2,000 on what was supposed to be this official assessment for the court. Then my lawyer, Gary Cole, dumped me as he said he had an important Ministry file that was soon going to court. He gave me a "break" on my outstanding fees and then blew me off.

He referred me to a Rebecca Fallen, a new lawyer who took a look at our thick file, charged me for two hours with her, and said she "can't take this on". Then I found another lawyer who said the same thing, and a third who wouldn't take my case, but referred me to a lawyer from my church. That lawyer said "this case is whacked and you need to get it sorted out". Five lawyers go to my church and all of them, one works with the Attorney General's office, agreed with that comment. All said there is no help in the Family Law system. My church minister, Reverend Frank, endured a similar situation with his divorce. He was a retired lawyer and just said he would "pray for you (me)".

Finally, I found Michelle Guel who was new and really hungry for work. She was my fourth lawyer! She got things done and was cheaper because she was relatively inexperienced. We had a hearing and my affidavits were already done. I was the claimant; Shelby the defendant. I was desperate to get a real parenting schedule in place; this was crazy. Michelle got us in front of a judge but right away he said, "you know, you guys don't want to go to court. I am not going to accept this assessment from this lady (i.e., Ms. Ny) who is not qualified to do one. What is it you are seeking?" If he had read our case, he'd know that I just wanted to be an equal parent with a schedule that stuck and could be enforced. The result was this judge giving the Sundays, on weekends when I had my kids, and I was also allowed to go to Nova Scotia with the boys, as my dad was ill with cancer. The judge said we needed to have a "real" assessment done so that meant more big dollars I didn't have.

We all went for two weeks to the Maritimes; the four kids, Mona and me. That was last year, 2011. We stayed with my brother as approved by the judge. Then, upon returning to Victoria, we were supposed to have this reassessment done followed by a "judicial case conference" with a judge.

At least I had a good lawyer now but of course, that didn't last. Michelle got offered a great job in Vancouver and left me with a referral for her colleague, Dan McLure. I made an appointment with him right away. Mr. McLure was an older fellow and wanted $7,000 up front, $5,000 for the reassessment and $2,000 as a retainer for his services. I couldn't swing it, so we went elsewhere.

Diane Davis was a lawyer Mona was familiar with so we hired her. She thought our case would be straight forward since it was just about parenting time and scheduling. She also knew personally Shelby and Tamara's lawyer. By fall 2011 nothing was moving forward because all our proposals were refused by the opposing party. At least we got a schedule over the Christmas holidays and I had my kids Christmas morning.

The year before, 2010, Jared had shown attitude again when he was gifted from me a used iPod for Christmas. He wanted a new one so he called his mom and went back to their place mid-day. Two days later, on December 27th, he called his mom again to come get him from my home. This made no sense as the six of us had planned a fun day together and Jared had seemed keen to go. He waited at the curb for his mom and Tamara and sure enough, they drove by and took him while the rest of us were packing up my car. They also took Carson, saying that they would not separate the boys. Both of my boys got along well with Mona and her girls, so this was another deliberate action to thwart any positive time they might have had with our blended family.

Diane had been negotiating with Karin Saccher, lawyer for Shelby and Tamara, when suddenly we got notice that Karin dumped them. Then we heard that we were scheduled for a judicial case conference in April, 2012. Shelby and Tamara had retained a new lawyer, Michel Butters, a local public talk-show figure, and he represented them at the case conference. On behalf of his clients, he told the judge that they would not entertain any of my parenting proposals. Instead, here is the schedule they were demanding: I pick up the boys after school on Wednesday and keep them Thursday. They return to their moms' on Friday by 8:00 in the evening. On my weekends I would keep them until Sunday at 7:00 p.m.

If I didn't agree to this schedule, they were going to go for Child Maintenance. I had paid child support (i.e., Maintenance) from 2004-2007 until we became 50/50 equal parents. My concerns were that there was no negotiating to give the boys the easiest transition; and I felt it opened the door to my being held to pay Child Maintenance if mom managed to get more than 50% parenting time. Sure enough, as soon as the ink dried on that Parenting Order, Mr. Butters sent notice that my ex and Tamara were seeking child support.

Diane wrote Michel Butters that both of them would need to recuse themselves from this application since both parties had agreed to *no child support* in the previous Order. Diane was furious and let Butters know she would hold his feet to the fire. To date, I have heard nothing further on this matter.

Shelby's and my salaries are about the same. We always paid half each for the kids' expenses and we submitted receipts to each other. But recently, Shelby has not paid me back her share of the gymnastics fee from two months ago. She also owes me half of the $341 that I paid for a saxophone for Jared, a purchase she agreed to up-front. I paid it all because I want my son to be involved in positive activities. If it was the other way around, Shelby and Tamara would be demanding that I pay up immediately.

I am tapped out financially. I can manage to pay my bills and no lawyers are hassling me for money these days, but that could change in an instant. Maybe I need to file for bankruptcy; I don't know. Last year, Mona and I started a support group for blended families. We want people to know it is okay to reach out for help.

It is really hard for me to re-live all the anxiety, fear and overall stress of the past eight years. The fact is that lawyers are not trained to deal with mental health issues; they don't even know anything about them, yet they are managing these complex custody cases involving *exactly those issues*! My counselor has told me that I am beaten down; I have almost believed that I am a horrible person, that I need to regain my self-love. Minimizing the conflict by agreeing readily to my ex's bizarre proposals and decisions has not served my boys' or my best interests.

I have spent about $40,000 on lawyers thus far. If I had gone to court, my costs would have been through the roof. Both Jared and Carson are doing well academically; great, in fact. I am very involved with my kids' schools. Last year, I volunteered with Carson's French Immersion class every Friday to help the kids with conversation. They even recognized me for that at the end of the school year, which was really nice. I always made sure to leave the school before lunchtime though. That is when Tamara starts her shift as supervisor and I didn't, and don't, want any further incidents. Carson has just two years left at that school.

Jared is in a middle school and I am on its Central Music Parents Association. We went on an overnight band trip this past June and I go to every one of his concerts. Last Wednesday, Jared's birthday, I chaperoned his class to the beach. The teacher asked me to go since the kids "readily engage with you (me)."

2017

Wow, here it is five years later and so much has happened. For starters, On March 13th, 2015, Jared came to live with Mona and me full-time. This occurred after his mom banned him from going on two band trips, one to Tennessee and the other to Denmark. These were consequences from his showing up stoned at her home at the beginning of the year. Shelby did let me know about her punishment, so I consulted with four psychologists and addiction counselors. They disagreed with her consequences, but when

Shelby and I discussed it over our first coffee together in 12 years, Shelby held fast to her decision.

Jared had an argument with Shelby about her decision regarding his missing the band trips during which, apparently, Tamara hit him. His school counselor reported this to a social worker and the result was his moving in with us. Mona and I went to court to get permission for Jared to go on his trips and we succeeded. He and I attended an addiction-counseling program and it turned out he was using because of his stress over the conflict going on between his parents. In the summer of 2015, Jared went for five weeks to stay with my family in Nova Scotia. This was a happy, productive, and healthy time for him. During his absence, Mona and I looked for a house to rent together where we could all be a family.

In June of 2016, Jared, who now lives with us, posted a GoFundMe campaign to raise money for a camera that his stepmother, Tamara, sold on eBay or online elsewhere. She also sold his snowboard last winter, stating that it was "a family snowboard" so she had a right to do so. Tamara also took Jared's bike that he used to move to my house in 2015. And recently, she launched a court case against his band teacher.

I let Jared, then 16, know that I thought GoFundMe was inappropriate as a personal fundraising tool for his "cause". I also thought he should have the police investigate the details of the sale of his belongings. He also pasted this campaign on Facebook and got some nasty replies from his mother's friends. A couple months later, I sent a blanket email to all the alienated parents from your study in hopes that some of them could give me advice about whether to make Jared remove his campaign. I wanted to be supportive, but I did not want to antagonize his mother, nor allow him to make money with zero effort on his part.

Jared remains a straight-A student who regularly performs on the saxophone with his rhythm and blues band. I am grateful that Jared continues to live with us full time, and I have attempted to foster his relationship with his mom, but it seems she now wants little to do with him. Carson is not faring as well. He has expressed a desire to stay only with his moms and does not want to come to my house. When I suggest we spend time together, he texts me back that he is "too busy". This was not an issue until 2016. Before then, he always enjoyed time with Mona, the girls, his brother and me and was eager to be included in family events. My youngest son is now severely alienated from us, and I am not sure what to do about this.

Maybe my story will provide some hope, as I never thought Jared would move in with us. We watched both boys go down the path of parental alienation where, unfortunately, Carson has ended up. I now know, though, that this too may change over time. I can only pray he comes back to us.

DAVID

CHAPTER 11

DAVID

I have one daughter, Brielle, who is almost 15. She was born in December of 1997 and her mother and I separated in 2003. Sheila, my ex-wife, and I were married for seven and a half years, together for 19 years. Brielle was our miracle baby; she was ten weeks premature and weighed three pounds, two ounces. After 9 ultrasounds during pregnancy and a week in hospital following birth, she came home. She is a gift from God, as all children are. Her mother, Sheila, had a lot of pregnancy complications, so it was a rough time. We weren't even trying to have a baby, but I am so grateful for our daughter. Every year Brielle gets more amazing; her beauty is inner as well as outer. I have pictures of her up in my shop since the time she was born.

Sheila had trouble nursing and felt inadequate because we knew breastfeeding was the way to go for the child's sake. I am sorry now that I encouraged her to try for almost three months; that probably stressed her out more. I was not the best husband for her. She came from a dysfunctional family with a very controlling father and I was not a very good listener. But I cared for and loved her, never laid a hand on her, and provided for our family as best I could.

When Sheila began to go to counseling, I thought it was kind of crazy, and I now take responsibility for my ignorance. I did go to counseling with her though; I wanted us to stay a family and I did love her. I didn't know she had already made up her mind to leave the relationship. One of Sheila's friends was in a relationship with an awful, abusive man and they had three children together. I believe this woman was toxic to our relationship as she really hated men.

Sheila stayed home for five years with our daughter, which was great. When Brielle started school at age five, I asked Sheila whether she planned to go back to work. We were really struggling financially and I suggested she waitress (her previous line of work) a couple evenings a week to help pay our bills. She did, but instead of two or three, Sheila immediately went to work five nights a week.

At least we could tag-team the parenting that way. I worked days and she, nights. But when she got off work around midnight or the wee hours, she always went to bed in our spare bedroom. For seven months we argued about that. We had no time together, but I guess she wanted it that way. She stopped cooking dinners, ever, and when Brielle would cry, Sheila waited for me to pick her up. When Brielle would make a fuss at the dinner table, Sheila sometimes just picked up her plate and went downstairs, away from us. Soon Brielle started copying this behaviour until I told her, "Young lady, this is not appropriate behaviour during dinnertime. It is family time". This was undoubtedly confusing to our little girl, whose mother was choosing to avoid sitting with us.

Sheila said I was controlling, but I never made her do anything, didn't ask questions about her friends or what she did in her free time. I was frustrated that she came home late after work though; way after her shift had ended. I asked her whether she wanted to be a mother and as a result, she started to make dinner for Brielle, but I was to fend for myself. At least our daughter got fed, and I was fine with cooking for myself as I had often cooked for us all.

One day I came home from work and Sheila announced she was leaving me the next day. My wife said she did not love me. I begged her to leave Brielle with me; I couldn't imagine going on living without my daughter. Besides, her school was right across the street and the last thing she needed was more disruption in her short life.

On February 8th, 2003, Sheila left and said I could pick up Brielle later at her sister's house. I went there at 6:15 p.m., retrieved Brielle and went home. So began the next two and a half years of sheer hell. When I needed babysitting, I relied on my parents. Sheila's parents were divorced and both lived in Calgary. Brielle had such a hard time. My parents said she would stare at a

photo of Sheila and me together and tell her grandparents how much she loved us both. For the next 18 months, Sheila would take Brielle a couple overnights per week.

I found out later that Sheila, 13 days before she left, had signed papers necessary to put the house I had bought into her name. I decided to seek out a family mediator. I told him I was stuck because my wife would not settle on a split of our finances. We, as yet, did not have a Separation Agreement. Sheila was working, then went back to school, but did not contribute to Brielle's care. The mediator drew up an agreement which I ran by the lawyer I hired; Janet Hendersen. She was all about the money and charged me $450 per hour. It was a whole lot more than I could afford.

By 2005, Sheila was showing up at my place unannounced to get Brielle sometimes as she still had a house-key. I allowed that in order to avoid friction between us. One day I came home from work and Sheila was there with Brielle. She had picked her up from her beloved after-school caregiver, Mama Sue. I presented Sheila with the draft separation agreement and told her everything was in it that she had said she wanted. She wanted half our house, half my RRSPs and half my business. I am a sole proprietor, so she basically wanted half of me. I was already paying for her existence as well as my daughter's.

Sheila could take as long as needed and run the agreement by her own lawyer. I told her that. She came over a few days later, crying, to say that her lawyer thought she was a complete idiot. There was a total of $13,000 she still owed me, but I had forgiven that debt in the agreement as well as giving her the shirt off my back. Apparently, this was still not enough so she was using the crocodile-tears trick on me.

I told Sheila I just wanted to move on and if we let the lawyers fight this out, we would both be hamstrung and poor forever. *The lawyers get fatter and the children thinner.* In the end Sheila signed on the dotted line and I decided to re-mortgage our house to buy her out. That way, Brielle and I could keep the only home she knew. So now I was maxed-out to the ears financially with a crying daughter at home. But Sheila was resentful that I had a house and she didn't. And within a short time, she spent all the money I gave her from our Agreement.

Even though our Separation Agreement states that our child's expenses will be proportionately shared, that became a problem right away. We supposedly had 50/50 shared custody but, in reality, I had Brielle about 70% of the time.

I voluntarily enrolled in the Parenting After Separation course. Then I also took the courses "About Dads", "Anatomy of Anger", and a few others. When Brielle was six and a half, she and I enrolled in the Caught in the Middle course offered through the British Columbia government. Around the same time, we started with my church's Rainbow program, which does not focus on religion, but helps families experiencing psychological and emotional grief. We went for three years and Brielle loved it.

Probably we would have continued, but there is so much demand for that program, we couldn't get into a fourth year. I talked to counselors through Brielle's school, other parents, lawyers, retired judges who come into my shop as customers, a very wide range of people. I figured I needed all the advice I could get.

We went through some really tough stuff. I would walk for miles and miles with Brielle in a stroller and we'd greet neighbours as we went. It was great, but there was no mom for my daughter. One time Brielle got really verbally abusive with me, which I will not tolerate. I saw it as her frustration with everything but in any case, I gave her a swat on the bum and sent her to her room. She was then about 7 years old. Ten minutes later, I knocked on her door and she let me in. She was on her top bunk and let me climb up beside her. I told her that I knew our situation was very hard on her but it was not okay to be disrespectful. She looked at me and asked why her mom left her. I explained to Brielle that her mom had left *me*, not her. I did not say negative things to my daughter about my ex-wife. We sat and cried and hugged and made a pact to never go to bed mad. I reminded her that her mom also loves her very much.

Sheila came with me to the hospital for the results of Brielle's assessment of learning disabilities (she is borderline Attention Deficit, ADHD). Afterward, Sheila announced that she had a barbeque to attend so would not be able to take Brielle. It was her scheduled night…one of only two, and I knew Brielle would be crushed. I was so mad I had to just walk away. Then I retrieved my girl and I had to straight-out lie to her in order to protect her heart. I told her that mom had something urgent she had to attend to and she was very sorry. It seemed like that event was soon forgotten, but in a way I think Brielle has it all simmering in her subconscious.

There were other occasions like the one I just mentioned but basically, the situation remained the same with my having Brielle five nights, Sheila two, until Brielle was 12. Then I got a lawyer. I could not afford to raise Brielle single-handedly without some help from her mother. I was paying for everything and my ex was working. To rub salt into the wound, Sheila even said to me once "You are doing such a great job with our daughter. She is doing so well." My lawyer said that since I had Brielle 75% of the time, I could make unilateral decisions for her. I changed her school to one I felt served her needs best and she did well there. I went to court twice, but that same judge ate me alive both times. She is now retired; I would buy the court transcript if it wasn't so expensive.

Jane, my lawyer, gave me bad advice. She was mad that I had done some legal work without her input and told me our Separation Agreement would not stand up in court. She said it was a stupid thing to do. I reminded her that I could not afford her fee of $350 or $400 an hour. If I had stayed with Jane, I'd have lost my house and my daughter and I would be living in my car by now. I fired her and got another lawyer.

Margaret became my next lawyer; she is one of my customers. She said I should not have changed my daughter's school without Sheila's approval. Well, Sheila did know by then and had no problem with it. She was glad Brielle was doing well there. I was the one involved with that school, volunteering, on the parent's council, and the principal said "I wouldn't even know the woman (Sheila); I just see you here all the time". Just as I was leaving the appointment at Margaret's office, my phone rang and it was Sheila. Apparently Sheila's dad had just committed suicide and I think she found him. She's the only one who watches out for her dad; her sisters are all over the place, dope-smokers and irresponsible to the core. I called Margaret back and let her know I wanted to put my case on hold for now. I didn't want to cause any extra stress on Sheila.

Three months later I wanted Margaret to serve Sheila that we were going to court. But instead, Margaret took no action for seven months and eventually I got served by Sheila's lawyer! That made me a Defendant, a definite disadvantage in the family law system. Sheila was painting me as a control freak, because I wanted her to contribute to our daughter's expenses. I fired Margaret, who was good at padding her bank account but was morally bereft.

We attended a Family Case Conference prior to obtaining a court date. It was held in Justice Chappie's chambers; she was an excellent and tough judge. She told my new lawyer, Jon Stalwart, to let me talk. I told her what was happening and what Sheila was proposing. She said her paramount concern was how the child felt. She decided that my ex and I would have a Child's View Report done. I was thrilled. Finally, Brielle could let the judge know what she wanted.

I had talked with another well known lawyer friend of mine who warned me about a former lawyer, June Wharter, who did Child's View reports. He thought she exhibited much bias against fathers and I should try to get someone else. In any case, we did get assigned to Ms. Wharter. I brought all of Brielle's financial, educational, medical, and psychological records to our meeting. I told her Sheila was smoking dope at her place, and I did not agree with that behaviour in our daughter's presence. I smelled it on her sometimes.

For example, one morning Sheila had dropped 7-year-old Brielle back at my place at 6:30 in the morning. I just put a quilt over her and let her sleep beside me. I had to get up for work and get her off to school soon. Well, that morning all I could smell was THC as my daughter breathed on me. Even though we both smoked pot occasionally in our early years, I implored Sheila to quit when she became pregnant. She wouldn't; I did, and for good. Sheila must have smoked marijuana on the drive over to my house that day in order for Brielle to be still exhaling it. I immediately called her doctor, took Brielle in, and asked for blood and urine tests. I wanted to be sure she did not have this drug in her system and if it was, I wanted that on record. They did the tests on Brielle but not until two days later. Of course, the tests came back all clear by then. After the report was complete, we went to court in early 2009.

Judge Kaye presided. She listened while Sheila used my own records against me and cried. Judges always fall for the mom's tears. She made it sound like she and her father were so close, but in fact, she told me she used to hate him. Her lawyer even made my church attendance look sketchy, stating that I only started going two years after Sheila left us. In fact, this was true, but I went because I was pretty broken, and it has helped me a lot to get back to my spiritual roots. The judge didn't care about the 36 times I bent my schedule to serve Sheila's vacation plans, nor all the arguments and inappropriate punishments (e.g., at the age of seven, sent to the backyard in a bathrobe one evening because she was fighting, actually fighting, with Sheila. That time I made Brielle go in and apologize to her mother) Sheila meted out to Brielle, nor my records showing I had paid $28,000 by then just for Brielle's schooling.

When it was my turn in court, my four pages of recorded incidents were given only two minutes of rebuttal time. I was supposed to get 15 minutes, but before we went into court, I couldn't confirm anything with my lawyer, Jon. He was occupied on the phone with his other clients. Judge Kaye cut me down, said I was controlling, and said to forget about getting Child Support. I was derided for being an involved father and the decision was to reduce my parenting time to an actual 50% from 70%. There was no mention that Sheila only ever wanted minimal time with Brielle. But what killed me was that the judge gave Sheila full decision-making authority over Brielle; education, medical, everything! Sheila was to pay half for Brielle's continued enrolment at the Christian school she loves, but she could pull Brielle whenever she wanted and put her instead into the public system. So much for *"best interests of the child"*.

I later showed Judge Kaye's decision to one of the service staff who told me she had never seen such a one-sided ruling in her life. Wharter's "report" depicted Sheila's boyfriend as a model "step-father" and the two of them as a unified, positive couple. The so-called Child's View report was, in this staff's view, a "hatchet-job" and was more of a Child Custody and Access report, riddled with her bias against me. It stated that I was unbalanced and couldn't move on, while Brielle's mother had a wonderful new life. Sheila went back to school and is engaged. I am self-employed and have been for over 27 years and don't have the luxury to close shop and return to school, even if I wanted to.

After we left the courtroom, I felt like the walking dead, and then-my lawyer, Darryl, commented that, being a long weekend, he needed to get going pretty soon. We met for about five minutes and he suggested I appeal the court decision. Brielle was at my place and I had to go home and tell her I couldn't have her and her friends over as planned to go to the Provincial Museum the next day. Judge Kaye had laid out, starting immediately, exactly when I would have my parenting time. Brielle wanted to know why I was cancelling on her. She was confused and distraught.

Shortly thereafter in June, I got a summons to court from Sheila's lawyer. She sure didn't waste time to come after me. I was already in breach of the Court Order because it was based on the public-school calendar; Brielle was enrolled in a Christian school. I was crying when I phoned my lawyer, Darryl, desperate not to lose my daughter. He told me I had nothing to worry about... well, it has been three years since that day and my ex has continued harassing me over everything to do with our daughter.

Sure enough, a couple years ago, Sheila told Brielle she was going to move her to a public inner-city middle school. Brielle asked me why she had to go and said she didn't want to leave her school and all her friends. I went to court to try and keep Brielle in her school, but I got the same judge who ripped me apart last time. My daughter even wrote a letter to the judge, imploring her to prevent the move. The school counselor also wrote on her behalf, saying that Brielle needed stability and a move would cause her unnecessary hardship. Nevertheless, Judge Kaye wagged her finger at me and told me I was toxic to my daughter. Afterward, the sheriff on duty in court that day told me that this judge was the reason many people appeal court decisions. My lawyer said to me, "You can never, ever go in front of that judge again". Judge Kaye has since retired.

Brielle was moved to the public school, but eventually, since she's a social kid, she adjusted okay. Her grades dropped badly at first but they have slowly crept up again. Darryl tried his best; I think he might even have a conscience. I told him I was financially tapped out and couldn't pay him for any more legal action. I then got a bill from his office for $1,700. What?!

I wrote him a letter saying that he had seen what happened to me in court. He knew I had no money. But I offered to pay him what I apparently owed as I was able, a little at a time. There was no way I could pay the entire amount. There was no response from Darryl, and when I called his office to follow up, my number was blocked. That was almost three years ago and I have heard nothing since. Darryl never got paid the rest of my debts owing. I think he gave up, and his ego was crushed by that judge. He should have been able to help me in court, but Judge Kaye stomped all over him.

I pay Sheila $160 per month in Child Support; meanwhile, she frequently requests extra "child care". My cheques to her have sometimes expired before she gets around to cashing them. She and her new husband have dual incomes so I am struggling financially while she benefits on all counts. Sheila and I are court-ordered not to speak by phone, but she calls me all the time asking for help with Brielle and announcing when she has plans that will require the forfeiting of my court-ordered parenting time. First, she will tell Brielle about an activity she has planned for them so our daughter gets excited. Then she calls and tells me to give up my time and if I deny this request, I am a bad dad and my daughter is disappointed.

Two weeks ago, I sought advice from my sixth lawyer. Court-directed parenting and money instructions are difficult to make sense of and the *family law system is a vending machine.* You just keep feeding the system but nothing good ever comes from it. I noticed in my bank statements that five of my cheques to Sheila were not cashed, so I wanted to know what to do. She had previously waited and then cashed my cheque months later, when I had changed my bank for a better mortgage. That time my cheque came back NSF (nonsufficient funds) so my ex called to yell at me about what a useless piece of shit I am. Each time she wants something, Sheila threatens me with further court action.

In January of this year, Brielle told me she wanted to move back in with me and go back to her old school. Then she told her mom and step-dad and they freaked! I was supposed to be picking my daughter up at 5:30 for the weekend but at 4:10 p.m., I got a call from Brielle's cell phone. She was very upset, shouting into the phone that she was hiding under her bed at Mom's house. She said *"I am afraid, Dad! I am going to get hurt, Dad …help me!"* At the same time, I could hear my ex shouting that she was going to put me in jail for this. For what, I wondered? I should have phoned the police but didn't.

Instead, I called family healthcare workers, Child Protection, any professionals I thought might intervene. At 5:30 p.m., as per the schedule, Sheila dropped Brielle off at my place. I encouraged Brielle to speak with her school counselor. That woman then called Sheila to get her side of the story. Sheila had said I was making Brielle change schools. Brielle set her straight and said her dad (me) just wants her to be happy and safe. At least the school and the others I called put Mom on notice for her dishonest portrayal of my daughter's wishes and my involvement. By the end of this school year, Brielle's and her mom's relationship seemed to smooth out to a degree.

"It has never been a matter of what strategically I can use for my child... it is about honouring my child. I don't own her, she is not my property, but she has been treated as property. I love being a dad. I love my daughter. To me there is just really nothing better. I think it is one of the biggest blessings anyone could ever have. So many years could have been good ones if the legal system had paid attention to what was really going on."

ARNIE

CHAPTER 12

ARNIE

This is my 12th year dealing with lawyers, and I have spent almost $250,000 on them. I have also noticed a predictable bias against men in the family court system. If you are a dad, you are going to have a hard time if your marriage fails.

The fact is that the family court system is a sandbox run by judges for lawyers, clerks and countless thousands of staffers. The toys, shovels and widgets in that sandbox are non-custodial parents and their children. Divorce is a billion-dollar industry. I believe, based on my experience, that in the eyes of the judiciary, if you a male, you are evil and don't have a chance.

Most of us have conscientiously raised our children, provided for their needs, supported them with love and positive direction until such time as our partners decide to leave and take as much as they can both emotionally and financially.

I have a total of six children from two marriages. I love my kids more than anything. From my first marriage, I have three grown children. That marriage lasted 25 years. From the second marriage, I have three more: aged 14, 12 and 10 years. I've been separated since 2006 after 14 years of being together.

2017

My eldest child today is nearly 50. The others are 45 and 35 respectively. My first wife said to me that "You are a lousy husband, but a great dad". I think that might have been true.

My older kids hated me since I had left their mother. Today, our relationships have healed to an extent, but I doubt they will ever forgive me for my "transgression". My older son has remained basically estranged from me but his older sisters tolerate me. They were fed so much negativity by their mother about me. That first divorce dragged on for five years in court.

The second marriage is a divorce disaster as well. The issue is money and this has dragged on since 2006 until 2018 with no apparent resolution in site. This ex-wife will not settle and loves the attention and sympathy she gets from the courts and her friends.

The second three children, now all teenagers, have figured it out. The oldest works for me and will be going to college next term. The second is preparing for university while my younger son is enjoying his high school years.

I was able to get an Order to get them 3 weekends out of 4 *after five years in court*. I decided that it was the best I was going to get, so decided to work with what I had. What will never be replaced is the time and opportunity that they might have had if we had been able to gain at least equal time parenting and a reasonable distribution of assets.

If I could offer any advice to the parents who are currently in the court system, victims of parental alienation and defamation, trying to get some time with their children, it would be to try to get a mediated agreement away from judges and lawyers and spend the energy and money on their children. Of course, in parental alienation, a happy outcome is next to impossible.

I have expended nearly 20 years of my life involved in two divorces. What I can say is life is short, so try to end the conflict and cherish every moment you can with your children. They will come back to you.

TERRY

CHAPTER 13

TERRY

I have been divorced since 2000. We were married 14 years. My daughter, Rhonda, is 22, and I have two sons, Mark now 20, and Adam, 16. The trouble started early on, after Rhonda was born.

We had made a plan for us both to keep working after our first child was born so that we could pay down our mortgage. Then we would have another baby after a few years and Dana would stay home. We always wanted three children and agreed that this was a good way to parent but also pay off debt.

Anyway, once it was time for Dana to return to work, she didn't want to and so we started seeing a good marriage counselor. That counselor, Glenna, was unusual in that she believed in marriage; she wanted our marriage to survive. Lots of these co-called counselors just tell the couple to split without any helpful therapy whatsoever. She helped us re-establish our plan that Dana would be able to stay home, but not before the second child was born. We had also attended a few weekend workshops through our United Church before and after the kids were born. They were supposed to be focused on marriage strengthening and enrichment but seemed to be for couples experiencing infertility.

We enrolled our daughter into a daycare at the bottom of my office tower, which was really convenient. But my wife had trouble detaching enough to leave our baby every morning and the problem intensified. I could drop in mid-day to see how Rhonda was but often, the babies were just left alone in their cribs. I told Dana about this and we made the decision to pull her out and instead, on our friends' referral, we took Rhonda to very loving lady caregiver who couldn't have children of her own. Still, Dana was struggling, so we went back to counseling.

This time, our counselors were appointed through work and we cycled through a few of them. That's how I know many are anti-marriage. Within 17 months of Rhonda's birth, Dana delivered our second child, Mark. She had experienced a reproductive health scare before Rhonda, so we decided to try sooner than planned for another baby in case fertility became an issue. After that, Dana stayed home, but our marital troubles ramped up.

There was no mental illness in Dana's family that I know of, but I started to see that she craved sympathy by any means necessary. She came from a good family, but her parents had a lot of children so her mom stayed home. Dana's mom had her first child as a teenager and then that marriage was annulled. Her second husband parented that child and all the rest while working as a politician and farming. There seem to have been a few teenage pregnancies and convoluted family dynamics on Dana's side. The women in her family seemed to be good at getting men, but were also, within themselves, a little subculture of divorce. Dana had five sisters, and all except one married really nice guys, but all six women complain to each other incessantly about their husbands.

Mark was conceived very quickly after the agreement was signed, facilitated by Glenna, our original marriage counselor. We had agreed that Dana would stay home with the babies after the second child. When Mark was born Dana continued to have a strong interest in older child Rhonda, but gave minimal time and tenderness to baby Mark. Of the three children, Dana breast-fed the eldest, Rhonda, for more than six months and the youngest, Adam, over 12 months. But, as a baby, Mark was set aside. Mark was breast-fed less than three weeks. At the time I felt sad for Mark. His little heart was being starved before it was big enough to be broken. Nevertheless the only life Mark knew was his own. He became a patient and very caring, empathetic little boy.

As well as her large appetite for sympathy Dana had endless ailments, disorders, and pains. My then brother-in-law called the phenomenon "The Women of a Thousand and One Mysterious Diseases". I had no understanding of my wife's motives or intentions, yet it was evident that she was making mountains out of molehills. This deceitful manipulation was venomous. Sadly, it affected the children too. She would encourage them to misbehave and try to make me out as "bad" whenever I had to correct behaviours their mother was teaching or encouraging. This venom was very destructive of every relationship it touched. Adam had just turned two when Dana announced she was filing for divorce.

At the time of our divorce I had a strong and persistent sense that if I did not have a hand in raising the children, then I would have the task thrust on me after they outgrew their mother's control by their early teens. I was determined to prevent my three innocent children's lives from being torn apart by their mother and family courts. After hanging on through two years of humiliation, duress and extortion I worked to gain a tenuous 50/50 shared parenting arrangement with Dana. Co-parenting was not possible without Dana's co-operation, so some aspects of the Shared Parenting Plan were never implemented. Nevertheless, Dana eventually became cooperative about sharing the children with me.

Now, 12 years since our divorce, I can tell you that all three of my children are doing well; the older children are at university. Rhonda is taking dentistry and Mark is taking Engineering. Mark and Adam continue to split their time, weekly, between homes. All three children are tall, healthy, athletic, intelligent, and capable. Any parent would be proud of them, as I certainly am.

2017

It is now 17 years since settling the divorce. Dana divorced a second time and moved into a house a couple of kilometres away from my house, our former marital home. Rhonda is a dentist; she lives and works three hours away from my city. She lives in an apartment with her beau; one day in the future I hope to hear what their future plans are. Mark lives with his girlfriend in an apartment here in town. He finished his Civil Engineering degree and worked for a year and a half. He quit his engineering job nine months ago and recently returned to university enrolled in Education. Coming out of high school, Adam stumbled academically; this continued into his first year of university. He now appears to be flourishing and enjoying his area of study, plant science and breeding. He was rewarded with a job at the university this past summer and hopes to study one semester at the University of West Australia.

MARK

CHAPTER 14

MARK

From the beginning, my ex-wife made sure she maximized the amount of cash she could grab through our divorce. My sons, John now 16 and Kevin, 10, have been used by their mother as a means to that end. The Case Management judge assigned to us required me to disclose all my financial records; my ex however, has never had to. I have been completely honest about my money and all assets, but she has not. Had I refused to disclose, I would have been found in contempt of court and thrown in jail. I have had five lawyers and they cost me $70,000. They also did not help me, or my sons, in any way.

In every court application, I included a request for a record of my ex's income, but that has repeatedly been ignored. Meanwhile, I got a Court Order requiring me to pay spousal support to her though she doesn't work and has been remarried for at least a couple of years. My ex concocted a story about how her second husband was injured fighting in the military overseas, so had to retire. His former wife, however, told me that he was never in combat, works in the military office and was never injured. According to his ex, this "veteran" had to leave the military because he refused to transfer. This is relevant since my ex, in her affidavit, tried to portray her second husband as some kind of war hero. She blatantly lied, but there was no penalty imposed by the court.

When a case gets assigned to morning chambers, as ours did, it is only allotted 15 minutes. If it instead goes to case management, you have one hour. In either case, there is no guarantee that the judge will read the background materials beforehand.

My lawyer for the case management meeting on July 27, 2011, reported that my income for the previous year was $10,000. I had earlier filed for an agreement with all my creditors, asking for leniency. I was left with all our credit card debt when my ex took off, and I had a huge Revenue Canada bill over $100,000 to be paid from equity on our house. The lawyers sunk their teeth right into that and I never saw any money from the house. I started to file procedures for bankruptcy. My efforts to get an adjustment on these due payments and accruing arrears of an additional $20,000 were refused. That judge, Justice D.J. Manderson in Edmonton, ruled that I should be making $60,000 a year and if I couldn't in Edmonton, then I needed to go north to work on the rigs or something like that. He said there was lots of money to be made up there.

At the time, I had been a realtor for 26 years. I worked construction for four years earlier in life, but had injuries and then surgery on both my shoulders. After my recovery, I took an employment re-training course through Workers' Compensation to find a line of work that did not require heavy lifting. Now, Justice Manderson was telling me, a 50 year old man with a total of 7.5 % disability pension, that I should go work the rigs up north. He was in a wheelchair, by the way.

Justice Manderson ordered that, on his assuming my annual income of $60,000, I would keep paying child support at that level, plus spousal support, plus another $200 per month towards accrued arrears with MEP (i.e., Maintenance Enforcement Program) of $23,000. He ordered this even though I had next to no income at the time. When he stated his Order, I jumped up in the courtroom and said, "It is THIS court that has put me in this situation and you are going to put me on the street!" Then I walked out of the courtroom. The judge yelled at my back, "You are in contempt! Get Security up here!" So, Security came running in and my lawyer came running after me, begging me to go back in and apologize to the judge. I refused, as Justice Manderson was a complete idiot.

I felt like the judge pushed me as far as he could to see what it would take to make me snap. The next words out of my lawyer's mouth were "How are you going to pay me?" Unbelievable! She, Christine Macdonald, was a new lawyer and I had hoped she wasn't as corrupt as the older ones. My earlier lawyer, Kathryn Kolbasa, was useless, so I had hired Christine to take over. Christine, though, was hired on referral from another lawyer at that firm. She was just supposed to get an adjustment to child and spousal support payments, yet she had phoned me repeatedly asking for extra background stuff on my case. I asked her why since I was only paying her for the adjustments application. Christine told me it was because my wife (soon to be ex) said it wasn't done, so I reminded her that she was supposed to do only what I hired her to do.

Christine, my lawyer, was working for my ex-wife at my expense. She was researching our Education Plan (RESP) and life insurance plan that would pay me $70,000 if my ex-wife died. My ex wanted to make sure I would get nothing if she died. But how would I care for my kids then?

After the Court Order by Manderson, I was worried sick that MEP would come down hard on me as it had before. Last time I had been in arrears, MEP garnished my wages up to 100%. Those were commission cheques and they are supposed to go to the real estate company I work for. Eventually, I got that insane punishment reduced to 30% garnishing, which was hard enough.

I know that MEP was communicating with my ex, but all I heard about was how much it was going to garnish from my income. My employer knew all about the payments since it was forced to comply with the MEP demand. MEP also took my driver's license…I am a realtor! At the same time, my ex was claiming to have income of $60,000, so I figure it was likely even more. Plus, she was getting child and spousal support, both of which she doesn't pay tax on, nor is held accountable for. So she makes more money than I do, gets two forms of extra cash, is remarried while I have no property, no vehicle, am bankrupt, and earn a tiny income.

Court had been July 27th, 2011 and her ex's lawyer failed to file the Order so on August 14th, I again had my driver's license revoked by MEP. My passport had already been seized earlier. Now I really couldn't do my job.

In February of this year, 2012, I got a Registered letter from MEP telling me to go to a financial review meeting. If I didn't go, it read, there would be a warrant out for my arrest. MEP wanted $600 toward arrears instead of the $1,400 the judge granted. It had apparently clued in to the fact that I was penniless. Even so, I told MEP I couldn't pay $600 and would have to borrow from my family. I had already done this in the past, so I was hoping not to have to ask them again. But MEP strong-armed me to get money from my family. I called Linda at MEP and told her I was not going to a financial meeting, so that she could order my arrest when I didn't have more money on hand.

I also wrote my ex-wife a letter, basically asking for mercy. She and her new husband responded that all arrears would be forgiven if I gave them the grandfather clock that I had bought after my parents died and we sold their land. That was many years before and I wanted to give that clock to my kids one day. It had sentimental value for me. My ex has the ultimate power to decide how much I have to pay and in what form. Don't forget that these negotiations for the payment of arrears was money that was supposed to be used for the well-being of my children.

I did agree to giving up the clock to make MEP go away. But when my ex phoned to say they were coming to pick it up, she had not nor would sign the agreement canceling my arrears. Then her husband took over and demanded I give up the clock and he would get it from me. I told him the same thing. I just wanted the agreement signed. I had already taken the clock apart and packaged it up for safe traveling. As punishment, my ex refused to give me parenting time with my kids for the next week.

I told my ex that I intended to seek justice. It was then she called the police on me, telling them "he sounds like he could be suicidal or is going to hurt us in order to get justice". A policeman called me at the office, asking if he could come see me and I agreed. When he arrived, I was finishing my court application for enforcement so that I could have my children as per the parenting plan. My ex had agreed to three hours over Christmas holidays, but I was supposed to have a week with them. She said since I hadn't given her the clock, I would not be allowed to see my boys.

The cop and I talked for a half hour and he saw that I was filing court applications. He asked about my statement that "I will seek justice until my last breath" and I assured him that was my intent through legal applications for court orders with teeth. At the end of our meeting that cop shook my hand and wished me luck.

Then I called MEP and told Linda that she and they were playing with my sanity. Guess that is the reason MEP has bullet-proof glass in its foyer. Out of the blue in March, MEP called me to say that my ex was "going off Maintenance". She must have gotten worried that I was really going to keep pushing for justice. Her lawyer finally filed the Court Order from last July 8 months later at the end of March.

I was rarely seeing my kids because I had no license and couldn't afford to take them anywhere. I had driven at times even so, in order to show clients houses in hopes that I might make a sale. What choice did I have? I know so many other guys who had to drive without a license or else face MEP's punishment of increased arrears. It's a disgusting organization.

Then another interesting twist happened. I think even MEP got worried that I might do something terrible because about a week after my meeting that cop, a lady cop and a nurse pulled up at my house in a white unmarked car. They said I had written a "threatening letter" and that they were just checking to see how I was. They asked if I was eating and sleeping okay, seriously! Well, not even one hour after they left, I got a phone call from MEP telling me that it had reinstated my driver's license all of a sudden. Maybe that was because my ex had notified MEP that she was signing off Maintenance, I don't know.

My ex carries that hammer with her every day now. She threatens to go back on MEP if she sees me with any type of property. My friend had his house caveated along with his vehicle and he went to MEP and handed over the keys to both. He couldn't manage the arrears. My ex holds that over me every single day. I got an email from her husband that said "If you harass us (and named himself, my ex, and my boys), we will take appropriate action". As if I would harass my kids. I have always been a loving, productive dad to them.

My ex has harassed me since the day of our separation. Even before the divorce, her parents would drive by my place and often her brother and her boyfriend at the time would follow me around to see what I was doing and where I was going. She even once texted me, saying she knew I was drinking something and wanted to know what it was. It was a Diet Coke, for God's sake! I haven't had a real drink in about three and a half years. I went to pubs for a while to drown my sorrows, but soon figured out that would make my problems a whole lot worse.

A couple days ago, I called and asked my sons if they would like to go to my family's reunion, but they said it would be too boring. They used to go willingly to events with me, but recently they refuse or don't answer my calls. I am trying to rebuild my business, and I have no money so I can't do expensive things with them. At least MEP seems to be off my back, at least for now. You know what's crazy: If I was arrested for driving impaired, under the Criminal Code of Canada, I could still get a breathalyzer machine and get to work, and I would be allowed to work during certain hours to support myself and my family.

I complained to the Law Society about my ex's lawyer's failure to file the Court Order for over seven months. That's why my license was wrongfully seized in the first place. The Law Society dismissed my complaint; no surprise there. I asked why my complaint was dismissed and the spokesman there said the Law Society does not have to explain its decisions.

I also filed with the Alberta Lawyers' Insurance Association (ALIA) but there too, my complaint was dismissed. And I wrote a complaint of misconduct against that lawyer. The conduct complaint committee has required that my ex's lawyer submit his whole case-file, but there's no deadline to do so that I know of. It was suggested by the Law Society that I file a lawsuit against that lawyer. Right. Hire a lawyer to sue another lawyer...in Family Court. And how would I pay for that, even if the system was legitimate?

This parental alienation and alienators number in the thousands, probably more, just in Canada. We need a class-action lawsuit to make it stop. You know, one day my 6-year-old son told me that his grandma says he and his brother should be nice to me when their mom is happy. But when she is unhappy with me (their dad), the boys should treat me badly. Can you imagine dumping that manipulative pressure on little kids? The kids are always the fall-out and the courts enable it.

Last year my older son Kevin said that his mom had a new husband and I said, "Well great, now you have two dads". He said that wasn't true because only I was his real dad. So he knows the difference. I wonder if he still feels that way. The connection between us is weaker because my ex is working them against me at every opportunity. My son has a cellphone but often doesn't answer, whether I text or phone. He pays for it himself from his part-time job earnings. Maybe he is just being 16 and rebellious.

I met Kevin for lunch recently, but his mom also showed up that day. Kevin saw her and immediately told me I had to go away. The next time I called him he said that his mom thought we were going for too many lunches, so she wouldn't allow them any more. I think he had been keeping our lunches to himself, but when his mom found out, she put a stop to it. He had enjoyed going with me until that time, but Mom saw fit to prevent her nine-year-old from seeing his dad.

I used to take Kevin to hockey tournaments out of town. At one of these, when he was only five or six and step-dad was just newly dating my ex, Kevin and I stayed in a hotel in Red Deer. When I hugged him goodnight, he began "grinding on my leg". I told him sharply that that was inappropriate. I asked him who he thought he could do that to and he said "Mom, Geoff (step-dad-to-be), and you". I asked Kevin when he had "hugged" Geoff like that and he said *"in mom's bed when she is at work"*. I went cold.

At home, Kevin did the "grinding hug" again, so I asked John if he had seen this behaviour. He said "yes" that he had seen Kevin do that grinding hug before. So I called Child Services in St. Albert. Their recommendation was that I write my ex a letter about what was happening and wait for her response. They said they didn't like getting involved between the parents. I wrote that letter and made sure there was no anger or other emotional in it, just concern. She wrote back that I was just bringing up shit and she didn't have to deal with that crap. I let Child Services know her response to me and as a result, they interviewed my ex. She and her husband said that it was an accident because Geoff thought it was Mom in bed. What a load of crap! Kevin told Child Services that he was naked in bed and his step-dad was grinding him. There were so many red flags, but that was the end. Child Services closed the book and I have been watching my son closely ever since. I haven't seen any further inappropriate behaviours or him withdrawing socially or anything, so I have to let it go. Maybe it was just a strange stage of my child acting out in some weird way; I'll never know.

After that interview with Child Services, Kevin told me he liked the woman who interviewed him but John, who was about 14, said "Fuck you, Dad". He had never sworn at me before, and I think he was just mad about being brought into the mess. I know I did the right thing but it must have planted a seed in my ex that she better get the kids away from me. She didn't like losing control and who knows if they were hiding something too? I dropped Kevin off and his grandmother answered the door, my ex's mother. I said to her that she needed to make sure my boys stayed out of that man's (mom's step-dad to be) bed and I pointed upstairs.

Just prior to my ex marrying Geoff, my son told me that they might be moving to Ottawa if Geoff took a new job there. His mom did ask me to sign a permission form so they could take our boys on a holiday to Mexico. I complied. They got married while in Mexico as I later found out from my sons. I was concerned that now they would be able to apply for a move out of province, even country, but fortunately that didn't happen. My ex didn't want to move. But it could still happen. Now that John is 16 I hope he could stay in Alberta if he so chose, but Kevin might have to go unless I successfully fought such a move in court.

I have a tenant now to help pay the bills, but that gives my boys more reason not to want to come over. I doubt they would want to live with me, even if their mother moved elsewhere. I don't talk about my financial situation with my kids because I don't want them to worry. They probably think I choose not to take them to nice places.

It's hard not to have support and people who can make your situation better. I do belong to a group called ECMAS (Equitable Child Maintenance and Access Society) here and we have held vigils for people who have lost their children due to parental alienation. I have written letters to the media and newspaper about the fact that Alison Redpath was the Justice Minister for four years and she allowed strong-arm tactics to enforce court orders. She had no clue about what is really happening in family courts. One of the ECMAS members had a son who was alienated from his kids and he was so bullied by MEP that he killed himself (Chapter 5: Gloria).

I know there are fathers who are not kind, loving examples to their children so I have seen both sides. There are alienated moms too and their exes make their lives just as hellish. It's crazy how the family law system just turns a blind eye to them all.

You can't be a Disneyland dad; you have to really love your children and spend loving time doing stuff with them. Just normal, every day stuff. I'm good at that. We always interacted positively, we laughed, we acted goofy, we cried and we talked about everything. We played hockey in the basement and basketball, baseball and dart tag outside… sometimes for three hours at a time. It was all free, so our entertainment was cheap but great. At first when I would see my boys after many days or weeks, they would come over with attitude, but it never took long for them to settle in and give up their tough-guy façade.

I came from a family of 12 kids. I was right in the middle so I am used to having very little material stuff and just having cheap fun using my imagination with basic household things that we turned into toys. When Kevin was only four, I'd drive up to his mom's to pick him and his brother up and I could hear him shouting excitedly, "Daddy's here! Daddy's here!" They need me in their life and I need them.

CHRIS

CHAPTER 15

CHRIS

I have a wonderful daughter, Katherine, who I am so proud of. She just turned 18. Her mother, Cara, and I dated a short while and the best part of that relationship was that we created Katherine. We didn't really love each other, but we were thrilled to be parents. At the time our baby was born, I had a business in Lethbridge, but we lived here, near Edmonton. I drove to Lethbridge to work for ten days and then I'd come home for four, but Cara did not want to move to Lethbridge. She wanted to stay close to where her own mother lived, so I was okay with that.

Cara had a couple of seasonal part-time jobs when we met. After we had Katherine in 1994, she worked on and off at the jail. Cara took a Criminal Justice course and she used that information to her advantage to manipulate the justice system when we separated.

One evening I drove a client to Calgary where his wife told me how her husband had started a business and was away a lot when their kids were young. I felt she wanted me to know that it was good that I worked hard for my family; it was the traditional thing to do. My wife wanted me at home, though, and she also wanted to stay home with our daughter. We agreed that we didn't want to put Katherine in daycare, so one of us would be the stay-at-home parent.

In hindsight, we married because we thought it was the right thing to do. Out of obligation and wanting to do right by our daughter, we likely stayed together way too long. We separated on February 3, 2002, although my wife claimed at mediation that we separated in May of 2000. The mediator, Kent Talon, asked my wife why she was living in my house (i.e., our family house, though I had paid for it before I even met Cara) if she was claiming that we were separated. I think the reason she said 2000 was because she started to date that same year. But she was still living with me in the family house then.

Cara said I chose my company over her, but I needed to make a living for all of us. She wanted to stay home, and said she would have committed suicide if it wasn't for Katherine. She didn't have post-partum depression, but she sure did hate me. I don't know why; maybe I didn't get it. I felt very confused as I thought I was doing what was necessary to keep our agreement of one parent at home. I changed my work schedule and hired a mechanic so I could do more work from home and not be away as much. That didn't help.

One day I got home and Cara handed me a little box full of my stuff and I asked her why. She didn't answer, but I kept my cool as I thought she might be suicidal. In October 2001, I began to stay at a motel whenever I came home, as I was overwhelmed with everything. Fortunately, I still had time with Katherine then. My stuff was still at the house, *my* house, and I was hoping we would still be together somehow. I thought I needed to be a better foundation for our family. Cara told me I had "ruined her life" and I was baffled. She was messed up before she met me, but I guess she meant that I didn't do everything she wanted. Cara is ten years younger than I am; I don't know if that was a factor. When Katherine was born, Cara was only 21.

Looking back, my wife told me that her dad had taken off with another woman and left her mother when Cara was young. Then, many years later, her dad returned and her mom took Cara's father back. When Cara was 25 or 26, she told me how she still resented her father for his behaviour. I'd notice that Cara and her two sisters often ridiculed their dad when he would say anything at family gatherings. It seemed her mother still loved him, but there was something very dysfunctional in the family dynamic. Her parents seemed at odds as much as if they were divorced and living apart. So, I'm no psychologist, but I think she redirected her anger for her dad towards me instead.

Cara also told me she felt rejected by me. Maybe that's why she began to alienate Katherine from me. It was redirection again… this time of my alleged rejection of my wife? After we split, Cara's affidavits spewed "extreme hatred" toward me.

In October, 2001, I was at the house to see Cara and Katherine when Cara got a phone call. She left the room and closed the door behind her. I later called the number where that call originated and I got a man's voicemail. That seemed fishy but I let it go. On February 2nd, 2003, I found out Cara had a boyfriend. I called that phone number again after Cara told me we were finished and the man answered. He said "Cara isn't here right now". I drove home from Lethbridge and asked her parents to act as mediators. I was dumb enough to want to reconcile, but it was clear immediately that Cara did not. So, I asked her for shared custody and parenting of Katherine. Cara's parents agreed that it would be important not to make Katherine part of our "tug of war".

I agreed that we would divide our assets in half, excluding the house. I would pay Cara child support, but she would have to support herself. She was with another man! She began crying but that was the end of the conversation. Her parents said I would always be welcome there as was Katherine. Several hours later, I picked up Katherine from Cara's sister's house. We got a movie, and went back to Cara's parents' place to watch it together. Our daughter was happy, but when we arrived at her grandparents' home, Katherine went into a back room right away. A few minutes later, she emerged and asked me "Why are you making my mommy go to work and now she won't be with me?" This was literally only hours after her parents said to keep Katherine out of the middle. I was immediately the bad guy. It turned out that Cara was in that back room lying on the bed and crying. I asked my daughter to go join her grandparents while I talked to her mom. I told Cara what Katherine had just said to me. Katherine was just seven and a half years old then.

From that day onward, Cara spewed her hatred toward me. This was before our mediation, so I tried to set up a parenting schedule with Cara's input. It was a disaster because Cara would cancel at the last minute or call to tell me that "Katherine doesn't want to see you". Sometimes Katherine herself would phone me and say whether and when I could pick her up. Then I would ask if I could speak to her mother. Cara would not talk to me or would come on the line with a very hostile tone. I said some mean and rude things to her on the phone in my frustration; I admit that and I am sorry for those words. But she was keeping me from our daughter intentionally, and I was terrified of losing my little girl.

I did see Katherine a few times. Once I picked her up from her grandma's, but Katherine said she wanted to go with me, and her grandma too. She was already confused and hesitating to spend time with me. Cara and Katherine were spending much time in Greg's, her boyfriend's, house and Cara was telling people that I wasn't part of my daughter's life. She said I was living in Lethbridge when in fact I was still traveling back and forth regularly. I, myself, am a child of divorce, though my parents never said anything negative about each other after they separated. That said, I was still traumatized by their divorce, so I knew that Katherine was having a hard time.

It was Cara who called first, asking me if I would attend mediation. Of course, I agreed. Kent, the mediator, suggested right away that I have "short, frequent visits" with my daughter. I asked him why I would agree to that when I was an equal parent and had always been very involved in my daughter's life. Where the hell did he come up with this idea that short, frequent visits were appropriate? He made it seem like my daughter didn't know me or I was dangerous or something. Anyway, I did agree to do for one month as Kent suggested. Then, we all agreed that my time with Katherine would increase and it would include overnights. This was a dark time for me. I remember going to a movie theatre by myself and not even watching the movie. That happened a few times and then I stopped going out altogether. Fortunately, time does heal to an extent and I came out of my funk; I had to.

We each made up the following month's schedule, but Cara's version had me spending even less time with Katherine than in that first month trial period. There was no reason for this, especially since I had quit work (I was off for seven months to deal with the stress of our divorce) so was available any time. We went back to Kent who, when Cara would not budge on my parenting time, advised that we go to court. Cara wanted me to pick up Katherine from school one afternoon a week and spend a few hours with her until 7:30 p.m. Then on Sundays I could visit her from noon until 5:00 p.m. I then asked for every second weekend, but she still refused.

By three weeks after the mediation agreement, I was picking up Katherine on Wednesdays and Sundays weekly, but in a subsequent affidavit, Cara wrote that my allotted time of 12:30-7:00 p.m. was too long. Cara would be in Calgary, visiting somebody, and she would leave around 8:00 a.m. to drive to Edmonton where she was supposed to drop off Katherine with me by 12:30 p.m. But then she would say it was too long a day for Katherine, so therefore my daughter should not have to see me that same day.

I suppose I was a tad cocky because I thought court would mean justice served and I would get my daughter back. I stupidly thought any judge would see that Cara was alienating me from Katherine and the parenting-time issue would be resolved for good. What a bad joke!

Soon after, I hired a lawyer since Cara ignored our mediated agreement. I had even agreed to pick up Katherine at the Dairy Queen, but she and her mother failed to show up. I asked my lawyer for interim access thinking it could then be changed later. The first lawyer I tried grilled me to the point that I felt like a criminal and was actually crying. She said she was only trying to get all the facts before she decided whether to represent me. I left her office. On the same office floor in Edmonton, I saw another lawyer's office and remembered her name as someone I had gone to school with. She is a few years older than I am, but I knew she was a kind-hearted person. I retained her after telling her my story. Unfortunately, Sheri Hostford did not understand parental alienation and in fact, I didn't either before that point in time. Sheri served Cara with papers and we went to court in late 2002. Cara's lawyer, Kathy Zareniuk, tried to make me out as a deadbeat saying that I was unemployed, had no house, was a transient and so on. Ms. Zareniuk worked at the same firm as a senior lawyer in Calgary who had been in a lot of trouble. He had been involved in a high-profile parental alienation case of three children in which one parent murdered the other. Zareniuk is one of many disciples of these big liars. They learn quickly how to milk every dollar out of their clients.

The judge in that parental alienation/murder case, McPhiersen I think was his name, stated that "the natural love for the mother…" (or father, in my case) "…evaporates because in the child's mind that parent has become unworthy". There were a couple books that I knew of written about that case: "Deny, Deny, Deny; A Canadian Tragedy"; and "Above the Law". I read those out of interest long before my own experience with parental alienation. So, similarly, I had no second chance with Katherine because she had already been brainwashed to have a closed mind toward me. Cara was diabolical in her quest to have me eliminated from my daughter's life and mind. Katherine closed ranks around her mother and excluded me.

Our case was stalled over and over and Justice Madam Trussle allowed this. Ms. Zareniuk made no effort to settle our case or reach any compromise. She just kept writing up whatever Cara told her to. Big billable hours, so I'm sure Zareniuk's firm was thrilled with her work. I do believe, however, that my lawyers, Sheri Hostford and Michelle Read did try to resolve my case. I know Sheri tried to get together, off the record, with Cara's lawyer to figure out a solution about a year after our court case began. I think Zareniuk backed out because Sheri seemed very upset and surprised about her doing so. Sheri asked me to agree to a family assessment and I did.

In court in 2002, Sheri Hostford asked for a family assessment and said I was in agreement. She also told Judge Paxton how we had been to mediation, but Cara would not abide by the terms. Mediation is a tricky thing, because it does not officially stand up in court. But here it was relevant, and Judge Paxton shut down Zareniuk's attempt to silence Sheri. The judge gave me some better access to Katherine...at least on paper. But he did not investigate any of the claims Cara made about me, such as that she was afraid of me, that I was basically a derelict, and so on. Cara got away with all her lies, and they were repeated by her lawyer.

We did go to a psychologist, Jay Mullen, who was supposed to do the family assessment. By this time, Katherine would sometimes be crying when Cara dropped her off with me. I knew Ms. Mullen would have her work cut out for her, figuring out what was happening to our daughter. I went a couple times on my own and then Jay wanted to see both Katherine and me. She said we needed 15 to 30-minute appointments with her. The first time Jay got together with both Katherine and I, we drove in her car to Dairy Queen. That was Ms. Mullen's idea, not ours. We were driving there and Katherine was punching me every time she saw a "punch-buggy"; that was our little game. My daughter was seven years old then. I felt like I was a lab rat and Mullen was watching my every move, even though I was supposed to "act and talk normally with your daughter".

Katherine told me about a birthday party she had attended and after lunch at the DQ, I told her where the bathroom was and she went on her own. As soon as my daughter was out of earshot, Jay said to me "The mother is playing games, isn't she?" I was surprised that Jay had already clued in to what was going on. We still needed 30 more visits though, for some reason, and I paid $1,300 for those. The judge had said the costs would be 50/50 shared, but Cara only paid $900. Jay Mullen was supposed to have a report on my family and an appointment schedule ready before Katherine went back to school in September, but she did not. I found out later that this psychologist, Mullen, has a history of failing to meet such deadlines.

The part of the assessment involving me was seven hours of tests. I was asked all about my family background and I photocopied all that I could. Some forms said DO NOT COPY but others had no restrictions so I did copy those. I got the test report later but when I showed Ms. Mullen, she clearly had no idea about its content. *She hadn't even read it*! I told my lawyer, Sheri, about this and Sheri responded by calling a 3-way meeting between the two lawyers and Jay Mullen. Then Sheri phoned me, but I didn't ask much, since I was driving at the time. It was October 6, 2002. Here is part of the written assessment's contents written by Ms. Mullen: "Cara (*pseudonym) took advantage of the situation. Cara's eyes well up with tears when she says she wants Katherine's father in her life. Cara's actions don't match her words". This is not from the actual report since it was yet completed.

There had been a 4-way appointment between us two parents, Katherine and Jay Mullen. At that meeting, Jay mentioned that Katherine had a knot in her stomach because of all her stress. I almost broke into tears when I heard that, poor kid. An hour after that, I was supposed to meet Katherine and Cara, so that Katherine could come with me for a visit. I did the civil thing and greeted them both when I parked, but Cara just looked straight ahead and ignored me. She clearly couldn't care less that our daughter's stomach was in knots due to our situation. That event really stuck with me.

I was relieved as I felt that I would be exonerated after the report was written with that content. I thought this was the end of my need for legal intervention to help my daughter and me. It turned out, though, to be only the beginning of my hell! None of the above content ever showed up in the report. I have no idea why or how it was omitted. She only noted that Katherine suffered separation anxiety when away from her mother. Then Ms. Mullen referred me to another psychologist.

The next psychologist was Bonny Hover and she at least seemed like a good person. In the end though, she was as disingenuous as Mullen. Katherine told her that she was allowed to read her mother's affidavits, and Ms. Hoven did nothing to stop this behaviour. Katherine was not supposed to, ever, be privy to either of our affidavits. Ms. Hoven interviewed Cara, her parents, and her two sisters, as I found out later. It took Bonny until March of 2004 before she stated that I should have Katherine sometimes for overnights. Cara kept repeating that I didn't have overnights and therefore I guess her plan was to retain that status quo. Cara said the reason was that Katherine was afraid of me and traumatized and *she doesn't know me*. In her affidavit, Cara wrote that I was like a "fun uncle". Really? But one she is terrified of? That was so hurtful in so many ways.

One day when she was in Grade 2, Katherine was playing in the schoolyard when I arrived there. Cara was also nearby. Katherine was so happy to see us both in one place and started showing off stuff she could do on the monkey bars. She would run up to me, and then her mom, excitedly shouting "Look what I can do, you guys!" Of course, Cara was continually trying to keep me away from our daughter's school because my presence ruined her façade of being a poor single mother. She was already with another guy and as I found out over time, there had been other affairs too.

One afternoon, about 10 minutes after I picked up Katherine for our joint appointment with Jay Mullen, Cara phoned my cell. She yelled at me that I did not have her permission for our daughter to attend the appointment. I had, however, let Cara know ahead of time by written notice. Then Cara asked to talk to Katherine. After she hung up, Katherine informed me that her mom had told her to tell Ms. Mullen "the truth" that she (Katherine) only wanted to see me on Sundays and Wednesdays. So mom was definitely coaching her along the way. When we went to see Bonny Hoven, it was the same thing. Katherine would be silent and deep in thought before the appointment. I believe she was trying to plan how to answer Ms. Hoven's questions. I once overheard my daughter talking on the phone beside Ms. Hoven's office. She was saying "They did all the talking, mom, so I couldn't say that" and "Mom, I couldn't get…". After the appointments, Katherine would be her joking, seemingly happy self again.

During this period of time, Katherine seemed to think I had not been a part of her life, so I wrote some memories down on paper. For instance, in her Grade 3 year, Katherine had parent-teacher interviews, which both Cara and I attended together. We met with several of her teachers, but Cara was very rude and acted as if I wasn't even present. The teachers probably thought I was a dead-beat dad. There, I didn't have one second to talk with Katherine. Cara was hovering around her the whole time.

Another time when Katherine was in Grade 2 or 3, Cara asked that I pick up her up from the school rather than the court-ordered McDonald's. But when I arrived at school, Cara was there and she immediately grabbed Katherine, took her down the hall, and left the school with me standing dumbfounded at its office. I called Cara's house and her boyfriend answered. I asked to speak to her and he said she was not home, she was at McDonald's. Then I called my lawyer. She said to just go get Katherine at McDonald's so I went there.

Later, my daughter was on the track team, so I stepped up when the coach asked for volunteers at a track meet. I attended, but Katherine did not show up. What kid misses a track meet unless she is sick? I found out that her mother took her out of school that day and to the lake instead. I also volunteered for a skating event at Katherine's school. When I showed up with my skates on, as the other parent volunteers had, her teacher bee-lined over to me and said I couldn't skate with the class as Cara had not given me permission to be there. But, I was not required to get her permission and again, I was made out to look a fool. I don't blame the teacher, as he was just doing what he thought our court order required as per Cara's instructions.

The orthodontist was another manipulation by Cara. She told me Katherine needed braces so I agreed to help pay for them. But Cara wanted me to send her cash and then she said she would send the money to the orthodontist. I asked her why it wouldn't be simpler for me just to pay directly for the work. I had no insurance. I asked Cara if she had dental insurance and she said she did not. She was so mad that I would not send her additional cash every month, supposedly for this orthodontist. My lawyer wrote hers and stated "This is not a windfall for you. This is for the child." Cara took me to court for more Child Support but the judge refused. He knew I was paying my correct support every month and had always done so. That's where I found out that she did, in fact, have dental insurance. *Katherine's mother was trying to make money on the insurance by taking extra cash on the side from me.*

After 13 months with Sheri Hostford as my lawyer, I changed counsel as I needed someone tougher. The next one was Michelle Read. I had earlier been referred to her, but I was in such a panic to get help and she was too busy to take my case for a few months. That's why I hired Sheri instead. Ms. Read understands parental alienation and she told me she would have acted differently on my case. She added that we needed to fix the mess and so we waited for Bonny Hoven's report for the judge. *Judges rely heavily on what these psychologists write.*

Finally, Ms. Hoven sent her report stating that there was no reason Katherine could not have overnights at my home. Ms. Read could now petition the court for more shared parenting and I was encouraged. It was 2005 when I received a letter from Legal Aid. Apparently, Cara had dropped off Katherine at their office so she could be interviewed to maybe get her own lawyer. So here was ten-and-a-half-year-old Katherine having to tell a stranger that she needed a lawyer. That "interview" was nothing more than my daughter repeating the content of Cara's affidavits as per her coach; *her mother.* I need to reiterate in this interview that I understand my daughter felt she had no choice as she saw it then. She had to do her mother's bidding or suffer her wrath. Katherine was assigned her own lawyer.

I had noticed the increasing distance between my daughter and me since she was about 10. By then, the alienation tactics were taking hold and Katherine just became more despondent with me. She was more withdrawn and angry whenever she did have time at my place. By the age of 12, she told me I was the "bad side of the family". My family had commented to me that Katherine was rude and needed some discipline. I tried to be more of a disciplinarian with her. For example, there was one time she dumped ripped-up paper all over her room at my house. I asked her to pick it up and put it in the garbage. She refused and wanted to go to the neighbours' house to play. Not until the room got cleaned up, was my comment to her.

As a result, she was mad at me and wanted to call her mom. I allowed her to and there were several calls before Katherine finally cleaned up her room. She mouthed off to me so I sent her to her room until she could be civil. She ran out of the house and I went after her. When I caught up, she kicked and bit me and pulled my hair. I tried to subdue her but was repeating, "Stop it! Stop it!" to no avail. You can imagine how Cara took that news. She made a huge deal of it, but the psychologist, Bonny Hoven, called it a dust-up and Cara had to back down. Nevertheless, Cara wrote in her affidavit that I was a child-abuser.

When Katherine was 12, I got an email that Cara also sent her Legal Aid lawyer. That one really hurt because, on it, she had listed Katherine's surname as her boyfriend's. When I read that, I cried that day, right in my lawyer's office. It was pretty clear to me that Cara's plan was to replace me as Katherine's father. I was to be entirely *erased* from her life. A friend of mine in a similar situation saw a family photo that had been taken when he was still with his wife and their children. The ex-wife had since removed my friend's face and replaced it with her boyfriend's; can you believe it?! This is abnormal behaviour; not just anger, that's for sure.

At one point Katherine confided in me that she was having health problems and her mother had taken her to a doctor on referral. Cara told her she might need surgery. When Cara arrived to pick up our daughter, I asked her what the situation was and how I could help. My inquiry turned out to be a mistake as Cara yelled at me that it was not my business, right in front of Katherine. My daughter had shared with me, and I guess I got her in trouble with Mom as a result.

Legal Aid took on Katherine without knowing anything about the other (my) side of her story. Her lawyer became a powerful instrument in accelerating the alienation between my daughter and me. That lawyer would not talk to me and just said the matter was before the court. I called my MLA who was also Premier of Alberta then: Ed Stelman. His office and the "Queen's Printer" informed me that Legal Aid receives some government funding. Well, lawyer Lois Sine of Legal Aid wrote me that being the biological father did *not* give me parenting time nor half of summer holidays. She added that I was *not necessarily* a "real" father to Katherine. That letter caused me to miss the next three days of work as I was so discouraged.

I should add that fortunately my boss was being very flexible with my work time, which allowed me to attend court, counselling, and other appointments as I tried to keep my life afloat. I spent so many hours reading and writing emails and letters that it became another job in itself. I really believed the legal system would help, that I just had to keep plugging away. I was not about to behave badly as that would provide ammunition against my case to be an equal parent.

Thanks to the enabling of Legal Aid and Lois Sine, my daughter's and my relationship continued to deteriorate. On the few occasions Katherine was with me, she stayed in her room. Justice Trussle had ordered one overnight a week and Cara had to bring her to my place, but once she arrived, Katherine would not come out of her room. I even took meals to her door. I invited her to go to her grandma's for Christmas, but she refused. When I would sometimes pick her up at her mom's, Katherine, between the ages of 10 and 13, made me wait a long time before she would appear at the door. It started as 20 minutes but became 90 from when I would ring the doorbell until she would come out. Then she wouldn't get out of my truck, once we arrived at my house.

By this time, I had been assigned to Steven Carton, another psychologist. I would have been okay with paying big dollars for his help if it actually did help, but of course it, and he, did not. Justice Trussle, in 2007, had commented that Cara's affidavit showed the "worst case of parental alienation" she had ever seen. Madame Trussle ordered Cara to undo the damage she had caused. She instructed me to go to Steven Carton and Cara to go to Sheila

Vandersand, both working at the same practice. Katherine was to go to another psychologist, Josie Sikes, who was horrible. This was all decided and I was to pay 50% of all fees; I had no say in which counselor my daughter, or I, would see. I guess Justice Trussle felt that Bonny Hoven had done all she could and we needed other "experts" involved. And after that court hearing, Lois Sine quit as Katherine's lawyer. I guess she figured out that she had been duped by Cara.

The point was to eventually put all three of us, Cara, Katherine, and me, in the same room at counselling. My lawyer, Michelle Read, intended to have Cara apologize to me in front of our daughter. We had a court order for this to occur, but Cara never went to Sheila Vandersand; not even once. The court order was completely ignored by my ex-wife. I, however, did meet with Steven Carton for some counselling. I also called Ms. Sikes, asking when I could meet with her to find out her experience, whether she understood parental alienation, and such. She was offended immediately, even though I had asked Steven Carton the same questions and he replied without hesitation. Ms. Sikes had precisely *no* experience.

I told Mr. Carton that I had had a difficult conversation with my daughter, after she and I visited my mother at the hospital. My mom was very sick and passed away shortly after. Katherine said some untrue and harsh things that day to my mom, and I wanted her to know the truth. I told my daughter I did not know that her mom was seeing Greg when she was still married to me. I told her that most kids did not have lawyers and I told her a couple other things. Well, Mr. Carton responded to my confession with "Well, you blew it".

Another day, while attempting to pick up Katherine at Ms. Sikes' office as per usual, I saw Josie Sikes and mentioned the awful things Katherine had said to her grandma at the hospital. She didn't say one word; just kept staring forward with that blank look on her face. She had no idea about parental alienation, nor how my daughter was being manipulated to hate me, and the rest of my family.

That office had moved to a new location and Ms. Sikes supposedly left me a message to that effect, but I didn't get it. I went to the old office instead and saw it was gone. I called the psychologists' office number, got the new address, and raced over there. Then I called Cara to let her know I would be late picking up our daughter. I was so worried that if I showed up late, that would be used against me in court. Cara answered the phone and laughed, saying, "Boy, that's a long distance to drive and there is no appointment, by the way". That's when I encountered Ms. Sikes and I asked her for a copy of the letter she had written to the lawyers. She told me to get it from my lawyer instead and I asked why. She then told me to leave or she would call Security. I got the hell out of there.

In the meantime, Justice Trussle retired and we were assigned to Justice Sanderson. I told Michelle, my lawyer, that I would not pay Sikes one more dime. Cara was in breach of the court order already, and this Josie Sikes was a waste of my money. Michelle took that to Justice Sanderson. At the meeting with him, my ex's lawyer and Michelle Read, Judge Sanderson seemed to disrespect the opposing lawyer. So, maybe Madame Trussle had filled him in on my case. All he did, though, was state that he needed a week to think about Cara's breach of the court order.

I don't think Sanderson thought about it at all. At the next week's meeting, Justice Sanderson simply asked both lawyers what they recommended as a solution. The Legal Aid lawyer wanted Katherine to undergo an "evaluation" done by yet another psychologist. Apparently Bonny Hoven's earlier evaluation report was now completely dismissed. Judge Sanderson ordered the evaluation against my will. So Katherine was sent to a Greg Pickton and he reported what Katherine told him. She said I had not been in her life; I recently decided to be a "real" parent; I left her at the age of 4; she didn't want to see me, etcetera.

Before Mr. Pickton's evaluation, I had called him and told him to expect Katherine to say such things. I had videos and cards from my daughter showing that I had, indeed, been an involved and positive influence in Katherine's life; always. He got paid $750 to write a letter that ignored all my evidence and took Katherine's statements as accurate. The only real part of his "evaluation" was its mention that she did not want to come to the two or three appointments they had. She wanted to be at school. It must have been horrible for her with all those damned people involved.

I bought six tickets for Katherine's high school graduation, but I was not invited. Two of my sisters went and so did my dad and they all brought presents for her. We went to the ceremony and then sat by ourselves at a table. My sister saw Katherine in the hallway standing by herself. I debated whether I should ask my daughter to dance with me for the special father-daughter dance. I decided not to, as my sisters thought Katherine might freak out. Instead, one of my sisters approached her in the hall and told her we all missed her. Katherine then told my sister she missed us too. My sister asked her if she wanted to see me and she said she did. So I went out to the hall, hugged her, but couldn't talk; I was too choked up. Katherine said "I'm glad you came, Dad". Now I know she does want me, want us, in her life. I felt like my daughter was a hostage, someone I hadn't seen in years until she was set free.

Last year, I sent Katherine a birthday card. She wrote me a thank you card. That's when I sent her, six months ago now, the other birthday gifts and cards that she only just recently picked up at the post office. Regardless, she was appreciative and said she had stopped by my place to thank me in person. I had sent gift cards and so on for years but never even knew if she ever received them. Finally, I stopped sending things to her. A couple weeks ago, though, Katherine and I finally had a nice phone conversation.

I agree with paying child support, and I know I have to pay Katherine's way through university, but I'd like to send it to her directly once she turns 18. I know there are other guys who have managed to get a court order to pay their kids directly at age of majority. I've already written Katherine that I would like to do that. I had an opportunity after when she sent me the thank you card, so I wrote her a reply. I let her know that my grandfather had died, encouraged her to finish high school, and mentioned I could pay her directly once she went to post-secondary. With any luck, Katherine will move out of her mother's home by then.

Even if she takes a year off and then goes back to school, I'm fine with that. But it is very hard for me to send cheques to her mother given the ongoing alienation campaign.

Our relationship still hangs by a thread, damaged forever. There were four years during which I did not see my daughter at all. Those years are lost to us. That day in court in 2008 when Judge Sanderson refused to enforce the court order was a turning point. He enabled Katherine to be held hostage by her mother. Before this happened to me, I felt that guys who weren't allowed to see their kids must have done something bad. They were probably bad fathers. Now I know this can happen to anyone whose ex is an alienator.

RENE

CHAPTER 16

RENE

My daughter's name was legally changed to Laila, without my knowledge, when she was 4 years old. I will never know how her mother achieved that. Her surname, too, was changed from mine. I think it is my ex-mother-in-law's ex-second husband's last name that she uses now. I believe my ex-wife went to Saskatchewan to change our daughter's name. There, at the time, you didn't need the father's permission. I think my ex claimed I was violent and she was afraid of me. "Laila" is now 17 years old and I have not been in contact with her for years.

Sarah, my ex-wife, goes by two first names interchangeably but I'll use this one consistently for clarity. We got married later in life; I was about 42 and she was ten years younger. We lived in Victoria where the economy was weak and we struggled financially. I lived in that city 30 years and it was always tough to make money. We were together about a year before we married, and soon after, had our daughter.

I was working at a residential exterior painting job, which led to repetitive strain injury that affected my health permanently. Sarah was looking after our new baby while I was working so we were both exhausted all the time. She went on unemployment insurance for six months following Sarah's arrival. We lived in a place that was very noisy, motorcycles and dogs mostly, and that paved the way to our marriage breakdown.

I found out she had been having an affair with one of my close friends during our first separation. Had I known about the affair earlier, there's no way I would have reconciled with my wife. I got angry and poured beer on her. In hindsight, that was a really stupid thing to do. Living alone for five or six months had been okay with me and I got used to being sort of single. But when Sarah started to refuse my access to our daughter, I was really broken up about it. That's why I lost it with the beer incident. Laila was only 3 years old then. We broke up but later reunited and bought a mobile home together.

The problem then was our combined income was still too low to pay the bills. We couldn't afford the place. Sarah was from Manitoba where there had been steady work, so she was shocked to find Victoria not lucrative. We split up yet again and that time, I left our home. I was really exhausted in my head so I began to see a counselor. She seemed helpful and encouraged me to communicate positively with Sarah for our daughter's sake. I tried phoning her but there was bickering and then Sarah started screaming at me. Next thing I knew, Sarah's lawyer had a restraining order put on me. I challenged that by representing myself in court and was successful. But I could only get supervised access to Laila because I had poured beer on my ex-wife's head. I was okay with that since I had been stupid. I hoped that with time the Order would be lifted so I was compliant in every way. I really thought things were going to get better. No way.

Soon the phone calls started and wouldn't stop. Sarah kept calling me, saying that she wanted to sell the mobile home and needed to hide from me. She had taken Laila with her. She sounded wild; that's the best word I can think of. I re-read my Court Order to make sure I wasn't doing anything wrong, and I wasn't. Sarah harassed me and then abandoned the mobile home. She went into hiding with our daughter somewhere in the city. I believed I needed to go to the Supreme Court to get specified access to Laila.

At the time, I was a tenant in a house *with a woman who beat up her husband*. He had bruises on various parts of his body, inflicted by her while he tried to block her kicks and punches. I saw this woman repeatedly hit her man, and there was blood on his face. There were quite a few incidents of this abuse. I tried to help calm things down there, but the abuse problems remained. Finally, I had to distance myself from that couple. I told the woman she was crazy and I got the hell out of there. I found out later that the abusive woman had years earlier been dumped by her ex in England and he got sole custody of their child.

I went to my friend's house, as I needed a roof over my head. Shortly after, the abused man phoned me asking if I would help him move out of their house; I did. He went back to his abusive wife a couple times and even went to jail when the cops accused him of being the violent one. The wife got a new boyfriend and he went to jail because of her too. So now she had a real vendetta against me because I helped these men and even testified in court for them about what I witnessed.

In the mean time, I did go to court to get specified access. I unsuccessfully tried to get a mobility clause put into the Order too. I thought, correctly as it turned out, that Sarah would bolt with Laila. Sarah was working with the RCMP at the time, so I'll bet the judge figured she was stable and honest. I also went to our local newspaper about my experience with Family Law and was interviewed by Jody, a columnist there. I got my own lawyer but the judge just granted me increased supervised access. I was also told to write a report about all my visits with Laila. Well, there weren't any because Sarah kept her away from me, despite the Order.

The night after my court appearance, I got a phone call from the police telling me they had arrested my mother-in-law. Apparently, *she had paid $5,000 to undercover cops to have me killed*! The connection is that the abusive woman told my mother-in-law that I planned to murder her whole family. The Times-Colonist newspaper picked up the story. Here it is: "Grandma who Sought Hitman Escapes Jail Time" (Author's note: I was shown and read this article).

I ran back to that judge immediately after my mother-in-law was arrested. The judge granted me a Stay of Arrears since Maintenance Enforcement (FMEP in British Columbia) was threatening to seize my driver's license. My daughter was missing, but FMEP was only interested in getting my money. I was in arrears because I had been laid off and now there was a lot of interest owing as well. I saw that judge in the court washroom after court and I told him my mother-in-law really did try to kill me. He said "Am I ever glad I don't have your problems". Judges don't care; they seem to be nice people but have no investment in doing the right thing. It's just another case, in every case.

So really, the next four years went by without my knowing where my little girl was. I searched everywhere, dealt with lawyers, courts, the RCMP, and the Missing Children's Society of Canada. I knew Sarah's family lived in Winnipeg, so I also tried contacting them. I could not find Laila. The stress and terror of those years is indescribable. I had to go on antidepressants and anti-anxiety medications just to survive.

Throughout those four years I had a job and somehow made it to work every day; I had to. It was really hard. I still have problems; I'll never be free after what I've endured. I am haunted.

I asked at gas stations where her picture was posted as a Missing Child. Finally, one gas attendant told me they had seen Laila only 90 minutes earlier. And then the Missing Children Society phoned and said they had found my daughter. My heart leapt! They were living in Edmonton and of course, both had different names since Sarah had changed them.

The next day I drove from Victoria to Alberta and learned the ropes at the courthouse. I got a process server to deliver the court summons. Back I went to court after applying successfully for Legal Aid. I got a lawyer assigned for Laila but that lawyer knew nothing. I did all the work in Winnipeg, went back to Victoria, and that way finally got a conference arranged with all parties. The judge gave me specified access though Sarah and her lawyer fought hard against that. One lawyer, Zella Harmon, especially made my life hell. She painted me in court as if I was the abuser and made up shit in court such as my throwing frying pans and such. Over the next few years, there would be at least five psychologists involved in our case following that court decision. There were also several supervisors designated for whenever I had parenting time with Laila.

My truck was my home in those days. I had no money and was trying to pay lawyers and Maintenance. All this was 11 years ago now; in 2001. Laila was born in 1995. So my daughter was six or seven by the time I was reunited with her. That first meeting was in a psychologist, Dr. Canna's, office. I was in the waiting room filled with trepidation about who would walk through the door. In came a little girl, a normal-looking kid and my eyes just popped. I had not laid eyes on her in six years and here was Laila, in front of me… finally. She was a bit shy, but we were able to chat and she became more comfortable with me, even that first day. Thankfully, Sarah was kept in another room, so Laila was not directly affected by her mother's control.

That first appointment to reunite Laila with me was a happy one. I have photos of it and we were clearly getting along well already. There were about seven more weekly follow-up visits at Dr. Canna's office. The first three were positive; Laila seemed okay and she began to call me "Dad." I was able to let go of some of my anger and anxiety about the past and the people who had enabled the alienation. I was so exhausted; I needed to rise above the past. The fourth visit was very different. All of a sudden, I saw a big change in Laila. She entered the room, turned her back and would not talk to me.

From that day forward, Laila was increasingly negative and distant from me. She would say "none of your business" if I so much as asked her what she would like to do. One time when Laila was maybe 11, she hit me with a book. Then I pushed her away so she began her "little girl cry" and ran to her room upstairs. My ex immediately ran to her (I still had only supervised visits), called the police, but fortunately my supervisor cleared me of the accusations.

Recently, I found out that a year after Laila turned her back on me, after six years of not seeing her, that woman who hated my guts for testifying against her was at the house with my ex. Sarah is very gullible and when that woman started to befriend her, Sarah must have encouraged the friendship. It was over Christmas and that was when I re-met Laila the first time. That woman was drunk for the entire week at Sarah's place. She could manipulate my ex to get near me for the sole purpose of attacking me. Sarah still doesn't see the manipulation of that woman and instead, picked up her traits and assaulted me in any way possible. So now I had two women after me all the time. *Both of them must want me dead.*

In the case of my ex, Sarah wants me dead because I am male and a former boyfriend of hers had beaten her up. She even said that if she had trouble with another man, she would "grind him into the ground". That crazy other woman taught her how to hurt me; *really* hurt me. Finally, I had so much stress I could not work properly and was fired twice for being distracted on the job. Even now I have a sense of forgetfulness that is certainly not normal. At my current job, I've been written up about it since I sometimes forget to do important things. I'm a maintenance man so memory-loss is very problematic. I don't blame my boss; I am a safety hazard. He just tells me to work on separating my life stress from my work responsibilities, and I am trying very hard to do that.

I am a musician. There are pictures over there (Author's note: he showed me some of them) of me playing my fiddle. My family is largely a group of fiddlers, but I also play guitar. I used to make my living playing the bass guitar, but it was a lifestyle that involved too much drinking. I quit and started a regular job and played in bands only on weekends. That 12-string guitar has been my way to survive all these years without my daughter. Ten years of practise and people say they've never seen anyone play that instrument so well. I hope I can audition for a Canadian talent television show. That would help me a lot.

After many years, I had to stop wishing to see Laila. It was killing me. My distraction of music kept me going, but I was dangerously depressed. Not only was I rarely seeing Laila since our "reunification" at the psychologist's office, she had turned mean and it was *so* painful. Each visit also cost me $200 that I could not afford. I paid for five visits up front, but then I said I was done; enough of the charade that I was her dad. On my final visit with

Laila, I lasted five minutes and then I jumped up and told the psychologist I couldn't do it anymore.

I had also been in contact with a couple of researchers, like you, who said they would help. One was James Holey, a sociologist and he was a good resource. He's retired now, but I still call him sometimes, just to talk. That guy is a saint! Everyone involved with my case, James included, knew and said that Sarah was coaching Laila to hate and abuse me. My daughter once called me "a diseased male"; wonder where she learned that term?

At work one day three years ago I had a mini-stroke. I suddenly lost the ability to speak. I couldn't think through what I wanted to say. The words didn't come. My boss was talking about a microwave oven, but I couldn't process his sentences. I was in a sort of spell. Weirdly enough, it passed as quickly as it came on and my boss noted that I had had a mini-stroke. I went for a lot of medical tests, but since they were after the event, they all came up negative.

I had not been able to memorize much, if at all, for the last 8 years. I believe it was due to my overwhelming stress-level, most recently ramped up by Sarah's demand that I pay her $40,000. I couldn't memorize the songs I loved to play. But after my stroke, all of a sudden I could remember lyrics again. Now I memorize songs every week. I think I am somewhat bipolar now; if I am not playing and memorizing, I sink into a depression episode. Maybe I have a weak spot in my brain now that I will always have to be aware and protective of.

I'm not kidding that I have learned to play "I Will Survive", "Staying Alive" and "Turn Me Loose" because of what's happened in my life. I am too exhausted to fight anymore. I've spent so much time and money in courts. I have no idea if Laila is still in school. I need to find out if and when she graduates for the basic reason that I can stop paying Child Support. I won't be asked to go to her graduation, that's for sure.

Since she was five years old, Laila has been on anti-depressants. She lives in a house I'm pretty sure her mother bought; that showed up in the court records. Sarah is working full-time and I saw she is driving a new car. I doubt Laila will move out; her mother will always enable her and likely, she'll inherit that house one day. Sarah may be an attentive parent, but she has made a career of portraying me as a degenerate.

I am 60 years old now. I have to have a life. I have a lot of bitterness that I want to get rid of. My daughter is gone. She is 17 now and lives two blocks away. I've seen her from a distance, once last year at Safeway with her mother, but she has never tried to contact me since I gave up those psychologist's office visits. At Safeway, I said "Hi Laila," but when she saw me she immediately skipped away, calling Sarah over to look at something. I have not seen her anywhere since.

I need to tell you that *one of my concerns is the idea of the government using my (and other targeted parents') experiences as an industry for the educated.* How do I know that any good will come of my telling you my raw story? I am so tired of nobody helping any of us. It's criminal.

CARLA

CHAPTER 17

CARLA

I am the mother of seven children; four boys aged 23, 21, 20 and 17, and three girls now 16, 14 and 12. In all, I used two lawyers and spent about $10,000. For the vast majority of my case, I self-represented.

I had all seven of my children within 11 years. My story really starts when I was living in Toronto, doing well in my job there, but became unintentionally pregnant with my oldest son, Jason. I was 23 at the time and decided to keep my baby. Jason, himself, is now 23 years old. That relationship ended amicably with my deciding to return to Alberta as a single mother. Jason's father has never been difficult in terms of our shared parenting.

Shortly after I moved, I was reintroduced through some friends to a man, Gerry, whom I had met years before. I agreed to go on a date with him. He proposed marriage to me on that first date. Now I kick myself remembering that and how it should have been a red flag. A couple months of dating and there were red flags everywhere. He was living in northern Alberta. Knowing what I know now, Gerry targeted me from the start. I was vulnerable with a 3-month-old baby and had little money or family supports. He wanted a wife to bolster his public image, and he seemed to have everything I needed in a husband and father for Jason.

Eight months after we started dating, we were married. Even before the wedding, Gerry was controlling. He had adoption papers drawn up so that Jason's father was prohibited from any contact with him. Jason's father had been in the picture earlier but still lived in Toronto. Gerry made sure he was now permanently removed from Jason's life.

I went along with whatever Gerry suggested. He was charismatic, wealthy and seemingly together in all respects. On our honeymoon I got pregnant and soon after Gerry moved us to Fort McMurray. He was then practicing as a dentist and also was super-involved with his church. I didn't know anything about that church and it all looked like "Little House on the Prairie", frozen in time and very nice. Within three months of moving there, however, Gerry made me wear a head covering, take out my earrings and other jewelry and submit to wearing only modest dresses. I realized that the church community believed and practiced women's absolute submission and obedience to their husbands. It was a full-blown cult.

The cult, I'll call it the Assimilation, was not affiliated with any other religious organization. Gerry was the leader. I became alienated from all my friends and family as Gerry controlled every aspect of my life. He knew mind-control techniques and used them to convince me this was the right thing to do. Eventually, Gerry also used these same techniques to program my children to hate me. He incorporated God and the Bible, good and evil, black and white thinking in every communication and deed.

He convinced me that my family members were evil and agents of Satan. They were a threat to my children's well being because they are Catholic which, according to Gerry, is not even Christian. My family would ruin my children who could otherwise learn the ways of the Assimilation and become world leaders. Gerry said my children had "the only light" but my family wanted to extinguish it.

I suppose our relationship was always rocky because I could not totally submit to my husband. I was, and am, a naturally curious person who loves learning. I always sought to understand people and phenomena, but here was someone who wanted to completely control my every move. I think at one point I actually made a conscious decision to "let go of my mind". I lost my identity and just gave up in order to avoid going crazy.

Cults can attract and recruit very intelligent but idealistic people. These sorts of people are targeted to do the work of the cult and expand its membership. Gerry and I kept getting pregnant and I had more babies over the next several years. After my second baby was born, I asked my doctor for birth-control pills. When I brought them home and showed Gerry, thinking this was a good idea to stop our family growing so fast, he freaked out. He told me that the doctor was trying to control God's plan for me. He reminded me that I was to submit my body to him and to God at all times.

The Bible teaching he frequently used was about Leah's women, who learned to be helping, obedient slaves to their husbands. Gerry valued me less than he did our children, and he gave them a sense of entitlement over me. This worldview fractured the bond between my children and me, since I was seen as an instrument of both God and my husband, not as a unique and separate person. I now run a support group for ex-members of cults, people raised and recruited into extremist religious sects, such as the Jehovah's Witnesses, whose victims are similarly kept from bonding properly with their mothers. It was also difficult for me to bond with my children, as I had to "let them go to Jesus" all the time. My influence was minimal and unimportant.

My mother tried to investigate the Assimilation, but the harder she tried to convince me it was dangerous, the harder I clung to the cult and to Gerry. A couple times we went into Edmonton to shop and my husband allowed me to meet with my mother and sisters in the mall. Of course, he would prime me beforehand with comments like these: "You know your family is going to try to pull you away from God and our church family. Ignore them and stay true to us". One time my family together said to me "We love you, we care about you, and we are really concerned about you. We don't like Gerry". I jumped up in the restaurant where we were having lunch and I ran to the bathroom, crying. I couldn't stop crying and didn't want to come out. Finally, I did, but coldly told them I needed to go "home" which meant back to the cult.

I was alienated from my real family first; by Gerry. The kids were just babies then and I was straddling the normal world *and* the cult. The techniques used to alienate create opposing thoughts and therefore, inner conflict. It's not so much that the alienated person doesn't care about his or her other family members, it's that you have a cognitive distance from them while your heart still loves them. Psychologically then, it was paramount that I stay away from my normal family members because what they would say to me (i.e., the truth!) caused a war in my head. Years later, a psychologist told me that kids between about 12 and 14 years old cannot handle two opposing views. They will usually choose one parent or view over the other one in order to reduce their stress.

After I had my first two babies, I intentionally lost all contact with my family outside the cult for 12 whole years. At home with Gerry, we had no media influences, no television, radio or computers and we even moved out to an acreage far from any neighbours. That isolation was only interrupted by visits from other women who were also members of the Assimilation. We only talked about banal stuff; we were taught not to even talk to our husbands unless they asked us to.

Finally, I came to realize that I was trapped. There was no way out and I had to relinquish myself entirely to motherhood. I began to homeschool my children and tried to engage them with topics outside the cult. I had them do chore charts and learn responsibility for helping around the house. We were in church four days a week, but I started noticing that Gerry's preaching indicated abnormal cognitive processes. Each week home-school parents were supposed to attend a meeting with each other to discuss the curriculum, but Gerry would often fall asleep there. I thought perhaps he was hard of hearing, but he just sloughed it off and said I was better in those meetings than he was.

When my second son, Tom, started schooling, our home-school supervisor recommended we take him for testing as he appeared to have ADD (Attention Deficit Disorder). Well, Tom had ADHD and certainly exhibited hyperactivity. I had thought he was a genius and had not taken his quirky, energetic behaviour seriously. The psychiatrist said Tom had likely inherited at least the predisposition for ADHD from one of his parents. After the diagnosis, Gerry began to make a big joke of Tom's ADHD and announced it to the whole congregation at church.

I noticed then that Gerry was self-medicating with a bunch of pills he got from his dental practice. They included caffeine, stimulants, Percocet, and other pain meds. Gerry also had behaviours consistent with OCD (Obsessive-Compulsive Disorder). He had a routine based on every 15 minutes of each day, which he would post on the wall for all to see. I was his puppet; *his mind became mine*. The babies kept coming, so I kind of pushed my psychological pain aside.

During my baby-making years, I had three miscarriages: one was twins and the other two were single fetuses. Had I delivered them, I would now have 12 children. Gerry never helped at home but my kids did, as they were old enough to. I trained them to be responsible. They worked hard and eventually we raised chickens and goats and had a big organic garden. I also learned to make soap and yogurt from an Encyclopedia of Country Living I was allowed to own. I might have pursued those goals even if I hadn't been controlled by a cult, but as it happened, my activities kept me sane. Gerry was very abusive to the kids. He physically disciplined them and didn't know when to stop. Sometimes he would whip them with a tree branch and I tried to intervene a few times. When I did so, pleading with him to stop hitting, he would openly chastise and belittle me.

When Tom was seven years old, Gerry told him in anger, "You are the most manipulative, wicked boy that ever lived" and I remember thinking, "He's just a child!" My husband lacked compassion and did not seem to love his children. Even when I was in childbirth, he would show me no sympathy nor support in any way. I believed I was weak. Once, Jason broke his arm and Gerry told him, "Stop your whining and get moving". Jason was seven at the time; still shaken from his traumatic skating accident.

There was no one I could tell my doubts to and everyone in the cult revered Gerry as the *godliest of men*. He would "save" them and lead them to "the only light". I still believed that God would change my husband for the better. Though he told me he didn't even like the people in his church, he sure portrayed himself as a loving servant of God and the perfect husband and father.

Each church service, we all sat in a pew, the girls in matching dresses and the boys with matching ties, all of which I had made. We each had a Bible open on our laps. That's what religion is anyway, a façade, so it wasn't that weird for me to behave that way in church. After all, my husband was the role model for everyone.

I wanted my kids to learn resiliency after all they endured. I made sure we had animals and they looked after them well. My children needed to understand responsibility, empathy, compassion and to hold on to what was left of their hearts. We helped people less fortunate and we brought in babysitters sometimes so my girls, especially, would keep their hearts intact. I was so worried my kids would grow up to be heartless.

By the time I had seven kids under the age of 13 things in the cult started to crater and some members left for good. That's when I started to really notice Gerry's narcissism and borderline personality traits, though I didn't know those terms yet. Gerry was reacting badly when members of the Assimilation would so much as buy a car without getting Gerry's permission. He would tell all the other members about this person and how wicked his or her behaviour was. His intent was to turn everyone else against that poor victim. He would even excommunicate such people because they undermined his authority. I witnessed this behaviour for years. If a person made Gerry mad, for any reason, that person became the next target. Often, the targeted member would leave before Gerry ran him or her out of the cult. It was very sick, all of it.

When other parents came to Gerry for advice about their children, Gerry presented himself as an expert. Though our kids were still small, he would advise parents on how to manage their teenagers' behaviour. He especially liked to espouse his pretend expertise when teenagers were rebelling against the cult's extreme legalism. In reality, of course, those teenagers had every right to rebel against Gerry's crazy doctrine. They would run away at 16, use drugs, and try to fight against the shackles they lived in. In response, Gerry told their parents to "Kick them out and never let them come back".

I started to look for passages in the Bible about loving one another and I challenged Gerry on some of his rhetoric. I asked him if God would want parents to cast out their children. He was so angry and then wouldn't talk to me. In one instance, I saw him alienate one spouse from the other and they separated for six years as a result. I did talk to them and told them I thought Gerry was crazy. They reunited, had two more children, and have been living happily away from the Assimilation ever since.

By 2004, I started to sneak away to an internet café, so I could research this cult of control. I began to understand that my husband was incapable of loving anyone and in fact he hated everyone. Gerry would mock me, roll his eyes, and tell the kids I was evil. I tried to become an "outside observer" and to watch as if I was in an out-of-body experience. To live in it was just too emotionally painful. When he would return from work, the kids would run to him and would ignore me. They no longer kissed nor hugged me. The girls were still pretty young, so weren't as convinced I was evil. When I finally got away, my youngest girl was eight.

He found our phone bills and phoned every person I had called. That's how he found out I had phoned women's shelters and abuse hotlines. He told the staff who answered his calls that they had no permission to talk to his wife. He also had our kids spy on me, especially the two oldest boys. Both of them turned 100% against me while we were all still living under the same roof. Gerry cut off the phone line and all sources of money, so that I was helpless. It took me four years to get out of the Assimilation, but the last two weeks there involved the police.

One evening in 2004, the RCMP were looking for a missing person and randomly showed up at our house. One officer told me to let her know if I saw anyone hiding in the bushes or whatever and she gave me her card. Subsequently, I phoned her to tell her my story. That officer wanted me to come to the police station to write a statement. The problem was that I was not allowed to leave my house. That officer told me she believed me. I found the courage to go anyway and I did write that statement. The officers on duty read it and warned that if Gerry found me at the police station or found out I was trying to escape he would likely kill the children and/or me. He said Gerry sounded "textbook" and they needed to get me away from him immediately.

So it was the RCMP that contacted a lawyer who got me into Special Chambers. There, I was granted an "ex parte" restraining order valid for three weeks. Gerry knew nothing about all this. The court gave me sole custody of all seven children, full possession of our home, the vehicle, and my husband was made to pay me $2,000. The money was to help me get settled, as I had no access to family funds. I used it to flee with the kids to some friends I still had in Calgary. The police supervised us while I hurriedly packed up some of our things and our dog and cat. It was so traumatic on all of us. We showed up at my mother's house with a few groceries. I was a battered, terrified woman with seven children in tow. My mom had lost all those years when we were alienated from her too. She didn't know my kids, nor they her. My mother is the most loving person who would do anything for anybody, yet Gerry convinced my children that their grandmother was evil. It makes me so sad to think of all my kids have missed in their short lives; their ability to bond with people, to trust people, and form relationships has not developed as it should have.

Gerry got his own lawyer quickly and then requested that I return to the family house and he would move out. I was to be excommunicated from the "church" but Gerry said he would let me parent the kids there. I refused, as there was no way I could do it and be safe. I had a panic attack at the thought. And then Gerry suggested we "share the house". He said I would have my own room with a lock on the door and I'd parent our children through the week. Then, on weekends, I was supposed to go live in a townhouse while he parented on his own. I would still be doing all the work. Are you kidding me? That's the proposal Gerry's lawyer brought into court.

The two lawyers then negotiated a compromise. I would relocate to Edmonton from Calgary and Gerry and I would share custody. I agreed. My three girls would go to their dad's twice a month. Jason, my eldest, immediately was taken back full-time into his dad's clutches. He did not come to my place at all. Tom followed his brother's lead two months later. When the kids were at my house, Gerry was phoning them constantly. Once I was grocery shopping and my mom was staying with the kids while I was out. During that 45-minute absence, Gerry called the police, telling them I had abandoned my children. Then he called me, asking if I wanted him to remove the kids before the police came and took them. My ex did everything in those early months to convince the children I was unsafe as a parent. He told Jason I was going to invite pedophiles into my home and made up other bizarre tales too.

I contacted Dr. Randy Rand, who is one of the most knowledgeable experts in this field and he told me that as long as my kids still had contact with their father, his influence would prevent their healing from the alienation Gerry had caused. I did not want to hear that but it has been true… completely. Dr. Rand also worked with Dr. Richard Warshak in California. I said to those two men, "I need you guys to quickly create a family intervention model". They did and it is known as the "Family Bridges" program.

My goal was to re-establish some normalcy in my children's lives. I had lost two of my kids but still had four at home with me most of the time. I hoped they could become critical thinkers and find some joy in life. Love was not modelled in our house. I needed to regain my self-worth. On weekends when the kids went to their father's, I attended seminars, did five years of training in the "Thrive Model", a recovery program that subsequently has changed my life for the better. I also went back to school for a Masters in Counseling degree.

I had been granted a Court Order which demanded the boys spend some time with their mother. The court was shocked that they were so completely alienated from me. My lawyer, Michelle

Reft, instructed me to show the boys the Order with the judge's signature. Jason, who was 14, and Tom, who was 12, then showed up at my door one day after having zero contact with me for eight years. They didn't want to come in and started quoting obscure Bible verses. Jason read the Order, looked at me, and said in a cold voice, "This Court Order is signed by a woman. It's not even worth the paper it's written on. We don't have to pay attention to that".

Michelle, my Edmonton lawyer, then got a counselor in Calgary involved, Dr. Lawrence Fang. Ms. Reft had previously worked with pathological cases and she specializes in high-conflict divorce. She knew she needed to be ten steps ahead of Gerry in his warped thinking. So Michelle convinced Gerry that Dr. Fang would help him and thereby manipulated my con-artist ex into agreeing to see this counselor.

We started going to Dr. Fang, all of us, for the next year and a half. Some appointments were for just me, or just Gerry, or with the boys individually or with each of us separately. We would drive to Calgary, the boys fighting the entire way. They saw me as *the devil*. Police even came to my house a few times when the boys were out of control. Dr. Fang witnessed all this mess and documented everything. He is an expert witness in court, so I waited anxiously for his recommendation about what was best for these children.

I waited so long for Lawrence Fang's final report. By the end of those 18 months, the boys would still not talk to me. Even though Jason and Tom were instructed to spend some weekends with me, they only did so for a couple months. After then, they told me they were old enough to make their own decisions and they stopped visiting me altogether. Gerry made sure the boys always "had other plans" on weekends when they were scheduled to be with me. He also had them each write an affidavit about why they did not want to see me.

Though Jason and Tom had always been home-schooled, Gerry now put them in a Christian, and then a public, school so he could claim they were "busy with activities" there. I enrolled my younger two sons in a public school and kept the girls home-schooled for one more year while they adjusted to their new environment. Then they entered the public system.

During the time we were all awaiting Fang's report, I noticed my younger boys, Zane and Norm, beginning to act more and more like their older brothers. They were rebelling, refusing to listen to me, and doing whatever they wanted in my house. I would try to provide boundaries but they would laugh and say they didn't have to listen to me. They were 13 and 11 years old then.

I lined up some top psychologists and parental alienation experts and read everything on the subject that I could find. I wanted to be ready to deprogram and reunify with my boys when Dr. Fang's report was released. I gave Dr. Fang the phone numbers of Drs. Rand and Warshak. I wanted him to agree to their attending the Family Bridges program and I needed his permission. Fang told me I had developed my parenting plan like a university paper. I noted the abuse, cult leadership, alienation and everything I lived through. I believed that Dr. Fang could direct our family in a productive way, toward healing. Gerry, all this time, was indeed paying Child Support as per the federal guidelines. That made him look cooperative and he knew it.

Finally, Michelle phoned me to say that things were going to go a bit differently than I had hoped. Where was the report Dr. Fang was supposed to have done? Apparently, my lawyer Michelle, Gerry's lawyer Terry Hopper, and Lawrence Fang had had a secret meeting at either the Calgary, Edmonton, or Fort McMurray airport. Nothing from that meeting was written down or recorded so it was just a verbal deal. Lawrence told the others that Gerry was narcissistic so would never benefit from counseling so it was pointless to request a judge to Order that. He recommended Gerry be asked to his face whether he badmouthed the mother (me). I did ask Gerry and he said that he did.

We didn't even have to investigate parental alienation; Gerry admitted he was trying to destroy my children's relationship with me. His rationale was that the alienation was his "responsibility as a man of God. I have to warn my children about evil".

In summary, Dr. Fang's so-called report after 18 months stated that there was no help available through counselling. He said that if I could take the two eldest boys to him and cut off access to their father, "someone" would kill himself, kill someone else, or otherwise do a lot of permanent damage. Lawrence saw that my boys were fragile, unstable, so he recommended no change in residency. The boys would remain with their father in the cult.

Michelle told me I had lost my fight for Jason and Tom and I needed to let them go. She and I both cried. We all had to pretend that Gerry was the winner, so that he would not punish the other 5 kids for their relationship with me. I had to stroke Gerry's ego to keep him from flying off the handle and to keep him working and paying support.

I feel I had to sacrifice my sons to protect the girls. I was to hand over Zane and Norm so that I could keep my three daughters. I refused to give up the younger two at first, but Dr. Fang assured me that it was already too late for them. He saw that they were completely alienated from me in their heads. Maybe I had denied that because I love them, even when Zane and Norm stole things from me, spied on my computer and sent my files to their dad.

Dr. Rand had seen a case in which an 11 year old boy was so turned against his father that he shot him dead from the backseat of his dad's car while he and his sister were on their way to dad's house. He works with cases involving children trained to kill in terrorist camps. If you can learn to hate your mother who gave birth to you, who loves you unconditionally, then you are capable of anything. Such children lack a conscience. But some can still feel love, they can love their animals, but they have no trust in other humans outside their psychological prison.

Each time my kids went to stay with their dad, they came back angrier with me. One by one Gerry reclaimed his children and they stopped coming back to me. When my youngest boy, Norm, came home after spending much of the summer with Gerry, he told me that when he finished Grade 9 he wanted to go live with his dad. I was in the middle of washing dishes and completely exhausted. I turned to him and I said, "If you want to leave here, perhaps you should just go now". Maybe he had thought I would beg him to stay, but I was done with that behaviour. Norm replied that he didn't feel like leaving yet. So the next day we together went to see Kathy Lytton, his lawyer and she drew up the Access Orders. I told her that I thought Norm would be better off moving now at the start of Grade 9, instead of at the end of the school year. That way he'd have time to meet new friends before high school. By this point in our relationship, Norm had been stealing from me, was usually disrespectful and a psychologist, Ms. Channer, had told me she was concerned he might be a sociopath.

Norm left our house and immediately the girls and I were relieved and felt safer than we had in years. My three daughters had a couple years of peace after that. We could listen to music, dance, have fun and not be constantly chastised for our *just being present*. I had a girlfriend come and live in our basement, which helped me a lot financially. That was back in 2008.

In those two years, I heard nothing from my boys… nothing at all. The girls were still going back and forth to Gerry's, so I'd send along birthday and Christmas presents and cards, but there was never any response. My phone calls and texts were ignored. The girls did not talk about life with their dad and brothers. I didn't ask, as I wanted them to be children without the added stress between their parents. Over those two years, I tried my best to show my daughters that life is good, it's not about dodging your responsibilities and your fears, it is about being intentional and creative. They took dance and they loved competing in it. They were very athletic and good at everything they tried. I saw their confidence improving: they were popular at school, and they smiled and laughed more frequently. At least, they did until Jason came back.

At Thanksgiving, two years ago (2010), my 20-year-old son Jason called me and said Gerry had kicked him out of the house. He had been living mostly on his own working as a contractor. A couple times he came to Edmonton to party with his friends and he would call to ask if he could come and visit his sisters. We met a couple times and I brought the girls along. It seemed to go well and he could see the love I still had for him. But then on Thanksgiving he showed up at my house during a dinner party I was having. I invited him in, but he declined. I knew it was because he had been taught that you should not enter the house of a "sinner". Here he had been partying with his friends, but apparently *that* was not sinning. He could not, however, enter the home of his mom and sisters.

We went for a walk together instead. He told me all the things his father had taught him to believe about me. He had been so thoroughly brainwashed and alienated from me for so long. I made sure to calmly respond which I had learned to do through my own inner work. I told Jason the truth and I told him his dad had threatened that if I ever left him, he was going to tell you kids that I "killed the babies" (referring to my miscarriages). He said he was shocked and that he needed to think about everything he had been told by Gerry. Jason looked at me and said, "Mom, if what you say is true, do you know how huge this is?" He said that after I left his dad, Gerry spewed venomous words about me around the church. I have even had people from the church show up at my door, saying "you seem nice," and "oh my gosh, you are not evil after all." Jason had a girlfriend at the time when he came to see me. I found out later she was the catalyst who encouraged his reuniting with me.

Following my conversation with Jason that day, he went back to his own place but met up with his dad at a Tim Horton's soon after. Apparently, he told Gerry he had come to see me and that he was shocked that his own father was a liar. Gerry said to Jason, "You need to get your Bible out, you need to pray, you need to get with God". In response, Jason said "F--- your Bible! You say you are my dad, but you don't come to my hockey games. You don't really care about me, and I don't think you actually care about anybody". I guess they had a huge argument right there and then. Gerry was telling Jason to keep his voice down, looking around to see if anyone he knew was in the coffee shop. Finally, Gerry grabbed Jason and pushed him outside to get away from the staring people inside. Jason yelled that he didn't ever want to see Gerry again.

When he got home, my son called me while I was driving in my truck with the three girls. Poor guy was sobbing his heart out, so I put him on speaker and we told him we loved him.

Jason said his dad was like the anti-Christ and that he *was* the person he warned his own congregation about. For the next two months or so, Jason called me frequently, sometimes in the middle of the night, asking about different events that he remembered and wondering how he had been duped by his father. Everything Gerry had dumped on Jason was beginning to unravel. Jason was seeing the truth. Those phone conversations were sometimes a couple hours long, one was six hours, and I really felt Jason was having a breakdown of sorts. He lost his job because he was rambling on at work about his warped life in the cult, and they basically thought he must be inventing it all.

I encouraged my son to come back and live with us. I said he could have the whole basement and we would help him get back on track. Then I phoned Dr. Hindmarch and got Jason in as a new client. He was a helpful therapist and gave Jason the book "Man's Search for Meaning". I know he read it thoroughly and since has bought it as a gift for some of his friends. It is a powerful book because it was written by Viktor Frankl, a psychiatrist and neurologist who was imprisoned in and survived one of the Nazi death camps. Jason was still like a 13-year-old in the emotional sense, but a six-foot-two teenager; he had been *frozen in time* since I left his father. He was really struggling with his past, but he was trying so hard.

The girls and I had lived in peace for two years and now we had their troubled brother living with us. I saw that the girls and he were connected, cared about each other, but I also began to see them pulling away from my son. I didn't realize it at the time, but Gerry was working our daughters toward disowning their brother. He planted the seeds of doubt in the girls' minds, telling them Jason was a drug addict, that he was not "one of us". My daughter's dad told them to let Jason go and that he would never come back. Over time, I noticed when Jason would come home my girls would retreat to their rooms and shut their doors. My girls turned on their brother. Gerry was unsuccessful converting me to his sick ideology, but he kept trying to totally control the minds of my children.

The weird thing is this: Jason is so big-hearted and loving that he didn't notice his sisters' rejecting him. But at dinner sometimes, the girls would tell me that Jason was too messed up and I needed to have him move out. I reminded them about compassion but eventually, my three daughters who were thirteen, eleven and nine then, disowned their brother. The next event that slammed Jason was when Gerry tried to sue him for the truck the two of them had co-signed to purchase. Jason would receive legal letters, which really increased his and my stress. I felt almost as if I was back living under the control of my ex-husband and it was scary for us both. I think Gerry hated the fact that Jason had returned to me, so he made him pay dearly for that.

His father's rejection tormented Jason. People who knew me would comment on how great my son was doing and how wonderful it was that he had broken away from the cult. I, however, saw the damage Gerry had caused. I saw Jason's meltdowns, how he couldn't get out of bed for three days, was becoming dissociative, and exhibited extreme PTSD (Post-Traumatic Stress Disorder) symptomology. Dr. Hindmarch did his best, but Jason stopped going to see him. He found the therapy just too painful. On Father's Day, he still often disappears and goes on a multi-day partying binge with his friends. Fortunately, he hasn't turned suicidal but just distracts himself as much as he can.

Now Jason lives with his girlfriend, since he moved out of my house. It's not going well and she's not a great influence on him. He seems to be doing okay though. I spent yesterday with him, which is always precious time together. I have suggested he come back and live in my basement. He knows he needs to dump his girlfriend, and I hope that happens soon. He's 23 now.

My other three boys are still living in their father's home. I have heard nothing from them in eight years. Tom is now almost 22. The last scheduled visit with him involved my driving up to get him in Fort McMurray. My girls came with me. 14-year-old Tom got in the car and said to me, in front of his sisters, "Fuck off! You are going to hell. You are such a bitch, why don't you just kill yourself? We would all be better off because you are wrecking our family".

My third son, Zane, was another interesting case. The kids' lawyer, Kathy Lytton, arranged to have him finish high school in Edmonton, so he would be away from his dad's influence more of the time. It was a bit of an experiment for a year and it didn't work. This decision was out of Gerry's hands because the kids were quite close to Kathy and would text and phone her. But after Zane spent most of the summer with his dad as per the Access Order, he never came back home to Edmonton. Kathy was furious but hamstrung. Zane never came back and now at 20, works in a fishing village somewhere. He supposedly plans to go to school to become a plumber. Tom, I've heard, is a process operator at an oil refinery here in Alberta. My youngest boy, Norm, is graduating high school this year. He is 17, a year older than my eldest daughter, Sybil.

Sybil is starting Grade 10 in Fort McMurray, but all her earlier life has been here in Edmonton. She came for a visit last weekend, stayed with her best friend's family two nights and the last night with me. When I picked her up from her friend's house, everyone there was crying; the mom, her friend, some other visiting friends, and her boyfriend. The mom took me aside and asked why Sybil had to go back up north. I told her how Sybil said she wanted to go north so as to keep peace with her father. That mom suggested that I allow Sybil to live with her friend's family during the week and then she could live with me on weekends. This could actually work because just two weeks before our court date, Kathy Lytton called Gerry, whom she has never met face to face, and asked about permitting Sybil to stay in Edmonton. You know what he said? He would trade Sybil for Sheila (my youngest who is 12 years old); in other words, Sybil could stay as long as I no longer saw Sheila.

My children have been pawns most of their lives. Gerry even said to his congregation that "people are pawns in a chess game, it is all about strategy'. I knew by now about pathological parenting, about psychopaths, so I had to keep ten steps ahead of Gerry's every move. It never ended.

I did ask Sybil if she would like to stay with her friend's family during the week and come to my place on weekends. She hesitated but then said "No, it's okay mom, I'll go back". The poor kid was under so much pressure. My middle daughter, Thea, who is 14, seemed like she had a shot at weathering the alienation and pressure to move north to dad's. But she left too. Kathy Lytton told me one time that Thea had the most promise of any of my girls and it would be the end of Kathy's career if Thea left me. Well, she did; with her sisters when none of them returned after the visit with Gerry. Today, they all have phones, so at least I can text and remind them I love and miss them.

I was very close to my youngest daughter, Sheila, but that got used against me too. Gerry told her sisters that I preferred Sheila, that I wasn't spanking her when she needed it. A few months after Jason moved in with us, Sheila began to really fly off the rails. She would even throw things at me, shouting, "I hate you, I hate you, I hate you!" I had been dating a wonderful man for a couple years by then and of course, Gerry knew because the girls would tell him. Sheila was anxious to meet Steve, my boyfriend's, daughter who was coming from Eastern Europe. They had been Skyping via a translator and were excited to meet in person. I flew to Europe with Steve and we brought her back with us. But Sheila had stayed with Gerry for a week while I was away and now, she came to the door a changed person. My daughter stared at her new "friend" as if she had two heads, wouldn't talk to her or Steve, and then ran out the door to get away from us. Those incidents kept getting more frequent and more intense, but I documented everything for Ms. Lytton.

Finally, I drew up a "contract" between my girls and me to be respectful to each other. I did that because Sheila had called me such names as "a hot bitch" and was kicking me. Sheila and I signed that contract and I gave a copy to Kathy Lytton. That just ramped up Sheila's aggression and I was soon covered in bruises. The last straw was her punching me in the stomach so hard that I got the wind knocked out of me. At that, I drove the other girls to school and Sheila and I directly to see Kathy. I asked Sheila to let Ms. Lytton know what had happened at home. After a 20-minute private conversation between Sheila and her lawyer, Ms. Lytton, Kathy called me in and reported that she was concerned that Sheila had become a ditto of her father.

That's when the court date was set. Ms. Lytton wanted Sheila in anger-management and to be sent to a school in another province where she would be away from the influence of her father. Sheila had told Ms. Lytton she wanted to stay with her father and hated her mother. I wrote up a thorough 72-point A to Z affidavit starting from the restraining order through every child getting picked up by Gerry and disappearing from my life. I never used the word "alienation". First, there was a teleconference in early June this year with Kathy Lytton and me in her office, Gerry's lawyer, and Justice Rose. Kathy, as the children's lawyer, explained her concerns. She stated how our children were spending more and more time with their father and less and less with me. They were becoming hostile and withdrawn as a result. Kathy proposed my idea to get a psychological evaluation done on all three girls. Then she asked Justice Rose for a 10-minute break and went in another room. I found out after that she had talked with Gerry's lawyer in private and they negotiated a deal.

The two lawyers made a deal and then brought the judge back on the line in Kathy's office. They announced the girls were to be evaluated as per my request. Kathy was working for the girls, but she also cared about me. She was worried about the kids with me because they had become abusive but she also knew they were increasingly damaged while under the influence of their father. Justice Rose ordered that the girls' evaluations be done and reported on in the next six weeks, before August 15th. She recommended Dr. Lynda Torns.

Lynda Torns conducted separate, three-hour interviews with each of my girls and subsequently reported that they all wanted to live with dad. She also reported that Sybil had told her I said her dad raped her, and that no one liked me. When Sybil came to Edmonton that weekend to visit her friends and me, I asked her about those statements. She admitted that she was repeating the words of her father and knew perfectly well that I was well liked, had many good friends, and was/am a loving person. Ms. Torns wrote all that stuff without any background on our family history. She did, however, note that the girls all showed "significant anxiety", coping mechanisms, and Thea, particularly, was emotionally "flat". Following our court appearance, Ms. Torns hugged me and apologized for the "bad report" which certainly had damaging results, especially for my girls.

The only court appearance I ever had was two weeks ago. In 8 years, I never entered a courtroom. When you don't have money, you don't go to court. You talk to the judge on the phone! That's what we did all those years. But now, prior to the court date, Sheila was sleeping in my bed, holding on to me. My daughter, who had hurt me repeatedly, kicked and punched me, was now clinging to me every night. Thea did not get dressed for two weeks during that time. Sybil hung out with her boyfriend and her other friends as much as she could. All the girls were so stressed, they even had skin sores, they were so afraid. Then the psychologist, Ms. Torns', assessment report came and I was devastated.

I thought about failing to show up in court. I had no hope for my kids or me. I figured the judge would just align with Ms. Torns' report and leave the girls with Gerry for good. The night before, I had dinner with Jason and he offered to write a statement on my behalf. He also promised to come to court, even though he knew his dad would be present. The next morning about 8:00 a.m., I called Jason as I had heard nothing since we said goodnight. I asked if I would be seeing him at the courthouse in a couple hours. He announced that he had had a "big fight" with his girlfriend until 5:00 that morning so he hadn't had a chance to write anything for court. I just told him it was okay and that I understood.

I drove to my office to print my documents for court and when I checked my Inbox, there was a statement from my son. *Jason had come through*! That was so brave of him and I will never forget it. He had summarized everything and typed it up in 20 minutes.

He recounted his whole story, including this comment: "The first thing my dad told me (Jason) when I arrived at his doorstep was the reason my mom left was because she wanted me to commit suicide".

Justice Rose, sister of the only other judge to have been on our case, Justice Nathan, presided again. Gerry's lawyer had requested that the judge throw out my affidavit since it was "old news". Regardless, Justice Rose entered the courtroom with my affidavit in hand. Kathy Lytton had made sure of that. The judge read Jason's statement, then looked at Gerry, and her face was incredulous. She slowly said, "Everyone must remain calm here today". Then Ms. Torns gave her report and Jason's statement was entered as an Exhibit. Gerry's lawyer read what Jason had written, but did not show it to Gerry. I still don't know if Gerry has read it. I am going to make sure, though, that all three girls get a copy.

When it was my turn to speak, I told the court that I wanted to respond to what Gerry's lawyer had claimed about me. I stated that the psychologist's report by Ms. Torn was full of falsehoods the girls had told her. They had simply repeated Gerry's lies about what I allegedly said. For instance, he told my girls that I had diagnosed them all with ADD and dyslexia. In fact, Sybil *is* dyslexic while two others have ADD, all three of whom were diagnosed and treated by mental- health professionals. I don't claim to be a mental-health worker, but I do know that my ex-husband, in his role as leader, paid people at his church to cover up sexual abuse and that *is* all documented.

I told the court how three of my children, the ones who have learning disabilities, have been hit the hardest by their father's alienation and warped worldview. They lack empathy and seemingly, a conscience. One daughter struggles academically, but she is scraping through. She plans to go to a trade school and become an aesthetician. Sheila wants to be a doctor or dentist and she clearly has the intelligence. I recalled aloud how Gerry had threatened that if I left him, he would take all my children away and that is exactly what happened. I know I was concise, clear and articulate that day in court.

Justice Rose then asked me, "What do you want?" I said I wanted my girls to have 180 days completely away from their father and their brothers. During that time, we would all be in intensive counselling face-to-face so we could openly discuss and resolve our issues and misunderstandings. I said, "Your Honour, please give my daughters the tools to resolve conflicts because they have grown up in a cult which values excommunication and shunning. These girls have been poisoned against their eldest brother, Jason, and me. They have been on a speeding train, and thank you for stopping that train, toward destruction. Please let these passengers get off and take a different train, a good train". Then the judge asked Ms. Torns for a response.

Lynda Torns stated that she had not known about Jason or the history of our case. Nevertheless, she did not think my idea would work because it was "too late as the girls are so against [me]. It is best they just live with their dad". At that, Justice Rose asked what I thought and I just agreed… so did Ms. Lytton. My girls were too alienated for anything to work, outside of extreme deprogramming therapy and clearly the judge was not going to order that. The lawyers then talked together and decided to keep the girls together. They all went back to live with their father.

Justice Rose ordered that the girls get cell phones, that I be invited to Norm's high school graduation (I had not been at any of our other kids' graduations), and that Gerry inform me immediately when there is urgent information about our kids. I asked for those things since my boys had been in rollover car accidents and had broken bones, yet nobody had notified me.

After court, my younger sons took the girls to my house and Sheila broke in without my knowledge. She took a bunch of their stuff and off they went back up north. Since they all got cell phones, I have been in touch, but have only heard back from Sybil. On paper, I have parenting access, but in reality, it is up to the kids. Justice Rose ordered Gerry to drive the kids down to my place for weekend visits, but I know it won't happen.

You know, children caught in parental alienation have been damaged. Their own personal development has been thwarted, they are forced to grow up too soon and they are not mature enough to understand what has happened or is happening to them. They become hardened, cynical, and judgmental; they have lost much of their heart. I know I did the best I could and I will always love them.

JASON

CHAPTER 18

JASON

I actually have two daughters, Brandy, who is almost thirteen, and April, who is eight years old. My girls have different mothers. There are no issues between April's mom and me, so my youngest daughter is doing very well. She excels at school, has nice friends, and moves almost seamlessly between her parents' homes. April's mom and I actively co-parent, communication is open and her boyfriend and I get along well. Similarly, my common-law wife Dierdre, has a smooth relationship with my ex-wife. As soon as April's mom and I separated, we went into mediation, worked out the parenting guidelines, and stuck to them.

Recently, Dierdre's mother came for a visit, so we asked April's mom if we could have her at our place that weekend, even though it was not our scheduled weekend. There was no problem at all. The two sets of parents have a give and take relationship and it's just fantastic… for us as well as for April. We have always made "best interests of the child" our priority and April is a positive, secure, loving and intelligent child as a result.

The story involving my eldest daughter, Brandy is far different. Brandy says she hates me. She has deteriorated over the years since her mother and I split. The parental alienation started immediately. Brandy was taught that her mother was her only loving and important parent; in fact, I was only considered a bother, not a parent. It's interesting to me that Brandy's mother, Jeanne, has an older child, Lyn, from an earlier relationship with another man. That child's father was similarly driven out of his daughter's life by Jeanne as were the girl's paternal grandparents. I was not married to Jeanne, but we lived together when Brandy was born. Our relationship had been rocky and we might have separated earlier had our daughter not come along. I was not told Jeanne had stopped using birth control, so her pregnancy was a bit of a shock. We decided then to try and make it work, so we could be united for our baby. I am a chef so my hours are long and often in the evenings. Jeanne didn't like that, although I had always been in that line of work.

I would come home from work to two babies whose diapers needed changing, who were often hungry, and who had not napped. In those days, Brandy was tiny and her half-sister, Lyn, was three years old. Jeanne would be lying on the couch and nothing would have been done around the house. I wondered what she was possibly doing all day in my absence. Jeanne got her back up when I asked that question one day, flew off the handle, and became violent towards me. I had had all I could take so we separated. Brandy was two and a half by then.

There is no documentation that I know of to show that Jeanne has mental health issues but it seems apparent that she did, and does. Some of our friends lived with Jeanne over the years, so I know from them that her behaviour was frequently bizarre and unpredictable. She, herself, was adopted so I know very little about her family of origin.

We were living in sliding-scale rental housing before we split up. I was not making enough money for us to live elsewhere. At our separation though, Jeanne moved in to one of the rental properties her father owned, so the kids were in acceptable housing. I moved in with my brother and slept on his couch. Right away I was paying child support, and there was barely anything left over so I could eat. But as you know, the Maintenance Enforcement Program (MEP) doesn't care about what happens to the Debtor (Author's note: At the time of writing, MEP now refers to the Debtor as a Payor).

I had gone to a government office to fill out the primary form necessary for shared custody. I checked off the appropriate boxes and as it appeared from that point forward everything about parenting would be shared. I even got advice from the clerk there, pretty straight forward. After signing and dating the form, I submitted it and returned to work. After all, if I miss any work, I don't get paid. My work is mostly event-based, so I couldn't ask for a regular parenting schedule. Instead, it was supposed to be that I would be able to share time and see Brandy as much as I could when I was off work; and work around my event schedule… fairly straight forward.

When I did have Brandy, I always took Lyn too, since I also cared for and looked after her as if she were my own. That little girl did not remember her real father because he had been stricken from her life. I was glad to take both girls and they were happy to come along with us. Years later, Lyn told me her mother said her dad was a "druggie and his parents were good-for-nothings". I still remember one time when she was younger, those grandparents showed up at our house with a hand-carved toy chest for Lyn, and Jeanne slammed the door in their faces.

At that time, I half-believed Jeanne's lies. Today, Lyn is 16, but she has never seen her biological father. We tried to find Lyn's father, but, to date, we have been unsuccessful. We were hoping to collaborate in court to substantiate Jeanne's track record and instability.

For the first while, I saw the girls every chance I got. I would call and make a "booking" with Jeanne and I always gave her lots of advance notice. That usually worked out until one day when Jeanne found out I had a girlfriend. Although my girlfriend tried to keep as distant from parenting Brandy as possible to avoid rocking the boat, there were times when Jeanne would cancel or change plans without notice or reason. My then-girlfriend would encourage me to put my foot down. As soon as I spoke up about wanting to stick to the agreed-upon "visit", Jeanne would become extremely angry.

Up to that point, I had avoided lawyers and the legal system. I couldn't afford a lawyer, so I depended on free legal assistance at the courthouse and some mediation. Brandy was still doing okay then, so I married April's mother. For a while, we saw the girls every second weekend. April's mom handled all the scheduling. Soon though, we heard that Jeanne had failed to pay her utility bills and her power, water, electricity all got turned off. I could have reported her to Child and Family Services then because Jeanne was not providing the necessities of life to her daughters. Jeanne had a boyfriend then who has since become her husband. Why they couldn't pay their utilities is still a mystery.

When the girls came to our house, April's mom and I saw they were dirty, poorly dressed in clothes that were too small or torn, and they didn't talk much. They did not admit right away that they could not shower or have their laundry done because their water had been shut off. Later that night, they did let us know about their situation at mom's. I called over there and asked Jeanne if I could help by keeping the girls a week at a time while she and her boyfriend got back on their feet. To our surprise, Jeanne agreed. That worked for almost two years. We had three kids by then, since April's mom and I had our baby, April, together.

In 2007, April's mom and I separated. April was 3, Brandy was 8, and Lyn was 11. We co-parented smoothly from the start, but a year later, I had serious medical problems. I broke my back and I had brain surgery. As a result, I lost almost two years of work. Fortunately, I was eligible for long-term disability, which saved me. I'm now doing a lot better, but my surgeries took a long time to recover from. I am epileptic, but the weird thing is it did not manifest until adulthood. Having to deal with nonstop stress over Brandy and the parental alienation by Jeanne increased the frequency and severity of my seizures. I am back at work now and very glad to be earning a paycheque again.

While I was sick, I couldn't manage to look after the girls as often. I am still prohibited from driving until enough time has elapsed post-surgery that the doctors declare me seizure-free. In November of 2009, I met Dierdre. She soon became concerned over my girls and my chronic high-stress. Dierdre felt the situation needed to be resolved for good so I could recover and Brandy, and indirectly, Lyn, would have peace. Dierdre and I moved closer to Jeanne's place so we could walk the two blocks to pick up Brandy and Lyn. Their school is also close-by, so the move was very helpful. That allowed me to resume the one-week on one-week off parenting schedule.

You would think our move would have been good news to Jeanne as well. But instead she freaked out! The almost-equal parenting schedule meant less child support for her. With a week's notice, Brandy, not Jeanne, happened to mention that her mother and new husband were moving to the other end of the city; the opposite end to where Dierdre and I had recently moved. To make the decision even crazier, Jeanne's job was in the north end of the city… so was Lyn's school.

When Jeanne moved to the other end of the city, that's when the parental alienation really ramped up. Dierdre and I moved to our current home right before school started in the fall of 2010, and my ex and her spouse moved away right after. The summer had gone well. From May until September the girls could walk between our homes, visit either parent, and I could drive them back to Jeanne's if it was raining, or they needed to be back at a certain time. We had the girls for half of July, but Jeanne was beginning to make that difficult. In August she wanted to take Lyn and Brandy to British Columbia for two weeks and I agreed. I thought we could just make up the lost parenting time later and it was good to show flexibility in our schedule.

The day Jeanne and the girls left for BC there was a horrible vehicle accident on the highway going west and I was terrified it involved them. I called Jeanne and her husband's cell phones, texted Lyn, but no one ever returned my calls. Then I called the nephew of Jeanne's husband, who was also living at their house. Finally, many days later, that nephew got hold of Jeanne and she called him back. She apologized (via the nephew) for not returning any of my calls and said her phone had dropped in a toilet somewhere. The story continued that her husband's phone was also out of commission because he had spilled coffee on it, Lyn's cell was too expensive to text me from, and Jeanne's mother had terminated her landline just before their visit. All I had asked was for someone to let me know they were all okay.

I called Child Protective Services one night because the Justice Office downtown instructed me to when I filed the original legal application. The clerk seemed interested and listened while I recounted the trauma my daughter has endured and the difficulty I have had trying to access information on, or just to see, Brandy. As soon as I brought up the issue of parental alienation, however, the clerk referred me instead to Child and Family Services at Alberta Justice. I called that organization's child abuse hotline and got a female lawyer on the phone. Again, the "advice" I got was that Brandy would be 18 in a few years so it would be best to just leave things as they are. The lawyer said my daughter had a mind of her own and could move out at 18 if she pleased. She had no idea about the cult-like brainwashing and enmeshment of the alienator.

Once Jeanne was back in town, I initiated mediation so that we could settle our parenting arrangements. The Alberta Government mediator-clerk was there to help arrange and draft an agreement. Every time I suggested appointment dates and times, however, Jeanne professed to be busy and unable to attend. Many delays later, we finally met with a mediator. But even then, she left early after 30 minutes, saying she had to get back to work. After three of these shortened visits, the mediator did manage to hammer out an agreement that stated Dierdre and I would have the girls at our place every second weekend at least. Since they had moved far away from us, the one week schedule alternating between homes wouldn't work. Jeanne told us that "I can do whatever the hell I like, I am the mother". She (Jeanne) told the mediator that "the agreement terms are not binding so I can wipe my ass with it".

Jeanne made sure the parenting agreement did not work. She made it increasingly difficult for me to see Brandy *and* Lyn, which was hard on all of us, including April, their little sister. This included ongoing harassment during pickup and drop off times by her then-husband, including simply bumping pick up and drop off times by half-hour segments either way *each time and every scheduled day*. Even in the dead of winter, Jeanne was relentless.

I then hired a lawyer, Brett Dyson, who was expensive, but he seemed to know his stuff. He had successfully dealt with alienation cases before. He told us that his recent case, similar to ours, cost the targeted parent $80,000 before it was resolved. We sure didn't have that kind of money. Brett would suggest one strategy, then change his mind to go in another direction, and it was all very confusing.

In January, we served Jeanne with a Parenting Order; she flatly refused, so we had to go to court. In fact, Jeanne told me I was never going to see Brandy again, since I had gotten a lawyer involved. Then, that same night, I called their house to talk to my daughter "which was an ongoing nightly routine since separation" and my ex's husband said to me, "Call here again and we will charge you with harassment". I phoned the police myself to find out if they could charge me as per their threat; I was told they could indeed. From that day, I had absolutely no contact or communication with my daughter, Brandy.

By the summer of 2011, I had not seen my daughter for six months, and she now stated that she didn't want to see me either. The alienation was abrupt and complete; Brandy refused contact with us all including her little sister, April. Finally, we got an appearance with a judge and were granted the official Parenting Order. That judge included in his Order that there was to be reunification between Brandy and me via a psychologist (since Jeanne claimed Brandy wanted nothing to do with me, the now-alleged *abusive* father). Each of the parents were to pay half for the cost of this therapy. We paid about $1,500 for our share. As per her usual tactics, Jeanne had to be chased down to attend the sessions she had agreed to and that were court-ordered. The psychologist and I agreed to let Jeanne make the session appointments so she would have no reason to renege. Still, Jeanne failed to attend half those appointments.

The counselor, Janet Maarten, was helpful and we have stuck with her. Actually, we have an appointment with her this evening.

At the time of our Parenting Order, the counselling wasn't that useful since half the appointments were missed. Jeanne was supposed to drop Brandy at Ms. Maarten's office for those sessions. We missed a whole month of appointments because Brandy's mother made excuses to cancel. After a year of Jeanne's noncompliance with the Parenting Order, we had spent almost $7,000 on counselling and I had not seen my daughter in that entire year.

Jeanne then openly refused to cooperate with any counselling. She said she didn't care if it was court-ordered. I told my lawyer, Brett, that Diedre and I would take on the entire cost of reunification counselling. This is where the Family Law system really breaks down: Brett said he already had put a Court Order in place so what was the point of putting another Order on top of that one? Jeanne was in direct violation of the Order, but there was nothing that could be done to enforce her paying her share of counselling and making sure it continued. Unbelievable!

Brandy is 12 years old now. Her mother has caused the parental alienation, refused to comply with a Court Order, and has walked away scot-free. Meanwhile Dierdre and I have paid for everything, and I still lost my daughter. There have been absolutely no consequences for the alienator. I continue to try and contact Brandy and her mother by email and text. Jeanne's replies are always "We feel it's best she not see you" and "She does not want to see you at this time".

When I used to see her every second weekend, Brandy and I also maintained daily communication by phone. I would call her on nights that I wasn't with her to ask how her day went and to tell her I love her. This continued until I was completely severed from her life when she was 11. Even as I could feel her withdrawing from me as the alienation took a tighter hold on her, Brandy would still sometimes reach out. She would ask me for materials to make something, a gift, for me. She and Lyn asked me what my favourite colours were. Then they made a painting for me. Those thoughtful presents happened right up until the last time I saw my daughter.

Diedre and I wanted to push in court for real reunification and perhaps full custody. But the bills kept piling up, and we were completely broke. It is so hard on Dierdre and me and our relationship. We sometimes hit the point where our stress level is through the roof. But we are staying together because we are each other's support through this hell.

My second court date was June 25th of this year (2012) so just a few weeks ago. The judge at our earlier pre-trial saw that my alienated daughter, Brandy, will soon be 13. In his wisdom, or not, he stated that to change my daughter's living arrangements now so she would be with us more often would only cause her more stress. He even said he thought my daughter might run away or kill herself if she was moved. That judge didn't care whether she was living in an abusive or neglectful home with her mother; he still was just fine with leaving her there and leaving me out of her life.

My lawyer suggested we ask for a bilateral psychological assessment to the tune of another $40,000. Then I would have legal fees on top of that. He also thought we should now go through Queen's Bench rather than Provincial Court. We have already spent $12,000, most of it on counselling, yet the alienation just gets worse. But it seems more useful to invest in reunification than in lawyers and judges.

Ms. Maarten alone has met several times with Brandy to date. She has even shown her videos, made by Dr. Richard Warshak, about how it's okay to love both parents. Janet Maarten has seen parental alienation prior to our case. She now insists that Brandy and I meet together in the sessions with her. Thus far, my daughter has remained withdrawn, uncommunicative, and has missed some of these appointments. It's hard to see one's daughter, who used to be so open, loving and demonstrative, sit slouched and silent as far away from me as she can possibly get, then in one session even turn to screaming and pulling her hair saying "I hate my father".

How can she hate someone who she doesn't even live with and rarely sees? I've barely even had a chance to take her under my wing in life. This got me thinking why she would even say this, so I started researching some more when I found this quote that I've seen on a website, by Canadian Justice Minister John Gomery, which states "A child has to be taught to hate". Now let that sink in a moment.

But, at last week's session, Brandy showed some improvement. Her posture wasn't as closed off, she talked some, and even showed animation in her face. She told me a little about her new school and her friends. We didn't go back to the past. I didn't want her to start using her mother's words such as my "interrogating" her and "I don't have to talk to you". And there were abuse allegations too: Jeanne had told the counselor, and written in her affidavit, that Dierdre tied Brandy to a chair to make her eat; that I held Brandy's head underwater while she was swimming; and that we locked her in our basement. You know what? We don't even have a door to our basement! No one ever questioned these allegations, but I'm sure they became cemented into my daughter's head.

I have hope for counselling with Janet Maarten, but the problem continues with Jeanne neglecting to bring Brandy. In such instances, the session is a waste of Janet's *and* my time while my daughter is encouraged to see Dad as just an inconvenience. Jeanne offers rewards to Brandy that directly conflict with the time she is supposed to attend counselling with me. For example, when there is a session booked, Jeanne will tell my daughter that they won't be able to go to a movie as planned.

We pay a retainer for the counselling, and then Janet uses it up as sessions occur. So if Brandy doesn't show up, there is no cost to us. We pay the entire amount, but can't bring Brandy with us as she supposedly doesn't want to see me. Sometimes Jeanne, her husband, Lyn, and her step-children all show up to Dr. Maarten's office with Brandy in tow. I think it's an attempt for them to appear as a happy "Brady Bunch". It got to the point that Janet told them directly to bring only Brandy.

There is a limit to what Dr. Maarten can achieve though she wants Jeanne and I to effectively and smoothly co-parent. Jeanne does not want that and does everything in her power to destroy any relationship I might have with my daughter. Ms. Maarten does not realize how deep the alienation goes. It is hard to believe unless you are living it. Janet tried to talk to Jeanne about being more co-operative for Brandy's sake. But Jeanne doesn't care how Brandy fares. It is all about her power and control over me. We will see how tonight's session goes. Brandy and I are supposed to meet with Janet tonight because Jeanne cancelled last night's session.

Years ago, I went online and Googled my ex-wife's behaviour to find out why she would not co-operate with me in parenting. I was also concerned by Brandy's increasing social withdrawal, especially when she is with me. I did an online quiz and scored off the charts in terms of the extent of parental alienation. I had never heard of Parental Alienation before and the more I read into it, the mannerisms and characteristics of my children match and sew together the pieces of the puzzle. I knew I required help, but I knew not where and how since I don't have primary or shared custody. I only have only a mutually agreed-upon arrangement to share visitation with my children's mothers. There is no access enforcement agency, no independent review agency that actually oversees and looks out for the best interests of the children.

Since moving to the south end of the city, Brandy's school grades have crashed, she and Lyn skip classes regularly, and my daughter's former A's have become F's. Recently, Lyn dropped completely out of high school. There is an online program called School Zone where parents can find out the attendance and grades of their children. I made the mistake of questioning Jeanne about all the absences I saw and next thing I knew, she had the school update Brandy's file to show "ill" instead. I want to support my daughter in her learning. Dierdre's employer has a program that offers summer jobs and subsidizes dependents in post-secondary, which could make university accessible. To date, Brandy is not achieving the foundational knowledge that could help her succeed in life.

The relationship between Brandy and April is sad. They were so close, but on the last few visits, Brandy was clearly working on April to alienate me as she has done. We noticed April becoming withdrawn and snarky with us, which is very unusual for her. Even April's mom noticed her negative comments about and toward me. We got together and decided that until Brandy can be "deprogrammed", it is dangerous for her to influence April. April is stuck in the middle and none of it is her fault.

I pay my Child Support religiously and have no arrears. It is an ongoing struggle to make ends meet, but I don't want that issue revisited by MEP. No doubt MEP would find a way to wring more money out of me to send to my alienator ex-wife, who dresses my daughter in old hand-me-downs and can't be bothered to get her daughters to school.

When asked about why she hates me, my daughter Brandy hesitated and in a cold voice with no facial expression, she told me "I can't tell you" and then, "Lyn and my mom aren't here, so I can't tell you".

2017

Our story is ongoing. This year alone Brandy and I have reunited, but had a falling-out on several separate occasions. One falling out was when I asked for her assistance with the FOIP request on her file. In hindsight, this request was too soon in our rebuilding phase. She became very angry on the phone, said I was a bad father and had fed her cow liver, as well as reiterating the alleged abuse she suffered at my hands. Then her boyfriend came on the line and shouted insults at me as well.

She has come back to me a couple of times in need of some dental work. I took Brandy to her first dental visit in the longest time. Brandy has been under my benefits since she was born. She had been to dentists before, but her mom stopped taking her when braces were recommended. Due to dental neglect, she now needs braces and three teeth extracted. Had I not been alienated from my daughter, her dental issues could very well have been corrected earlier or prevented. All the good money thrown at the court system and "reunification therapy" could have paid for dental care and then some.

As for the stepfather (Jeanne's husband) who has mentally, physically and emotionally abused her, he was criminally charged and pleaded guilty last March. Brandy's stepfather received 90 days in jail, 10 months' probation, is now a registered Sex Offender who cannot be around children for ten years, and had another charge dismissed of assault on a minor.

I, her real father, on the other hand, have spent all my savings and then some and suffered a life-long emotional toll due to parental alienation at the hand of Brandy's mother, Jeanne. My daughter carries a multitude of negative effects and will require years of psychological therapy, at an exorbitant expense, if and when she decides to become healthy.

Fortunately, I have a family support network and another daughter who loves me very much. I can't imagine other alienated parents in their grief and burden who lack in such support. I will always remember the precious times we had following our brief reunification.

Brandy was sent to a foster home at one point as I later found out. This was due to an investigator's visit to Jeanne and her husband's (the abusive stepfather) home. I questioned MEP as to why I was not contacted when my daughter was placed into a foster home yet was required to continue paying Maintenance to Jeanne. How was this failure-to-disclose not fraud? I was told by MEP that "these things are often overlooked" and it was simply brushed off as an administrative oversight. The staff member I spoke to even mentioned that other clients had been in far worse administrative situations!

My phone call to the crisis line years ago was laughed off by the lawyer on the crisis line when I mentioned my daughter being alienated from me. My call was also never recorded. I guess they don't track, record, or log Crisis Conversations and calls. This blatantly *highlights the need for sufficient training in parental alienation and intervention for family unit caseworkers.*

Our story is continually ongoing. Looking back on the years I can only reflect on the positive impact that the tiny intervention had on my daughter. She still stays in touch occasionally and reaches out over Facebook. I reply with positive loving word of support and encouragement; something she is still getting used to. I look forward to the day where we can put the past behind us and move beyond this. I am hopeful that future generations will never have to go through this.

April, on the other hand, continues to excel at school and is a loving, positive girl. She, her mother, and I together demonstrate that co-parenting from the beginning works. This is a true testament to "best interests of the child".

Lyn finally connected with her real father and enjoys having established contact, finding out their similarities and piecing together the commonalties in our stories as fathers and what we have gone through with Jeanne, her mother. It was this reunion where she learned of all her mother's lies and she encouraged Brandy to get back in touch with me. I haven't had the pleasure of meeting Lyn's father yet, but one day I would like to.

Just recently, in 2018, Brandy has become more accustomed to spending time with us. She is doing much better, enjoying reuniting with April, and I feel tentatively hopeful for her… and for our whole family.

To all the parents who are going through this or who have yet to:

"Keep your wits about you, your heart close, as it is a long process, especially on those long painful nights and during holiday seasons. Keep your head and chin up, never ex-bash. Be graceful; seek to accomplish everything in the best interest of your children. Oh, and compromise; don't let some stranger "court judge" try and settle things that grown adults should settle together through mindful compromise and compassion for the long-term best interests of the children."

KATH

CHAPTER 19

KATH

My husband, Bob, was abusive and systematically alienated me from both our children: Melanie, 21, and Matthew, now 23. We married in 1986 and not long into our marriage the abuse began. The incidents included his breaking my arm in 1998, which was the last straw. Whenever I phoned the police, nothing was done because Bob works in law enforcement.

That year, 1998, Bob moved out and left me in our marital home with both kids. I was a stay-at-home mother for years after giving up my teaching career. From the time of our separation, Bob did pay basic child support but not spousal support. The kids were in Grade Four and Grade One then. I was suffering from Battered Spouse Syndrome, so I neglected to obtain legal advice or help of any kind. My self-esteem was destroyed. My children were always my first priority and I did everything that I could for them.

The first three years of separation the kids stayed with me and they saw little of their father. He showed up at his convenience. Then he served me with divorce papers, so we went to court. The result was he had to start paying me spousal support. My lawyer was Mr. Short and he was wonderful.

One day though, my daughter ran away from school when she was looking for me. Someone reported seeing her on the street with no shoes on and called an ambulance. When I got that call about Melanie I phoned Bob to let him know and see if he could help find her. He called CARRT (Child at Risk Response Team) and soon Social Services showed up at my house. The social worker told me she felt Bob was trying to control me from the outside. She advised me to get a "barracuda of a lawyer" as Bob was apparently going to try to obtain full custody of our children. I hired Raine Cochon to represent me. I told her how Bob was abusive to the children and me, that he worked shiftwork, and had rarely seen the kids in three years.

One day I called Bob and asked if he could pick up Matthew from hockey. He did, but when I arrived at his condo that evening to pick up my son, Bob's girlfriend was in the parking lot and she approached me. She tried to prevent my ringing the doorbell. Bob swung it open and hit me with the door, badly bruising my arm. The next day the girlfriend filed a false police report saying I had assaulted her and the police came to my house again. Since Bob was high up in law enforcement, he could spin the truth and get his henchmen after me.

So, I was wrongly charged with assault. I had filed a police report of the assault causing bodily harm (to me) and had three medical reports documenting the injuries to my arm. Regardless of this, the police came into my home and, in front of my children, placed me under arrest and wrongly charged me. I had to get mug shots and fingerprints. When this fiasco occurred, Raine Cochard dropped my case and gave it to Crystal Baker. She, then, was "too busy" when we had to go to court to see where the kids would live. Instead, Raine gave my file to Desiree Berinski. After a couple of months, it somehow went back to Crystal Baker.

For the next six months, I had politicians and other people write to the police about how I had been wronged. Eventually, a Justice of the Peace at the courthouse actually read the medical reports from that night and Bob's girlfriend was then charged with assault and making a false police report. It wasn't long before my charges were dropped. But Bob's girlfriend's charges were also dropped!

Since Bob now had to pay spousal support, I believe he was motivated to seek custody of the kids. He told his lawyer he wanted a custody assessment and he told Melanie and Matthew that I had assaulted his girlfriend. The irony was that Bob used to tell me how excellent a mother I was. I taught them to read before they were even in school and I played hockey with Matthew. Now here he was trying to convince the law that I was mentally unwell. I had suffered from depression due to the years of abuse at the hands of my husband, but I was certainly a competent, good mother.

A custody evaluator was assigned to our case. Her name was Carla Shander. Well, the first question she asked me was why I drove my son to school every day. They had to get to school on time and Matthew has to carry his musical instrument back and forth to school, that's why. But Ms. Shander was mad that I dared ask her the reason for her line of questioning. I realized later that she had earlier met with my ex, who had no doubt told her my kids should be walking to school.

Ms. Shander suggested we each have the children half time until the trial. By then, I had already spent $18,000 on lawyers and therapists. She also recommended I attend a course over the next three months to help me get mentally strong again. In the meantime, Bob should keep the kids at his home. I live two blocks from their school, their friends were nearby, and I had a close relationship with both Melanie and Matthew. In court, Justice Trassle agreed with Shander's recommendations.

My lawyer, Ms. Berinski, was livid. She knew Bob was a shift-worker so the kids would be alone while he was working, even on his night shifts. My kids were in Grades 4 and 7 then. My children were very upset when they found out what the judge had directed. They didn't want to live with their father. Melanie was so distraught that I had to take her to our doctor the next morning. The court ordered that my kids came to my house three of every four weekends. Sometimes Melanie didn't want to go back, but her dad would phone and remind her she had to. But then he'd show up a few hours late to get her. Two weeks later we were back in court as Bob felt I was not facilitating his parenting access. The judge cut back my parenting time. Bob's lawyer, Mitchell Pollard, was very aggressive, and it appeared that he and Bob would do and say anything to win in court.

One day the school phoned me saying that Bob had agreed to be a parent supervisor on a field trip, but had not shown up. The teacher asked me to go instead so I did. It was December and when I got to school, I saw my daughter in a short skirt with bare legs and a spring jacket. I was mortified! Melanie should not have been with her dad; he did not look after her properly. I mentioned this to another parent and next thing I knew, I was back in court again for "saying bad stuff" about Bob in public. Now my access became part of Saturday, overnight, and then part of Sunday twice a month. There had not even been an affidavit by the person who reported I badmouthed Bob. It was all hearsay at best, yet I was punished and my kids were again the big losers. I was not even allowed to phone my kids except for ten minutes every Tuesday at 7:00 p.m. And guess what?! When I would phone they would inevitably be "unavailable".

When Melanie was with me and it was near time to return to her dad's, I would notice her getting tense and irritable. She locked herself in the bathroom once because she didn't want to go back with Bob. My lawyer told me to make sure I took my kids back to their father's, or I would lose all parenting access. So, I did, but sometimes I would have to carry Melanie out to the car.

I went back to court several times to try and increase my time with my children. I had no money, but I had to pay lawyers. Thankfully, my mom helped me pay those legal bills. I tried to enroll in that course the judge directed me to take, but the facilitator wouldn't accept me. Also, my doctor disagreed that it was appropriate. The facilitator said since we were in litigation, the course was useless. Here was my lawyer telling me I had to take a course, but it was impossible to actually take it. It was crazy-making behaviour, as I had nowhere to turn.

Finally, my lawyer called my doctor and begged her to recommend me for another class at a different hospital. I got in, but I was with a bunch of ex-psychiatric patients, some of whom had been suicidal. We sat around in a group and were supposed to talk about our problems. But, I was court-ordered to say nothing negative about Bob, so I just sat silently. I went to those classes for six weeks and then we got to the following phase, which was to be a more-intense six weeks. At that point the facilitators discharged me because "ethically, we can't keep you here". Upon informing my lawyer of this turn of events, she reminded me I had to finish the course or the judge would rescind all parenting time. I can't even describe to you the frustration I felt.

Next, I went to a psychiatrist, one who had previously dealt with Bob. I was told by my social worker friend that he could help me with my depression and hopefully regain some custody of my children. The psychiatrist had written his report on Bob, finding him to be very intimidating to women and children. He acknowledged that I had been the primary caregiver of our children and that he was unclear on why they were sent to live with Bob. I thought my seeing this psychiatrist and a social-worker for my anxiety would show my commitment to getting well and getting my children back.

I hired a second custody evaluator, Dan Frazier, but had to pay out of my own pocket for him. I borrowed the $7,000 required so I could get an assessment that actually was accurate, unlike Shander's. I was not even working at the time. Mr. Frazier said he wanted to talk with our children at least twice to get a good understanding of what was going on. But as soon as Bob got wind of this, his lawyer shut us down, telling Justice Trassle that another custody assessment was a waste of time. Mr. Frazier had, in the meantime, read our file and found my behaviour was well within normal limits, but Bob scored high on deceit behaviour. Dan Frazier said Shander's report was so significantly flawed that it should be invalid. Yet, it decided our fate.

The judge appointed a lawyer, Jake Hoffer, for my children. On her first visit with him, Melanie told me she let Jake know she had been hit by her father. She said she was hit in the face, dragged down the stairs, pinned to the ground and yelled at directly in her face. Bob had been angry that Melanie wanted to be with me and did not want to be with him and his girlfriend.

Melanie kicked him back. She was ten years old and her lawyer responded by telling her that her story sounded false as her father would not abuse her. A child's attorney is a mandated reporter to the court, so Jake Hoffer should have reported this assault.

Back in court yet again, Mr. Hoffer finally told the judge that Bob was hitting the kids, badmouthing their mother, the kids were very stressed as a result and they wanted to be with me. This went on another two years, though it was supposed to have been three months, with the kids spending most of their time with their dad and very little with me. The court did nothing to help our situation.

My lawyer had Justice Trassle removed and replaced by Justice More. Each time we went to court, I tried to gain parenting time and each time, Bob and his aggressive lawyer said and wrote whatever they thought would be in their favour, regardless of my children's suffering. The kids had to stay with their father. Both Melanie and Matthew were always asking when they could "come home". Matthew told me his dad said they could be with me when I gave up my spousal support and went back to work full-time. I was working part-time with a special-needs child then.

Melanie got so skinny in those years and Matthew had developed IBS (Irritable Bowel Syndrome) with all the ongoing stress ramped up by the legal system. My lawyer, Bob's lawyer, and Justice More got together to decide what to do. Bob's lawyer disagreed that Melanie needed more time with me, so nothing changed. Someone called Social Services who agreed with Ms. Shander's report that Melanie did not have a good relationship with her father. They also opened a file on Bob, who was found to have physically abused the children and neglected them. Thanks to Social Services, I thought I might finally have the clout to get my children back. But still nothing changed. The Courts left my children with their father who was abusing and neglecting them.

Matthew was beginning to show signs of parental alienation in a major way. He was turning against me, phoning Bob whenever I would discipline him. My lawyer pressured me to give up my spousal support as then Bob might agree to my having the children without having to go to a trial. I needed that money, though, as I was only able to work part-time due to my ongoing neurological condition. Plus, I felt that spousal support and access to my children were, as they should be, separate issues.

I did give up my spousal support. I felt pressured to do so even by my lawyer, who was soon moving out of the country. It was unjust for a judge to even allow a mother with no employment to waive her spousal support for the return of her children. I was desperate and so were my children. Giving up my spousal support was my only hope of getting my children back. I had no idea how I would survive without spousal support, but at least I could help my kids. Both Melanie and Matthew asked me over and over again when they could come home. Although the children were supposed to return the day after we signed documents, Bob did not return them as scheduled and it was two whole weeks before they made it back to my place. I called the police, but they would not help. Finally, when Bob brought Melanie and Matthew back, they were changed forever. They became mean-spirited and when I called them on their behaviour, Matthew threatened to go live with his dad.

By 2005, when Matthew was 16, his father bought him a junker vehicle to drive and he decided to live full-time with Bob. Melanie meantime, was okay with half time at each parent's house. I had started teaching part-time to make ends meet. Soon though, in early 2006, Melanie did not return from her dad's either. Bob never did pay the correct amount of child support. I believe that his motivation to manipulate the kids to live with him was that he didn't want to pay anything. After everything I had done, gone through and given up to get my dear children back, my kids, again, were gone. Bob also got a "No Contact Order" from the judge so I could not even phone my own children or I would be arrested.

For the next couple of years, I did not see my children except on a very few special occasions but I could not fight any more. I had no money and my Legal Aid lawyer said there was no point, since my kids were teenagers. My kids no longer fought to see me; they had turned against me. Matthew, seven years later, has not told me where he lives, but I know he is out on his own and has been for a few years. I don't even know where he works. Melanie lives in British Columbia now and she talks to me sometimes. I don't know where she works either, though. She tells me about her boyfriend and I help her with her schoolwork, but my relationship with both kids is very strained at best.

Bob has not paid a cent for either of our children's university fees. Matthew worked two jobs to get through university and Melanie is still trying to make ends meet as a student. Over the years, my parents and I put money away in RESPs (Registered Education Savings Plan) for my kids but Bob never contributed.

I have told judges that I am a teacher. I am given responsibility for 30-plus children on a daily basis. How were my children sent to live with their father and given very little time with me for over two years? How am I prevented from contacting my own children? Do they not see the absurdity of this situation? No one has ever accused me of being a poor mother. Even Ms. Shander, the custody evaluator, commented that the children and I had a very close bond.

I was the primary caregiver while my children were growing up and nobody pays attention to that fact. Melanie, with all she has been through, is on the Dean's List, and Matthew has some kind of academic scholarship. They are both brilliant. I have told my kids that with a good education, they will not have people telling them how to live. I encouraged Melanie to be independent and not look for a man to support her. My story reminds me of the book, written by Pamela Richardson, called "A Kidnapped Mind". Her son killed himself because his father manipulated him to the point that the teenaged boy gave up.

2017

When my children do speak to me and since the No Contact Order expired, I have continued to support them financially, emotionally and academically. Both Matthew and Melanie acknowledge this through cards and even the odd gift. But they seem to forget that I am a kind and caring mother and their brainwashed perception of me is still apparent.

I have continued to be left out of my dear children's lives and most special occasions, as has my ailing elderly mother, who they loved dearly.

In 2015 and again in 2016, I took Bob to court for back-pay of Child Support and of Spousal Support, which I had given up under duress in exchange for the return of my children. Documents signed under duress are not valid. I hoped to set a precedent so children can no longer be used as pawns to get the best "deal". I lost my case. Matthew still will not say where he lives or works; he spoke to me last on my birthday a year ago.

My daughter did *not* invite me to her university graduation so I had to argue with her to be able to go, which was very disheartening. Recently, Melanie visited her grandma and me in June for five days, but never stayed at my place.

My narcissistic, controlling abusive ex-husband, did his best to turn our children into his clones. I have missed out on much of their lives and they have missed out on so much time with me. My mother, their grandmother also needlessly missed out on time with her only grandchildren and suffered so much because of this atrocity. She passed away earlier this year without so much as a single visit in hospital from either Melanie or Matthew. However, I have put my children in God's care and continue to pray that He will heal them of the brainwashing that has been inflicted on them since they were young. I hope that one day they will again see me as their loving and caring mother, include me in their lives and that our close relationship will be restored. I forgive because that is what I need to do.

GREG

CHAPTER 20

GREG

I was married for ten years, but we separated in 2005. My wife, Terry, and I had three children of the marriage, a girl now 16, and boy and girl twins who are now 12 years old. Our marriage was troubled early on. She wanted full control of all decisions for our family. I had suggested we attend counselling, but she wouldn't go. I wanted to work out our problems so we could be a family together. But I was hit by my wife four or five times. It was all I could do to defend myself without hurting her. I knew I would end up in jail if I did so. Hurting other people was also against my values. The last time it happened, I had my daughter on my lap while I was reading to her. Terry started yelling at me because I wanted to delay a discussion she wanted to have until I was finished the book. So, Terry took a swing at me. She almost hit our little girl and I knew it was time to get out of there.

At the time, I was a truck driver and making decent money. Terry was also working. By informal agreement, I left the home and our kids in the care of their mother. I was worried, but there was no evidence suggesting Terry would hurt them. I filled my two short-box pickup trucks but left the house fully furnished. I took a table, a bed, clothes and my cookware; that's all. All my tools and stuff were left in her garage.

I gave my wife $1,000 per month in Child Support. A couple months into our separation, she wanted to be friends or even more. One night she invited me to her, formerly our, house. In the meantime, my buddy called me with free passes to a bar opening so he and I went there instead. I told Terry "I got a better offer" and my life has never been the same since I made that comment.

We went to mediation at Terry's request within seven or eight months. The mediator, an older lady, was awesome and she listened carefully to both parties. She had been a family lawyer earlier in life so she knew the manipulation tactics people use to get what they want. After about 20 minutes of discussion, she had already figured out what my ex was all about. Clearly, we were not going to reach an agreement other than with the Child Support. But when I was served with the divorce papers, I got mad. The first step I took was to look up the Federal Child Support Guidelines and it turned out I was overpaying. I adjusted the amount to $850 in line with that chart.

Terry had a lawyer named Iola Sachene from a big firm in town. I was terrified because a friend's wife had told me that "that woman" would bury me, the lawyers were so ferocious at that firm. I decided to have a consultation with a family lawyer and that gave me some much-needed information about how to proceed. That didn't last long, however, as she took a promotion and dropped me as a client. The couple of meetings with this lawyer cost me about $5,000 and after that, I decided to self-represent. Nobody will take as much interest in your case as you will, I thought to myself. I also couldn't afford more legal fees.

Right after I reduced the amount of Child Support, Terry decided that instead of my seeing my kids every weekend, I would not see them at all. She said I was not paying for my kids so I wouldn't see them. I reminded her that I was paying exactly what I was supposed to and besides, Child Support and Access were treated by our *useless* legal system as totally separate issues. In fact, I had overpaid her by $150 each month until I checked out the Child Support Guidelines. But I didn't go after her for repayment for those seven months. Her response to me was to block my phone number on her landline so now I could not even phone my kids.

Once in a while Terry would phone me and the conversation would start off okay. But within a minute or two, she would start yelling and swearing at me and then hang up. Sometimes then she'd call me back and start the pattern all over. At mediation, we were asked why we were there and I told our mediator that I wanted to see my kids. She was shocked that I had been reduced from an occasional parent every weekend to not seeing any of them now in over a month.

No doubt at Terry's initial interview with the mediator, she had painted me as some kind of freaking monster but the mediator was now seeing clearly that I was a reasonable dad who just wanted to parent my kids. I was asked why I left the marriage so I related the incident where my daughter almost got hit when Terry swung at me. At that point, Terry joined our session and the mediator said, "Dad would like to see his kids and why is that not happening"? Terry told her it was because I was not paying what I used to. The mediator decided that I was to get the kids that very weekend, but Terry said that wouldn't happen because "we already have plans" (the kids and her). The mediator stepped right in and sternly told Terry that the kids were to go with me for the weekend or Terry would go to jail.

The kids did go with me and we enjoyed our time together. From there it was pretty smooth sailing until Maintenance Enforcement decided to seize my driver's license. I blame MEP more than I do Terry in that instance. MEP has its own rules regarding Section 7 extraordinary expenses. My ex-wife had placed the kids in before- and after-school care as she was working. My share of that cost was 60%, so Terry would submit a bill to MEP for $600 per month and *bam*! $360 would disappear from my bank account. I tried to reason with her showing her that I was to pay 60% after-tax and that there was software available that would calculate tax benefits and each of our portions for free. That software showed that I should be paying $190 instead and because of that reduction, which was supposed to be accurate, my arrears with MEP accumulated. That's when MEP pulled my license.

My income had also been reduced after the busy summer season of driving a gravel truck ended, yet MEP held my income level at the highest amount. It was harder and harder for me to pay my share. When MEP calculates your income and your "owed costs", it's really difficult to get them to recalculate if your income gets reduced. If, however, your income goes up, you can bet MEP is all over that in a nanosecond to increase your payments.

Without my driver's license, I was in big trouble since I drive for a living. I play by the rules, though, so I complied. At the time I was living in the south end of Edmonton while Terry remained in the north with our kids. One weekend, she dropped off Nikki, Matt and Cathy and I noticed right away that all three were acting weird. They were about thirteen and nine years old. I asked them what was up because they seemed really ill at ease. I made some snacks for them and then asked what the matter was. Nikki blurted out that her mom had said I didn't want them. My kids reported to me that their mother said "Your father is a big loser and can't even afford to pay for you". They related some other stuff Terry had told them and it just blew my mind!

I thought about how to handle this news and then sat down with them to discuss it. I said "You know what? Even when you guys were cookie-snatchers, carpet-crawlers, whatever, we never talked down to you and we talk to you as people because you are all very smart. You know that your mom and I don't like each other much, but I have never run her down in any way. I give you full credit for having and using your own brains and you can form your own opinions. You know I love you and would do anything for you; so would your mom. She has been inconvenienced by having to bring you three here this weekend, so she was just venting. Don't be mad at us for that; it's just what happened". Then I walked into another room and let them sit by themselves for a half hour. I could feel the tension leave that room. A while after, all three came and joined me with hugs all round. They told me "we know you love us, Dad".

The "Parenting After Separation" course was useful and I had taken it right away after we split up. It is common sense, but really useful, reminding parents to communicate with each other and not use their kids as messengers or spies. That really stuck with me and I vowed to never do that. But my kids shared that "Mom said to tell you she took that stupid, fucking course". They actually used those same *exact* words.

I tried texting and emailing since phone calls always ended up aggressively. I found that by letting go of my anger, I could better manage hers by not reacting. When I saw a strange truck in our family's driveway, that hurt. The kids told me that mom had a boyfriend. I kept it together, but it was still painful. A couple years after we separated, Terry moved away from our marital home. She tried to remove my name from the title, so she could get all the profit. I refused, so then we had to go to court. Both of us were self-represented and I offered her a sweetheart of a deal. She refused. I had offered my ex full ownership of our marital house on two conditions: that she gave me back $45,000 when she sold it, and that she keep it until all the kids were 18 years old.

Terry's refusal was bizarre, given her stated preference for staying in that house in that same neighbourhood until the kids were grown. Now she was saying I was keeping her tied down. I got a letter from her demanding that I instead pay all legal fees, get only $40,000 from the house sale, and allow her to sell whenever she felt like it. This proposal would require her giving me only 90 days notice of when she was moving and only if she was moving more than 75 kilometres away.

Her lawyer, Ron Hawk, would not be able to represent me simultaneously so I would have to retain someone for the couple hours it would take to sign any agreement. Extra cost would be incurred to do so, but I agreed anyway. I wanted an agreement signed. Ron spent a long time explaining to me what I already knew and then I told him to save his breath; I was not signing Terry's amended terms.

Ron said that since I was paying him, we still had time on the clock so could discuss next steps. He told me I was getting a raw deal and he anyway, would have advised me not to sign. His clients, he said, wanted one of two things, depending on their sex;

either wife wanted to get as much money as possible out of her ex, or husband wanted to pay as little as possible to get rid of his ex.

From that point, I told Terry I would fight for every penny since I was verging on destitution by then in any case. She represented herself again and applied for full house ownership, but she only got half. Of course, she also asked for an extra $20,000 from the sale of the house to repay money her dad had gifted us during our marriage. The judge granted her that. I asked to get some occupational rent in compensation since Terry's boyfriend had been living for free in our house the past two years. The judge disallowed that. Today, my ex and her boyfriend live in a fancy house in an expensive area of St. Albert. I live here, in a basement suite, owned by my friend who took pity on me.

Over the next while I lost my driver's license twice to MEP, saw my kids less than every second weekend, and tried to keep moving forward. Christmas is always a hard time for me and since the kids are older now, I can't get an Order for specified access. Terry lets me see them as she feels like it and usually I'm alone during the holidays. Last year I had Nikki, Matt and Cathy for a few hours Christmas morning but had to return them to their mother by noon. I took them back to Terry's as per her demand, went back to my basement, and drank away the rest of the day.

My self-destructive behaviour would distract me a little from my overwhelming sadness, but a few hours into it, I'd be feeling even worse. That day, I cried and cried and then decided to get out of there, got in my truck, and drove out of town. I got nailed by the cops. I told Terry I had gotten an impaired charge. The point was, though, that I didn't even care anymore. I felt I had nothing to lose. If I had been killed, oh well. Fortunately, I didn't kill anyone else though. I thought about suicide, but couldn't bring myself to do that to my kids or my girlfriend, Laurie.

Laurie lives in the U.S., but she is as supportive as possible. She has an eight-year-old son and could move here and get work, but she won't leave her child without his dad. She understands that kids need both their parents.

My kids have had some very lean Christmases and birthdays since I have no money to spend on them. They understand and love me anyway. Last year I was able to give them each a bigger present, basically technology, but just used and older versions of XBox and cellphones. They were thrilled and those gifts, especially the game-player, are used a lot when my kids are here.

Nikki, my oldest girl, talks openly to me and we are very close. Matt is like I was at his age, kind of rebellious, and my younger daughter, Cathy, is very quiet and withdrawn. When Nikki was born, we came home from the hospital the same day, and she was sleeping through the night within the first week. Terry was a great mom, and I loved playing with our baby. I have an old VHS tape that I recorded of our early days with Nikki. She and I watched it recently and it just made me so sad. I used to be able to stop my daughter from crying so easily, I would play patty-cake with her, and to this day, I can do that and she still laughs. Terry and I had albums with all the photos of our kids with us. She took them all. I've asked her to borrow them to make digital copies for myself, but she won't let me.

After we finished our day in court, I sat down with Terry and told her I hoped the tough times were behind us now, so we could each move on positively for our kids. She talked a good game that day, but within two months, she was making it difficult for me to see our kids. Once she knew about my impaired, she told me "your life circumstances do not dictate what I am going to do on my weekends, asshole".

Nikki works at a part-time job close to my place, so spends extra time here when she can but that just makes Terry angrier. She sees dropping Nikki or the twins at my place as a favour to me, even though the kids want and need to see me. I've been accused of being too slack with my kids. I have reasonable rules and boundaries, but it seems like when they are at Terry's, our kids do a lot of housework. I was on the phone with then 12-year-old Nikki in the evening while she was doing and folding the family's laundry, cooking and cleaning.

Nikki called one night to ask if she could come to my home because she was fighting with her mom. I told her she needed to work things out with her mother, but if they both needed time apart, it was okay. I would need to ask Terry first if that was the case. I phoned Terry who said that yes, she was going to drop off Nikki in ten minutes. Nice notice! Sure enough, there my daughter stood at my doorstep a few minutes later and it was clear she had been crying a lot. Mom was long gone already. I hugged her and asked what had happened. Apparently, Nikki and her friend tried to go to a movie, which was sold out. They could get into the later showing but she would need a ride home from mom at 11:00 p.m., not 9:00 as they had agreed. That caused the argument. Terry just picked her up at the theatre immediately, so she didn't see any movie that night. The last straw was Nikki telling me that *her own mother* called her "a fucking little whore".

I left Nikki in my house and went outside to talk to Terry. She admitted she had called our daughter that name "because I was mad". She thought that was an acceptable excuse… unbelievable! I told Terry that Nikki was going to stay with me the rest of that weekend. Terry's response to me was that our daughter could stay full-time with me if she didn't get her act together. I let her know that would be just fine, but of course it never happened.

So that's where I am. I see my kids sometimes when it's convenient for their mother. They are great kids, but stressed-out all the time. I try to make a living but am rendered penniless by the unfair payments demanded of me while Terry benefits in a huge way. I have lost wages, sleep, time at work, and three years of driving time due to MEP's penalties. The impaired driving was my own stupid fault because I was distraught. I am behind in my rent to my friend and am trying to sell my truck. I just want to be a good dad and for my kids to come out of this mess and somehow be okay.

RAINA

CHAPTER 21

RAINA

I am a mother of five children. Their father and I separated four years ago, in 2008. My partner (boyfriend) Paul, who is here with me today, used to work with my ex and me. He observed our family dynamic over 12 years. When we were married, my husband, Kim, used to denigrate me in front of our kids and I had very little self-esteem. He and I had a business together but whenever he would meet with Paul, Kim would tell him how incompetent I was. Our business made money, but I never saw any of it.

Paul saw Kim and I go to restaurants where I would be afraid to even order tea while Kim had a steak dinner. We went to counselling over eight years to try to resolve our conflict issues. Finally, that counselor told us he couldn't fix our problem and referred us to someone else. As time went on, I was getting stronger and more able to stand up to Kim and he resented that. He grew more controlling and aggressive. When the counselor gave up on us, our marriage fell apart. By July of 2007, I told Paul that I needed to get a divorce from Kim.

In November that same year, my second-eldest son got into a knife-fight with his dad in our kitchen. I called the police who handcuffed and took Kim to their station. My son, Seth, had been skipping school and one night we got a call about that. Kim confronted Seth and I went upstairs to bed. I heard a crash a few minutes later and ran downstairs. Kim had smashed Seth's XBox and it was in pieces on the floor. Seth freaked out and I guess that's when he grabbed the knife.

By this time, we were with a second counselor and our marriage was not improving. Kim asked me whether I planned to divorce him, and I didn't answer. The following spring I asked my husband for $500 to pay for our daughter's dance. The monthly allowance he allocated to me did not cover the whole amount. I paid all the household bills with that allowance but the bank accounts were in Kim's name only. I couldn't directly access money. By writing out a ledger showing Kim how much and on what I spent the allowance, I hoped he would see that I didn't have enough to make ends meet. He refused to pay extra for the dance lessons so I got the money from my mom.

I had already produced five children and I didn't want any more. I was also a gestational diabetic, which was an added complication. Kim made an appointment to get a vasectomy but then kept cancelling and re-booking it until finally I refused to sleep in the same bed with him. That's when he suggested we go out for coffee and talk. We did and that's when he told me he was now with-holding my allowance. I didn't care, so he started buying the groceries and paying the bills for our family.

Kim had confided in me, after our second son was born, that he was sexually abused by his own brother from age 8 to 12. That made him wary of leaving our kids with an uncle to babysit them. With this second counselor, Kim didn't want to talk about that and was angry in our sessions. After we went a few times, Kim announced he was not returning to her and wanted us to attend a session with a social worker instead. It was spring of 2008 and at that initial appointment, I told the social worker and Kim that I was done and wanted a divorce.

We had a mediator who got a parenting schedule and the money issues worked out. I did some reading and found a Calgary lawyer named Ron Faulter, self-proclaimed expert on difficult divorces and parental alienation. Since my two eldest boys were living with their dad and refused to see me, I consulted Ron. He never did get a divorce decree, just a signed agreement after repeated stalling to get maximum billable hours.

After the divorce, life kind of calmed down. My eldest son was a bit messed up over it all and for a while he went to live with my parents, then later with his dad, Kim. Seth became involved in drugs, once assaulted me, then also went to live with his dad. Seth was already in the court system since the knife-fight episode and had a probation officer monitoring him. I had the three younger children with me.

I was doing okay with the three younger children, Andrew, Carlene and Ella, but had not seen Seth or my eldest boy in many months. My parents decided to hold a birthday dinner for Seth in mid-2010 and he arrived with his girlfriend. We were all finally together. Soon after, though, I got a mean email from Seth, telling me I was a clueless mother and his vitriolic tone was unreal. He was so filled with hate towards me.

The younger three kids and I went to Hawaii on a business trip. Paul was there too as he still worked with us. Everybody had a great time but when we returned, all my kids went back to their dad's for the next ten days. When my third son, Andrew, returned to my place, he was distant from, and critical of, me. Soon he left entirely and went to live with his two older brothers and dad. I knew that Kim read the affidavits and court orders to the boys, even though we are instructed by the courts not to do that. The boys told me that they knew I "stole $16,000" when in fact it was our household money and I needed some of it just to survive after we split.

In the fall, my eldest daughter Carlene, began to argue relentlessly with me over everything. At Christmas, I still had the two girls but the three boys refused to come to my house. Early in the new year, I took Ella to her soccer game and when I got home, Carlene had taken off to her oldest brother's place. She actually moved in with Kim too and left a note to that effect on her bed.

Paul and I were together by this time so we started to organize for court which was held on February 1st, 2011. We enlisted Joseph Goldman, a consultant who lives in Toronto and Florida, to help us prepare. I had talked to him by phone a year or so earlier and sent him $2,000 for his advice on how to proceed to get the kids back. He told us to meet with a mediator and we had a bilateral assessment done by Dr. Hyndmarsh. The mediator sent Kim a letter asking for Section 7 expenses for the kids and a parenting schedule. When he received it, Kim phoned my lawyer, Kara Schwartz, and sent her a bill for $907. He claimed he was representing himself so his time was worth money too.

I had recorded phone calls from the kids in which they called me a "fucking bitch" and worse. I gave copies of these to Kara on Joseph's advice. Joseph told us we needed to get the kids into deprogramming via psychological therapy; Section 7 expenses were not as important. My ex-husband showed up to court with our eldest son. Kim read a prepared statement stating that his ex-wife is crazy and needs a psychiatric assessment. It went on that all our kids agreed with their father. Kara, my lawyer, said "Whoa… we have not even seen this information. Is it an affidavit?" But Judge Leah allowed it anyway. At least the judge then said, looking at Kim, "I know there is something going on here and I will tell you, sir, that you had better not be weaponizing your kids against their mother".

We got an Order in place that demanded Carol Shander as our therapist. Joseph Goldman had talked to her by phone and thought she sounded knowledgeable about parental alienation. Ms. Shander, according to the judge, was supposed to do an "intervention". But on the weekend when it was to happen, Shander was in another province, citing Kim's non-payment of her retainer as the reason. Kim kept stalling instead of paying as per Shander's request though I had thrown in my portion right after the judge ruled for the intervention. My kids needed help *now*!

Kim continued to stall so Carol Shander continued to sit on her thumbs instead of doing the intervention. My middle son, Andrew, and one of his sisters, Ella, begrudgingly came to stay at my house for the weekend. Upon arrival, Andrew was already livid. Paul was not to be at my place when the kids were with me because Kim had told the judge they hated Paul. In truth, they had spent some time with Paul and it was really fun and positive. Both kids came in the house, ate supper, and immediately afterward Andrew took off, saying "I'm out of here". On the way out to his soccer game, he handed me a note before slamming the door which said "You are not invited to any of my games. I don't want to see you there". My parents, his grandparents, were at my house too and Andrew told them they were welcome to go watch his game but I was not to accompany them.

My parents made it clear they would not be comfortable attending his games without me which made Andrew even angrier. Over time, my parents had to increasingly step in as the kids became more hostile toward me. When they stood up for me and told our kids their behaviour was unacceptable and unfounded, they were erased from their grandchildren's lives.

I phoned Andrew's soccer coach and asked to have him benched. I told the coach that Andrew had serious discipline issues with me so he should be taken out of the game. When he came back to my place after the game, Andrew yelled that he hated me, I was dead to him, and even worse stuff. He ran upstairs, slammed his door so hard that pictures fell off the wall and broke. I called my parents and they thought I should phone the police. I did and they came but Andrew had also phoned them. At least the cop backed me and told Andrew he had to stay at my house for the weekend. Finally, the female cop got Andrew calmed down while the other officer and I joined the two of them in our living-room. The woman cop asked Andrew to tell me what he wanted to say and he apologized and admitted his behaviour was inappropriate. I was very encouraged to hear that.

The minute the police left my house, though, Andrew went berserk again. The rest of the weekend was hellish; the police got called twice more. Andrew and Ella tackled me to get my cellphone at one point. Ella had been okay with me until then. She was just observing the others' hatred toward me and she finally jumped on board with them.

We went to Ella's soccer game and all the kids sat with their dad. When we got home and they were in bed, I finally relaxed a bit and started watching television. But the police showed up at my house because Kim had called them. He said our kids had emailed him that I was threatening them. No police report ever got filed.

A few days later Carol Shander came back into town and started the intervention. In the meantime, Kim had met with her, no doubt told her his story about the weekend as being my fault, and paid her retainer… finally. I met with Carol, planning to tell her about the weekend, but she spent two hours talking about herself and her so-called expertise. She said she wasn't going to read our affidavits so it was clear she would not have the history on our family. I re-read the retainer contract and sure enough, in small print it says that Carol Shander does not look at history of a case.

Ms. Shander did a report which was quite biased against me. She requested of the judge that she become our "parenting coordinator" which would entail a lot more money as well as more psychologists brought into our case. My parents had already cashed in some of their investments to pay my lawyer, Kara. The high legal bill was mostly due to Kim's stalling and stalling while the lawyers cashed in.

It would have been better to have one consistent judge assigned to our case instead of Leah followed by Action. Kara asked Justice Action if she had all the details of our case from Justice Leah. *Nope.* She said "that never got to my desk". I wrote another affidavit and we went back to court. Justice Action asked Carol Shander to attend. All she did was regurgitate the report she had written, which was inaccurate to begin with. Shander acknowledged that Ella might stay with me. But we were so long getting a court date that by the time we did so, Ella was out the door.

Now we are waiting to go back to court again. Kara Schwartz wants us to keep Shander since the court listens to her but I'm worried since she has shown major bias against me. The kids have their own lawyer, Kathy Lytton, since our last court appearance so I guess Kim must be paying for her. Legal Aid pays for the first 30 hours of legally representing the kids. Well, Lytton billed for about 30 hours in the first week! She also requested of the court that the intervention continue with another 25 hours spent with

Carol Shander. This is to be at shared cost between the parents. There is to be a psychologist assigned to each family member while Shander coordinates the entire process.

I took my 15-year-old daughter for a haircut today. She stills wants to see me when other people leave us alone. And Ella gets to decide when to spend time with me. She stays at my place Monday through Friday, sees Kim on Saturdays, and Sundays are random as she calls them. In the new year, Paul and I plan to take the two girls and my parents on a trip. We have already talked to them about it and they are keen to go.

When we needed help, we went to the legal system. We needed the court to step in and make sure my children had access and a relationship with both parents. The older boys should have been kept away from their sisters until they stopped brainwashing them to hate me, their mother. They needed a psychologist to understand and act on the alienation in progress. All this estrangement and alienation could have been avoided if the family law system actually cared about kids and families.

KIER

CHAPTER 22

KIER

My two sons mean everything to me. The eldest, Khan, is 7 and my little guy, Sher, is just 3. I was married to their mother, Mita, for almost ten years. We separated in early 2011, so my boys were 5 years old and 8 months old then. We had a verbal argument on December 30, 2010, and I left the house to cool off for a while. I came back later and thought we were okay. But in January, I found out my wife had filed an assault complaint against me the day of our argument.

The morning of January 6th, Mita called the police while I was at work. After work, I went as I usually did to our restaurant business. There, around 8:00 p.m., the police phoned and asked me where I was. I told them I was doing an errand, but could be back at our business in about half an hour. When I arrived, I expected to be questioned about our argument, but instead the police arrested me on the spot. Although I was terrified, I went cooperatively with them, as I wanted no trouble.

I was kept overnight in a cell, but the next day made bail and got out by 1:00 p.m. My wife had, apparently, not returned to our house the night I was in jail. I had made a phone call from the police station, so my mom knew I had been arrested. The police told me when I was released that I was not allowed to go back home. What was I supposed to do, as I had no clothes or any of my belongings? My mom lives with us, but even though she was at our house, I could not go there.

I phoned some friends, and they had Mom call my cellphone. She told me she wanted to get away from the house and Mita. My friend picked her up with all her clothes and a few of mine. I stayed with these friends in Edmonton for about a month and drove my mother to my sister's home in Calgary. She stayed there for four months.

Since Mita and I were an arranged marriage; I phoned her parents in India on the advice of a mediator there. He thought it best I ask them what to do. They thought that if Mita would withdraw the assault charge, we could reconcile with counselling. I was doubtful and didn't trust her. In the meantime, I was served at our business with divorce papers. I had no home, but Mita and the boys stayed in our house.

On January 25th, my mentor told me the best thing would be for me to give my wife everything she wanted and move out permanently. Mita was asking for $4,500 a month in child support. I offered her the entire house, all our assets including our business, cars, everything. My condition was that I wanted custody of one of our boys and she could have custody of the other. Of course, they would still have time together, but officially, we would each have sole custody of one child.

Mita said no way, so I hired a lawyer, Ryan Koch. He sent the official offer through Mita's lawyer, Jason Tome. Mita said she still wanted the $4,500 a month, part child and part spousal support, based on my income at the time.

She and I were both involved in our business and I still own it, but I never go there. Mita always got money from there, but she was not on the official payroll, so it was tax-free for her. Since we separated, Mita would call the police every time I tried to go to the restaurant. I felt I had to file an Access Order, so I would at least be able to see my kids. I did that at the end of January. I hadn't seen them for a whole month.

Fortunately, I was granted police assistance so I could go back to my house and get my stuff. I was so glad to see my boys, and they had missed me too. The baby had changed a lot already in that month I was absent. My 5-year-old son cried and hugged me for a long time, asking me, "Papa, when are you coming home?" I had no answer for him.

Mita tried all this time to prevent my seeing our kids. How could she do this to them? She knows exactly how to manipulate me to get what she wants. She doesn't mind using our kids for that purpose.

I asked my lawyer to set up a regular parenting schedule, but since he was out of town, he sent me over to his colleague. I sent their office an email saying I knew my rights and I needed access to my children right away. This lawyer communicated through Jason Tome, Mita's lawyer. He responded that "my client" doesn't agree with your request because you are without a home right now, so she proposes 2.5 hours visitation each weekday (i.e., 5:00-7:30 p.m.) and 3:00-7:00 p.m. on Saturdays and Sundays. Mr. Tome added that if I did not agree to those terms, I would not see my boys at all.

I had to agree as I needed time with my sons, but the hours were outrageous. These are two little boys, a baby and a kindergartener. Mita also prevented my parents from having any access to their grandchildren. When the boys were with me, my parents had to leave and go to a friend's. The way it worked was that Mita had the boys at the front of the restaurant, and I would get them there for my big 150-minute visit.

The next time I had the boys, I took them to my friends' where my parents were and they had a little visit, despite Mita's terms. Soon after, I got a letter from Jason Tome telling me that despite his (at Mita's instruction) recommendations, the kids had seen their grandparents. If I persisted in "such behaviour", he would take me to court and would make sure the kids did not see them and my access would also be terminated.

My lawyer, Ryan Koch, wrote back that grandparents have a right to see their grandchildren under the law. Since Tome got that letter, there has been no further issue with my parents visiting with the boys.

I had taken a one-month leave from work in January when my marriage fell apart. Now I went back after using up all my "vacation time". I had been unable to get disability-leave approved. As soon as Mita heard I was back at work, her lawyer sent mine a letter terminating my parenting time Mondays through Wednesdays, effective immediately. It was just a letter, not a court order, and there was no explanation.

The way I found out about this change was when I went to pick up my kids as usual on a Tuesday and they were not at the restaurant, nor was their mother. I waited outside for a while but nobody showed up. I went home and phoned my lawyer the next morning. His assistant said "oh sorry, we have a letter here stating that you are now to see your kids Thursday and Friday for two and a half hours each, and weekends for four hours each day." And to make things even worse, Mita would sometimes not allow the kids to come with me because she would say they were "sick" or "too tired".

One day when Mita had claimed the boys were too sick to see me, I had three of my friends stop by their house and both kids were just fine. My parents also went to the house and found the same thing. Mita was lying but of course, despite five witnesses stating that my children were healthy, the court ignored this information. I was paying child and spousal support to my ex-wife while she was busy finding ways to reduce my access to our kids.

February 8th, 2011, we finally went to court. The subsequent court order allowed me "liberal, generous access to the children" which didn't mean squat as far as my ex was concerned. By June I fired my lawyer as I had done enough research by then to do a way better job than he had done for me. What a waste of money; $10,000 to make our situation worse.

In the fall, I hired a new lawyer and we went back to court. Mita told the judge she needed more money from me, but I was able to show that all her demands were unreasonable. My company's Christmas party was coming up in November, so I had asked Mita for the boys overnight and I would take them back to her on Sunday. She refused. But the judge allowed me the weekend with my boys. Khan, Sher and I attended my company's party, but I had to go to court to make that happen. It cost a lot, but I didn't care as long as I had my boys.

My parents helped me a lot when I had my kids, but when they went to India for some visiting, I was on my own. I managed fine and got everything done. My intention was to have the boys a more equitable amount of time each week. Mita, however, likes to party on the weekend so she would decide at the last minute or change plans on me depending on what she wanted to do each weekend. Sometimes she'd call me, asking if I could keep Khan and Sher until 5:00 p.m. instead of 3:00 so she could have more time on Sunday without the kids. I always agreed as it gave me more time with them, even though it only happened at their mother's convenience.

Mita believes me to be the babysitter but at least I get my boys then. At the time, she was trying to restrict me from taking the kids to visit my sister in Calgary. Mita failed when my lawyer asked her in court whether my sister was unstable, had a criminal record, or such. If not, then why was Mita requesting a restriction? My ex-wife wanted me to give her two weeks notice if I planned to take the boys out of Edmonton. She had no such restriction on her own travel with them.

For the Family Day weekend in February, Mita asked me to look after Khan and Sher as she wanted to fly to Vancouver. I said it would be great and since my parents were still away, I could take the boys to Calgary to visit their aunt and family. I emailed this plan to Mita so I would have it on record. She, though, never responded to my email. When she flew home from Vancouver, she filed a legal claim that I had taken my kids out of Edmonton without her permission.

Then one day I picked up the kids after school and was to take them to their mother's home by 7:30 p.m. But we got to the restaurant 15 minutes late as a result of falling asleep on my couch. When we arrived, no one was there so I took my boys back to my home. I received several emails from Mita then, telling me to drop the boys at her house immediately. I reminded her that I could not since she had conditions in the court order that forbade me to go to her house. I suggested she pick up the boys from my place. She refused.

I took my kids to school that next day. Next thing I knew, Mita was going after me again through the court, stating that I was not complying with our parenting schedule. Fortunately, my lawyer did a good job cross-examining Mita who clearly showed her goal was to maintain control over all parenting time and the kids. She said I was often late picking up or dropping off the boys, but then had no evidence. The judge lifted the condition of my keeping away from her home too. Now I can pick up and drop the kids directly with their mother.

In March of 2012, we were scheduled again for a court date so I could see more of my kids. Mita continued to make it extremely difficult to do so. The court date was for the 4th but again there was stalling from her lawyer and the date got postponed to March 22nd, and then again to April 17th. By this time, I was desperate for time with Khan and Sher. I know that lawyers are not allowed to stall but they do it all the time; *all* the time.

This time in court, Justice Robert J. Hope actually said to my ex-wife that her intention seems to want to be "the sole *owner* of the children and to manipulate the children's father. Further, you need to tell me if [me] is a criminal, an addict, an alcoholic or something, because you have not proposed a single reason why the judicial system should not support equal custody." I recorded that statement by the judge. It was the first time we had been in front of that judge, but he knew exactly what was going on.

The resulting court order specified my parenting access. The judge allowed me to pick up and drop the boys via their school, so that I wouldn't have to deal with Mita. Now I pick up Khan from school and Sher from his daycare and then the next day their mother does the same. It is one week at each of our homes, the way it should have been by default from the start.

I still have my lawyer and pay her $2,500 per month on retainer. She charges me $300 an hour, and I never know when I'll need her to do some work on my behalf. It is money well spent for my peace of mind and my boys' well-being.

Mita went back to work part-time, and I no longer pay her spousal support. But she is still after me for more child support. She also wants a retroactive sum of money for child and spousal support dating back to the beginning of 2011. By claiming that she did not receive spousal earlier this year, Mita thinks she can make a claim. But I have proof that I paid as I was supposed to. In fact, I paid through MEP, so it is documented by that program. I showed proof to my lawyer, along with proof that when we separated, Mita stole $24,000 from our bank account without my knowledge. In her original affidavit, my ex-wife claimed I had taken all our money when in fact she had. If my first lawyer, Mr. Ryan Koch, had done his job, a lot of this added hassle could have been eliminated.

Recently, I wanted to get passports for my boys, so I emailed their mother and asked her to sign the necessary forms. She said she would only do so if the passports remained in her custody. I asked her why she needed to have them but she did not email a response to my question. So I went back to my lawyer, and we proposed that each parent keep one of our kids' passports. Mita refused so we filed to go back to court again. Soon after, her lawyer agreed for Mita to sign the passport applications. We gave her three days to sign and if she did not obey, I got a court order that allowed me to be the sole signing authority for my boys' passports. Mita took a week to sign, but eventually she did and I got my children's passports.

Now, Mita drops off Sher at his daycare at 9:30 in the morning on Fridays when I am off work and scheduled to parent my kids. Then I have to pick him up a half hour later, which is ridiculous. Why can I not have him the entire day? But Mita made this a big deal, and we had to go to court for that too. The first time I called the daycare operator and told her I would be by at 10:00 a.m. to get my son, Mita was just dropping Sher off. When she heard I would soon be over to get him, she took our boy back with her! I followed her and videotaped it all. She did not go home but instead to our business. I am required to pick up and drop off at the daycare at our common access point. From 10:00 that morning until 3:00 in the afternoon, I sat in front of the daycare for five hours, waiting until Mita brought Sher back so I could pick him up. The whole day was wasted so that Mita could exert her power over me.

It didn't end there either. My ex-wife then arranged to get Fridays off work, so I would no longer be able to take Sher those days. Our two lawyers got together and unofficially changed the court order, so that I would now have to pick up Sher at the restaurant. I'm complying with that, as I do not want any more days in court. The only reasons for this change are to make my life as difficult as possible and to restrict my time with our sons.

When I am at work, my mom cares for Sher during the day and for Khan before and after school. It works smoothly and she is happy to have time with her grandsons. My lawyer has made it clear to Mita that if she wants to keep after me for more money, she will be required to pay me rent for living in my house. I still pay the mortgage and my ex-wife pays the utilities. It was Justice Hope who ordered that Mita pay her own utilities, since I am already paying for my own home. Paying for hers would constitute hardship for me and be totally unethical. She tried, nonetheless, to get me to pay everything for her, but thankfully this judge understands Mita's ongoing manipulation.

I have read that some States lay criminal charges if you don't comply with a Parenting Order or make access difficult and unmanageable. I don't know why we do not have that legislation in Canada. All along my ex-wife knew I really love my kids and the only way she can harm me is to keep them from me. I know that I have to remain vigilant, or she will take them away from me altogether.

SARAH

CHAPTER 23

SARAH

I am an intersexed parent with a form of gender chimerism (born with both functioning sex organs) who identifies and lives as a female. I am also the biological father of Hannah, a 13-year-old girl. Since 1999, I have been embroiled in a bitter custody case as a result of my child's biological mother's discrimination toward me. Hannah's mother stated to me shortly after our separation, "Whenever I find a father that could be better than you, I will do whatever I can to ruin your life and make sure you never become a parent again".

My friend is with me today, as I am deaf. She will translate for me so I can tell you my story.

When we separated, my common-law partner, mother of our daughter, was filled with hatred for me. She began dating men a short time later and from that point, never let up her quest to destroy Hannah's relationship with me, her father.

Hannah's mother insisted on supervised access, so I had no time alone with our daughter. Even with this outrageous caveat on my parenting time with her, Hannah's mother was still not satisfied. She would only permit members of her own family to act as a supervisor for visits. Those she permitted were instructed to enforce on me her will, rules, boundaries, expectations and such. I was rendered helpless as a parent to my child. I had always been a loving, positive parent, yet her mother only saw that I was unfit, simply because I am intersexed/chimera person; therefore, somehow anomalous.

A couple years after we split, Hannah's mother became pregnant by another man. I hoped that meant things would calm down, as Hannah's mother would be preoccupied with the new baby. Not so. For the next four years, every time she disagreed with any decision I made regarding our daughter, she filed a claim and we went to court. One terrible accusation Hannah's mother made was that I sexually abused my daughter. The police called me one night, telling me they were launching an abuse investigation. As a result, poor Hannah underwent all kinds of internal and external medical exams, as well as numerous psychological tests. When all tests came back negative and had cleared me of any *and all* wrong-doing, Hannah's mother just went to other "professionals", looking for someone who would believe her and agree that I was aggressive and highly abusive. All these tests in themselves were a form of abuse inflicted on my little girl. It was noted by one such professional that the continued tests and examinations the mother had insisted on could be considered abuse by the mother.

Finally, Hannah's mother found a social worker who said he did an "assessment" and "interview" of our child. This man, who was a licensed social worker for the Alberta Government Child and Youth Services, was in a conflict of interest position. For some reason, he also did her assessment in his own home and alone with her.

This social worker did not record nor document the supposed meeting with Hannah yet stated to the court that it did, in fact, take place. In court, he insisted that my daughter be removed from my custody. The judge ordered that my regular "visitation" be terminated.

I had called my lawyer asking for enforcement of my Court Ordered parenting time. In response, Hannah's mother freaked and had me arrested. It took a whole month before I was told I was being charged with abuse. It turned out that Hannah's mother's new spouse had made the abuse accusation. The charges against me turned my blood cold and sent me into a deep depression, which included suicidal ideation. I was separated from my daughter, falsely arrested and charged with allegations of abuse, even though the court knew *damned well* I was innocent.

The judge gave a "slap on the wrist" to the social worker for his lax protocol and questioned the methods used under the authority of the Department of Social Services. On July 22, 2004, I was to have an unsupervised visit with my daughter. The judge allowed an overnight, so her mother dropped her off at my place even earlier than we had agreed. I took Hannah to the Capital Exhibition and we stayed and watched the fireworks that evening. We had such an excellent day together!

The following morning, Hannah asked me why her mother hated me so much. All I could think of to say was that some parents don't get along. Then she asked me *"why does my new daddy think you're a fag?"* Until that time, I had not even been aware that Hannah's mother was in a new relationship, much less that she was pregnant. I let my daughter know that it is wrong to call other people names; always. I told her she could decide on her own what the truth was.

When Hannah's mother arrived to pick her up, I asked whether she and her new partner had indeed said those things about me. She got very angry with me, said "Yeah, so what?!" and that it was her right to say whatever she wanted to. The new partner was present at the time and scolded Hannah for saying "I love you" to me. He also let her know that I was not to be her father anymore.

Two weeks later, Hannah's mother phoned to tell me our daughter was "too sick" to have her visit with me. I asked to speak to her on the phone and her mother refused. This had also happened in the past several times. Whenever Hannah's mother cancelled a visit, she would disallow Hannah from contacting me.

Each visit became more difficult as Hannah's mother tried to make them as few as possible and she and her partner were instilling negative ideas in my daughter's head. On a few occasions, my ex complained that Hannah's behaviour was oppositional, rude, and antisocial toward them, other kids and adults. Yet when she visited me, my daughter listened, was respectful, asked questions and was happy to spend time with her grandparents and other members of my extended family. Hannah was excited to see me and always cried when she had to go home to her mother and "new dad's".

During these years, I was undergoing major changes in my own personal identity. I withheld that information from Hannah, planning to explain it to her one day when she was mature enough to understand. Due to the genetic conflict my own body had been going through, it ended up being determined medically that I had to be one gender. I knew this would complicate matters more as I was transitioning to the female gender; this was a lot for a child to take in. Regardless, Hannah's mother and spouse decided to tell Hannah from their homophobic, transphobic point of view. Even to this day, Hannah is very homophobic and transphobic.

Their campaign of denigration and obvious repugnance of me, in my daughter's mind, turned me from a loving and beloved parent into a monster. In court, Hannah's mother's spouse said that Hannah now referred to me as "that thing". She was five years old then.

From my understanding of children, a five-year-old knows who her parents are and must be brainwashed to drastically change their view of a parent. My child stopped altogether believing I was her parent and became convinced that I was evil, her head filled with false memories to support that perception.

Hannah hates me; I have rarely seen her in years and only when it was by accident on her part. She avoids all communication with me and professes a deep hatred, the depths of which I could never have imagined.

2017

Hannah is now an adult. She is also now a mother and I am now a grandparent. The campaign of parental alienation hasn't ended. In fact, it was expanded to include my role as a grandparent. I have been prevented from access to my granddaughter. Hannah stated that when the child grows up, she will tell her how horrible I am and to ensure permanent severance of the relationship.

As an alienated parent, I also lay partial culpability on the courts, the judges and lawyers involved, and the family law system, which refuses to recognize parental alienation as child abuse.

In 2011, I wrote my own book, entitled "Parental Alienation: Understanding a Dark Truth", based on my history of maltreatment and the damage done to my family.

Over the course of 13 years, I went through over 200 court appearances, 44 JDRs (Judicial Dispute Resolutions), 100-plus court orders, variances and agreements and countless "examinations" on Hannah that even the courts ordered. In the end I was cleared of all wrongs, but the damage had already been done. It would have been more humane if I had been murdered physically, instead of parentally and socially. As a parent and a person, the therapy I am now in will be ongoing in the very long-term. I am now on disability, too scared to go back out in the world, and because of this hatred that Hannah's mother has caused, I will never recover who and what I am; a parent.

I hope that my narrative sheds light on the damage done, the irrevocable damage done, to children raised by a parent to hate their other parent. Hannah is half me, but she hates and denies that half. She has had a difficult childhood and adolescence. How will she be able to form positive, loving relationships and be accepting of people for their hearts instead? I fear for her future.

HAILEY

CHAPTER 24

HAILEY

My husband, Karl, and I had a baby boy almost a year ago. In addition, Karl has a little girl, born in 2009, from an earlier three-month-long relationship to Brenda. Recently, we found out that Brenda just had a new baby with another man.

I met Karl in Calgary and soon after, we moved to Lethbridge. A few months after we began dating, Brenda informed Karl that she was pregnant and he was the father. He asked her for a paternity test and she agreed if he would pay for it. While he was saving money for this, Brenda wrote his parents a letter. Karl was unaware of her doing this. The letter said that Karl was "rejecting his baby", that they were the grandparents, and that she wanted Karl to be a part of the baby's and her life. Brenda wrote that she didn't want anything else, just wanted them to know the situation. Karl's parents had met Brenda only once or twice at most. As a result of this letter, Karl's parents paid for the $800 paternity test and it was positive that Karl was the father. He wanted to be involved with the baby from that moment to this day. But this is when the manipulation began. Brenda wanted to improve her lot in life by using their baby as a negotiating tactic.

Karl's daughter, Emma, was about 6 months old when he first met her. She was with Brenda at a Hepatitis-C clinic where he was working as a security guard. Brenda and Emma were coincidentally there being inoculated due to a disease breakout-scare at a local McDonald's. There had been a plan for Karl to meet his daughter about a week later, so this surprise meeting caught him off guard.

After that first meeting, Brenda insisted that Emma only see her father at her place, not at our house. I was not invited to go along so only Karl visited her. I made no fuss since I thought the important thing was for father and daughter to bond. There was no legal involvement at first, but as time went by, Brenda made it increasingly difficult for Karl to see his daughter.

We decided to hire a lawyer to get a Parenting Order put in place. We hoped that a regular schedule would alleviate the access issue. Our combined income then was less than $46,000, but it was too much to be eligible for Legal Aid. We needed to go to court but that costs about $10,000 a day. There was no way we could afford that.

Our lawyer, Kelly, and Karl sat down with Brenda's Legal Aid lawyer and got her to hammer out a parenting schedule. So we were paying $215 per month to Brenda in Child Support plus legal fees while she paid nothing and collected from us. The maximum parenting time Brenda would agree to was 15 hours *per month*. That amounted to every other Saturday; period. Karl signed that agreement since we had no money to fight the terms.

Brenda's best friend was a woman named Christy and they spent much of their time together. This concerned us because Christy had four kids from different fathers, was at the time in an abusive relationship, and had one of her children taken away by the government when she actually tried to *murder* it. She was also living in a tent-trailer. It was our business since Brenda often left Emma in the "care" of Christy and her abusive husband.

One evening Karl and I were out for dinner with my parents. Christy had, in the meantime, texted Karl's brother with the message that she had a "surprise" for him. A few minutes later, she dropped off Emma at his house. Neil, Karl's brother, told Christy that Emma was neither his child, nor his responsibility. Christy left that 8-month-old baby girl with him anyway. It was

Hallowe'en and apparently Brenda and Christy wanted to go to a big party.

Karl and I went home after dinner and found the baby with Neil. Of course, baby Emma stayed with us overnight, but it was the first time she had done so. Luckily, we had some baby supplies because we had been hoping to have Emma for overnights in the future. The baby had been left with Neil without so much as an extra diaper. According to Neil, Emma had a full, wet diaper when she arrived unannounced. *This was total neglect.*

The next day Brenda showed up and got Emma from us. Then, the same evening, she phoned Karl to tell him that Emma had been airlifted to the Calgary Children's Hospital and was on a respirator. We had no idea what was going on. Brenda tried to tell Karl that Emma had eaten something off *our* floor, which had caused her to have either an allergic reaction, or she was poisoned by drugs in *our* house. What a load of crap!

Then Brenda's story changed to the hospital's having drug-tested Emma and found "general narcotics" in her system. Karl works at the hospital so he went over there and asked the staff when the most recent airlift transfer had occurred. The hospital staff told him there had been only one airlift that day and the time did not coincide with Brenda's story about Emma being sent to Calgary. We then called the Children's and every other hospital in Calgary. There was no record of Emma having been admitted.

Karl then phoned Brenda and asked her what was going on. She told him she had obtained a "No Contact Order" so she could not give him any information about the baby; another total lie. She didn't stop there either. Brenda then said she had changed Emma's surname so that we could not find her. And then Brenda really did disappear with Emma for four whole days.

We called the non-emergency police line and asked if there was something they could do to find out if Emma was okay and where she was. The officer told us they could not charge Brenda with anything, but they would go to her house, talk to her, and see what was going on. They did go over, but she did not answer the door. Next, they called her cellphone and she answered. The entire lie blew apart then. Brenda came clean that the whole story was fabricated. But there was nothing we could do since we were not legal guardians.

Another time, Brenda told Karl she had been "seeing" some guy and just found out he had been charged with being part of a pedophilia trafficking ring. Karl was freaking out with that news! She went on to say that Emma had been alone in a bedroom with this fellow and she wondered whether he had been taking photographs of the little girl. Brenda "offered" to give the name of her boyfriend to Karl so he could "go beat him up". Karl said he didn't want to do that and did not want to get arrested. He asked Brenda what she was going to do to fix the situation so Emma would be safe. She said she had called the police, they had arrested the pedophile, but he had been released the following day. Then she said her babysitter had reported that that guy was stalking the house when Brenda was not home.

Karl was also told that Brenda was taking Emma to Calgary while she obtained a restraining order against the stalker/pedophile/ex-boyfriend. This also did not happen. Karl had the police check and they confirmed that nothing had been filed or charged on that man.

Here we are now, trying to get access to Emma's medical records because we want to know what is actually true about Karl's daughter. Emma is only 3 years old. Kelly, our lawyer, advised us to document everything, but we need proof. Brenda has claimed that Emma has celiac disease and has been tested for that. We don't think that is the case, nor has she likely been tested. We have also been told by her mother that Emma is allergic to gluten, strawberries and laundry detergent, so we have to buy special products off the internet and hand-wash her clothes.

Maybe the stupidest thing Brenda has lied about is Emma's supposed allergy to grain-fed animals. We should, accordingly, buy only specially produced beef. What does that even mean? What would one feed a cow if not grain?

One time, Brenda claimed to have moved to Winnipeg with Emma and she gave Karl her new, but *nonexistent*, address. She said she had already lived there a month. We drove by her "former" house in our city and saw her shoveling snow that very day.

She also supposedly went to the United States for three months, so we didn't see Emma at all during that time and it was over Christmas. She said she went with her "mom" though she had told us earlier in time that she did not know the whereabouts of either of her parents. And she told us she took Emma with her to Italy, but that story changed to her staying home while Emma went to Italy with Brenda's "mom".

We don't know whether Brenda has a job. She has claimed to have several and has claimed to work at a school sometimes, but we think she is just on welfare. She admitted in court that she got welfare, as she probably knew she would get caught in that lie. She did not work prior to having Emma, so would not have qualified for Employment Assistance. We have no access to Brenda's medical records, but it seems pretty likely that she has some psychiatric history.

Recently, Brenda did, for sure, have a baby because we have seen it. When she went into labour, she called Karl and asked us to take Emma, which we gladly did. Brenda lives with the father of this baby so Karl went to his house and picked up Emma. She stayed with us for six days after Brenda's "water broke" as she told us. Her story later was that even though her water broke, the hospital "kept on sending me home with morphine". Clearly, that too was a lie. Over the last three of those six days, Brenda was phoning Karl, saying that she didn't think she was actually in labour after all, so could she come and get Emma? We told her we thought it best for Emma to stay with us for a bit longer, but Brenda just showed up to our house and took Emma back with her. She kept her two days ad then dropped her with us again; this time for four more days.

Brenda told us she had a scheduled C-section for the next Saturday at 8:00 a.m. Both Karl and I were working that day, so we had Karl's parents go to the hospital and get Emma from Brenda. Brenda showed up late, and then when my mother-in-law asked her where she needed to check-in, Brenda told her she didn't need to. Karl's parents wisely took Emma and got out of there. Outside, they saw Brenda's boyfriend Jack, father of the baby-to-be, sitting in his car. They watched for a few minutes to see if Jack went into the hospital. He did not. In fact, soon Brenda came out of the hospital and got in the car and the two of them drove away.

Karl called Brenda with this information. She said her C-section had been changed to Sunday. That was the next day and happened to be my birthday. We called Brenda and were told the baby had been born and was in the "ICU" (she must have meant the neonatal intensive care unit; NICU). She said her baby had breathing trouble because her C-section had been complicated. Yet the baby supposedly weighed ten pounds! Karl asked for Brenda's room number and we went to the hospital to bring her flowers. It turned out that Brenda had never even been admitted. When questioned, Brenda on her cellphone told Karl that she had been sent to the NICU to be close to the baby. First of all, they don't do that and second of all, she would not be using her cellphone in the NICU.

Poor little Emma was missing her mom after ten days with us. She would ask us when her mommy was coming for her. We had to tell her that Mommy was having a baby. Finally, Brenda called to say her friend was coming to get Emma. We had never met this friend. A car pulled up to our house and Brenda was in the driver's seat. There was no sign of a baby. I decided to go out to the car with Emma's bag to see what the situation was. Her friend, who weighs about 300 pounds, blocked my way and grabbed the bag. Emma got into her mom's car.

A little while later, Karl went to McDonald's and guess who he saw in there? Brenda was there, still pregnant, with Emma in tow, and there was no sign of her friend. Karl said nothing to her and left.

Some friends of ours work in Labour and Delivery at the hospital in town and they reported that Brenda did, indeed, have her baby a week later. It was about six pounds and healthy though Brenda told us it was very sick and was losing weight. The lies continue.

The other part of our story involves money. We started to pay child support when Emma was six months old as soon as Karl found out he was her father. Karl was instructed to pay $215 a month. He was making about $2,000 monthly; I was pregnant and on Employment Insurance. We paid Brenda in cash and got receipts from her. Unbeknownst to us, Brenda had registered Karl with MEP (i.e., Maintenance Enforcement Program) but continued to accept our cash. Then we got a notice from MEP stating that we owed four months retroactive child support covering the months before the paternity test was done. MEP sent us many letters, charging us interest for "arrears" while we were already paying Brenda. Karl tried for weeks to get a staff member at MEP on the phone. He left a lot of voicemail messages to no avail.

Then Karl's wages began to get garnished every month. They took 40% of his paycheque every single month! I checked out MEP's website under Information for Creditors, and found this statement: *"Please don't lie because this can cause unfair fault on your debtor"*. Unbelievable! This gave power to the so-called creditor and possibly the idea to lie as well.

I had to get financial help from my parents just so we could make ends meet. We had our own baby by then. After a few months, we were apparently "paid up" in arrears so MEP became a bit more receptive to our position. We got somebody there on the phone who instructed us to send MEP the receipts Brenda had given us; then after a month or two someone would get back to us.

MEP sent a notice to Brenda after it received our receipts, explaining to her our position and asking her to sign a document confirming that she had accepted cash from us. She did; but later told MEP we had forged her initials on that document. When we found that out, Karl phoned her and threatened to take legal action against her. She backed down and called MEP, admitting that she lied. Instead of sending our much-needed overpayment back to us, MEP just kept it as a cushion of child support to be allocated to Brenda over time. There was no penalty for her deliberately getting overpaid.

MEP, however, made it clear to Karl that if he so much as missed one payment, paid it late, or it was one penny short, he would get a *ten-year garnishment of his wages.* MEP sat on our money and made interest on it. For about six more months following our paying off the arrears, MEP was taking child support from Karl twice a month. Every single paycheque was garnished so now we were really broke. My parents are accountants and thankfully got us through that precarious time. Finally, when Karl's Human Resources department and Karl succeeded in waking up MEP, it ceased the double payments but kept our money. So… even though we had at least an extra six months of payments sitting in their coffers, Karl continued to have his paycheques garnished until the entire year was up.

MEP told us that its garnishment was to be for 12 months, then it would reconsider for future. In the meantime, Brenda accumulated money, did not have to pay tax on the extra income, and kept receiving welfare. She also did not disclose that she was living with Jack in his house. And we worry that if MEP or the government gets wind of her dishonesty and wants repayment from her, what will happen to Emma's care?

Our two lawyers had made up the initial parenting agreement, but a year or so later we asked to go to mediation. Brenda's lawyer must have advised her to attend. But mediation doesn't stand up in court, so it's kind of useless if both parties don't want to cooperate. Karl asked for more time with Emma and stated that he believed he and I had proven ourselves worthy parents. He also requested Emma's medical records. There was a judge who made suggestions, but no court order could be issued since this wasn't a court appearance. He scolded Brenda for her lies, false allegations, misrepresentation of her financial situation, and calling the police a number of times on us for no reason.

The mediator/judge gave Karl more time with Emma on a trial basis. He told Brenda to "suck it up" and adjust to it unless she could find a reason to change the new parenting arrangement. He inadvertently suggested she find a reason. We had Emma more after then, but Brenda would prohibit overnights, telling us and the mediator that she doesn't trust us. We have our own baby, for God's sake, and we had Emma with us for ten straight days while Brenda was supposedly having her baby.

Just three weeks ago, we took Emma back to Brenda's at the usual scheduled time, but no one answered her door, her phone or the texts Karl sent her. We went back to the car and waited outside Jack's house. Then Karl decided to go around the house and found Brenda in the backyard, sitting on her doorstep with her baby. I joined Karl and asked Brenda why she did not answer her door or phone. She said "Oh, my phone died, I guess." Of course this wasn't true. Anyone with a dead phone plugs it in at home.

From what we observe, Emma seems happy enough to see her mother when she gets back to her house, but she is a very needy child. I feel she may be neglected much of the time. She once showed up to our home with bruises on her body in "unusual places" (i.e., her jaw, a few on the inside of one thigh, and a bunch along her spine) and I took pictures of them. My job is with children, so I know what sort of bruising is natural. A psychologist looked at those photos and told us they showed "suspicious bruising". She also told us, though, that Child Welfare would not take action unless we had a series of evidence photos over time. Fortunately, to date we have not seen any more bruising since that one incident.

I keep a big and thorough file of everything that has to do with Emma so the photos are in there too. Emma can talk more clearly now as she gets older. We hope she will tell us what she is experiencing if she needs help in any way. She has already told us that "Mommy is always tired." She seems more excited to see Jack than her mother when she goes back to their house. Jack seems like an okay dad from what we can tell. He is the new baby's father and seems to be fairly level-headed.

When Emma comes to our place, she loves to spend time with our son, Luke. He is almost a year old now and he wants to follow her around everywhere. Emma also loves to see grandma and grandpa and play with our animals. We have a dog, cat, and bunny. Brenda once had a Rottweiler puppy, but she left it unattended in her yard and it got hit by a car. You know what the saddest part is? This little girl deserves to have a happy home with each of her parents. If our spending money on lawyers would help give her that, we would happily be poor to keep paying them. But we have spent about $8,000 so far plus a $5,000 retainer up front to hire one. We haven't even gone to court.

We still have not seen Emma's medical records because we don't have official guardianship. If anything happened to Brenda, her secondary guardian is "mom", some unknown person who Brenda supposedly went with on a trip to Europe. Karl is not named on Emma's birth certificate. He is her father and he loves her. We both love her. We pay child support as well as legal fees to try to help her as best we can.

JERRY

CHAPTER 25

JERRY

My partner, Terry, and I met in 2008. She is here with me today. I have a daughter, Samantha, who is 11 years old, from my marriage. We had our daughter together when my wife already had two kids, Nancy, 21, and Michael, 17, from an earlier relationship. Samantha's mother, Barbara, and I were married for 18 years and separated in July of 2005. I moved right away to Texas, working for an oil company and sent child support north every month to my ex for all three kids.

To give you some idea of the dynamic between my former wife and me, one time she decided to be angry with me and did not speak a word to me for the next three weeks. After that time, the ice began to melt a little so I asked her what the matter was. I said I needed to know so I would not make her so mad in future. She said this: "I am still so mad at you because of something you did to me in a dream I had."

I once had a business in Medicine Hat which failed. When I left for Texas I took all that debt with me. Fortunately, I was able to consolidate it so that my ex and the kids could stay in our marital house. My ex got my half of the house, plus its $160,000 in equity, a $6,000 tent trailer, and a two-year-old car, which was paid off. Up until then, my relationship with all three of our kids was excellent.

When I went to Texas, I was truly suffering separation anxiety. Basically, I ran away and put myself into exile. I didn't communicate with my family at all. But in the first year there, I flew my kids down to visit me for ten days. There were also two visits here in Alberta when I managed to fly home to see them. Our Separation Agreement stated that I was to have "free and generous access" to my children. And we had joint custody.

In 2007, I was making about $55,000 American, but Barbara claimed it was $75,000. She obtained our divorce while I was in Texas. The divorce gave my ex-wife sole custody, $1,100 in child support, and $400 in spousal support, per month. Not only were my payments now $1,500 a month, but my out-of-country cheques would have a 25-day hold on them. So, a couple times, my cheques bounced by the time Barbara cashed them. From then on, I started sending her money orders instead, but I was already fined $2,000 for insufficient fund penalties.

I decided to move back to Alberta in August 2007 when my job ran out in Texas and I could not renew my three-year work Visa. I closed all my American bank accounts. My ex remarried in September 2007 and I felt I did not want some stranger raising my kids. I phoned my kids who told me they had just returned from "mom's wedding". Barbara went out with this guy for *three dates* and then they married. Apparently, he was a semi-retired businessman whose wife had recently died of cancer. By late fall, I was back in Alberta, but in another city four and a half hours away from my kids.

Then one day I got a phone call from MEP, *the Gestapo arm of the provincial government*. I was told that I was starting with arrears to the tune of $29,000! My ex did not disclose any of the payments I made to her between 2005 and 2008. So, the first thing I had to do was negotiate with MEP big-time so I could keep my driver's license. My job was long-haul driving for a big company, so I have a Class One license. Each time I wanted to see my kids I had to drive to Medicine Hat from my city. I saw them twice the winter I came back to Alberta; once in January and again in March. Besides the gas, I had to stay in a hotel there, so visits were expensive.

I was with Terry by this time and we were able to persuade Barbara to let us have Samantha for the May long weekend in

Calgary. From the moment they met, Barbara referred to Terry as my "flavour of the week". She also told our kids that I cheated on her for 18 years and that I didn't love them. Meanwhile, my ex was cashing in on spousal support and child support for three kids, one an 18-year-old daughter no longer living at home. Nancy, my eldest, got a tattoo when she turned 18, so her mother threw her out of the house. It was a windfall for Barbara.

Nancy was visiting us frequently. Child support to her mother remained in place unless we went to court. So I was paying $1,500 a month, my eldest did not live at her mother's, and Barbara had already been remarried for a year and a half.

That September long weekend Barbara and her new husband were in Calgary so she "offered" to "let" me have Samantha from Saturday at 11:00 a.m. until Sunday at 6:00 p.m. I made sure to pick up Sam right on time Saturday morning, but that evening, Barbara left me a voicemail saying she changed her plans and wanted Samantha brought back to her by noon on Sunday. Barbara also changed the venue at which I was to meet her to transfer Samantha. It was now to be the opposite end of the city and about as inconvenient for me as possible. I called Barbara back and told her we had an agreed-upon plan and I would abide by that original drop-off time, 6:00 p.m., and place.

When I arrived at 6:00 p.m. Sunday to transfer Samantha back to her mother, Barbara was spitting nails. She yelled at me, and in Sam's presence, "you will never fucking see your daughter again"! My current spouse, Terry, and her son also witnessed Barbara's threat. As a result of this incident, Terry and I filed a claim in 2008 to get an active Custody Order, a parenting schedule, from the court. We self-represented to save the little money we had. The claim had to be made in Medicine Hat, since that's where the kids lived with their mother. Barbara hired a lawyer for our court date of October 9th. We hoped to eliminate spousal support and the so-called child support for a child who was an adult living independently.

Barbara's lawyer knew well how to stall the process, so he called for mediation before any filing of documents for court. He also tried to make me pay for my ex's legal fees. We met with the judge who directed mediation. Soon after, Barbara one day called the police, saying I had kidnapped my children! In fact, all three of my kids had been on the way to our place for Thanksgiving weekend. This would have been a first, and they were all keen to come. Nancy was able to come with us of her own free will since she is an adult. The other two, though, were subject to their mother's whims. Terry and I picked up all the kids after school, her son included, and we stopped off at Dairy Queen to confirm the plan with Barbara. Instead, Barbara showed up with the cops, yelled at the kids to go with her and that they were all grounded.

The police told us "this looks like a domestic; just go home." I think they see what is going on. They just can't help because their hands are tied. From that day forward, each child has been systematically alienated from us. We no longer see either of the two oldest kids and Samantha is actively being groomed to hate Terry and me.

Samantha is happy as a lark when she is with us, but as the time nears for her to go back to mommy's house, she starts to complain of her stomach hurting. The older two kids visited us for a while, but Michael even told us that if he went against his mother's wishes to see us, he paid dearly for it when he went back to her home.

Since 2008, when the legal involvement began, Barbara forbade Samantha from visiting me, her father. Barbara told me not to buy her presents or try in any way to contact her. If I phoned, no one would pick up or Barbara would tell me Samantha was "too busy". We were able to have Michael take presents to her, but for all we know, they got thrown in the garbage. I have never had a Christmas with all three of my kids, four including my step-son Laughlin, since the time of our separation 7 years ago.

Mediation never happened as Barbara refused to go. It made no sense. She could have enjoyed her life and shared our kids. She was remarried and had lots of money. I always wanted to smooth out parenting terms for our children's sake. It was not to be.

In 2009, I got laid off from my trucking job and had to go on Employment Insurance. But MEP kept docking my bank accounts

$1,500 a month anyway. I have no benefits, but fortunately, Terry can have all three of the children and me under her healthcare umbrella. Barbara could get benefits for our kids under her own health plan at work, but since there is a cost to her, she has consistently refused.

I did finally get a Court Order, which reduced my child support to $400 a month and spousal support terminated. We also got a credit of $6,000 to my MEP file. Now I have Samantha officially every second weekend. That was great news and we celebrated Sam's birthday together. Nancy, that evening, told us her wisdom teeth were really bothering her and she needed them taken out. Well, thankfully, we now had full coverage via Terry's work benefits. A couple days later, Nancy phoned me, crying because her mother told her it was "illegal for *The Skank* to cover your medical or dental costs." This, supposedly, was because Terry and I are not officially married.

I let my daughter know that she could, in fact, get her wisdom teeth out using Terry's coverage and she did. One of Nancy's friends drove her to Lethbridge for the surgery. Barbara, meanwhile, refused to drive Nancy there or home because she was getting her teeth out on Terry's benefit plan. The poor kid had an emergency extraction of all four teeth and was sedated, yet her mother would not help her get the care she needed.

After that incident, Barbara began showing Nancy her court documents and my MEP file. She told her how I was "a deadbeat and behind on his payments by $29,000". She also told our daughter that I did not pay child support, I was abusive, I was a cheater, etcetera.

Barbara was ordered by the judge to meet me halfway between our home cities, about two hours' drive for each of us, on the weekends I was scheduled to have Samantha. But we would drive to Cluny, to the agreed-upon transition point, and Barbara would not show. Then she would text and say she had to cancel the visit for a multitude of invented reasons. Sometimes, I'd get the text about 15 minutes before I was to meet her with Sam. When I asked why the cancellation, she would tell me it was none of my business.

Terry and I barely had enough money for food and we were spending lots of gas money for nothing. In nine months, we saw Samantha four times. In December of 2009, Barbara successfully petitioned the court to have me drive to Medicine Hat every other visit so she would only have to drive to meet me once a month. The judge allowed this, even though it meant many more driving hours for me, and a hotel each time I went to that city. I agreed to those terms just so I could see my daughter.

For one of the first visits with Samantha after the new "visitation terms" were put in place, we got a cheap hotel with a kitchenette. Barbara then texted us that Sam had a birthday party elsewhere so could only spend time with us after it was over, late Saturday afternoon. I offered to take her there and back, since it was to be our weekend. Barbara refused, saying I was not allowed to go to the party venue. In fact, my allotted parenting time was from 8:00 Friday evening through Sunday at 6:00 p.m. Barbara said she put Sam to bed at 7:30 p.m., so we thought that was why we could not see her until after the birthday party on Saturday. The message to Sam was that she could not attend the birthday party because I was not allowed to take her there. You can imagine how angry my daughter was… at us.

Barbara forbade me from attending Sam's soccer games, her usual church, birthday parties or friends' houses; all of these. I was not clearly not supposed to be a part of her life. Samantha sees us as interfering in her normal life, so any time spent with us is a downer.

Samantha has no relationship now with her extended family on my side. Barbara has destroyed that too, telling Sam that her grandma is bad and so are her cousins, aunts and uncles. We never pry to get information from Sam, but sometimes she inadvertently comes out with negative comments about my family.

I was asked to provide a travel letter of permission so Barbara and her husband could take all three of our kids to Mexico. It was about that time that Nancy stopped talking to us. She phoned me from a new cell number. I thought it was one of Terry's clients, and Nancy got really mad that I didn't recognize her voice. That was the last time I heard from her until Michael's graduation. Regarding the letter, I told Barbara I would provide it when she gave me the passport, flight numbers and dates of travel. She refused to do so, even though this is a standard requirement for Customs. She told the kids that I would not sign the letter. Soon after, I got an email from Michael dismissing me from his life because "you won't give me permission to go to Mexico." I messaged him back to let him know I was just waiting for the vacation details.

Then Barbara took us to court, saying I was denying their right to travel. The judge chastised me for not providing the letter. But he did tell Barbara to give me the required information. The judge even told her not to alienate me from my children. Too bad the kids did not hear that exchange in court.

I attended Michael's graduation, even though I was purposely not invited. My son completely ignored me there. He had turned on me over the course of two weeks, from the time Barbara started telling lies about my history with her, MEP, and everything else. He texted Laughlin, who he was on good terms with, and told him what a loser I was. He also told Laughlin that I stole $6,000 from his mother, Barbara.

In early 2010, Barbara began serving me with court documents, getting Sam to deliver them as her own personal courier. One time, Barbara's husband, Craig, showed up with Samantha to transfer her to us for the weekend. The poor kid tried to hand over the papers but I held my hands up and told her that no, her step-dad needed to do that himself. So Barbara's husband jumped out of the car, pushed Sam, grabbed the documents from her hands, and shoved them at my chest. He yelled in my face "Consider yourself served!" This was in the middle of a parking lot and Terry witnessed the whole incident. Then Craig threw the car into drive, spun the tires in the gravel and took off.

Since then, Barbara's husband will text me, writing that I am not to correspond or otherwise communicate with his wife. He has even instructed me to only correspond via his cell phone. He calls me an "asshole" among other derogatory terms. I still try to be civil; if in Medicine Hat, I will offer to pick up Sam there so they won't have to drive to the exchange point. This saves them a long drive. But every time, if I am even able to reach one of them, they instruct me to go to the meeting point instead. They would rather be hugely inconvenienced than cooperate on any level with me. This has happened even in minus-29 degree weather!

Barbara's current lawyer, Noelle Strandt, took Barbara's money but, in the end, fired her for disobedience. Every time, Ms. Strandt went up against us in court, she lost. And we were self-representing. She charged me once with contempt when I failed to attend a court appearance. I had not been informed of that hearing date. The judge, as a result, sent our case to Special Chambers so I had to hire a lawyer in Medicine Hat. Terry and I had no idea how to proceed through Special Chambers.

Terry quickly sent me $3,000 so we could retain a lawyer and that Special Chambers appearance actually gave us the current visitation schedule; every second weekend and joint custody. In court, we also presented that Barbara had been getting reimbursed for the kids' medical and dental costs but was claiming I was not reimbursing her under Section 7 (extraordinary expenses). Our lawyer was a smooth-talker and was making a killing in fees but at least he read our file and called it "a classic case of a woman scorned". The judge also gave us police enforcement. Of course, Barbara denied us Christmas access as a result of her ramped-up anger. She took off to Regina to see her parents who have become accomplices in her manipulation.

We found out that Barbara and the kids had left town by phoning her parents' number from a different cell number. She had blocked mine but when I called her via the other number, she picked up right away. I asked to speak to Samantha. Within a few seconds, Barbara caught on that it was me and she immediately hung up. That gave us confirmation that she had taken the kids to Regina. Our next step was to call the RCMP. The police called their office in that city and soon officers were at the grandparents' house.

Although we hoped the police enforcement would show Barbara that she needed to abide by the court order, she did not. In fact, the very next month in January, Barbara arranged for Nancy to fly to Vancouver with Samantha. It was my scheduled weekend with Sam. I received no communication at all from Barbara. Instead, I went to Sam's school to pick her up and found out she had gone to the coast with her sister. The next two scheduled visits Barbara also denied my access. This was before the new Court Order was stamped, so my ex knew she could get away with noncompliance.

The new Court Order specified that a journal was to be kept and shared by the parents, Barbara and me. This way, each of us would write events and important information for the other parent and it would be taken between houses along with Sam. That February, I wrote Barbara asking whether we needed to renew Samantha's passport since we planned to take her to Disneyland in November after our wedding. She did not write back. I write her again a few times and still got no response at all. Finally, I had to get our lawyers involved.

The summer of 2011, Barbara tried her best to prevent my week with Samantha. She went to the police and told them we were illegally keeping her daughter, and she wanted them to come and arrest me. Instead, the constable who took Barbara's call penalized her. We started to prepare court documents and did research on parental alienation. Sam was so stressed out. She would cry when she had to go back to her mom and step-dad's house. Samantha even asked Terry directly if she could her help stay with Dad and Terry. We talked to people we knew in the Child Welfare department and tried to think of ways to fix this mess.

Terry looked into Practice Note 7 interventions on the Alberta Courts website. We asked for that too on our legal claim. We wanted to get psychological assessments done and we knew social workers who did that kind of work. In August, Justice Kerke in Medicine Hat ordered Samantha's passport, the Practice Note 7, and directed that all reports from those assessments go straight to him. We were self-representing. Barbara's new lawyer turned our application around to make it look as if it was Barbara and her who requested the Practice Note 7 intervention. So Kerke asked us whether we objected; of course we didn't. If that judge had read our application, he would have seen that we initiated the request for an intervention. Justice Kerke is a circuit judge, so he gets assigned whatever cases are happening on days he is in town. We have had so many different judges, and half the time they don't even read the background materials before court. In Texas, people elect their judges, which is so much more ethical.

Justice Kerke said he was only aware of one therapist who was qualified to do the intervention; the one my ex's lawyer was requesting. To that I said, Your Honour, on the Court of Queen's Bench website there is a list of appropriate therapists, including the one we recommend who has a Master's degree and expertise in this area. He then wanted to see the list, which I showed to him. But he decided we would proceed with a Bonnie Ruse-Widemann, the woman Barbara's lawyer suggested. His rationale was that "she is a friend of the court".

The intervention took forever and started in October. In the meantime, we got married and Samantha came with us to California as planned. Her mother phoned her twice a day for the 10 days Sam was with us. On the day of our wedding, Barbara phoned Sam three times. For comparisons, on two previous vacations with us, Samantha's mother did not call her once in 17 days over Christmas holidays nor at Easter, when we had Sam for three weeks.

Our wedding was wonderful but my two elder kids, Nancy and Michael, refused to come. We had Samantha and Laughlin with us at least. They danced and had fun and it was so great to see Sam having fun with everyone there.

Since we got home, Barbara is now refusing to allow Sam to wear her eyeglasses when she comes to see us. According to my daughter, her mother told her she had to leave them at home because otherwise her father (me) would steal them. Recently, Samantha has begun to balk at visiting us. She says she would rather stay with her mother. Barbara is very strictly religious and she hasn't let Sam dance at her house. But suddenly my daughter says that she is allowed to dance, listen to music, and have friends over. She also says she wants nothing to do with us. We had given her a photo taken of us tobogganing almost two years ago. She wanted to take it back to Medicine Hat, which she did. Now Sam has written in the journal, a year after I wrote her asking about it, that she will never keep a picture of us in her mom's house. She added that if we wanted to look for the tobogganing picture, we would have to go to the dump to find it.

This year, in January, I finally went to the child psychologist supposedly doing the assessments for court. I told Ms. Ruse-Widemann that I was supposed to have Samantha that upcoming weekend. And that I emailed Barbara several days before to let her know I could pick up Sam from school as I planned to be in Medicine Hat that day for work. This would mean Barbara did not have to make the long drive with Sam to meet me. No response from my ex.

Bonnie assured me that Barbara would allow my plan, so I should go ahead and pick up my daughter on Friday. It was a super-cold day, almost minus-30. I called and texted and emailed Barbara that day and she never got back to me. So, I literally followed her car to our meeting place two hours away. Then Sam got out of her mother's car and into mine, and we drove the rest of the way to my place. Bonnie has no idea what she is dealing with. She does not recognize parental alienation, or the mental state of the mother of my children.

In February, Bonnie apparently met with Barbara, but she refused to give consent for Sam to talk to her. Finally, she did sign her permission. We were scheduled to have Sam over the Easter break. But when we got the journal back, Barbara wrote that she and her husband had purchased plane tickets to take Sam on a "family vacation". She also wrote that if we wanted to fight her on this, we would have to go to court.

The evening we were supposed to have Samantha, we drove as usual to the meeting place and Terry's friend, a Child Welfare employee, came with us. We expected there to be a no-show and then we would file kidnapping charges against Barbara and Craig. To our amazement and only 20 minutes late, a truck we had never seen before pulled up and Samantha got out.

We went home and then heard from Sam that the week prior she had been dropped off at her "uncle's" (Craig's brother's) though she barely knows him. She said she spent the whole week there, went to work with him and played video games all day at his office. She was not allowed to bring her homework along she said. This was the first we'd heard about this. Barbara would rather have our daughter stay with a little-known, new male relative than with her father.

This time I figured Barbara and her husband had gone on holiday without Samantha. I wondered who would be there when I took her back to the meeting place on Sunday. That uncle could be a pedophile for all I know and I'm supposed to leave my 11-year-old daughter with him? But in the journal, Barbara wrote that she would be there, so I sure hoped that would be true. On Sunday, at the meeting place, Barbara did not show up. The uncle did; so I asked Sam to stay in my car. She started to cry because she didn't know what to do. We left and drove to the RCMP precinct. They advised us that we did the right thing in keeping my daughter.

Once Barbara was back in town, she got Sam back with no problem. Ms. Ruse-Widemann did nothing to protect her, or to prevent Barbara's future breaching of the Court Order. A couple weeks later, I got served with court documents demanding my 2009 tax return (the court already had my 2010 return) and notice that MEP was recalculating my child support. This was nothing short of legal bullying.

Once again, we had to hire a lawyer, but this one was helpful. She answered all our questions, but it cost us $6,000. Justice Kerke also received Ms. Ruse-Widemann's report on the "assessments" which stated that there was evidence of "mild to moderate parental alienation". The report said that Samantha told Bonnie that we did not feed her at our house or when we went to Disneyland. We have witnesses including Terry's mother who saw that little girl eat a lot while we were away, as she does at our home. Sam also said that I left her mother very poor and that Barbara is always stressed because of what I did to her. She repeatedly referred to me by my first name, not Dad. Four months prior to this "assessment", she was always hugging and telling me, as well as Terry, that she loved us, and she always called me Dad.

Barbara remains in contempt of the court order, yet she continues to get away with it. She is supposed to keep us apprised of, and share, school and medical information and records, but she hasn't done so. We have another court date coming up this Friday, and Justice Kerke has requested to be our case manager. But our lawyer wants another $1,000 before then. Until we pay her, she won't so much as talk for a minute on the phone to us. She told us we could not have our case file from her unless she was no longer representing us. We fired her.

We found a website about a program in the States called "New Ways for Families". It is in the pilot-stage with a mandate to detect and expose situations of parental alienation. I am meeting tomorrow in Medicine Hat with one of the three counselors in that program. If it seems worthy, we can proceed for the most part via Skype after that. We have managed to get this program court-ordered.

There will be six sessions between my assigned counselor and me, and Barbara will also have six sessions with her assigned counselor. Then both parents meet together with the counselors and then Samantha will be included a few sessions after that. It sounds interesting, but I'm not sure how well these counselors really understand parental alienation. If they all meet together, then Barbara's lies will be exposed for sure. We now want to get primary care of Sam since she really needs us, and needs parenting. Barbara needs some kind of treatment; anger management at the very least. She is a hostile parent and from what we can see, *likely an undiagnosed narcissist.*

Today, Samantha is doing well at school. She gets all As and Bs. Michael, too, is in Engineering and doing very well. He actually emailed me the other day, but called me by my first name, not Dad. Michael then proceeded to tell me to "stop lying to" Samantha. I think he truly believes he is a warrior for his poor mother. If I phone their house, Craig will often pick up the phone now. When I ask to speak to Sam, though, he yells to her and she tells me she doesn't want to talk to me. Before the alienation progressed so far, Sam used to hide in the basement in order to talk to me on the phone. Now she has just given up, and I don't blame her.

Our hope is that this New Ways for Families will help us be a family. My kids all need help and I will be glad to cooperate however I can and am allowed. I believe that if all the assessments are done, compared, with interviews done and observed, the parental alienation history will be obvious and severe. I have given up on reuniting with my older two kids for the most part. I hope I am wrong, but I can't see their figuring out what really happened to them and the depth of their brainwashing. Samantha, though, might have a hope if the intervention provides her the support that she needs.

CRAIG

CHAPTER 26

CRAIG

I'm a father of three kids and I've been going through parental alienation for five years now. I do have to tell you that today is actually the first day I have had any hope for the future with my kids. My eldest son is nine and a half years old; his name is Emery. My middle child is a seven and a half year old daughter, Brittany. My youngest boy is Cale; almost five. My ex and I married in 2001 and split in 2007. I met Paula, who would become my wife, through her grandfather at a church function. He was heavily involved in some Christian circle, as was his family including Paula. When we split up, it must have been a black eye on her family's image.

We first lived near Red Deer, the town in which I went to high school, but moved to Medicine Hat a couple years into our marriage. A teaching job came available in Medicine Hat (aka: The Hat) and Paula's parents lived nearby in Brooks. I had an opportunity to go instead to Slave Lake, which would have been great, but there was no way Paula would go there. In our marriage, we made decisions together, as long as Paula made our final decision. She wanted to stay home with the kids and always did so. There was no reason she couldn't consider moving elsewhere, but she clearly wanted instead to be near her parents.

Emery was born here before we moved to The Hat. Britt was born in Brooks and Cale, in The Hat. We had been going to counselling pretty much from the start of our marriage because Paula wanted it. Her friends suggested the counselor who was in Calgary. I noticed that as soon as the counselor started, in our sessions, to ask questions of my wife that were up close and personal, Paula decided we didn't need to go any longer. We also went to a counselor in The Hat which was okay, but he moved away so it ended. And then we went to another counselor.

Three years into our marriage, Paula said she needed to visit her parents in Brooks, so she left me with the kids for the weekend. Her deciding to leave with Emery a toddler and Britt only a few months old was kind of stressful and probably a catalyst later to her leaving me permanently. Paula had been spanking Emery repeatedly because he would not get into bed; he was 2 years old! I intervened and kind of pushed Paula away from my son. She stopped halfway out of his bedroom and said to me, "What are you doing?" I told her I needed to separate her from our son.

This was as physical as our relationship ever got, but Paula told me I abused her and she was going to use it against me. After that episode, she did not spank the kids again, but she had no idea how to discipline them without corporal punishment. I wanted to go to counselling then so she could work through her anger and we could develop good strategies for disciplining our children in a healthy way. We did go to that third therapist, and I thought we made good progress. He was very good and really tried to help keep us stay together.

After six years of turmoil in our marriage, Paula left in July of 2007. She gave me a week's notice, but I was fine with her leaving. I did not understand the significance of what she told me. In fact, I thought she was just trying to manipulate me again, as she often did, by giving me an ultimatum or a threat. She left on a Friday while I was at work; I didn't know this was her plan. I guess she got a bunch of friends and/or family to help her by sneaking into the house because they took all kinds of stuff with them.

It was all so crazy and Paula took Emery, Britt and baby Cale with her. When I returned home that evening, my kids were gone and so was my wife. She left a hand-written note telling me to look on the computer where I would find another note. Paula's note on our computer told me that this was a sudden choice, her leaving me, because she "couldn't take it anymore". But surfing the internet, I also found an actual letter from her to me, a letter written some time prior to that day. I didn't read that letter when I found it; I was too overwhelmed because my family was gone.

Anyway, my wife had apparently gone to stay with friends for a few weeks. Strangely though, a week after she left our home she went camping with her parents and all our kids. You see, several days before our separation I had asked for, and gotten, a week's vacation and asked Paula if our family could go camping together. She didn't want to go, so instead, I had gone camping with Emery and Britt. 18-month-old Cale had the sniffles, so Paula insisted he stay home with her. We had a great time and when I got home with the two eldest kids, Paula urged me to talk with our counselor, and I did.

I also got together with our neighbour, Brad, and we talked half the night. I have no idea what all Paula had told him, but I'm pretty sure that after our lengthy conversation, he had a very different view of what was going on with my wife and me. My wife thrived when she had all the attention; people around her were her puppets and she is a master manipulator.

Before Paula went camping with our kids, she asked my permission to take them out of the city. I refused, but she took them anyway. I think she was testing the waters to see what she could get away with. She later took them to another city without my knowledge. The weekend before she moved with our kids to Red Deer, she asked me to look after them. It was a Thursday night and she wanted to drop them with me on Friday. I was desperate to see Emery, Britt and Cale, but I was scheduled to work that whole weekend. I managed, however, to get the office staff to cover for me; they have been wonderful. They gave me the whole weekend off, so I finally had a couple of great days with my kids. The night Paula was to pick up the kids, she called and very sweetly asked me if I would go to a "family birthday party". That was the night, while I was at the party, she cleaned out the house and took off with the kids to Red Deer.

At some point after she left, Paula came back to our house, again while I was away, and made a video while touring around it. I guess she wanted to figure out what she planned to claim as hers. Unbeknownst to me, Paula had been granted an Ex-Parte Restraining Order against me. On a Thursday evening, a police cruiser showed up in my driveway and the officer came to the door. He served me with papers and watched me read them. He had no hostility toward me and just asked, "Do you understand the terms?" I was in tears, just like I am now, but I managed to respond that yes, I understood that there was a Restraining Order on me and I could not see my children. He talked to me a bit, in a nice way, and then left. I immediately went over to my neighbours' house. Thank God for them; I don't know what I would have done without their support. I even asked them whether they thought maybe I was a bad person, but they assured me I was good. I needed to hear that. Just to have somebody I trusted tell me I was okay meant so much.

Then we went to court. I hate conflict, and being before a judge, especially without legal representation, was traumatic! Barney Harrelson was Paula's counsel at the time. Mr. Harrelson, though, seemed like an honest guy and after that hearing, he ceased to represent Paula. Our hearing was adjourned for a few weeks and I was instructed to get a lawyer.

A few days later, Paula showed up at the house with her brother in tow. Due to the Restraining Order against me, I said they were not allowed in, but I would bring the court-ordered items on her list outside to her. Since I refused to let them into the house, Paula's brother called the police who soon came and supervised Paula's assets grab. The officer was not pleasant to me, no doubt judging me as an abusive husband.

I think Paula had to call me an abuser to save face for her family, since they are devout Christians. They would not have been supportive had they known the truth about her. Close to the time she left me, she goaded me one night to the point where she was asking me, seriously asking me, to hit her. Now I realize she needed a reason to leave, but I did not give her one. Instead, I walked away, but punched a hole in one wall of our house. That's as abusive as I ever got. Everyone who knows me knows I am not "that kind of guy".

My brother-in-law advised me to give his sister some space for a couple weeks while she "settled into her new life". I believe she had concocted a story about being a poor, abused woman and it was working for her. After a couple weeks, I called my brother-in-law again and he told me Paula needed more time. I asked to see my kids and he said "no". Her brother told me the kids would call me at specific hours so I stayed close to my cellphone. But no one phoned me and when I tried calling them, my brother-in-law would answer and tell me the kids were busy. In the meantime, I had not talked to my wife at all and even my emails were ignored.

A few weeks later in mid-August, I drove by the house where my wife said she was living with our kids and outside I saw a man. I was driving a bus at the time, and Paula's new street address in Red Deer was on my route. I called her landline and a man answered the phone. He said his name was Jim Smythe and he was a social worker. Apparently, he and his wife were the friends Paula and the kids had moved in with. Jim seemed surprised that I did not know my wife had left town, nor where she was staying.

Within a month or two at most after Paula left me, she had a boyfriend. From my understanding, it was her parents who set that up. There are more things her parents did that did not impress me. On Labour Day, I was served with papers instructing me to be in Red Deer court the following Wednesday, in two days time. I was still working and living in Medicine Hat then. I had not seen my kids in at least a month by the time we went back to court. Cale was only one, Britt was just 2 and Emery 4 years old.

On the recommendation of a friend, I called a lawyer named Sandra Scripten in Didsbury and told her what was happening in my case. She said that I had a clause in the Court Order that needed to be "dealt with today". Ms. Scripten assured me that with one phone call to Paula's lawyer, she could solve the access problem.

I believed my case was pretty much open-and-shut since Paula had left with the kids and moved to another city without my knowledge or permission. It was abduction. But Ms. Scripten told me I would have to go through the Attorney General's office to have Paula charged with abduction of our kids. I was fine with that, as I didn't know any better. I thought we would get justice. In hindsight, I don't think Sandra had a good impression of me; I badly needed a lawyer, so she probably assumed I was a bad man.

Once I even asked my lawyer if suicide was the best thing to do. I was only half serious but I sure was distraught at the time. She looked at me with obvious surprise, and I told her I wasn't actually thinking of offing myself. I am a teacher, for God's sake, entrusted with children every day, but here was my estranged wife telling people I was abusive and who knows what else. All she had to do was suggest I was an abuser and instantly I got screwed out of being a father. Once I had Ms. Scripten, Paula started using tactics to delay our next court appearance.

I had that lawyer, Sandra, for 3 years. She figured out the big picture, how we were both being manipulated by Paula, but she couldn't do much. In court, Paula told the judge I was abusive and that her psychologist (I had never seen *that* person) had agreed that I was, so I should not be allowed access to our children. Ms. Scripten asked Paula's lawyer for evidence by documentation, yet it was never produced. That's because proof of my abuse doesn't exist. Nevertheless, the judge refused my parenting time request and again, I did not see my kids for weeks.

Paula also registered with MEP (Maintenance Enforcement Program) soon after our separation. I had been paying regularly with post-dated cheques, but now MEP took over. I was harassed by that organization on a regular basis. Last year, I got a bill for $800 per child for the month of July, yet I had the kids at my place for 2 of those 4 weeks! I have also had my wages garnished even though I was late paying because MEP changed my due date from last of the month to first of the month. I had to pay on a Friday and again on a Monday. Eventually that error got fixed, but it took several months and I was out-of-pocket that whole time. MEP issues continue today, and I have an upcoming Viva Voce court hearing to deal with those on October 1st.

During those years and to this day, my neighbours have been my saviours. They and I would have each other over for supper. The woman, Susan, had tried to be friends with Paula during our marriage. After our separation, the minute Paula got wind that Susan and her husband were supporting me, she completely severed ties to them both. She "unfriended" Susan on Facebook and never connected with either again. Susan and Paula had another mutual friend who kept up with Paula for a while but he, too, was eventually snubbed when he started asking my wife for verification of her claims against me.

Finally, at another court hearing, the judge granted me some parenting time. I think it was every second week from Wednesday to Sunday. I was living 4 hours away from my kids since Paula had gone to live in Red Deer. But I told the judge I would drive both ways. I knew that if he ordered that we meet halfway between our cities, Paula would either be late or fail to show up at all. So we began to transition the kids between our homes, but there was drama every single time. If I went to Paula's sister's house to get our kids, my brother-in-law and Paula would yell at me to get off their property or the like. I got a friend of mine to come and stand on the sidewalk out front to "supervise" the exchange and often the police would be there too. My friend's or the police's presence kept the exchange fairly civil. A few times Paula drove to Medicine Hat with Emery, Britt, and Cale, but she would only drop off our kids with me when police were sitting in the back alley, supposedly supervising.

I was so relieved to be seeing my children again, but it has been so needlessly difficult, especially for Emery. On more than one occasion, when he was dropped back to his mother's house, he would stand behind me in tears. He didn't want to go, but there was nothing I could do. Paula would bring Britt and put her in my car while I was still in the driver's seat. She would carry Britt to my car, open the backseat door, and lean in. I held out my arms and my little girl just reached for me and clung to me. I couldn't even pick up my kids without my estranged wife's interference.

I cried too, for a year and a half, every day. I had to keep hoping that things would smooth out for the kids', as well as my, sakes.

All three of our kids have been living stuck between their parents; all of it is unnecessary, self-serving drama on their mother's part. I do know that Paula has spanked the kids since she and I separated; the kids have told me without my asking. The grandparents on Paula's side are very involved and they always support her point of view. They also are accomplices in keeping our kids away from me. Of course, if you asked Paula, she would tell you our children just don't want to see or go anywhere with me.

But every time I did get to spend some time with Emery, Britt, and Cale, they kind of switched personalities within a day at most and were soon happy, calm and obedient children again. They were, and are, affectionate with me and we do all sorts of good, outdoorsy, healthy things together. They loved it when I helped out at their school and the school staff and I got along very well. One fall, the kids and I attended my dad's wedding in Vancouver, and we all had an amazing time together. Paula brought them to the airport for our flight but, she also brought plain-clothes police (which I didn't mind as witnesses are always welcome) along. Their mother did not even hug, kiss, or say goodbye to our three kids. She just left them with me and took off.

The year after our separation there was a bilateral assessment done by Glenna Luxor, who works in Calgary. She was unbelievably biased in her interpretation of the results so Paula came out smelling like a rose. Whatever Paula told Ms. Luxor was taken as fact without any evidence. I paid for most of that assessment; it was about $10,000. And then, 4 years later, we had another assessment done by this same biased psychologist who had no clue what or whom she was actually dealing with. This time, since Paula asked for it, she also paid for that so-called assessment.

For example, Luxor concluded that since the kids moved around a lot in her office during their session and I had driven them there, whereas they had sat still on chairs when their mother dropped them at her office, Paula was the better parent. Luxor claimed that Paula clearly had more control and discipline over the kids. She also stated in her 20 or 30 page "report" that Paula had a good relationship with her own mother. In fact, my wife had told me she never had a good relationship with her mother, and I was not clear on the reason for that. Anyway, without an opportunity to cross-examine her claims, my point of view and history were ignored in Luxor's report.

Recently, Paula moved again, this time to Calgary. She left our children with her parents in Red Deer. Now I have been granted a clause in the latest Court Order that prohibits the kids from moving out of that city. Paula asked me last summer if she could move and I said "no". That was on a Saturday and by Monday, she moved anyway, but left the kids. I realize now that the reason she wanted the second assessment by Luxor was to give her the power to move our children to Calgary.

This summer, I have been continually, but unsuccessfully, trying to get some time with Emery, Britt and Cale. I called Ms. Luxor to let her know that parental alienation was the real story. In an email to me, she wrote that she *did* know about that! Why she didn't act two years ago on that knowledge, as is her professional duty, is beyond me. I'm waiting now for the recent "assessment report" to be released. Ms. Luxor actually phoned me earlier today and she says it will be in the mail tomorrow. I'm anxious to read it, but I do have hope that it may be more accurate than the last one was. There is no reason why a judge would allow Paula to take my kids to Calgary. Ms. Luxor told me today that the report is "favourable" to me. I guess I will have to wait and see.

Perhaps Glenna Luxor has now learned about parental alienation. She sure didn't know about it four years ago and her first "report" allowed Paula to ramp up the alienation and cause extreme emotional stress on our kids and me. It cost me $10,000 to pay someone to enable their mother to mess up my kids' lives.

I am hopeful, but really scared that if Paula doesn't get her way in court via this assessment, she will get really angry. A couple years ago, when I was granted increased parenting time, Paula emerged from court absolutely livid. From then on, she ramped up the alienation tactics. She never admitted to being the instigator of the deterioration of my relationship with our children. Instead, she would ask each child, in front of both their parents, whether they wanted to go with me or stay with her. You can imagine the no-win situation this puts little kids in. They were regularly made to choose between us, and they always chose her. I let it go because I did not want to ever pressure Emery, Britt, or Cale.

The last time we were in court, the judge actually scolded Paula for her alienation behaviours, but that had no effect on her. She continued to make allegations against me, so she could keep our house, but at least the judge ordered that it be sold. She wasn't even living in it. She was at her boyfriend's place and that's why she has moved to Calgary now.

Paula took me to court once when she decided to obtain spousal support. Fortunately, the judge realized that to pay spousal along with child support would bankrupt me. She was refused. As a result, Paula started taking in other people's kids as a sort of day-home and then later, she went to work full-time in a commissioned sales position. I was very pleased since I hoped that meant the kids would socialize and make some new friends, but that didn't happen. Within a short time, Paula fabricated a story that our children's caregiver was unreliable, maybe even a criminal, since she claimed there was a police report on the poor woman. Of course, as per usual, the court asked Paula for proof of that report and she answered that she couldn't find it but knew it existed. That's when Paula started leaving the kids with their grandparents every day instead and paid them to babysit. Grandpa had lost his job so I just wonder whether that was part of the reason.

For the last two years, my former in-laws take care of our kids in their basement suite while I, their father, hardly ever see them. Paula lives in Calgary and apparently works for her former pastor. She says she had to move there as she had maxed-out her earning potential in Red Deer. So far, the court does not know she is living away from our kids in another city. The assessment by Ms. Luxor should expose that.

This year, I have only had Emery overnight once and that was back in the spring. He arrived with a cellphone, which I later found out about. It was 10:30 that evening and I walked into my 9-year-old's bedroom. Suddenly a phone buzzed and I realized he had one. I asked Emery if I could borrow it, and when I returned it, not 5 minutes later, my son was already asleep. It was apparent that since I took the phone, he had peace and separation from his mother's control. At the end of the weekend, I checked his texting history and found that Emery's texts included: "I am upset"; "I don't want to stay here"; I don't think I can handle it here". And Paula had responded with: "Are you scared?;" and "if you are scared, you can call 9-1-1."

I am not aware of mental illness in her family's history, but I really wonder. As far as I can tell, Paula's behaviour is completely centred on her *narcissistic worldview* and everyone else is a pawn in her attention seeking. I believe that when I lost my job in 2007, (my mom also died that year), I was vulnerable and without a big paycheque so that catalyzed our separation. Paula had no desire to earn a living and expected that I would serve her in all ways for life.

Altogether, I was in court 19 times in the first couple years following our separation. I even got a police enforcement clause, but that just ramped up my kids' confusion and allowed Paula to reinforce their belief that I was bad. Then I pulled the plug on the legal action. Paula was ignoring the Court Orders anyway, so what was the point of my paying lawyers for a job that resulted in no improvement? The Family Law system actually enabled greater harm on my kids. For sometimes as long as six months, I did not see any of my children and the only way I could was by volunteering at their school. Eventually though, Paula even prevented me from going there by telling the staff that I was an abuser.

I arranged exchanges of the kids through the Women's Outreach program and a staff-member there proved somewhat helpful. One of us would bring Emery, Britt, and Cale to the Centre and the other would drive up and take the kids from there. There was a surveillance camera on-site and that staff member observed Paula's and my behaviour during the exchanges. She told me she was concerned and would talk to all three of our children in her office. From her meeting with them, she said it was apparent that they were "being coached by mom". This woman reported in a letter to Ms. Luxor that the kids had said that I killed their family pet (I *did* kill their fish by accident) and used buzz words and terms that would be unknowable otherwise to children of that age.

In my job, I often see kids who have no contact with one parent, usually their dad. In one recent case, I know of two kids in my class whose mother left the dad and those kids have had zero contact with him since. I know the dad through work and he is an excellent person, as far as I can tell. I asked his daughter if maybe her dad could help her with a project she was working on. The result was that the girl came back to see me after school and brought her mother along. They said I was not to speak of the girl's father. The three kids in that family are all teenagers and none of them has any relationship with their father.

My family's case is, sadly, a common one. I have called Social Services and other agencies and each time, I am told there is nothing I can do because Paula is the "primary parent". Even some of my kids' teachers have reached out to me, as they are worried about my kids' performance, or lack thereof, at school. They have also talked to Paula, but according to these teachers, their comments fall on deaf ears.

Don't get me wrong; some of these judges are excellent, well-meaning people who can read the situation quickly and accurately. But a lot of them are not familiar with the complexity of parental alienation so don't make appropriate or useful orders. Often, judges bend over backwards to give women who are unrepresented a lot of leeway and benefit of the doubt based on their verbal testimony. Men, however, get slammed. There is no investigation or any cross-examination of claims.

Now, I am awaiting Ms. Luxor's report, worried sick about the consequences, worried about my kids' mental health, and now pay an $82 school busing fee (though my kids don't take the bus, mom drives them) for my kids and another $640 for their childcare. On top of those costs, I pay Child Support and have MEP breathing down my neck. I have to email and ask Paula whenever I want to see my kids and she has the power to veto any parenting time she feels like. She took Cale out of school this year at the age of six, telling the judge she feels he is "too brilliant" to need to attend. It has been five whole years since my wife and I separated, and the situation with our children is worse than ever. I can't begin to explain the toll it has taken on Emery, Britt, Cale and me.

I have not pursued another relationship, as I am afraid of what could happen. I am probably not someone to invest in at this point either, since I am sad and poor. I can be upbeat on the occasions I do see my kids, but those times are very rare indeed. The money-pit that is legal action goes unregulated and destroys lives while lining the pockets of family lawyers. I have spent approximately $50,000 in my case thus far, and now I self-represent as the lesser of all evils. So far, I am still standing, but I'm not sure how well my children will come out of their horrendous childhood.

JOHN

CHAPTER 27

JOHN

I have four children; two daughters and two sons. My eldest is Garrett who is 20; next is 18-year-old Ayla, then Shari who is 16 and my youngest, Mick, who is 12. By the time we split in 2008, my wife and I had been struggling for some time in our relationship; I won't deny that. I had a very loving relationship with all my kids and believe it or not, with my wife too. We separated after a big argument following Garrett's running away with his girlfriend. He had gotten into a lot of trouble at school and this was kind of the final straw. Garrett had taken some marijuana to school, got caught, and I took some privileges away from him as punishment. Roberta, my wife, was furious that I punished him and told me to leave the house.

Until the time Roberta kicked me out, she had held a full-time job, while I was a stay-at-home dad during the day. I did, however, work 12-hour shifts at my job 4 nights a week. That way, I could raise my kids and be present while still providing for my family. It was kind of exhausting, but I love and want to be with my children. That is how our parenting worked for the entirety of our marriage.

Once I got the kids off to school in the mornings, I could sleep for a while. That way, I was still available by phone if any of my children needed me during their school day. A few times, stuff did happen and I could immediately get up to the school and deal with it. I was pretty much the only disciplinarian- as Roberta was emotionally unavailable and not that interested in being a mom. Looking back, I don't really think my wife cared about her children much at all. Maybe I misinterpreted our whole relationship... it may have just been convenient to have the kids as long as I provided caregiving, housekeeping and money for our household.

Over the years, though, there had been several instances where my wife left the kids and me and was gone for a couple weeks. Roberta never gave me any explanation, other than where she would be staying. It seemed like she just went and spent time with some girlfriends. Then she would call me, first saying she was returning home, but later changing her mind, saying she didn't want to get back together. I was completely confused, as I always loved her. Even this last, *final*, time when I had to move out, she called me and wanted to get back together. I had Mick and the girls with me after the separation, but after about four months, Roberta got Child and Family Services to help her take them from me.

When Roberta told me to leave, I did so and took the younger three kids. Garrett had run away. Only about 3 days after I left, my wife allowed Garrett, who was 15 at the time, to move back into the house and cohabitate with his 14-year-old girlfriend, Michelle. Within a few months they were pregnant, but Michelle miscarried. Garrett and Michelle are still together and have another baby who is the absolute love of my life. My granddaughter is 7 months old now. She's named after a beautiful flower... and that is exactly what she is.

The first while after we split, my wife kept stringing me along, telling me she wanted to meet to discuss custody, access and money stuff. When the kids were with me they would just pick up the phone whenever they wanted to talk to their mom or go see her. They did go back and forth without a problem but were with me more of the time, since I was home during the day. I had moved us all into my sister's house; she lives close by and she and her husband had a three-bedroom suite downstairs. It worked fine and we were quite comfortable there.

A couple months after our separation, Roberta made allegations of abuse against me. There was absolutely no reason or history of abuse. These charges shocked and blindsided me. She was able to easily get a Restraining Order by showing up at court by herself, telling the judge I was too controlling and would not let her take the bus. The Order was good for 20 days. Then we both faced a different judge at a judicial review and that guy threw out the Restraining Order. He even called it ridiculous and couldn't believe my wife had been granted it in the first place.

You know, I've got to tell you: Before this happened to me, I always believed that any woman claiming domestic violence was telling the truth. Domestic violence and abuse are horrendous things when they actually happen. But now, if I hear someone tell me about a case, I wonder whether that case is real, or instead, a manipulation tactic that appears to always work in family courts.

So, after our separation, Roberta had Garrett and his girlfriend, Michelle, living with her. There were no parental boundaries in place. Garrett was drinking, using drugs, and I had no contact whatsoever with him. That's when the allegations of abuse began. There was a snowball effect; first, one charge, then more and more. My wife wrote that I was physically and mentally abusive to her, physically and emotionally abusive to our kids, that I am an alcoholic and a drug-abuser. All of her charges against me were made in her affidavits, without my knowledge. Within a few weeks, Roberta was in court telling some judge that the kids didn't want me in their lives.

I am from Newfoundland so of course I enjoy beer occasionally. I have also smoked a joint of pot now and again but my wife, on the other hand, was a chronic marijuana smoker every day. As long as she kept it away from the kids, I kept quiet about her habit. Then suddenly I became the target of all Roberta's hostility. One day I was driving my car with Ayla in the seat beside me when she blurted out "I know you used to beat Mom all the time". I told her that was absolutely untrue. My daughter was 14 at the time. My wife and I had then been separated only two and a half months.

Just two more months later, both Ayla and Shari refused to see me at all. They both went to live full-time with their mom and I had only Mick left with me. The court order reinforced the girls' decision, but the judge thought Mick should be with me, given the at-risk behaviour of his older brother, Garrett. Even during the 18 months Mick was with me, though, he still continued visiting his mother regularly. For Mick, that back and forth parenting pattern between our homes has somewhat continued to this day.

Mick told me that the other three kids, Roberta, and Roberta's best friend, had confronted him in her living-room. Right after we separated, my wife had quit her $65,000 a year job. Instead, she went to work cleaning houses for this divorced "best friend" for $25,000 a year. This group told Mick to sit on the coffee table and they surrounded him, telling him stories about why he should not live, or have contact, with me. My own children encouraged their brother to sever ties with me. They said I am a horrible person and they were supposedly afraid I would hurt Mick.

That incident happened a mere four months after his mother's and my separation. My son was eight years old. Mick phoned me in tears from his mom's house right after it happened and asked that I come get him. I did so. He said that at first the others were not going to let him come with me but then they relented. To this day, Mick is very insightful. All my kids are smart; Ayla is currently at university on scholarships. They all used to be Honours students, even Garrett, before he dropped out of school.

When Roberta went to court to gain custody of our daughters, the judge also appointed a lawyer for the children. Legal Aid paid for that lawyer; her name is Carol Krand and the judge actually recommended her. The next thing I knew, there was a Judicial Dispute Resolution (JDR) hearing, and that's when I heard Michelle and Garrett were pregnant. The judge had heard, somehow, that some disturbing things were happening at my ex-wife's home. My 15-year-old son and his 14-year-old girlfriend were smoking pot with Roberta. My ex offered no response when these claims were made at the JDR. Nonetheless, the judge decided to get Child and Family Services involved, while still granting custody to the mother of our children.

It didn't take long for Child and Family Services to come after me. Fortunately, I kept every single scrap of paperwork they wrote over the next six months; stuff that claimed I was angry and apparently abusive. The social worker was Kirk Brauer and then his file on me went to some criminologist guy named James Billy. Even though my younger three kids never said they wanted to disown me, the "report" from Child and Family Services claimed they did. Only Ayla was furious with me, and that's because Roberta told her I thought there was "something wrong" with her.

Ayla didn't get any counselling for her anger. She still has extreme anger toward me, yet I have never done anything to warrant this hostility. Ayla is 18 now and she absolutely believes that I am a liar and was abusive to her mother. Even though she cannot name any incident in which anything like that ever happened (because it didn't), she hangs on to her false belief. She is completely brainwashed against me. Both she and Garrett have told Child and Family Services that I beat up their mother and them too. Shari has never said a word against me.

The file report done by Brauer and Billy was opened and shut once they realized there was zero evidence to back the abuse allegations against me. Child and Family Services, though, got involved a second time after the girls were taken away from me. We went back to court. I was worried about my kids' welfare living with my ex-wife and wanted us all to get family counselling at the very least. My affidavit stated that my kids were in trouble, they needed help, and I was being prevented from helping them. I probably didn't help my own case much at times when I got so frustrated with the Family Law system. I said I couldn't believe that these so-called intelligent lawyers and judges were just blindly following along with accusations made without evidence. Nobody looked at the facts; *nobody.*

Child and Family Services made me go for a psychological and parenting assessment. Brauer claimed that I was paranoid, as I thought my phone calls with my children were being recorded.

Judge Lipting ordered the assessment. Of course, there was no ordered or even suggested assessment on my ex-wife. The assessment report, written by Dr. Sally Durrell, showed I was completely normal, but was living with a lot of situational stress... *duh*! I was depressed for sure and went to counselling for it. Sometimes I still go now when I feel like talking about losing my kids and the defamation campaign against me.

Now and again I have recurrent bad dreams; they started again recently as I thought about coming to this interview and talking to you. In every dream, something bad happens to my kids and I am unable to help them.

On February 12th of 2009, we went back to court; the judge took Mick away from me. Though Mick had been living and doing well with me for a year, the judge ignored that. He ordered that my nine-year-old live full-time with his mother and that I have supervised visits only. His decision was based on the Child and Family Services report that stated Brauer believed me paranoid.

Only one month later, after Mick went to live with Roberta, he phoned me in tears. He told me his mom was recording his phone calls and when he asked her to stop, she refused, saying I am a bad person. I calmed him down, said I loved him and it didn't matter that she recorded our calls. But then I phoned Roberta directly, sent her an email and a text, but none were responded to. Finally, I did get her on the phone, and she said it was James Billy, the other guy from Child and Family Services, who had encouraged her to record our calls. While Roberta was on the phone with me, I could hear my two daughters in the background, saying things to Mick about how dangerous and scary I am. I got angry; I couldn't help it, I was so frustrated and worried about my kids.

I have all the transcripts from those recorded phone conversations. My lawyer got them and sure, I said some things I should not have, but seriously, *how far can a person be pushed*?! We tried to get the phone recordings stopped, but my ex continued with no penalty at all. I was sending emails to Roberta and to my kids, asking to see my girls and Mick. It was to no avail. Roberta apparently thought my attempts pretty funny; she said I was a joke and that if the kids were sent to live with me, they would all just run away. Now that I am back in contact with Shari and Garrett they have told me that Roberta's "best friend" was their instructor in what they should say to me to keep me away from them.

Despite Roberta's ongoing attempts to kill the relationship between my kids and me, Ayla phoned me in May of 2009 to say she wanted to visit with me. I was allowed twice a week supervised visits, but thus far, I had only seen Mick. James Billy and a few other former social workers had quit Child and Family Services and opened a business doing supervision for parents like me. They would hire social work students to do the actual supervising during visits at my home. Everything they wrote was super-biased in favour of Roberta. Once Mick and I were playing a game at my place. As he was getting ready to go back to his mother's, he said he was going to take the game there. Instead, I asked him to leave the game with me for next time he came for a visit. The social work student supervising wrote that: "Mr. (me) behaved in a mean way toward his son, disallowing him from taking a game home".

The supervised visits were a no-win situation. Another time at my place, Mick said his head was itchy, so I asked him if he was bathing or showering regularly. He told me he wasn't. I suggested he take a bath at least one a week and a shower every couple of days. Then he told me he thought he had lice so I had a good look. Sure enough, the poor kid was infested! I gave my sister a quick call, and she came right over with Nix, that medicated shampoo to get rid of lice. Then the supervisor asked to see the lice, so I pulled a comb through Mick's hair and showed her. I also took photos of them for proof. A few months later, the supervisor's report whitewashed the incident with "he (me) was apoplectic when he found a couple lice in his child's hair". I also saw a note the supervisor wrote to her boss accusing me of blaming the lice on Roberta's poor parenting. I did not do so. But, the reality is that if Roberta knew about the lice, she should have told me; and if she didn't know, why didn't she?

During the time I was subjected to supervised visits, phone-tapping, and nonstop defamation, I was very fragile and emotional.

The family law system was enabling the alienation campaign to destroy me as well as my relationship with my children. When we went back to court again, all those comments and lies written by the supervisors were used as ammunition against me. On one of the last visits I had with Mick before he came back to live with me, we had a barbeque in my yard. I invited my nephew, his wife and their little son, Mick's cousin. My parents came too and it was a beautiful day. We played with water and were having fun for maybe 15 minutes before I saw the supervisor's face turn ugly. She called me over and told me to make everyone leave except Mick. I asked why, and she said she was not authorized to include any of my family in the visit.

After that day, my kids were not permitted to see any of their paternal extended family. *Unbelievable*! Child and Family Services sent all four kids to the Sheriff King Centre for "abuse counselling". I had requested counselling but individually for general problems each child was having as a result of their parents' separation. My kids needed to be in a safe, comfortable environment to talk with an unbiased third-party whom they trusted. But nope, they got abuse counselling.

On July 8th, 2009, we went back to court again. I had exhausted all my finances so I was representing myself. I had tried Legal Aid, but their lawyer just told me to agree to all the charges against me to smooth the way forward. There was no way I would admit to things I never did. Justice Lipting, in all six of our court hearings, kept making terrible, biased decisions that hurt my kids and they hurt me. I wrote to the Chief Justice of Alberta about him. He was, shortly after, apparently removed from the bench. Lipting had seized our case, so he was the one consistently making all decisions.

In December of 2009, Justice Lipting, in court, stood up and told everyone in the room that I had complained about him. He said that even though he had done nothing wrong, he had talked to the Chief Justice and decided on his own, to recuse himself from our case. Then he added to Child and Family Services that if they chose to bring any future application against me, they would have to have someone else on the bench. Well, two weeks later we were back in court with a different judge and I got visitation back with all my kids. Three months later, I got full custody of Mick and he was tickled pink. He visits his mom and his siblings without any hassle, and I remind him both his parents love him dearly. I have also let him know that issues between his mom and me are not his fault or his problem. I want him to know what healthy relationships look like, to trust people, and to be kind.

I wish I could be as positive in my view of how Ayla and Shari are doing these days. Shari went through a long period of shoplifting and thankfully, she eventually got caught. I had not seen her before that most recent incident. I think it was almost 3 years that I did not see or speak with Shari, Ayla or Garrett. Just this past Christmas, I sent Garrett a note via Facebook, letting him know I loved him and that I knew he was doing well with Michelle and had a good job. I invited the two of them to come over during the holidays and said there were gifts under the tree for them. *You know what… they came*! My heart grew so big and I felt joy for the first time in years.

Garrett and Michelle not only visited me a few days after Christmas, they came over every day for a whole week. At the end of that week, they asked me to drive them home to the tiny basement room they had in an old house. It was awful and right then, I told them to pack up and come stay with me. They did and have been with me ever since. Three weeks ago, they finally moved out and got their own nice little apartment. It's all good; they need their own space now that they have their little daughter. I am so proud of them! I still worry because Garrett drinks too much and he's only 20, but there's not much I can say. Michelle is only 19 but a sweetie and she's good for my son. They are excellent parents.

Getting back to Shari, though, the way I found out about her stealing was when Roberta phoned me to say she was having problems with our daughter. Shari was 15 at the time; staying out overnight, sometimes gone for days at a time, skipping school and basically acting just at Garrett had a few years back. I told Roberta I wasn't sure what I could do, given that both my daughters refused to see me, and they lived with their mother full-time. My ex-wife had no clue what to do or how this could have happened. I *so* wanted to say "I told you so," but I kept my mouth shut. I just suggested she report Shari in case she was picked up on the streets or somewhere. It was a couple weeks later that Shari was arrested by the police for shoplifting.

I got a phone call from Shari at 5:00 one morning. She said "hello, Dad" and I, for a moment, couldn't think who it was. It had been a long time since a girl's voice had called me Dad. She immediately started to cry and told me her mom had kicked her out of the house. She asked to come see me and of course I agreed right away. She grabbed a taxi, came to my place, and stayed with me for several days. At first when she saw me, she was really nervous; I could feel it when I gave her a hug. I left her alone and just suggested she get her bearings and hang around my house for a couple days. I also encouraged her to phone her mom and try to figure things out with her.

Over the next few days, Shari relaxed, and began interacting pretty normally with me. Then she informed me she had worked things out with mom and was moving back there. She lasted three weeks back with Roberta until another early morning, this time 4:00, phone call to me. This time I told her to call me back in 15 minutes, as I wanted some clarification from my ex-wife. Roberta answered her cell phone and told me she had had enough and she wanted Shari out of her home for good. I said that was fine and to send Shari over by cab to my place; she did. Now it has been 5 months and Shari is still living with me. We are doing very well. She is going to high school, has not run away, is accountable and if I have any complaint, it's just that I sometimes have a hard time getting her to do her dishes. She lost most of last year when she was still at her mom's, earning only about two school credits, but this year she is really doing great.

Over the past months, I have tried emailing Roberta to arrange a time to pick up Shari's belongings. When she came to live with me, it all happened in the middle of the night and Shari only took her purse from mom's house. I've had no success via email, but once in a while I can get her by phone. I think Roberta wants to make sure there is no paper trail of her conversations with me. Although I now have both Mick and Shari living with me, I am unable to obtain their clothes and stuff from mom's house. If Mick goes to Roberta's house for the weekend, I never again see the clothes he took over there. So, I'm buying him clothes almost every other week as well as buying all Shari's stuff. And if Mick stays over at his mom's on a Sunday night and then goes to school directly on Monday morning, he will arrive there in the most garish outfits. It sounds petty, but I wonder why he is not supervised or provided with the appropriate clothes he needs.

Keep in mind that Roberta still receives child tax cheques. Our two youngest kids live with me, Ayla is at university and at her boyfriend's place most of the time, and Garrett lives with Michelle on their own. I'm buying clothes and other necessities all the time, so I suggested to Shari that she ask her mother for her portion of the cheques. That would really help me as I'm tapped right out. Next thing I knew, Roberta took me back to court, claiming that she needed more spousal and child support from me. I don't even know why I am paying spousal support, given that my ex-wife voluntarily quit her well-paying and full-time job. But I don't care about that. Our next court date is this coming November, so we'll see what the judge decides on that score. I am just thankful to have a relationship back with 3 of my kids; if only Ayla would see the light and let go of her huge anger toward me.

When I see Ayla, she spews venom and I cannot disagree with anything she says. If I try to, she immediately ramps up, her face gets red and swollen, her eyes narrow, and I feel like she wants to punch me in the face. It is a really scary thing to watch. There is no way to talk to Ayla and I worry constantly about her state of mind. The only time I hear from her is when she wants more money for school. Even then, she only sends an email with the amount she is demanding. My children think I have been maleficent in paying child support to their mother.

The truth is, I am registered with Maintenance Enforcement (MEP), so if I had not paid properly, God knows MEP would have been after me in a second. I would have had my driver's licence revoked, bank accounts seized, and probably been jailed. At first, after our separation, I paid Roberta cash, then money orders, but finally MEP got involved by the court order. I think that may be automatic when a case is deemed high-conflict.

The good thing about MEP is that I no longer have to deal with my ex-wife, other than via email, where our kids are concerned. The problem is that Roberta does not respond to my emails. For instance, recently I sent one asking her which weekend she would like to have Mick. There was no response until Mick phoned her and directly asked. Then she sent a confirmation of the dates she had promised him. We are supposed to have a regular schedule and I do keep my side of that. Roberta, however, changes it at last minute and whenever she finds it convenient for her own plans. Roberta is also supposed to call the kids every day, but often 10 or 12 days go by before she phones Mick. Since I never know when his mother will invite him over, I have a hard time scheduling anything involving Mick and his activities. If I suggest a new movie that Mick and I want to see, he will tell Roberta and next thing I know, he announces that he is going to his mom's and they are going to that *exact* movie.

For me, the most important thing is that my children all gain an education and skills to make a good living. So far, Garrett has not returned to school but I hope he does. I know that his girlfriend plans to go to business school. Right now, she works nights in a bar and that's tough as a mother. I watch my granddaughter quite often while Garett and Michelle are working, and I am always happy to do so. The odd weekend she stays at my place too.

My regret comes from all the years lost without my kids. All of it was completely unwarranted, and I blame the courts more than my ex-wife. They gave me time with Mick, took it away, gave it back, manipulated and enabled my children to hate, gave me phone privileges but no visitation, and then vice versa. The whole thing was absolute torture for me, and devastating for my kids, especially Ayla, who may never recover. I joined advocacy groups, wrote copious letters to legal people and mental health workers, and none of my efforts were helpful. I talked to Child and Social Services who assured me that James Billy had been removed from my file, but the next time we were in court, James Billy was still there. There was no new social worker put in place and in court, Mr. Billy's supervisor, Patricia Plank, outright denied she had told me she was replacing him.

Finally, after my complaint to the Chief Justice, a real social worker replaced James Billy. He had been making decisions affecting my family, and he wasn't even a social worker. Mr. Billy likely only spent a weekend retreat or a few classes becoming "accredited" and, until the Minister of Justice's Office removed him, he did a ton of damage.

Mick is doing well, despite his seemingly ADHD tendencies earlier. He is just a high-energy kid who was subjected to ongoing stress from his parents' issues. Since my ex was convinced Mick needed medication, I took him to our doctor who thoroughly examined him. The doctor said, "If Mick had ADD or ADHD, I'd have noticed symptoms by now and that is not the case. He is a completely normal, healthy boy." When I reported the results to Child and Family Services, the worker did not believe me and asked for contact information to verify the diagnosis. No problem and I gladly provided that. Sure enough, when the judge finally closed the Child and Family Services file on us, she also said she didn't want to see our case in front of the court again. When the Child and Family Services' lawyer then stood up to respond, the judge told him to sit down, as she was not finished speaking.

That judge was brilliant; I love that woman! In the 40-plus times I have been in court because of our divorce and the welfare of our children, this was the only time in which a judge spoke the truth and did her homework. I have averaged 10 court appearances *each year* and at one point, took a 10-month leave from my job to handle all the legal finagling that I had to do to defend myself and try to get help for my children. At times, I was barely even able to function due to my stress level. I was obsessed with proving the truth and was finally vindicated when Mick came to live full-time with me. I have remained flexible and open for shared parenting because I know my kids need both their parents. Even since Shari came to live with me, a reasonable Justice Crothers asked if I wanted sole custody of Shari, but I told him I believed shared custody was best for all my kids.

I have no money, still pay Roberta spousal and child support for my two younger kids who live with me, pay Ayla whenever she wants money, and support my grand-daughter however I can. But you know what? I don't care about money. Mick and I find cheap things to do and those things bring us closer together. We hike and fish, go for bike rides, and save up for the odd movie at a theatre. If I need a car, I can borrow one from my work without any problem. I rent a house with three bedrooms and a great yard. We are building our own beautiful flower garden out there too.

ORLIN

CHAPTER 28

ORLIN

I am from Eastern Europe and met my wife, Jordyn, while I was learning German. She was my teacher. We married in 1996 and afterward lived in Germany on student visas. I got a job there, and Jordyn was going to university. It had been my intention to also go to school, but I started working to support us both. We couldn't stay forever since I was working there, but it was a good move while we were there. The economy in our home country (we are both from the same one) was dismal after the collapse of the Eastern bloc countries. After four years of marriage, our son, Bryan, was born.

We knew we would have to leave Germany, so I thought perhaps we could immigrate to Canada. My English was better than Jordyn's then; her obvious strength was German. We both speak a few languages now. In 2000, we landed in Canada and obtained permanent residency. At first, all three of us arrived, but Jordyn and Bryan went back to Germany after a week. My wife wanted to finish her degree in Germany. She had switched Majors from Linguistics to Political Science shortly before our son was born. At the time, I was worried that it would be difficult in Canada for her to find a suitable job. But since she really wanted to do it, I agreed to support her until she finished that degree.

While they were back overseas, I planned to get settled in, find a job and a nice place to live in Canada. By that time, I thought

Jordyn and Bryan would be back with me and our new life would be a happy one. In Germany, schooling is paid for and child care is inexpensive and good. The downside of that is that many people become professional students who delay getting a real job.

Sometimes on the phone, Jordyn would joke with me that she would not need to work since she now had a child. I didn't take those comments seriously, but I should have. From that point on, in retrospect, Jordyn was looking for a way to gain prestige and power without actually having to work. Maybe she saw herself as some kind of politician, I don't know. We Skyped and emailed every day, often twice or more, but I was pretty overloaded with expectations.

I started in Canada in Toronto doing mostly menial labour, packing crates at distribution centres and that sort of thing. My background is an Architecture degree from my home country, but I wanted to move into Mechanical Engineering. Since I could not study in Germany, I decided to wait until Jordyn finished her degree, and then I would go to university in Canada. It was three years before my wife finished her degree. After the first year, I went to Germany and stayed for a couple months with her and our son. I kept our place in Toronto while I was gone. Jordyn had a big exam while I was visiting Germany, so I looked after Bryan while she studied. On two other occasions, my wife and child came to Toronto for a short time.

During those three years, life was really expensive. We had two rental places, were flying back and forth, paying a small fee for daycare, and subsisting on only my earnings. Fortunately, my job expanded into architectural technology after a year. I had a career path and wondered whether Jordyn was thinking about what she would do after school was completed. I asked her what her plan was for the future, and that's when our disagreements really started.

Jordyn told me that after completion of her degree, she had decided to begin a doctoral program in Political Science in Germany. I was flummoxed by this news; I thought she would be anxious to come to join me and was perhaps taking English to make herself more employable here. That was not the case. Pretty soon I started seeing public political forums online, which Jordyn regularly contributed to. They were based in our home country and she was interacting particularly with one journalist over there. Here I was on the other side of the Atlantic, trying to figure out what was happening in eastern Europe. Jordyn was not forthcoming about her activities, and our relationship became ever more strained. I had no option to go back and work in Germany as our citizens cannot get work visas there.

After six years of my wife and son living far away from me, I gave Jordyn an ultimatum. I told her it was time to decide; if she wanted to be with me, she needed to come to Canada. There was a practical reason too. If my wife did not arrive soon, she would lose her permanent residency status in Canada. When Jordyn and Bryan had come over to visit me, my wife was appalled that I lived in a basement suite but that was all I could afford. It was, in fact, a boarding house.

As it turned out, Jordyn never took the doctoral program seriously. She was instead looking for some kind of political position in either Germany or our home country that would anchor her there. Even though she was a temporary resident of Germany, and even though the economy in our country was the reason we left there, Jordyn seemed to believe she could somehow parachute into a high-level, high-paying job in a political Ministry. She had delusions of grandeur, I realize now, and she was completely out of tune with real, possible job prospects.

Several times I was laid off in Ontario and had to take on a line of credit to continue sending money to my wife and child. I couldn't send money from unemployment benefits, so instead I used something called a Plus System. It allowed me to put money in an account and Jordyn got a card that let her withdraw from it overseas. That was a joint account, but Jordyn was draining it. I didn't mind for a while since she was raising our son alone, he was learning German, and they lived in better conditions than I did in Toronto.

Jordyn finally agreed to join me in Canada, and she promised she would look for work here. The alternative was for her to remain there, but for us to divorce; she said she wanted us to be a family. I hoped for a second child, but I guess that wasn't in the cards. We were both over 35 by the time Jordyn and Bryan arrived in Canada. Our son was 7 then; we had first separated around his first birthday and now he was starting Grade 2 with no knowledge of the English language.

Kids are amazing learners, though, and Bryan soon became functional in English. He still struggles with Language Arts, especially spelling, and a couple school counselors suggested he might be dyslexic. I think he just went through such a major transition in his childhood that he was thrown off base and had to catch up so much. When they arrived, Bryan had little support either, since I was working and his mother was pretty distracted. Jordyn wasn't working, but she spent her time continuing to write in political forums that concerned Europe. She made no effort to learn English or to drive. I can confirm that she cooked for us and took care of our household, but we had agreed that she needed to help pay the bills so we could get on our feet. Every day, I would take Bryan to the school bus stop and pick him up after so I could not work any overtime hours to increase my paycheque. After supper, I would tutor him with his homework. I was exhausted and our marriage was going down the tubes.

I don't know of any mental health issues in Jordyn's family, but in hindsight, I noticed a lot of manipulative traits and grandiose ideas. My wife was raised by her mother as a single parent; Jordyn did not know, for unknown reasons, her own father. As our conversations became more and more conflicted and damaging, we eventually started pushing and shoving each other. In November of 2006, I ran out of our home. By the following February, Bryan brought home a leaflet about the Sheriff King Centre and how it could help families dealing with hostility and violence. He probably mentioned at school how his parents were constantly shouting at each other. I filled out that form in hopes that we could receive counselling to resolve our problems at home.

That was the beginning of the real nightmare, however. After we had both signed the form Bryan brought home, Child and Family Services got involved and I was encouraged. First, Jordyn began counselling there on her own. As she attended more sessions, our situation at home actually ramped up and she became more aggressive toward me. She learned that if she left me, she could get Spousal and Child Support and have me thrown out of our home. It became increasingly clear that we needed to divorce and I calmed down and accepted that fact. I just wanted to be an equal parent for my son. I even packed my bags and told her I would leave without any resistance; we could work out the parenting schedule after.

About two weeks after we officially agreed to separate, I received notification that Jordyn filed an Emergency Protection Order (EPO) against me (Author's note: At the time of this interview, I visited the Divorce Claims floor of the Calgary Courts Centre and saw one of the wickets had a large sign hanging above it which read "Emergency Protection Orders here: No evidence required". That sign was removed by my next visit in 2015). That happened even though my wife and I were no longer in conflict; at least, I thought we had reached a truce. Things were going pretty smoothly with co-parenting Bryan, but we all still lived in the same house. One day I drove home, planning to pick up Bryan soon from school, but I found a police car in my driveway. I was handed the EPO and immediately moved out. The granted EPO was for a period of six months and I was only permitted to see Bryan at the Sheriff King Centre, by appointment.

In hindsight, Jordyn had probably first been reasonable with me because she was worried that I would file for divorce and the gravy train would end. But the EPO gave her power over me, and she gained a legal advantage by making me look bad. Jordyn claimed I abused her and my son. This was absurd since we had both been abusive with each other, but more importantly, I had never been abusive in any way toward Bryan. In fact, the first time I confronted my wife about her political forum involvement, she lost her mind and attacked me. I had bleeding nail scratches on my face and that's when I ran out of the house. She was angry because I was holding her to her promise to find work in Canada.

I did visit Bryan at the Sheriff King Centre. It was very humiliating, as it always had to be supervised. Jordyn assisted in setting up the visitation schedule there which undoubtedly made her look cooperative. Bryan was confused about why he had to meet me there with a stranger observing our interaction. After two visits, one being Christmas when I had to take his gifts to that Centre, I told the staff I was not an abuser and this situation was unacceptable and inappropriate. For the next three months I did not see my nine-year-old son; I wasn't even allowed to phone him.

Jordyn and Bryan soon moved out of the house since she could not afford the rent. She got a full-time job in a mall clothing store. The house stayed empty for a couple months, and then I moved back in. I had been living with friends from our home country who lived only two blocks away from our house. We had met them at Superstore, started talking when we overheard them speaking our home language, and really hit it off. It was lucky I could ask them for temporary boarding because I had nowhere else to go.

We went to court six months later, as soon as the EPO expired. I was paying child support, but the fight was on for her to try and get spousal support too. Jordyn wanted me to sign her version of a separation agreement, but there was no way I was going to do that. We needed to get a Parenting Agreement in place, but Jordyn tried her best to exclude me from being a parent. Bryan was 11 years old then. During the six-month EPO, I had to pay for babysitters for my son because I was not allowed near him. But now in court, the judge reinstated the parenting plan that had worked before; I picked up Bryan from school, sometimes also took him there, and we often had afternoons together. The judge's decision was a relief, but Jordyn was furious. Even though I was going to be supervising our son, helping him with his homework, and providing his transport to and from school, my ex-wife cared only that the judge refused her claim for spousal support.

I had a Legal Aid lawyer representing me then. She came from Castle and Associates but went on maternity leave just before the hearing. At least Legal Aid provided me with a replacement. The Court Order gave me 50/50 custody with no spousal support. I'll bet Jordyn had planned to remove me from our son's life and be a heroic "single parent" with benefits, just as her own mother had done, but it didn't work out that way. Thank God, the judge realized I am a good father.

There's another complication to the story as well. The lawyer Jordyn had recruited was a fellow member of the Church of Jesus Christ of Latter-Day Saints (LDS). My wife had never been a member of that Faith, or church. But neighbours invited her to attend when she gave them her sob-story about being a single mom, as she lives right across the street from that church. Soon she was a "member" and using nice people's sympathy for her own means. She had no money and was paying rent, so maybe her lawyer was representing her pro bono.

Anyway, after the judge's decision for 50/50 custody, Jordyn must have figured she needed to do something fast to avoid my gaining access to our son. The judge had also put a police enforcement clause in our agreement to ensure my ex-wife was compliant with the parenting schedule. But, within a week or perhaps two at most, my son turned from a loving, happy child into a boy who hated his father. I had been unable to see Bryan because he would be "busy" or "unavailable" or "sleeping", according to his mother, so one time I got fed up and did call the police to help me facilitate access to my son. Bryan had already been acting hostile toward me, but the police involvement made it much worse.

At one point, a school counselor informed me that Bryan was talking about suicide. That counselor sent him to the Children's Hospital here in Calgary, where there is a mental health program for troubled kids. Jordyn and I were both involved in their family counselling program as was Bryan. Sometimes we each had our own individual sessions too. Bryan had been kept in hospital, so it was closely monitored by staff. That was very good as both parents had to cooperate. There were sessions that Jordyn did not attend, however, even though they had been mandated by the court.

I couldn't stop praising the family counselor we had. Her name is Nancy Rotinski and she has a lot of background in court mediation. She also has a good grasp of psychology and family counselling. When I attended the Parenting after Separation course for High-Conflict cases, Nancy was one of the instructors. She told us that we needed to let go of the past and focus on a positive future for all our sakes, especially our son's.

Bryan's behaviour toward me, as a result of the family counselling, was improving, but once we completed the hospital's program, he quickly reverted back to his anger and hostility. For instance, he refused to see me, said he hated my house, and to "stop following me". My son told me he knew I had kicked him and his mother out of "their" home, and it was totally my fault that her life was ruined. He said that because of me, they could not go back to Germany where "we were happy". It was my fault that Bryan was not doing so well at school anymore; I was no good at helping him with homework; I had anger management issues; and so on. The brainwashing was all encompassing; Bryan spewing all the lies his mother was telling him.

I have a funny feeling that Child and Family Services was exacerbating and channeling Bryan's negative attitude toward me. At one point, I suggested that organization to Jordyn, hoping their staff would recognize and support our 50/50 parenting time arrangement. I made an appointment for our family to go to a counselling session there, but of course, Jordyn said Bryan did not want to attend.

Instead, I met with a female staffer, called an investigator, who came to my house (by then I was, and still am, living in a basement suite not far from where Bryan lives) and immediately said to me, "Well, it is very easy, you look very well-educated and are well-spoken. It is so easy for you to convince the judge you are not an abuser". She had no evidence against me but, nevertheless, did not hesitate to incriminate me. I told her my entire family and individual history, but she really didn't care to listen.

The 50/50 Parenting Order came into force in December of 2010. Until that point, I was seeing my son regularly and we had an excellent, loving relationship. As soon as Jordyn found out she could not avoid work forever and had to make a living somehow, she used our son as a means of coercing me into giving her a free ride. When that didn't work, she enacted a life-long vendetta against me. But the person who has suffered most, who will carry the unnecessary burden of his horrible childhood forever, is Bryan. My son could have enjoyed his growing-up years with both his parents, been happy and productive. The fact that we divorced should never have been used against him as a tool of revenge against his father.

TOM

CHAPTER 29

TOM

I have two daughters and a son. My eldest girl is eleve and her name is Valerie. My son, Quinn is nine and my little girl, Natasha, is eight years old. My kids' mother is a national of Thailand. Yesterday was the anniversary of the last time I saw my children... and that was only by chance. I was at an Edmonton mall on a Saturday, anxiously awaiting a court judgment, which was to come down on Monday, two days later. My kids' mom, Nora, appeared very nervous to see me. I think it was because she had already bought plane tickets to fly all four of them to Thailand if the judge ruled in her favour and allowed mobility. I didn't know this at the time, but she had purchased tickets far in advance of this upcoming court decision.

I had already reported two judges for misconduct to the Judicial Council of Canada, those being the associate Chief Justice and our case management Justice, Andrea More. Our 10-day trial had been a complete farce. Those with experience like me know that the very fact of reporting a judge to Judicial Council is going to anger some judges. Our case management Justice in the Court of Queen's Bench was so angry that right in court she said that she doesn't "give a fig for the Judicial Council or its rules", and then she wrote instructions to the clerks banning me from making any applications to the court.

This is a clear violation of the Canadian Charter of Rights and Freedoms and in the United States the Constitution trumps everything; here in Canada that's also supposedly the case. Yet oddly enough, the Maintenance Enforcement (MEP) Act, which seized my passport and driver's licence, restricted my ability to travel and judges are apparently unable to overturn this action. This should be an open and shut case where the Charter of Rights trumps the MEP Act.

When targeted parents such as I challenge MEP's seizure of their documents, they lose. I am not sure if this challenge has gone to the Supreme Court, but I do know that I am a well-educated, clear-thinking and rational person who is being punished for unknown reasons. I have experienced the trauma of losing my three kids, been falsely accused of violence and unheard by our supposed justice system. These things have had the effect of tearing me down in all personal ways. I can argue well with rock-solid evidence, but I am ignored and treated callously by the court. One judge, More, said in court that she had not read my affidavits with their supporting documentation, nor did she intend to. She strode into court announcing that she did not know our case history and planned "to start fresh". Now to me that is blatant judicial misconduct. Yet my complaint to the Judicial Council was dismissed.

A year earlier in 2011, another Justice assigned to our case, named Velt, was excellent and did try her best to get to the truth. She told my ex in court to stop her crying and that "You cannot make accusations of abuse unless you have evidence. Don't even come in this court unless you do." Justice Velt supported my application for a case management judge because our case had been so mismanaged thus far. But Justice More was assigned.

The result of her "case management" has been that half my paycheque goes to the other parent who is not working, not even trying to get a job, using the excuse that she is looking after the kids. Well, I want to look after my kids too, but I am not given that option. Two days after I saw my ex and my children at the mall, Justice More gave Nora mobility so she could leave the country with them. I tried desperately to get an injunction to stop this outrage but I failed. Shortly after and unbeknownst to me, Nora and my three kids got on a plane to Thailand and have been there ever since.

Her family has threatened to kill me if I go to Thailand and try to see my kids. MEP in accordance with the Family Law Act of Alberta has ordered that since Nora got custody, I have to pay thousands of dollars to this woman who is unemployed and lives in Thailand, yet receives child support as if she was a resident of Canada. This loophole allows scores of women from India, Laos, Burma, Thailand or anywhere with a lower cost of living than that in Canada to make huge money. All they have to do is win custody of their children (which is the outcome in 82% of cases in Canada), ask the court for mobility, then return to their country of origin with their children and their windfall.

When I initially met Nora, I was a senior programs manager making about $60,000. This income allowed us to have a maid, nanny, cook, driver, gardener, a big house and a very nice lifestyle. But now my family has left me in Canada as a sessional instructor at a university in Calgary, making about $2,300 a month and I have to pay Nora over $1,000 in Thailand. This disparity is mind-boggling. I barely get by and she is living a lavish lifestyle.

The government of Canada commissioned a report called "For the Sake of the Children", published in 1998, which offered to correct a lot of the disparities and harmful policy surrounding children of divorce and custody. This report was promptly swept under a rug and no measures were implemented from its recommendations. International cases, like mine, are becoming more common, but without appropriate legislation, they are a disaster.

You know, my case should never even have been an international one. My kids were born in Thailand, but we all moved to Canada in 2009. I was with my ex for 14 years and we had always talked about moving to Canada when the children were older. We felt the education system was far better in Canada, it was less polluted and there were more employment opportunities. In 2008, there was an economic downturn in Thailand, my work contract was not going to be renewed, and my father was dying of cancer.

My ex and I owned a bicycle shop in Thailand, but she rarely worked at all, even then. She has a Nursing degree, a Master's degree in Psychology, and she speaks excellent English, but she didn't want to work. Our relationship was always strained, I realize now I was consistently manipulated, but I felt our life was good there because I had time for my kids and I love being a dad more than anything. It was strange to me, but culturally acceptable in Thailand that my ex suggested repeatedly that I should get a "mia nois" (i.e., minor wife) since Nora wasn't interested in a real relationship with me. I was hurt because I loved her. Nonetheless, I moved back to Canada with the two older kids and Nora agreed to follow soon after. But it was eight months before she and six-year-old Natasha came to Canada.

For a while things were okay in Canada, and the kids did great at school and made friends easily. Nora and I were both happier when we were getting along, but soon she would begin her sabotage tactics again; it was almost a two-week cycle. She said on occasion that "I can make anyone like me; I can make anyone help me" and was very proud of that. One night she became angry and *stabbed me with a carving knife*! And if this wasn't bad enough, the kids were all present at the dinner table and witnessed the whole thing. When the police came, the officer's first words were to me, asking "What did you do to her to make her stab you?"

I blame myself for staying in the relationship, as it was abusive and I just took it in order to keep my family together. There wasn't any history of documented mental illness in her family, but she sure appeared to behave in bizarre ways. Eventually Nora was criminally charged for the knife assault, but managed to reserve her plea a total of 13 times…and with 13 different judges! Each court date I showed up having taken half a day off work and each time Nora didn't show and the court let her lawyer stall again. Finally, the charges against Nora were dropped and you know why? Our case manager, Judge More, got involved in the criminal charges, which she had no right to. I have letters between her and Zella Harmon, Nora's lawyer at the time because I was then self-representing. More was writing Harmon suggesting she talk to the criminal lawyer and Harmon agreed to! Our case manager was very worried that if my case got before a judge in court, it could go badly for Nora and she might even be sent back alone to Thailand. So they pushed hard for the Family Court date to be prior to the Criminal Court date… and they succeeded.

In the fall, Nora flew back to Thailand to supposedly pay our bike shop staff, the mortgage and take care of things there. I found out later she didn't use our money for these purposes and I had to cover all these costs myself. The court heard about this, but didn't care. Nora stayed for a while in Thailand, but agreed to my bringing the kids back. I became a full-time single father teaching at two different universities to make ends meet. I found out that Nora had a boyfriend in Thailand, so she was not in a hurry to come back to Canada. I decided against sponsoring her Canadian citizenship application.

When I gave Nora my decision over the phone, she demanded that I sponsor her and send her a plane ticket. I noted that she was not talking about fixing our relationship, or even asking about the kids; just demanding sponsorship. She then refused to fix her computer, which cost peanuts to do in Thailand, so I was no longer able to Skype with Natasha. Nora would call but usually didn't ask to speak with Quinn and Valerie, which I found disturbing, as I am desperate to talk regularly with my kids. Mahn, the children's nanny in Thailand, wrote in her affidavit that Nora unplugged the phones and disconnected the computers so I could not connect with my children.

Thankfully I had bought a duplex back in 2005 and now we lived there with my mom living on the other side. The kids' school was just a street away with no busy roads to cross. This worked out well as I could be home for my kids and my mom could cover the mornings and after school when needed. I took my kids tobogganing, to the symphony, on photography excursions, I really opened up their lives, but none of this was ever recognized by the court. In fact, Judge More accused me of being a "Disneyland

Dad". I had furniture from the Salvation Army and was somehow still able to make it work.

Once back in Canada, Nora said she didn't want a relationship with me, but suggested she live in a house nearby so we could co-parent. That discussion ended with her changing her mind and agreeing to live together and work on our relationship. That failed when Nora refused to help around the house, saying she was "on strike" because I wouldn't sponsor her. Within four days, she moved into the basement with all three children.

On January 6th, 2011, I went to pick up the children after school and was told their mother had taken them somewhere. The school staff treated me as if I was a felon. They didn't want to tell me that Nora had taken Valerie, Quinn and Natasha to a women's shelter… I can't imagine the story she must have told them about me. This was especially weird since we had been before Justice Velt on December 17th, 2010 and there had been no mention that Nora planned to remove the children from our home. Nora later admitted to Justice Velt that she knew back in November, 2010, that she was going to the shelter.

Justice Velt told Nora to find a shelter closer to my children's original school (north side of Edmonton) and me. But when Nora's lawyer stated that the shelter in the north end of the city was full, Velt agreed that Mom could stay where she was. Judge Velt reprimanded Nora's lawyer for not filing anything about domestic violence. Eventually, after I went to the Domestic Violence Intervention team in Calgary, they changed their minds and agreed that I was no abuser.

My ex got a lawyer who portrayed me as an unimportant person in the family. Her lawyer described Nora as a wonderful mother with a wonderful relationship with her children, but said my kids' love for me was due to it being "a biological thing", nothing to do with my being a good person and father. Nora filed Emergency Protection Orders against me on false pretences and openly lied to the court on many counts; in fact, on most counts. Under oath, though, she admitted I was a good father.

The taxpayers of Alberta funded Legal Aid lawyers and the Women's Emergency shelters that helped Nora concoct a story of abuse despite no evidence of my being abusive. Nora never earned a cent in Canada, never paid any tax, yet was given six different lawyers, a three-bedroom apartment in Calgary in order to "take care of her kids", free food, utilities, and full Alberta Health Care. But she wanted to go back to Thailand because, in her words, the Canadian support system wouldn't help her.

Kathy Linter, the kids' supposed lawyer, acted more as an agent for my ex and cared nothing about my kids. She said in court that the mother (Nora) was clearly a good parent by her dealing with the adversity of coming to Canada by finding agencies to support her. There was no acknowledgement of my whole gamut of responsibility. If a couple gets along okay they are usually awarded shared custody, but if it's a high-conflict situation, Mom has a 90% chance of getting a windfall and full custody. So creating conflicting and exploding conflict are great tools to get a judge to rule in the mother's favour. Judge More had refused to read my affidavits and then the trial judge, German, said in court he didn't believe any of my witnesses and didn't care what they had to say. If you are a good liar, like Nora is, then viva voce evidence is great. If you are a researcher and science guy like I am, affidavits onto which I can attach objective documents are better. We have judges and a court system that doesn't care much for affidavit evidence; so what is due process? They don't look at affidavits with evidence and they don't hear witness evidence, so it seems their decisions are just made by presumptions.

That summer my dad passed away, and even though Nora had gotten an Emergency Protection Order (EPO) against me (for unknown reasons, since it was she who broke into my house and car), the judge carved out a day to let my kids go to their grandpa's funeral with me. I found out Nora was living at a friend's house and the situation there was very bad for my children. The kids told me they were sleeping on the floor, and even the principal of their new school warned me that Valerie, Quinn and Natasha were not being cared for properly.

I called Social Services and reported my concern, but the worker I spoke with said there was nothing they could do because the kids were with their mother. The children were truant and their grades plummeted. They were getting bullied. Each begged me to come back to my house and go to their former school. So, again I see a double standard: If Nora called Social Services and reported the same thing, but with the kids living with me, can you imagine there not being an investigation? What really broke my heart was my children needed me to help them and I couldn't.

In fact, while they were living in the house the principal warned me about, my eldest, Valerie, ran away and tried to find my place. She did this twice that I know of. Both times Nora found her and took her back to that house. Valerie was also told by Nora to never speak of those events and in a therapist's report I have, that counselor stated that he tried to talk with Valerie to no avail about what happened when she ran away (which I had told the counselor about). Valerie just stared at the floor.

I tried to talk to our case manager Justice More about the children's welfare, but as usual, she refused to look at the problems and even stated she was not willing to discuss it with me. These kids were seven, eight and nine years old. Unbelievable!

I finally got a court date for December of 2011 to get this mess sorted out. It was arranged by my same dumb-ass lawyer who agreed to the outrageous Child Support, which I was still paying and was making me destitute. I subsequently fired him; his name was Ralph Barrie. He had made the trial date months earlier and at the time I asked him why the date would be so far away. His answer to me was that "we don't want the trial date right away anyways because it might be a judgment against you" and I was naïve enough to take his advice. I had an appeal date in November to lower my payments and I did successfully manage that on my own. My child support was cut in half, so at least I could survive. I sent a complaint to the Law Society about Barrie, but of course it was dismissed.

In the meantime, I was assigned another Legal Aid lawyer; this one was Barry McMurtry, who suggested we pursue a mutual restraining order. *What*? He said that by pursuing this I could get my EPO removed. But there was no history of my being abusive, so I said I didn't want to take this course of action. I had also spoken to Russ (see Chapter 4), a great adviser in Edmonton, who was very clear in dissuading me from this path. He thought *any* restraining order would haunt me in Family Court.

Nonetheless, McMurtry wrote a terrible affidavit, and although I told him I did not want a mutual restraining order, he said I had to because Legal Aid would not fund further action on my behalf. He also said I would not see my kids for three months unless I took his advice. Justice Borrow presided at the hearing in November, 2011, and had read our prior transcripts from the Justice of the Peace. Mr. Borrow said right away that he saw no emergency and there was no present threat. But McMurtry then suggested the mutual restraining order that I had told him not to suggest. Nora's lawyer was quick to portray Nora as the victim and at risk. Actually, Nora had called the police four different times on me and you know why… because I had our children's clothes that had Nora's name on them. Yes, *she had taken a marker and printed her name in their clothes so she could claim them as her possessions*. Of note, my mum had paid for all those clothes.

In the basement where Nora had been previously living with our kids, I later found a stack of lunch containers and three boxes of children's clothes that she had been hoarding. That explains why I had found it harder and harder to find what I needed to make lunches and clothe my children.

The hearing ended with the mutual Restraining Order in place for the next six months and the EPO was vacated. That's when the criminal charges against Nora were vacated as a result of this Order. I had no supports other than my useless lawyer, McMurtry, but Nora had a lawyer named Andre Percy, counselors, social workers, and a whole team paid to help her. She did such a good job of looking helpless and distraught, lots of tears and everything. Nora's lawyer, Percy, phoned me after the hearing to let me know that since there was now a mutual Restraining Order and "you are a threat to the kids," Nora was refusing to return our children to me.

Mr. Percy also tried to have my Child Support payments increased, but since our trial was pending, Judge More turned down that application. Since Nora had now taken the kids more than 50% of the time, I guess she thought that tactic would get her more money. Judge More finally did something right. On the other hand, Ms. More asked where my kids had slept the previous night and since they had been at my house, she said "no" to the proposed increase in Child Support. Pretty flimsy logic, I'd say, since I would have effectively lost my kids then if they had instead slept at their mother's. Andre Percy even fought my request to have access, as Nora had, to my children's medical and school records.

My mom reported to me that she had seen Nora googling how to move to Toronto and eventually back to Thailand. This totally freaked me out, so I immediately applied successfully to the court for an Order preventing either parent taking the children out of the country.

There was another snag in the process when Andre Percy screwed up my child support payments. He was the writer of the Court Order, so I asked him how to pay what the court said I had to. He said to give him cheques, which I delivered to his office and got a receipt for. This was November of 2011. Percy, though, apparently forgot to file the new Order. So MEP was on my case, harassing me with writs and garnishes, and didn't believe that I'd paid as I was supposed to. I sent MEP my receipts, but it still insisted I owed $1,200 a month. MEP wrote that I would lose my driver's license and passport and I was so terrified that I dreaded picking up my mail every day. I finally got an MLA (i.e., Member of the Legislative Assembly of Alberta), Peter Sanhier, to support me; not my own MLA, Tony Vanderbrink, as he had refused to help. Perhaps I got support from that office because their staff were familiar with brutal and unfair divorce proceedings, so they understood.

The day before our trial date, Legal Aid finally assigned me a lawyer, Greg Spectre. I met him for the first time the morning of the trial, and he asked immediately what my income was. In hindsight I should have fired him right then and there.

So it was at the trial of December 17, 2011 that Justice Adair German gave Nora her Mobility Order that enabled her to take my children permanently away from me. Zella Harmon told Judge German how Nora needed to go to Thailand. I was completely blind-sided by this request in court. German listened while my ex explained my children's truancy as "due to the harsh winter". My ex had no job or place to live in Thailand, but German didn't care about those details. Even though he contravened the Family Law Act, Judge German ruled as he pleased.

Of course I now had to appeal the decision. Yet another Judge, this time Justice Hive presided. He sat down and basically I ran the trial. The first thing I asked was whether the affidavits were present and the Justice said "no". So I started in about Mom claiming she was an abused woman and the harmful things she had actually done to the kids and all co-parenting attempts. I mentioned my Thailand affidavits and then realized this judge had read nothing. He then said he would "look at them" and all of a sudden, a court clerk came in and dropped them on his desk. Hive then quickly rifled through them and kept reining me in when he said I was straying off-topic. Then it was Nora's turn and Justice Hive never called her on her irrelevant questions, even when she was asking me what colour my kids' belts for Tai Kwon Do were. By the way, I knew the answer... I know my kids...very, very well.

In the afternoon my lawyer, Mr. Spectre, announced he had to leave early so I represented myself again... just another of many times. I noticed Nora's lawyer with a calculator at hand and he kept using it. I figure he was trying to make sure Nora would get the children 60% of the time so her Child Support payments could be maximized. I ended up with 40/60 parenting time. Interestingly too, the resultant Order read "All days shall be the mother's, but for these days which we are giving to the father," effectively making me a secondary caregiver. Of course, then there had to be yet another court appearance for a Confirmation Hearing on December 23rd, five days after the trial!

My lawyer, Greg Spectre, thought this a good idea to discuss Christmas access. And there was another court date in January too. I couldn't believe how frequent and pointless these court appearances were. These lawyers are making a fortune. I was trying to keep my job, I was behind in my marking, was distracted teaching my lectures and the whole time Nora was not even working, just planning her next legal assault on me. She also went to our kids' school a lot, so I heard, even on my parenting days. And she moved from her friends' place to a shelter and back again, dragging my kids behind her every time. But Social Services wouldn't look into the matter, since none of our children had bruises.

I missed my kids' Christmas concert because Nora decided to go on the day she knew I had planned to go. Since we had the mutual restraining order, we were not to be in the same place at the same time.

January 3rd was Valerie's birthday and all three of my kids were with me. But on January 6th, I called the school to let them know I was coming to pick up my kids and the secretary put me on hold. My blood ran cold. Then she came back on and told me the children had left the school. Nora had, without my knowledge, transferred them to Poller Meadow school, which is attached to the women's shelter. Later, Valerie told me she and the other two kids only found out that same morning that they were to go there and leave their usual school. I asked the school staff why they had not informed me that my kids were going to leave and they answered that it was because the mother had requested they not do so. I couldn't believe the depth of bias against me, and dads in general. I had always been involved with my kids, with their school and School Council, yet I was clearly a bystander in their eyes and the eyes of judges in my case. I wrote the school superintendent and his response was to blow me off.

I should have formally pursued a complaint against the Edmonton Public School Board since Justice Hive, at our trial, had directed there be an exchange of information about our kids' school and medical records. Instead, the Board enabled Nora to breach that Court Order, so both were in contempt by not sharing school information about my kids with me. That Order also said the parents would exchange a communication book, so each would know any developments and events about the kids as they regularly transferred between our homes. I bought and shared that book with Nora, but she never participated and eventually it never got returned to me. I bought a cell phone for the kids too, but as my children told me, their mom hid that phone.

Justice Hive's Order also stated that I was to get a phone number so I could contact my children. Nobody would give it to me, so I went to the police station with that Order. Guess what?! Nora came walking out of one of the interview rooms. When she saw me, she was clearly startled and ducked back into the room. One of the police officers from the domestic violence team asked me why I was stalking Nora. I showed her the Court Order. This officer requested a meeting at 7:00 a.m. for a couple days later. Another half-day of lost, unpaid work time, but I agreed. Finally, I got the phone number I needed from the John Howard Society.

A police officer and a social worker from the Domestic Violence Team, Sherry and Sheila, met with me and I presented all my evidence. They were shocked and kept saying they hadn't known all that stuff. They told me they had been under the impression I was "improperly emotional" because they had seen me when I was trying to get contact information on my children from the police station. But now I was bawling and they said, "we can work with you because you have proper emotions". Nora was trying to get me charged with domestic abuse, but the team began to understand her unstable history such as her knife-attack on me. But rather than help me, this team just backed away from my case, as it was too messy. Nora went on to find yet another agency to support her disingenuous agenda.

I went to the intake centre for domestic violence at the John Howard Society and it was clear they were not used to seeing men there. There was a big poster on the wall, which read "Stop Violence against Women and Children". It then listed a bunch of points about men being violent. I asked why the poster assumed men are always perpetrators, especially since the 2009 Statistics

Canada Domestic Violence report stated that 20% of domestic abuse calls to police are made by men who are being assaulted. I was abused, my life was threatened with a knife, I endured years of psychological abuse, but the poster excluded me. I took a picture of that poster and sent it to my MLA and Alberta Justice. The next time I was in the John Howard Society, that poster was gone, but there was, in its place, a sign prohibiting cameras on the property.

In February, I had a court hearing scheduled to try and quash the mutual restraining order. I was super-prepared no thanks to my lawyer, Greg Spectre, who had gone on vacation. He didn't want to help me anyway, as he said he was only doing the custody stuff. The morning of the hearing it was about minus-30 degrees and my car wouldn't start. After I got a boost, I rushed to the courthouse, but arrived 20 minutes late. I got there just in time to see Nora's lawyer emerging from the courtroom all smiles. I asked the court clerk what was going on and was told the judge had dismissed the case and I was to pay court costs.

I tried again for March and was assigned to a Justice Sanders. I had written on all my affidavits a request, basically begging, that the judge read them prior to the hearing. And Sanders said he had, so I was encouraged. The restraining order was probably going to be lifted and he gave me the go-ahead to file for the issues with parenting time. But when I got to court, Sanders was not presiding. Instead, there was a Justice Bounder who said Sanders couldn't make the hearing. I was shocked and dismayed because Bounder had not read anything about my case. All he did in court was set more court dates: March 4th to deal with the kids and school, April 15th to deal with the mutual restraining order, and in the meantime we were to discuss the application for case management.

Justice Reece, however, responded to the request for case management and she stated she didn't see a need for it. I then wrote her directly to show how we really needed case management. My lawyer, Mr. Spectre, had by then returned from vacation and freaked that I had written Justice Reece. I had done so because Reece was the Chief of Family Law Justice at the time, so she would be making the decision.

The March 4th court appearance happened but as usual, my lawyer Greg Spectre did not appear. He said he "can't make it; sorry." Justice Joan Velt presided and she was impressive. If only she had been involved in my case the whole time. She started by asking why we were in court and I told her how the kids had been moved, and to a new school as well, and they didn't like the situation, nor did I. Then Nora started to wipe tears away and asked if she could say something to the court. Justice Velt responded to her that, "I'm not buying this routine of yours for a second. You sit down and let your lawyer talk for you." Then she asked why the mother could not be relocated to a shelter in the north end near where I live and why the kids couldn't continue at their regular school in their regular neighbourhood with their friends and their dad nearby.

Justice Velt then announced lunch-break and told Nora and her lawyer, Mr. Percy, to find a shelter before we were to reconvene in the afternoon. She knew there was something fishy about Nora's story, the violence allegations by her, and so on. She did not shrug us off for another hearing, but instead told us to come back to chambers that very same afternoon; excellent.

I had a class to teach at noon so I requested we recommence proceedings at 1:30 p.m. and Justice Velt gave permission so I could do my job. In fact, she said "no problem".

When I returned to the courthouse, I found that Percy had been talking with the Justice and as usual, Nora had her supports there including somebody from the shelter and another social worker in tow. I, on the other hand, was by myself, as per usual. Justice Velt told me that Nora's lawyer had told her the north end shelter was full and other shelters wouldn't take a woman with three children so they would be staying at the distant one Nora had moved them to. I sensed that Justice Velt was feeling cooler toward me since Percy had talked to her at lunch break.

But at least the judge asked Mr. Percy if he had filed evidence against me, which he had not. Looking exasperated, Justice Velt threw herself back into her chair and asked why he had not followed procedure. She then looked at Nora and said "You had better not come back into this court without evidence of domestic abuse. I better be hearing some screaming and shouting, I better be seeing some photos of bruising or I will take it that this never happened." I felt there was to be some traction in my case finally since Justice Velt then asked for all my file numbers so the court could consolidate all my evidence. She said we had an upcoming court appearance with Justice Binder on March 24th and she wanted a complete affidavit by the week before so Justice Binder could be prepared by the hearing.

But Mr. Percy was to write up this Court Order, and he was the same guy who dragged his feet on the MEP Order. As a result of that screw-up, I had been wrongly penalized by MEP. Well, this new Order never did make it to the Justice. Apparently, Percy did file that Order, but somehow nobody could later find it.

I updated my lawyer, Mr. Spectre, who agreed to start writing up my affidavit for March 24th. I wrote the draft and it was 60 pages. When I gave it to Spectre, he thought it hilarious that it was so long. Well, I had to answer to all of Nora's allegations against me with solid evidence, all of which I provided. I got to see Nora's affidavit, and it had bank statements for the first time. She had way more money in her bank accounts than I did.

Then, out of the blue, I got a letter from Justice Reece telling me that although I had requested Justice Velt to "seize our case", Reece or Velt now refused. Justice Velt did write to Reece that she had heard our case and was very concerned. She recognized that I was being affected professionally and personally by the allegations against me, and felt case management would be essential to get to the heart of the matter. She also requested that the case be dealt with quickly since the children were continuing to be negatively affected. That letter from Reece also told me to take courses about High Conflict Parenting (which I did) and she assigned Justice Andrea More as our case manager.

I called Justice More's assistant to make sure my affidavit was there and More would read it and she assured me that would happen. But a bit later, she called me back to say they couldn't find my affidavit. Really; *60 pages of evidence somehow got lost? By the case manager's office?* After a couple more sleepless nights, I got called by More's assistant again to report that they had found my affidavit after all.

I had asked for a lawyer to represent my children, as was their right. But when I called Legal Aid to find out if one had been assigned, the staff told me that Nora had been in and had talked with them so they couldn't give me any information. *What*? I was the parent who had made the application for my children. So I called Greg Spectre and asked him to help. He agreed but never looked into this. It turned out that Justice Velt had stated in her letter to Justice Reece that Zella Harmon was to represent the kids; however, Kathy Linter was assigned instead. Nora knew this! She had whispered to Percy, her lawyer, at the March 4th hearing that despite his mention to Justice Velt that it would be Zella Harmon, Nora thought Linter would become the children's lawyer.

The day before the March 24th hearing, I got a phone call from my eldest, Valerie, who told me they had had a visit from their own lawyer, Ms. Linter. Nora had taken the kids to see her in her office the day before our hearing. I asked Valerie what they talked about and then the phone went dead. Valerie told me later that her mom had grabbed the phone away from her then.

I was panicking; I called my lawyer and he assured me I was just being paranoid. He said there had only been one meeting with Ms. Linter and my kids and the hearing would be fair and reasonable. But the next day, March 24th, changed my life and those of my kids forever. Greg Spectre introduced me, in the courtroom, to Ms. Linter. I held out my hand to shake hers and she didn't even look at me. She then went to sit with Andre Percy and Nora, after first hugging Nora, the mother of her clients. Why was she not sitting in the middle between the parents? She was clearly siding with Nora from the outset.

Mr. Spectre asked me to sit with him in case he needed help, as he was unfamiliar with my case, *having met me the day before*! And then Justice More walked in and announced she hadn't read the affidavits and had no plans to. Sixty pages; my affidavit might as well have been thrown in a fireplace. Spectre asked Justice More for permission to sit with him and she said it was okay but that he should "control your client". More showed such obvious bias against me; Percy was not asked to control *his* client. My lawyer, Spectre, should have asked for a half day to read all the affidavits, but instead, he let the proceedings continue.

Next, Justice More announced that she had been good friends with Kathy Linter for 12 years and was happy to see her. She also stated that Kathy Linter had a Master's Degree in Clinical Psychology, which More said was great training. Interestingly, the psychologist at our trial contradicted everything Linter said when I cross-examined him. This showed how out of her league Linter was. More asked to hear from the children's lawyer, and Linter said she hadn't read the history. She said she'd only met with the kids the day before for a couple hours, but it was the worst case she had seen in 30 years! Ms. Linter continued that I had assaulted Nora and she had only defended herself by stabbing me. Then she said that the kids told her that they always see their daddy with money, but their mommy never has money. Daddy is always pulling big bills out of his pocket. Do you think my children really said any of those things?

During this barrage, my lawyer said nothing. At one point, I spoke up and started to say to the judge, "Excuse me your Honour", but More reprimanded me and Linter continued to tear me to pieces. More was looking angrier by the second and then Percy, Mom's lawyer, told the judge I had absconded from Thailand with my children. According to him, poor Nora had to fly to Canada to get them back. Finally, I couldn't stand the lies anymore, and I stood up and said to the judge "That's not what happened. She gave me permission, and we were all going to move to Canada". Justice More stared at me, and said I'd better sit down and be quiet or I would be removed from the courtroom.

The earlier February decision by Justice Sander had overturned the mutual restraining Order and I had been able to attend two of my daughter, Valerie's, events: a field trip and her singing competition. They were just great and Valerie glowed, seeing both her parents on the field trip. She even asked, and we had a photo taken together. But even when our daughter was made so happy, Nora was angry because I had shown up. It interfered with her concocted story that I am a dangerous man.

So in court, Justice More decided to overturn Justice Sanders' decision in one sentence with "I am going to strike Justice Sanders' changes". More had no right to do this since she had not read or considered any of the evidence; Justice Sanders had. My lawyer should have appealed that decision immediately. Greg Spectre should have had More recused right then since her prejudice against me from the very beginning was profound. Instead, I was again punished for wanting to be with my kids.

It was then, after this first case management hearing, that Justice More decided we needed to go to trial. She said there would be a Practice Note 7 implemented (i.e., independent parenting experts are called upon for Interventions and Assessments when a Family Court reaches an impasse in a high-conflict case), a therapist would be assigned, and the parents would split the cost. Nora and I were instructed to each write yet another affidavit about how our children came to Canada.

Subsequently, there were at least five more case management hearings with Justice More before we even got to trial. During this time, she would not rule that my kids return to their regular school or scheduled time with me. The children's supposed legal representative, Kathy Linter, stated that she wanted control over which documents went to their therapist, Gram Clarge. I asked Greg to fix this, as Linter was interfering with the flow of knowledge, but he did nothing. Mr. Clarge met once with me, once with Nora, once with each of our three children, and then another time with each parent. Based on his superficial synopsis of the complex family dynamic, he wrote a "report".

During the May long weekend, Nora wanted to take our kids to a YMCA camp for children from abusive homes. It was my scheduled weekend with them, and I didn't want to lose this time. My former lawyer, Greg Spectre, had pushed me to agree to this. I would have not seen my kids for 20 straight days if I let Nora take them to the camp. The first I'd heard of this camp was from Valerie and when she asked me if she could go, I asked her to have her mom contact me so we could decide. Of course, Nora did not contact me. I wrote her an email asking if we could trade weekends and I would be okay with that, but she never responded. Then I texted her as it was almost the long weekend and my kids were still waiting to hear if they were going to camp or to my place. Finally, she texted back "Talk to your lawyer"; that was the whole message.

I called Mr. Spectre to find out that Justice More had sent a letter to him instructing that I had to give up my weekend so Nora could put them in that camp. Apparently it was not an Order as there had been no hearing, but Spectre said I had to go along with it. I didn't; I took my kids camping instead as we had planned. By Saturday afternoon, I got a call from my mother saying a police officer was looking to apprehend my kids. Remember that I had waited months and months to get to a hearing to reinstate my rightful time with my children and here was More writing a letter on Nora's behalf outside all court proceedings. It turned out that Zella Harmon, now Nora's lawyer, had written to More and Greg. She wrote that if there was no permission given for the kids to go to the YMCA camp, she was requesting that More "take care of this". And where was Kathy Linter in all this, the kids' supposed lawyer? Greg Spectre had Harmon's letter for two weeks and didn't tell me.

More also wrote in her "letter of instruction" that I was to get my time with the kids back in some way. Maybe she back-pedalled with this olive branch because Greg had written a letter of complaint to her that was then going to Judicial Council of Canada. I wrote to the Associate Chief Justice Rock in Edmonton as well. Justice Rock's response to me was that he did not expect his judges in case management to read the history of evidence unless there were applications in front of that judge at the time. Well there were! He also wrote that I should not write him again.

I fired Spectre and got a new lawyer, Henry Hannerson. First thing we did was make a pitch to Justice More for a full, bilateral assessment in this case, which is what Mr. Clarge was supposed to have done. More said "no". She said there was an imbalance of power between the parents; but I had zero power. When my lawyer argued that point, More just shut him down and said that I was to blame since Nora might be deported due to the knife attack on me. Hannerson told me he had never seen such inappropriate behaviour by a judge.

Leading up to our trial, Justice More, at our second or third hearing said she was surprised that I made the Parenting Application, not Nora. She somehow advised Zella Harmon to cross-file so that Nora would be an Applicant. I am the Applicant for Parenting, and I am the Applicant for the Mutual Restraining Order issues, but all of a sudden I was served with Parenting as a Respondent.

I knew from the outset that More was going to be biased against me. In our final hearing before the trial, More kicked me out of the courtroom. The reason was that I had prepared a Memorandum of Agreement and Ms. Harmon had signed it stating that we thought mediation would be useful. But Justice More blew up at me and said "No, we are going to trial." She interfered in the criminal case, and now she was insisting on a trial instead of the agreed mediation. This judge accused me of behaving inappropriately in her courtroom and not following her orders. She gave Henry, my lawyer, and me 12 hours to file everything for the trial. And she blocked my affidavits and other documents from being filed prior to the trial so she planned to prevent my evidence from being read and heard. I put together my financials and faxed them to Henry Hannerson and I wrote an application to have Justice More recused from the trial. I took that to the court clerk who refused to file it on the grounds that I had to talk to Justice More first. I figured at least Hannerson had sent my financials and everything to Zella Harmon. However, according to Harmon, my documents arrived too late, so were not filed before trial.

So we went into trial with Justice German. I would love to have that transcript from our 10-day trial, September 19-29th, 2011, but it would cost me $20,000. I could never find that kind of money. Hannerson was not prepared due to More's 12-hour deadline, so

I did the best I could. The resultant Order gave Nora mobility and most of the parenting rights including school decisions. German also confirmed Justice Hive's Order giving Nora a nine-straight-day stretch with our kids.

Child Support was set according to the Federal Guidelines, and she was also awarded retroactive spousal support of $1,900 a month from January 1st when she moved into the women's shelter. I was only making $2,000 a month, so I clearly could not pay this huge amount. Justice German decreed that as long as Nora stayed in Canada, I had to keep paying her spousal support in that amount… forever. This amounted to a total of $3,000 a month!

If Nora went back to Thailand, I would no longer have to pay spousal support as Justice German said he believed "she is a wonderful professional and I am sure she will find work there". He added that if I also went to Thailand, both spousal and child support would instead be up to the Thai courts. What I heard was this judge telling us to go back to Thailand and continue the fight there.

I had so many obligations in Canada and no money, so how would I go to Thailand? The Order would be a standing one, so if Nora again returned to Canada, I'd be obligated to pay the full amount again. To end this charade of a trial, German ruled that I pay all court costs too. The lawyers had not even asked for that provision, but he gave it to Nora anyway.

I had to keep Legal Aid and although the bills were accumulating there, I would lose its support if I declared bankruptcy. Also, to appeal German's Order, I needed Legal Aid funding. If Henry Hannerson had been a good lawyer, he would have filed a Stay immediately after Justice German's ruling came down. He didn't. Instead, he asked that our children stay in Canada with me while their mother went back to Thailand. Then she could apply from there to see if she would be allowed back in Canada. What a stupid plan and I looked like a heartless bastard. That was *not* what I had wanted. Hannerson was a nice guy, but clueless as my lawyer.

If Hannerson had filed an immediate Stay, we could have had a hearing for that purpose the next day and Nora would not have left the country with my children. I studied up the next day on how to file for an Appeal, and then it was my night with the kids. But I did not get to see them. I went to the police station to get a police enforcement clause activated, but I was told I could not. Justice More, once again, had interfered by her Order that I had given up the kids for 18 days. That meant the police were unable to help me. As I found out later, the Order went into effect on October 3rd and Nora fled the country with the kids on the 6th, the very next morning after I tried to get police enforcement. I didn't even get to say good-bye or give them their favourite toys; they were just gone.

Although judges are instructed to reduce conflict and help children regain some stability in their lives after their parents split, Justice German threw my kids' lives into a tailspin with a stroke of his pen.

I phoned the school asking where my kids were and was told nobody knew anything about their whereabouts. Two weeks of anguish later, I got a phone call from Valerie, who told me she and her siblings were in Thailand. Her mother had taken them to her family's village to live, a village to which they had never been. Valerie had secretly borrowed a phone to call me, without Nora's knowledge.

Valerie was 11 years old and had the sense to contact me, however she could. She told me her mother was telling them I would soon be visiting, but she knew perfectly well I could not travel to Thailand. MEP had taken my passport! Even though I wrote to MEP explaining my situation and asking for a reprieve, I was still supposed to pay over $900 to Nora every month and was unable to. You see, since Justice More was not recused from my file, her letter determining everything held fast, and there was nothing I could do to change it. When More got wind of my letter to MEP, she wrote the court stating that "Mr. (me) nor his counsel is allowed to make applications to any child support, to vary child support, to recuse me, to discuss Ms. Linter or Ms. Hardin". In turn, MEP advised me to take my request for relief back into court. How? Talk about being hamstrung.

MEP planned to take my driver's license too, but I was driving the Edmonton Transit bus then, trying to make ends meet. So I couldn't see my kids, but MEP was going to make damn sure I still paid Nora. In November another judge, Mr. Rock, said I could go to the Appeals Court if circumstances of my kids had changed. Well, they had! But, since Justice German had not specified where the kids were to live, Nora simply took them to her parents' village, not to Chiang Mai, where they had lived earlier in life.

I decided to go to an Appeal, so I worked as hard as I could, but was still accruing arrears with MEP as there was no way I could pay what the Court Order required. I thought the appeal would sort things out, but when I went to Legal Aid, I was turned down. No one would represent me. I submitted my whole story to a panel that decides whether refused cases should instead be granted Legal Aid support. Mr. Hannerson wrote a good letter on my behalf to those panelists too. I finally got funding for an appeal.

After months and months, Legal Aid found me a lawyer, Avril Kellen, but she thought it too much work to revisit my whole case. She said she'd inquire "off the record" about what could be done. Ms. Kellen looked over the Order as she hoped to find a mistake in its wording. This would constitute grounds to change its terms. So as I found out, appeals aren't based on judges making crappy Orders, they are based on mistakes found when making a crappy Order. It was late April by this time, six months after my kids were taken away, and Ms. Kellen told me she wanted to be released from my file.

She filed the Appeal application, but said she didn't want to do the factum. Now I am left to try and appeal my Order by myself, without representation and without any supports. I have been trying to get on my feet and rebuild my professional reputation, but at the same time I am psychologically devastated. Somehow, I have to get this appeal to go through.

I have been to court, with legal representation and without, about 40 times so far. A lawyer has never written a single application for me. The only affidavit a lawyer wrote on my behalf was for one review hearing, and he did a terrible job. But they all got paid even though I did all the work. My ex was never cross-examined in court and her lies were accepted as fact. One of my lawyers, Greg Spectre, even said "I have private clients paying me all this and you are just a Legal Aid client, so I don't want to go to the trouble." They wanted my case to be formulaic, simple and quick, take your weekends, pay your ex and go away. But I insisted that I love my kids, I need them and they need me, I love being a dad and I just want 50/50 parenting time, but all the legal individuals in my case thought "Oh God, this guy is going to be trouble." It has cost me a fortune; I've lost my children, all my savings, and my peace of mind. I have been diagnosed with PTSD (Post-Traumatic Stress Disorder) recently due to the trauma of having my children removed from my life.

Complaints with evidence showing a breach in the Lawyers Code of Conduct were completely dismissed by the Law Society of Alberta. I filed complaints with stellar documentation against three lawyers that I used and who messed my case up more each time. None went anywhere because they all protect each other. Craig Bush is a nice guy, but totally incompetent. He was the Director of Conduct, and he was completely useless. He had no idea how to manage and just told me there was nothing he could do. Even worse, Morris Dupont, then Complaints Manager for the Law Society in Edmonton, had not even finished processing my complaint about Rich Barrie from almost two years earlier; and there was also the one about Kathy Linter filed a few months ago. I'm sure by the 3rd they just decided I was the problem because on appeal, I was told by the decision panel each time that the lawyers were free to behave as they had. It's a shameful way to supposedly build credibility with the public.

I am proud that I always parented in ways that accounted for each child's individual differences, but also set standards for our family that we all agreed on. We worked as a team, the kids helped clean house, cook, accepted consequences and rewards together. We were an awesome team and my kids were polite, smart and kind to others.

"Being a dad was the best job I ever had. I loved it and I can't believe I got that taken away. I loved being a dad, I loved parenting and what hurts me so much right now is they have taken away my opportunity to be a parent to these kids and to help them grow into good people."

Early 2017

It has been a long and painful road and I'm still trying to resolve my family situation. Since Nora took off to Thailand with our kids in October of 2011, all three have faced an unending struggle to have a good life. It took me three years to get to Thailand to try and find my children. Alberta Court of Queen's Bench ruled that every aspect of the children's welfare was now assigned to the jurisdiction of Thailand. But, all money issues, such as child support, were to remain under Canadian jurisdiction. *If I was a serial killer, I would have received better treatment from the courts.* International law states that kids have a right to a relationship with their father; apparently that did not include my children. I finally got my passport back and immediately left Canada. If I was to return to Canada now, I would likely have MEP after me and I would probably be thrown in jail for the arrears still accruing against me.

Once I got to Thailand at the end of 2014, I went to the Canadian Consulate in Chiang Mai. There, I was told no one could help me access my children. They would not even help me find them! I applied for Legal Aid there, but was refused. I was penniless and my first goal was to get a job. After four months, I was able to get my bike shop back and that helped a lot. Then I obtained a job in Chiang Mai, but got laid off when the project was completed a year later. Now I am working with a company and have my two eldest children, Valerie, now 16, and Quinn, 14, living with me.

I was able to find my children thanks to Valerie's contacting me and my relationship with a few of Nora's relatives, our old friends and staff. My kids were not doing well in the village Nora had taken them to. I heard they were sleeping in a shack on the floor and their school was a long way from them. Natasha, 12 years old then, ran away once and when Nora found her, she pulled her out of school. For the next year, according to Nora, Natasha was "home schooled". Natasha had been trying to get to me, so her mother clearly had to rein her in. Once she was unable to mix with her friends at school, Natasha became increasing hostile to me; she was completely under the spell of her mother and remains so to this day.

My other two children begged to live with me, but when they too ran away to see me, Nora charged me with kidnapping. This charge went to court in Thailand. Valerie and Quinn talked with the judge and stated their desire to live with me. They were ignored and Nora remained the custodial parent. Eventually, my two eldest became too unruly with Nora, so she decided to allow them to live with me. Both are doing extremely well. Their grades have improved and they are cooperative helpers in our little family unit. We work and play together and they are kind and productive people. This is not the case with Natasha.

Nora had her lawyers propose a "deal" with me. *I was to give up Natasha in exchange for custody of the other two kids.* So their mother used Natasha as a bargaining chip so she could keep getting child support. Remember that Nora has no job, and Natasha is somehow home-schooled, isolated from peers and her dad. I am too tired and worn down to continue this fight. Nora signed a letter agreeing to my request for passports for Valerie and Quinn. Regularly, I drove five hours to Nora's family village for visits, but each time, my other kids and I noticed that Natasha was becoming increasingly like her mother, narcissistic and unfeeling toward us. The last time I saw Natasha was a few weeks ago, and it did not go well. She said she doesn't want anything to do with us.

Throughout these five long years, Nora has never stopped her legal quest to get more money from me. I wonder whether Zella Harmon is still representing her via Legal Aid at the expense of Alberta taxpayers? The court applications are still signed by Harmon, even though Nora has been living in Thailand since 2011. Interesting too that the Canadian government would not help me access my children as it claimed it has no jurisdiction in Thailand… just another double standard in favour of the alienator. Nora is a "cry-bully" and this has always worked in her favour. There is no possibility of our being able to co-parent or even parallel-parent because one of the parents has an overriding agenda that benefits herself at the expense of our youngest child. I have lost Natasha, but I am grateful to have my two eldest kids back.

Late 2017

In July, I arrived back in Canada with my two eldest children. Natasha was left behind with her mother, now completely brainwashed against us. She has lost her dad and her two siblings because the system allowed the cult-leader, Nora, to control her for the last 8 years. Valerie and Quinn are doing well and glad to be back in Canada. We are staying in Edmonton with my girlfriend, Mary, who has stood by me for almost 7 years. I need a job and I need to regain my peace. I am still in touch with Natasha via Skype once in a while, but she seems to be increasingly like her mother. I hear the same manipulative and mean words out of her mouth that I have heard from Nora for years. She told me a couple days ago that her mother intends to come to Canada.

If Nora comes here, I am so worried that our tenuous peace will again be shattered. I phoned the Legal Aid Centre in Edmonton for some free advice in case that happens. I want to be clear on my course of action if Nora decides to come after me again for Spousal and/or Child Support and if MEP penalizes me with arrears. Nora has been unemployed in Thailand for over three and a half years and has never been required to disclose her income. I, on the other hand, have worked and scrounged and tried to make a good life for my kids, but after 8 years, our future still hangs in the balance.

JIM

CHAPTER 30

JIM

2017

Hannah and I first met in the fall of 1992 and were married the following December. Shortly after we married we began meeting with a counselor. My wife and I both came from dysfunctional families of origin and we wanted to have a positive life together, a different one from what we each experienced growing up. Our extended families were not helpful and undermined our relationship from the start.

In 1995 our son was born at the conclusion of one of the most difficult times a newly married couple would ever have to deal with. A child in a group-home where I worked accused me of inappropriate behaviour. On March 1st, 12 days before the birth of our son, my week-long trial in Court of Queens Bench concluded. I was completely exonerated, but those 18 long months of accusation had taken a toll on me. I had been instructed by my counsel to refrain from speaking with anyone until my trial. Now, in hindsight, I can see how that period of forced isolation set the stage for mistrust between Hannah and me… mistrust she has never been able to overcome.

By 1997 the relationship with our families had become more strained so we decided to move to Medicine Hat. We had been staying with my mom and her husband, but she and Hannah did not get along. I felt caught in the middle, each of these women wanting me to take her side. In January of 1998 our eldest daughter, Erin, arrived into the world. Hannah was a good mother, but she dealt with postpartum depression. Over time, she felt somewhat better and in 2001, we had our second daughter, Lucy.

We moved again, this time to the USA, in the fall of 2003. I loved it, but my wife did not. Hannah and I began to argue frequently, and sometimes we even resorted to pushing each other. Both of us are to blame for that inappropriate behaviour. Also, prior to the move, we discovered that my brother's son (8 years old then) sexually abused our son, Mike, who was 7. Mike told us my nephew had also abused Erin. My mom sided with my brother and made the abuse seem trivial, an overreaction on Mike's and our part. To this day, I believe Mike feels responsible for the family separation. Should he ever read this narrative, I want him to know that at no time have I ever blamed him. In fact, my son did the right thing by telling his parents.

By spring of 2005, we moved back to Canada and settled in Lethbridge. Hannah's and my relationship remained rocky and the distance grew between us. I was working multiple jobs so Hannah could stay home with the kids. I wasn't home much and our children were finding their own independence. I began to get phone calls from my wife asking me to come home because she needed help. Many times, I arrived home to utter chaos and had to figure out what had happened prior to my getting there. I was supposed to bring peace back into our home. Our kids resented my intervening, no matter what parental strategies I tried to employ.

From 2003 through 2007, our family had virtually nothing to do with Hannah's extended family and only occasional contact with mine. In 2007, my mother wrote letters to our three oldest children acknowledging that our son had done the right thing in bringing to light his cousin's sexual misconduct. In June that same year, my mother gave us a sizable amount of money to help us purchase a home. I was not present when my mother made that big announcement and looking back now, I can see that this generous gift only reinforced to my family that I was an inadequate provider.

In August of 2006, our third daughter, Ava, was born, but we soon noticed she was not reaching developmental milestones as the other three kids had at similar age. In the spring of 2007 we learned that Ava has some developmental-delay issues that still remain only partially diagnosed. While this child is an absolute joy and blessing to our family, her delay has been difficult to navigate. Of all four children, it is Ava who has the closest bond with me. Hannah's and my break-up affected her most negatively, as she has been allowed very little time with me. In fact, in the limited time I have spent with Ava since May of 2014, I have observed her regressing in her development; she has lost weight and her school reported that she is not sleeping well. I learned that for months Ava would aimlessly wander the house calling for her "Dada" and then just break down and cry. Prior to my break-up with Hannah, and subsequent rare time with Ava ever since, she was beginning to communicate using basic sign language and could put multiple syllables together. She was also almost potty-trained. Much of this progress has since deteriorated.

Back to 2010, we began fund-raising efforts to take Ava to the States for intensive physiotherapy. In those five weeks in Florida, my wife and I witnessed our girl take her first steps just after her 4th birthday. During that time six of us lived in a two-bedroom motel room as we rallied together to cheer her on. I had been working in Calgary up to that point and the commute from our home frequently kept me away from my family. Via phone calls to Hannah and the kids, I heard of ongoing tension in the home with no resolution. When home, I felt more like a peacekeeper than a husband and father.

Between 2011 and 2014 there were many times when the police were called out to our house. Anytime Hannah felt like she could not handle things she called the police. We also went to counselling and had Child and Family Services investigate what was going on in our home. None of this helped in bringing peace into our home.

I became more isolated from my family as Hannah repeated to our children that the turmoil was all my fault.

Hannah and Mike became extremely enmeshed. Our son became physically as well as verbally abusive toward me. My wife and son had effectively removed me from any positive influence in my family. One Sunday evening in August of 2013, after an argument that involved Hannah, Mike and me, I called our pastor to come into our home for mediation and an outside perspective. He spent a couple of hours with us and was able to see some of the dysfunctionality. During the next few months he tried to help, but to no avail. This pastor even told members of his congregation to stay away from Hannah because she was "trouble". In follow up conversations with me, he also acknowledged that Hannah constantly slandered and spoke negatively about me to anyone who would listen to her. I was told by this man that he never heard me say anything negative about the hell I was living in.

We started family counseling at Crossroads Counseling Centre later in 2013. Hannah and our son Mike gave their perspective first on what was going on in our family. Then Hannah and I attended for marital counseling. The counseling quickly became a reason for us as a family to avoid discussion about anything. I expressed my concerns with the director of this counseling centre and was told he was "building a bridge of rapport" with my wife and son before he could resolve the division in our family. At one of my individual appointments the counselor asked me how I felt we were progressing and whether I was starting to see any changes at home. I told him that I felt even more isolated and alone, virtually ignored by my wife and children. When I walked into a room my family members would disperse to other parts of the home until I left that room. If this counselor was giving my wife and son some new skills to bring us together, then his counseling was failing miserably. I remember asking him if there was anything else that I could do, say, or become, that would help, and he told me repeatedly that there was nothing more I could do but be patient.

Hannah had me arrested on May 24th, 2014 after a two-day argument. Though we argued frequently and even physically abused each other by pushing and shoving, I had never sexually assaulted my wife, and yet these were the charges against me now. In fact, our counselor verified that Hannah told him that I was loving and kind. But I was now portrayed as evil; Hannah was self-declared innocent. Once, Hannah texted me that "if our son kills himself I will hold you personally responsible". On some ill-advised legal advice, I pleaded guilty to three counts of common assault and was placed on 12 months' probation. One of my conditions was to have no direct or indirect contact with Hannah. This made contact with our girls virtually impossible, as Hannah refused to allow them to contact me. Ava was, and remains, unable to speak for herself.

On October 22nd, 2014, I went to Ava's school to let them know I would attend the parenting meeting to be held there on October 30th. The staff member informed me that Hannah had already been there to tell them to exclude me from the meeting about our daughter. She offered me a subsequent, November 6th, date to meet alone with Ava's caregivers at the school. I was not in favour of this plan of two separate meetings, since it would significantly affect decisions for Ava's wellbeing with only Ava's mom present on October 30th. I then met with the assistant principal, Chris Sano, to discuss my concerns, but to no avail.

I also made an appointment to see Erin's school principal, Chris MacIntosh, to find out how she was faring at school. He turned around and informed Hannah of our upcoming meeting and she phoned the Lethbridge RCMP. On October 27th, a Constable Karan called to tell me the meeting with Mr. McIntosh for the 30th was cancelled and should I show up, the RCMP would arrest me. Hannah had told the detachment that I had a "No-Contact" Order disallowing me from any engagement with my children. This was a lie. Nevertheless, there was no meeting and Mr. McIntosh continued my banishment from the school. At my request, he did have Erin's report card and attendance records mailed to me.

On November 6th, I did attend the meeting about Ava with her school counsel

or. On the way out, I caught a glimpse of my little girl sitting in the library, but that was all I was allowed. The same afternoon,

I went to the community pool to watch Ava's swimming lesson from the side of the pool. As I sat there, two Lethbridge Regional Police officers approached and asked me to leave at Hannah's request. They said I was in breach of my probation Order, which was untrue. Though I was allowed only supervised visits with Ava then, her supervisor, Kerrie, was in the pool with her. One officer asked whether I had informed Hannah that I planned to go to the pool so I reminded him that contacting Hannah, my estranged wife, would indeed be a breach of my No Contact Order. Apparently, Hannah had driven through the pool parking lot, saw my vehicle there, and called the cops. I advised the officers that I had attended most of Ava's Thursday activities since September and without incident. At that, they left the building.

The very next day, however, the Lethbridge RCMP's Constable Derry phoned me, following up a phone call they had received from Lucy the day before. Constable Derry told me Lucy had been "near-hysterical" as she had seen me on the driveway of our family home, which I had been removed from. I had in fact been there to see if I could talk to Lucy, but changed my mind when I saw an unfamiliar vehicle in the garage. I had no prohibition clause preventing me from contact with my kids or being at or in my home, only no contact with Hannah. When I explained this to the Constable, she agreed that Lucy's behaviour seemed unusual and "heavily-influenced". Ms. Derry then apologized for the inconvenience and hung up.

On November 27th, 2014, Ava's school principal allowed me to have lunch with Ava and then go to the pool, but I was not allowed to swim with her. This Mr. Paya said he planned to attend and observe my visit. Ava was so happy to see me at lunch, she immediately climbed into my lap, threw her arms around me, and stayed there until the break was over. Mr. Paya, and all other staff in attendance, could not help but notice our positive interaction. I noticed Ava had lost weight, her teeth had yellowed, and her aides told me she had a poor appetite. Later, at the pool, Ava did her utmost to get my attention and, according to her aide, was more vocal than she had been in a long time. At 5:00 p.m. the same day,

Mr. Paya called me to apologize and said that after observing us during lunch and the swimming lesson, he knew this little girl needed her dad. He told me he would highly recommend that I be allowed into the pool with my daughter from then on. He also encouraged me to show up for lunch with Ava whenever it worked with my schedule. Mr. Paya said he would get a letter signed by Hannah, agreeing that she stay away from the school when I was there, to align with the No Contact Order between us.

That November, Kerrie, Ava's supervisor, asked to be removed as a supervisor for visits between Ava and me. She stated she could not deal with the hassles Hannah created. Kerrie's employer, Palliser School Division, advised her to remove herself from our family's file. In the summer of 2014 due to charges laid against me, I consented to supervised visits at the local YWCA Women's Shelter through its so-called "Safe Visitation" program. Why a father would have to attend a battered women's facility to see his child was puzzling to me as it seemed to be a "foxes guarding the henhouse" situation. When Kerrie heard about this she graciously agreed to be on a court-ordered document as a supervisor so that Ava could see her dad. When the school year started Hannah became so difficult to work with that after a handful of visits Kerrie had to stop supervision in order to keep her job. Kerrie worked with Ava for three years and knew she had a very close bond with her father. In September of 2016 Hannah stated under oath that she had Kerrie removed from working with Ava because Kerrie did something she did not agree with.

Hannah had bad-mouthed me at length to the Y so they scheduled visits with Ava during times that Hannah knew very well conflicted with my work schedule. When I notified the Y staff that I could not attend, they recorded those as "cancellations" and promptly removed their services from us. I was left with no supervisor and so could not see Ava.

Fortunately, my friend Clay arranged with Hannah to supervise two visits between my older girls and me in December of 2014. I had not seen either of them since the previous August. Clay wrote an affidavit including his difficulty in scheduling visits due to

Hannah's obstructionist agenda and the ludicrous directive for supervised visits. He could see there was absolutely no need for supervision when I was with my children.

Clay did report, though, that through his observations and some interaction with the girls it was apparent to him that Hannah did not want to see me and wanted to "inflict as much pain on him (me) as possible". In his opinion and from his contact with Hannah he could see she was playing the children against me. At my visit with the girls on December 28th, Erin told me to "give Mom sole custody and just walk away to make it easier on everyone". This behaviour from my daughters was so unlike them and I knew the brainwashing had to be extremely severe. That day was the last time I have seen or spoken with my teenage girls.

In 2015, I continued as before visiting with Ava on Thursdays for lunch and pool time afterward. On January 15th, I noticed Ava had some severe bruising on her back. Kerrie, and Ava's other aide Nala, also saw and photographed the injury. I notified the police who called Child and Family Services and Ava was taken to our family doctor. My concern was for Ava's safety since the injury was large, severe, and happened while my daughter was in the care of her mother. But that was the end of any follow-up. Hannah had reported I was breaching my terms of probation by underpaying Child Maintenance. In February I was charged with breach of probation for missing payments for child support. In fact, I was behind on my payments because I was having to take time off work to see Ava on Thursday afternoons. I let Mr. Paya know that I could no longer visit with my daughter on Thursdays since MEP required me to work to send Hannah more money. I told him how much I appreciated his understanding of the situation and his support of Ava's relationship with me.

I stopped seeing Ava at the school in March of that year due to the ongoing conflict that Hannah was creating at the school. Mr. Paya stated to me that it was causing too much drama for his staff and students to deal with our family situation. On June 23rd I attended the school to review how Ava's year ended. Mr. Paya refused to allow me to review her information citing FOIP concerns. Instead he read through daily communication, redacting information as he read. Why one parent was getting all information, while the other was not, caused some concern as my parental rights had never been taken away from me. What was way more concerning was that immediately after Ava was disallowed from seeing me, her behaviour in school dramatically changed. I was hearing words to describe a child, once the envy of all aides because of her sweet disposition, now described as defiant, not following direction, sad, not eating, and looking pale. My heart broke at that point and will only be repaired when both parents are equally involved in her life.

That June, I obtained a Court Order that directed mom to place my two teen daughters. Erin and Lucy, into counseling, with my involvement. I found out a year later in court that Lucy had been taken to one session and Erin to two or three. Hannah claimed on the stand she could not remember the exact number of sessions our girls attended. Mom stated that the girls did not want to go so she let them discontinue. I was completely unaware of any counseling taking place in spite of the direction from the court that I be involved. I was successful in making changes to my probation order to allow for third-party contact with Hannah in order to set up parenting time. When a mutual friend made contact to set up a visit Hannah called the RCMP who threatened to charge me with breach for making contact. When I explained the changes the officer still told me not to contact Hannah, even though I was legally entitled to. How was a father (me) expected to see his children when clearly the authorities were not on his side?

In August, Erin went to the RCMP, accusing me of molesting her multiple times when she was 3 years old and between 2007 and 2014. On October 15th, I was arrested and charged with sexual assault and sexual interference involving my eldest daughter. I spent Thursday through Monday locked up in the Correctional Centre as a result. This occurred one week prior to the termination date of my probation and came as no coincidence.

This was the second time I had wrongfully been arrested. On September 28th, 2015, I had been arrested and charged with breach of probation because I set up through mom's counsel, a visit to see my children. The Lethbridge constable unlawfully detained me for five hours, from 10:30 p.m. until 3:45 a.m., at which time I was finally allowed to call my lawyer. I did not see any of my children for the remainder of 2015. Without support of my friends and other alienated parents I have come to know, I am not sure I would have survived that year.

On January 5th 2016, we went to court. My new lawyer at the time, to her credit, had received my file a week before Christmas and it was 1,300 pages long! She did an admirable job in court and had our case adjourned until January 26th so she could better prepare. She read about my alleged abuse by my wife toward her and also Erin, my eldest. Hannah wanted me locked into the Safe Visitation Program offered at the "battered women's shelter". Even though, to this point, I still had court-ordered "reasonable and generous access" to my kids, it had been exactly five months since I had last been allowed to visit Ava. Now I was granted an upcoming "supervised" visit on February 26th, to occur at the Women's Shelter.

In the meantime, Hannah's and my house was illegally sold right under my nose. Hannah had apparently put it up for sale in hopes of making a nice profit for herself. When I found out, I read through the Real Estate Act and then called the broker who had facilitated the entire transference of ownership. The realtor claimed that I had had my rights as a property-owner removed so this was a legal transaction. But I had received notice from my own lawyer asking for my signature to finalize the sale. The realtor was in violation of their own Code of Conduct in the Act. Though I asked to negotiate and settle the terms so the house proceeds would be shared, the broker refused so we had to go to court for that too.

Erin turned 18 the next week. Though I knew I would not get to see her, I bought her a birthday card to put in a box I keep for her, as I do for my other children. I hope one day I will be able to give them these things so they will know they were always in my heart and thoughts. I discovered shortly thereafter that April 25th is Parental Alienation Awareness Day. I made an appointment to meet with the Mayor of Lethbridge in hopes of his learning what this issue is all about and helping us to get it fixed. A couple weeks after, a friend mentioned to me that I must be pretty overwhelmed with this mess. I laughed and said that I was so far *beyond* overwhelmed that I would welcome getting back to just being overwhelmed. I remained, and still remain, extremely tired and not sure how I would, and will, be able to keep juggling all of this.

I did get to see Ava on February 26th, 2016, but on March 2rd, a week later, I got a nasty email from Beryl Lambin, Manager of Domestic Violence Services at the YWCA along with a visit from two police officers. The subject heading was "Visit March 11 Caution". She falsely claimed that I made "inappropriate comments", and it didn't specify to whom, and "deliberately advanced into personal space" (again, whose?) twice for "attempted physical contacts". She wrote that "any threatening actions made by you towards any of the staff" would "continue to be reported to authorities and additional security will be exercised based on this conduct for all future visits". She reminded me that "safe-visitation services will remain indefinitely for Ava (pseudonym)'s safety. Then, "**only** the guitar has been authorized to bring in for a visit". I couldn't believe it! I had conducted myself professionally at the Y and finally had some time with my disabled daughter. Of course, as I played my guitar, which she loves, there were three adult women staring at us and I was not allowed to get close to my daughter, never mind try to give her a hug.

On April 1st, while awaiting Ava to come in for our visit, Ms. Lambin insisted I take my guitar out of the room. I told her that my legal counsel advised me to continue an activity that Ava really loves. I then closed my eyes and continued to play softly, waiting for Ava. Approximately 20 minutes later three police officers entered the room and placed me under arrest. Ms. Lambin had called them and wanted me charged with trespassing. She neglected to inform the police that this was my only, court-ordered, place to see my daughter. After being detained for nearly 30 minutes I was released and told to follow the rules. I thought to myself that this was a challenge as the rules keep changing to suit the needs of Hannah, not our children.

In May, I had another visit with Ava but sure enough, not 24 hours later, I got a follow-up email from that same YWCA manager, Ms. Lambin. This time she referred to my upcoming May 20th visit and wrote "To keep (Ava) safe from repeated events of protocol challenges that both disturb her and disrupt visit time, it has become necessary to exclude *any and all* (her emphases) personal items being brought in by you for visits. This restriction is the direct result of culminating breaches ranging from past inappropriate items, hostile actions and the aggression of attempted physical contacts with staff (necessitating police contact) to non-compliance with directives. As witnessed by 3 staff in the last visit, your refusal to comply with a very simple request - made both via email and in person - to limit your guitar strumming and singing to only when (Ava) is present in the Child Care Centre was an intentional provocation on your part and a needless act of defiance". Beryl Lambin continued with "It should be noted that allowing your guitar at a visit was a concession extended to you and that courtesy is now being revoked to eliminate further transgressions. As explained in the email sent you "additional renditions of your personal preferences during those 15-minute wait times – before (Ava) arrives and after she leaves – is an imposition on staff as a captive audience and obliges them beyond normal parameters for parent interaction. This request required only respectful consideration for staff on your part. You are welcome to choose from multiple child appropriate music selections provided on site. Personal or electronic music preferences cannot be brought in. As a correction to your statements in the last visit that "*My lawyer said I can...*" please be informed that an outside party or agency has no authority over any YWCA program, process or protocol in any context. Hiring legal counsel does not equate to entitlement of preferential accommodation regarding any facet of the program. You were also personally cautioned on the April 15th visit by the Lethbridge Regional Police to be of good behavior when accessing services at the YWCA".

I took my guitar to visits with my daughter because she responds well to music and my singing to her. Since she is non-verbal, she cannot express her desires or needs but she smiles and perks up when I am there and playing to her. After these emails by the Y's manager, I was appalled and so sad.

In June of 2016, my lawyer, David, informed me that he received a letter from the opposing party stating their concern that I was not availing myself of the generous offer to see Ava at the Y. This letter from Hannah's lawyer also claimed that my kids wished to change their counsel now and he suggested a lawyer that David was in the process of suing. David prepared an application and affidavit to get me out of the Safe Visitation program and used Ms. Lambin's emails to support my assertion that the program was biased.

Meanwhile, my criminal lawyer, who had represented me on the abuse charges, informed me that all charges against me would be dropped by month's end. That didn't happen though; I may never know why. This was my 3rd Father's Day and birthday without my kids and the ache in my heart grew more painful every day.

I called David. I had attempted to get a license plate for my vehicle but was refused by the nice lady I have dealt with there for years. MEP (Maintenance Enforcement Program) had placed a restriction on my ability to register a vehicle. This was ludicrous since I had in hand my Court Order which gave me a Stay of Proceedings on any arrears that might have been on my account. MEP, however, made me out to be a "deadbeat dad", even though the Stay was in place until a JDR (Judicial Dispute Resolution) hearing was to deal with my overpayment of Child Maintenance. I was left in panic mode at the Registry but had to wait until the next morning to call MEP for a retraction.

At the same time of my harassment by MEP, David informed me that my kids' new hotshot lawyer wanted to cancel the hearing scheduled for the following Monday. He asked the judge for "professional courtesy to get up to speed on the case". *Wow*! When I asked for professional courtesy for my 10-year-old daughter who had not seen her dad in months, I was told by the judge he understood my frustration and was going to push ahead with the questioning. The kids' lawyer would have to read the transcripts before that hearing on Monday. Finally, a judge that cared. Hannah was now working with her 4th lawyer.

In September, I obtained a Court Order reinstating my license and was told by a very helpful woman at MEP that it would take three to five working days to be implemented. My file was wiped clean of any arrears and I received a cheque from MEP, reimbursing me for penalties and interest I had paid over and above my Court Order's amount. This woman actually apologized to me and encouraged me to "hang in there". I felt very encouraged that some small bit of justice had actually been served.

My hope waned pretty fast though. On October 10th, 2016, I was arrested again and charged with breach of probation when I stopped to speak with one of my former neighbours who was outside doing yard work. The Order stated I must stay outside a one-block radius of the matrimonial home. But the house had been sold back in January and my family no longer lived there. When we arrived at the jail, the guard asked the police officer what I was charged with. The officer said it was an "active investigation" so he wanted me held until the bail hearing. The guard said they could not hold me as there were no charges and it was contrary to my Charter Rights to be held without a charge. But the officer insisted and the guard reluctantly agreed. He said to the officer, "We did not have this conversation" and held me until my defense counsel secured my release. My poor lawyer, David, left Thanksgiving dinner with his family to act on my behalf and I was very grateful indeed.

On October 21st, 2016, all charges against me by my daughter were Stayed and I entered into a Common-Law Peace Bond.

On December 10th, 2016, I sent a letter to an Alberta Member of the Legislature, Rick Fraser, summarizing my case since I had reason to believe he understood parental alienation. He might be just the politician to promote a Bill for default equal-parenting.

He did meet with me and seemed to listen well. He said he would do what he could.

My friends kept me whole and although I had another Christmas without my kids, I had seven offers to be with people and come for dinner. I worked doing snow removal instead to make some extra cash and kept busy until the end of the year to keep my mind off the dull ache that never goes away. Many times I just want to walk away and then I have this picture (which sadly is starting to fade a little) of my youngest daughter looking at me with her big brown eyes screaming... *DADDY DON'T GO* !!!!! God, I miss my kids so much.

In January of 2017, I met with David and, as a witness, the other lawyer in his office. David stated that I was a "difficult" client. I agreed with him but explained that my frustration was due to a general lack of progress on my file, no access time with almost 11-year-old Ava, nor a parenting plan for Lucy, who was then 15. David assured me he was doing his best and wanted me to "trust" that he would do his job.

I wrote a complaint to the Real Estate Council of Alberta regarding the illegal sale of my home. I mentioned this to David and his colleague who told me not to hold my breath. He said that since real estate agents are self governed, it is a toothless "kangaroo court." I respectfully said that any professional organization that is self-governed could be considered a kangaroo court; this after I asked whether lawyers are self-governed. Both lawyers laughed.

On the 17th, we were in court again. Kirk Shader was the counsel representing my children. In his statement and follow-up Order, filed on February 27th, Shader presented the following position: That Lucy and Ava (*who is non-verbal!*) had requested a change in children's counsel because of the lack of progress on their file; that he (Shader) was taking an "instructional advocacy approach" with his client, Lucy, and a "best interests approach" with Ava; that he met extensively with all four of my children; that both Mike and Erin reported physical and sexual abuse from their father (me); that Lucy, too, reported "significant mental abuse and manipulation" by me against her; that both a Ms. Witty and Beryl

Lambin of the Y staff claimed I acted "inappropriately" with Ava during supervised visits there; and that I declined visits with Ava through the YWCA's Safe Visitation Program since March of 2016.

Kirk Shader's recommendations included that Lucy have no contact whatsoever with me, and that I continue to have only supervised visits at the Y with Ava. To direct the court otherwise, said Shader, would put both girls in *significant harm's way*. Ava, in particular, they claimed was vulnerable to me since she is non-verbal. In the final paragraph of the filed Amicus addressed to Justice R. A. Gerk, Shader wrote that my "only barrier to same (access to Ava through the Y's Program) is his (my) own attitude, as a result of which he has deprived himself of any access to Ava (pseudonym) for the last year".

We were directed to go to a binding Judicial Dispute Resolution (JDR) meeting in a few weeks time with a different judge. David finally called Beryl Lambin at the YWCA to discover that I have, in fact, been telling the truth about the manipulative spin she and her staff have put on my visits with Ava.

In mid-February, David sent me notification that one of the Y staff supervising my visits with Ava had given some notes to Hannah. The notes claimed I had acted in a "sexual manner" with Ava during our visits. I felt like I had been run over by another truck, and this time I wasn't sure if I could get up again.

The advice I got from David was to canvas for a trial date. At trial, we could subpoena witnesses and ask some hard questions of the opposing side. Of course, Hannah's counsel from Legal Aid would balk at having to go to trial since they would have to do a lot of work to find proof instead of relying on her anecdotal "evidence." My ex had concocted such a massive file of misinformation about my character that without time to expose it as such, she would continue to build her case against me. I wanted a trial; if I had been guilty as charged, would I want to expose myself? My lawyer, too, was frustrated and said the counsel for Hannah had "drunk the Kool Aid". He believed that her goal was a full character assassination of me, and alienation from our kids.

In court, there was a bright spot when David was able to get a commitment for a trial though not for another 18 to 24 months. Even Justice Gerk talked about the "glacial speed of the system." I was ordered to pay $800 to my ex because I lost my application for three hours per week visitation with Ava. At least I was granted the ability to schedule my own visits with Ava at the Y, and Hannah was directed to bring my daughter as per that scheduling. David did a fantastic job and, for the first time, my side was heard, or so I thought.

The JDR, scheduled for Wednesday, March 22nd, 2017, with Justice Mariam, was cancelled. My ex's lawyer and Mr. Shader refused to deal with the Order so all three lawyers, including David, met and decided not to pursue the JDR. Coincidentally, David talked with Justice Mariam at a judicial dinner in Calgary and she told him she was concerned about my lack of access to my kids. Justice Mallard, who ordered our JDR in June 2015 was updated on the non-compliance of his Order and he subsequently requested a conversation with the lawyers the following week. I reminded David to tell that judge about the counseling for my girls that was ordered but ignored. That conversation did not happen and a mock JDR took its place.

I didn't know how much more I could take. The loneliness, heartache, and grief were, and are, *brutal*. It was getting harder to get out of bed and put on a happy face to try and take on each day. I refused to let my mind stay in dark places for extended periods of time but the frequency of trips there in a day were increasing. I went to a counselor in Lethbridge Domestic Violence who had assessed me in December of 2014 because of my probation order. I knew that when my family went to trial, he would be called in as an expert witness to speak to my mental state during this ordeal.

David figured that we would need five days in court to call all my witnesses and expose the lies of my children's mother. At that point, if I could only get two weekends a month and an evening or two a week with my kids, I would gladly sign everything else away. But I know Hannah will never stop her campaign to bury me.

I decided to phone Bryan Ludman, a lawyer in Toronto, since I had heard he really knows parental alienation and how to navigate through the filth to resolve it. I sent him the letter by Kirk Shader, the children's counsel, so he would know before our call what the situation looked like. He was helpful in terms of ideas to pursue, but since he works out of Alberta, there was not much he could otherwise do. It seems his heart is in the right place, so I hope he can help stop parental alienation, somehow.

Knowing that there are thousands of parents in Canada going through the hell I am gives me courage to carry on for my children's sake and for my own. There are so many people who really do understand the pain, dynamics and shit that I am dealing with. Some lawyers are actually fighting like hell to change a paradigm and system that causes more hurt than help under the guise of "the best interests of the child."

In April, David and I met with the CEO of the YWCA. Although I felt she remained set against my relationship with Ava, David did manage to set up four months of visits with her that would take us into September. I did speak about my concerns with the visits. David explained that all allegations against me were as yet unproven, seemingly aimed at keeping me away from my kids. We all agreed that open communication was the key to make the visits beneficial to Ava. After each visit there would be a debriefing time to make sure no issues arose from any of our perceptions.

I made a pitch to be able to play my guitar, as that was my primary communication with Ava. I explained how her hearing Dad play would reconnect us. It had then been 14 months since our last contact. The CEO and staff said they would talk about it. Ninety minutes after David and I left that meeting, I received an email from the YWCA further disallowing my guitar. It stated that we could discuss those terms at a later date, but this has yet to happen. At David's suggestion, I decided to donate a guitar to the Y, so there would always be one available in the visitation room there. Even if they would not accept a gift from me, a friend could donate it; who the donor was didn't matter.

David let me know that opposing counsel was intending to run up his bill in order to ruin me. That explained why they were being so difficult with his drafting of the last two court orders. David said that he had, to date, received eight letters from opposing counsel nit-picking about wording of the Orders, which were still not filed. My lawyer even dropped his rate and told me I could pay him each month whatever amount I could afford.

On April 23rd, I had a visit with "my precious girl" Ava; *finally.* I recorded the entire visit on the advice of my counsel. Ava barely recognized me. There were four "supervisors" in attendance: Eve, Harley, Carrie, and Harisa. Unbelievable. By the end of the visit, Ava hugged and kissed me, and my heart broke all over again. All four staff stayed for the so-called debriefing after Ava was taken away by one of them.

I wrote to David as soon as I got home. I had three main, and grave, concerns about my daughter's welfare. First, when I arrived at the Y, Ava appeared glassy-eyed, almost sedated. She was not focused and her vocalizations were minimal and limited to occasional shrieks. Ava was never on any drugs when I lived with her and the rest of my family, so if she was now being drugged, why and what were they? Second, my daughter had grown very little, but was entering puberty and was not potty-trained. It appeared she had significantly regressed in the year since I had seen her. Third, regarding the refusal to let me bring my guitar, the available musical instruments at the Y are simply just toys, and broken ones at that. When I asked Harley, one of the supervisors, for permission to bring my guitar the following week, I was told they would have to ask Hannah for her permission first. The answer was "no", of course. This again shows Hannah's sick pattern of abuse on her children.

I begged David to do something to change the terms of the visits. Four months of my short visits would not help Ava come out of her shell or make her safe. She would continue to deteriorate, right in front of my eyes, for unknown reasons. Even if Ava was put in a loving foster home, if the court would not let her live with me, she would still be better off than where she was then.

By mid-May of 2017, I had had three visits with Ava and she showed signs of coming back to life. There were now two supervisors present whenever I was at the Y and they, thankfully, stayed more in the background. On the last two visits, Ava toddled over to the toy guitar and brought it to me as soon as she entered our visitation room. She motioned to me by grabbing my hand and putting it on the guitar. Both supervisors agreed with me that Ava shows an affinity for music and they have no issue with my bringing in my own, real, guitar. Still, Ava's mother refuses so their hands are tied. I brought along Panda All-Natural licorice, Ava's favourite, with me on my last visit, but Hannah refused my giving her daughter any. I let the supervisors know that as uncomfortable as these visits were, I did appreciate their trying to cooperate with me.

In spite all the hassles, I was somewhat encouraged that Ava remembered me; she remembered that we connect through music; and at that point, it kept me going.

David drafted a new letter to the children's counsel, Kirk Shader, asking for a valid reason why my guitar remained prohibited. He also asked for validation regarding the exorbitant legal fees he charged for his retainer agreement. Shader had gone ahead and crafted his retainer terms with Hannah, without my knowledge or input. He had not disclosed this fact. Shader was acting as an advocate for my ex-wife, not for our children as was his job. David asked that Shader immediately recuse himself from our children's file. Failing to do so, my lawyer would bring an application to the court to have him removed, invalidate the retainer agreement, and pursue legal redress for his dishonesty. To date, this issue remains outstanding and unresolved.

On the 15th of May, David sent Mr. Shader the letter with our concerns. And on May 30th, I had another visit with Ava. On this occasion, my heart sank. The girl was obviously drugged, lethargic, drooling, and almost immobile. I went home and wrote a letter to the new manager, Ms. Lina Newton of the YWCA, who had apparently replaced Beryl Lambin. I detailed all my concerns about the neglect and apparent sedation of my daughter. I again asked if I could bring my guitar to future visits. But on June 6th, this was the reply I was emailed by Ms. Newton: "As a safe visitation site, our position is not to evaluate or assess. We provide a safe environment for a child and a parent to visit and ensure safety while they attend our site. As such, we will not be giving our opinions to parents as we are a neutral party and will remain so. Also, the guitar request will not be revisited at this time".

On June 16th, 2017, I wrote my lawyer a summary of my latest visit with Ava. The supervisor was Harisa, but there were two more, Eve and Harley, in attendance too. Ava came into the visitation room with Harisa ten minutes late. She then ushered Ava away ten minutes early so in total, I got 40 minutes with my daughter instead of the scheduled 60. Why… I have no idea. During our time together, I touched Ava's hair and immediately a supervisor reported it to Harisa, who had briefly turned her head. This supervisor was watching the CC video that is in the room. After that, Harisa moved into my personal space and remained there until she took Ava away. I had to remind Harisa to refer to me as "Dad", not *Jim*, to my daughter. I was told that notes from the visit would be given to me at my next Y visit, even though we had agreed they be available immediately following, as had happened up until then. At least that visit had shown Ava to be more animated again, more like her normal self, until she became sad-looking when told the visit with me was over.

A month had gone by with no response since David sent the letter to Kirk Shader. I was at a loss since neither lawyer seemed to be working for my children and my file was effectively stalled.

On the 20th of June, I went to Motor Vehicles to renew my license since I had only been renewed for one year, thanks to MEP's restrictions on me. The Stay of Enforcement should have enabled me to renew but instead, that day turned out to be my last day driving. My lawyer was to have my Child Maintenance payments to MEP recalculated to reflect my thousands of dollars of overpayments and align future payments with my actual income. He told me back in April that it would only take a few minutes but here I was, again penalized for an error beyond my control. I found out that *MEP had seized my license on June 2nd, but I only got that letter in my mailbox, dated June 3rd, on June 20th*. That letter gave me 21 days from June 3rd to make payment arrangements or lose my license.

But this was June 20th and I was told my license was revoked as of June 2nd. This made no sense. A MEP staff member had reassured me that there is a 45-day process before a person's license is seized. And the MEP website stated that it was a process that commenced after 60 days of the payor being in arrears. Bottom line was: I had an existing Court Order that read "There shall be a Stay of enforcement on arrears".

I really started to understand why fathers in such situations kill themselves. How the hell was I supposed to deal with the ongoing and unwarranted persecution? When I spoke with David at 6:00 p.m. the evening before, he promised to "take care of it" immediately, but that I would likely be walking to work for a week.

In addition, I got an email from Harisa at the Y, stating that visits with Ava were now to occur at 3:45 rather than 5:15 p.m. and on dates the program supervisors had chosen. There was no reason given. Harisa and all the supervisors, as well as Ava's mother, knew full well that I could not make 3:45 p.m. since I had to work. The Court Order gave me the right to set my own visitation schedule, which I had done without a problem until that June email blind-sided me. The ending of the email was a request to either confirm or decline the YWCA's schedule of dates and time.

In my utter frustration, I wanted to fire David, my lawyer. There had been no progress in getting my driver's license back, and now he wasn't returning my calls. I still believed his heart was in the right place, but nothing was happening. Hannah continued to alienate my children from me, Ava was doing poorly, and I was harassed beyond belief by MEP *and* the YWCA. I sent an email to David, begging him to please file a Contempt of Court Order against the Y, which had ignored Justice Gerk's Order from March 1st. And I asked him to report Kirk Shader to his governing body for misrepresentation of minor children and enabling Hannah's agenda to destroy me by using our children as pawns.

On June 28th, I sent a letter to Justices Mallard and Gerk, asking them to look into my case and enforce the granted terms of their court Orders. In response, I got a letter back from a court clerk advising me that judges do not read correspondence from, nor reply to, civilian letters.

At least I got a bit of good news from Harisa in response to my request for amended visitation times at the Y, additional visits during the week, and bringing my guitar. She agreed to Sundays from 1:45 to 3:15 p.m. though she did not provide a start date. There was also no mention of the other aspects of my request. I wrote Harisa back, confirming my agreement with the new schedule, and thanking her for being flexible. Only two visits ever occurred on a Sunday.

July was another shit-show. On the 6th, David wrote me that it "is apparent that our professional relationship has broken down. I have done my best to accommodate your circumstances in this matter, even to the detriment of my personal time and interests". And further on, "As a result of other commitments, I have had to set your matter aside while more pressing issues have had to be dealt with". I couldn't believe it. I responded to him and this is part of that email: " unless one experiences the horrid trauma of having children removed from your life (emotionally and physically kidnapped), and having your hands tied to help pay for them, you cannot possibly understand the desperation I feel. Not to mention having to rely on other people to not only try and understand the situation, but actually step up to the plate and do something about it. It is difficult most days to continue on, and I hear on a weekly basis of many who choose to make the difficult choice to give up the fight either by walking away and deserting their children or by ending their life. Those of us living this absolute nightmare are traumatized by this experience in ways that no one who is looking into our situations will EVER understand. It is a form of domestic violence that is sanctioned by the system under the guise of 'best interests.' I appreciate your efforts, but also feel that I require more urgency on my file, as a child with a disability is being destroyed in the time it is taking the law (system) to deal with this issue".

Then, on the 8th of July, I was handed, by David's assistant, a Withdrawal of Counsel Notice. It was not signed by David though, which seemed very odd. So, I wrote to Alberta's Minister of Justice, Kathy Gainey, with details about my four-year battle thus far to get help for my disabled daughter and be involved in her life. I attached my letter to Justices Mallard and Gerk. I respectfully requested intervention with teeth from the Justice Office.

A couple weeks later, just before my next visit with Ava scheduled for July 30th, I got a "cancellation notice" from Harisa at the Y that, "due to lack of staff availability", my visit was now cancelled. She also wrote that "you will be advised as to your next available visit date".

On August 10th, I was interviewed by "Victurus Libertus", located in Texas, for a 50-minute YouTube video on my experience with parental alienation. I was happy to share my story in hopes of creating awareness to the crisis and perhaps helping some other targeted parents.

I did not see any of my children through the rest of the 2017 summer. In September, the YWCA emailed me with a schedule of Friday visits, instead of the agreed Sundays, so again, I was unable to comply due to work commitments. I had not seen Lucy in almost three years; she was then 14, and I hadn't seen Ava, who was 11, since July 23rd.

Without legal counsel, I now proceeded alone to obtain a court date. It was set for October 17th so I advised opposing counsel for Hannah, Mr. Letourin, her 5th lawyer, of that on September 9th. In response, he advised me on September 18th that Hannah had requested I give permission for her to take Ava to Spokane, Washington. This is the content of that email from Hannah to her lawyer, Mr. Letourin: "Ava (pseudonym) is due for her appointment at Shriners Children's Hospital in Spokane Washington next week. I will need a travel authorization from September 25, 2017- September 28, 2017. See attached copy of previous one. This is not to be debated, as the appointment is booked, and travel arrangements have been made with the Shriners who drive Ava, and I. In addition, my former attorney had the travel authorization signed and returned within 2 days, and Mr. Holden (pseudonym) is familiar with this process. Please have this drawn up ASAP, have Jim sign it, and have it ready for me to pick up from your office no later than Thursday September 21, 2017".

I responded to Mr. Letourin that a specialty appointment such as the requested one for Ava would have been made some time before, so I was unclear on the reason why I was only informed at that late date. I was not opposed to the appointment but rather, being kept in the dark about it. Hannah's lawyer responded that he would meet with his client and told me to "please stand by". In the meantime, he requested that I sign the travel authorization for Ava.

On October 2nd, 2017, Mr. Letourin withdrew his services as Hannah's counsel. I never did sign the authorization and don't even know if Hannah took Ava to Spokane anyway.

On October 17th, Justice Gerk ordered my matter to be assigned to case management, after almost four whole years. In that time, my youngest, special-needs daughter, Ava, who was once closest to me, had seen her father for a total cumulative time of less than one week and mostly in a basement room of the YWCA, since May 2014.

In mid-November, still awaiting a case manager to take action on my file, I wrote the Case Coordinator who responded that case management would expedite the process and someone would be in touch with me soon. I wrote my politicians again about my situation. They expressed sympathy but did nothing else.

Finally, on December 6th, I had a meeting with Ms. Kathy Christoff, who was our assigned Case Manager. The purpose was for all parties to determine and agree on parenting time over the upcoming Christmas holidays. At that meeting, I learned that Kirk Shader would thereafter withdraw as my children's counsel. He claimed it was because he could not work for free. But when Hannah stated she would not budge from my minimal access during infrequent and supervised YWCA visits, Mr. Shader got up and left our meeting after agreeing with Hannah to no change in access regime.

Ms. Christoff, in the same meeting, then asked me how things were going and what my "end-game intentions" were. I told her that there was no progress on my file even though all false allegations against me had been laid to rest. It was still my hope, and I believe, Ava's and my right, to have 50/50 time together but after years of fighting, I would even accept just every second weekend and Wednesday; the apparent standard for disposable fathers. She took notes.

My ex-wife's 6th lawyer, Aaryn Reiner, then joined our conversation. He stated that since I had abused all of the older children (physically, sexually, emotionally and spiritually for many years), his client maintained that she wanted sole custody with professionally-supervised access for Dad (me) in the Safe Visitation program exclusively; forever. Mr. Reiner then went on to explain that because of Ava's diminished capacity she was unable to express any emotion regarding her father or her desire to be with her dad. Upon hearing that, I nearly cried and wanted to die.

The end result of the case management meeting to discuss access for a special-needs child to see her dad at Christmas... was no change. I did not see my children for the 4th Christmas in a row. There was no information on my other children, including Lucy, who was still a minor, yet I remain their legal guardian and pay their mother every month for their supposed care.

Ms. Christoff also decided to set a date for a seven...yes, seven-day trial to be held sometime in 2019. I have no idea why this is necessary given the obvious and simple resolution, which would be to order 50/50, or at least shared, parenting time. Christoff also made me responsible for extra, Section 7, expenses pertaining to my two minor children. These expenses will be incurred at Mom's discretion.

2018

This January began in much the same way as the previous four did. I was alone, and there was no facilitation of access for visits with Ava. I remained completely alienated from my other three children. On the 4th I wrote Mr. Reiner, asking who had taken over as counsel for my two minor children since Mr. Shader's withdrawal in December. I still have no information. To try to find out how Lucy and Ava are doing at school, I requested their records from their respective principals. On January 8th, I received a response from Lucy's principal asking for a meeting with me. He agreed to provide me with her report card then. I took that as a positive step and sure hope that there may be a light somewhere in this never-ending dark and lonely tunnel.

The response from Ava's school has been more favourable; however, they will not allow me at the school or provide me any day-to-day communication without informing Hannah who, based on past behaviour, will likely involve the police. The school cites "status quo" in refusing my legal right to be an involved parent in Ava's schooling. The way in which status quo can be changed when there are lies, manipulation and control from a parent who alienates children from the other parent, is a question that may never get answered.

On Monday, April 30th, I got an email from Dr. Giancarlo (*author*) who let me know she had been contacted the month before by a woman named "Ali Wise." This woman, who said she lives in Winnipeg, wrote Christine that she has a blog and had been in touch with me about my case. She asked Dr. Giancarlo to keep her correspondence about me confidential. Ms. Wise then went on to discredit me by writing how I was not to be trusted, was an abuser, and such. When Christine then asked Ms. Wise for her sources of information about me, she declined to elaborate and was not heard from again. It was apparent that all Ms. Wise's information was from an unknown source, who I later found out was either my ex-wife or a mutual friend of hers. I discovered that Ms. Wise was using a pseudonym and I was able to identify her real name.

Dr. Giancarlo cautioned Ms. "Wise" against spreading misinformation, even slander, about me. I was being blacklisted on public media by a third party without any evidence.

On Monday, June 11th, Dr. Giancarlo sent around an article posted by a family lawyer, Gene Colman, regarding Bill C-78, which has a mandate to initiate Child Custody Reform in Canada. The problem is: this bill would make things even worse for children, since it would ignore the brainwashing and abuse done to kids at the hands of their alienating parent. Instead, it proposes to give children choice in who they want to spend time with. Their targeted parent, like me, would be removed further from his or her children's lives since kids will take the path of least resistance every time. Denouncing mom or dad as an alienator would feel like a betrayal and they would suffer the wrath of that sick parent. They would also lose the rewards being handed out to them for rejecting their targeted parent. You see, that's what really happens on the ground.

On June 27th, I wrote to Kristine Allsbie, the lawyer appointed to represent my children. I reminded her that Justice Gerk directed, back in June of 2015, that my two older daughters receive counselling. But then under oath in September of 2016, their mother admitted that the girls had not followed through with counselling and only attended a few appointments. Justice Gerk's Order also stated that I be included in that counselling but, in fact, I never was.

On Friday, July 13th, I met with Syd Wilaf, a family violence counselor who assessed me back in December of 2014. I hoped to help him understand the emotional toll that this was taking on me, and other men, who just want to be dad. Also, Mr. Wilaf will testify at my trial in December this year, so he'll be able to show that I have been accountable for my actions and kept myself as sane as possible. I'm incredibly stressed; I've tested myself on PTSD questionnaires and come up positive every time. But I manage my stress with my healthy support systems.

On July 26th, I was supposed to have a supervised visit with Ava at the YWCA's Safe Visitation Program as per Justice Gerk's court restrictions. There, three staff were in attendance as if I was some dangerous dude, not just a dad visiting his daughter. I was accused of carrying a cell phone and berated for parking in the undesignated part of their parking lot. One of the attending staff, Ms. Burrals, terminated the visit and asked me to leave; I did. The following day I wrote to my Case Management Counsel, Christian

Cathay, telling her that I was not able to see my daughter, and that I had not had any visits in weeks, except once when Ms. Allsbie was away on vacation.

On August 30th, I received a letter from Justice Gerk with instructions for me on how to represent myself at our trial this December. I had declared myself as such since I had no luck with lawyers and had exactly zero dollars left to my name. At the end of Justice Gerk's letter, he wrote "Again, I urge you to begin your preparations for the trial as soon as you can. I know very well how important your child is to you." So now I await my trial in December, collecting as thorough a paper trail as I can. For instance, I've contacted my children's schools for updates on their progress and will continue to do so.

I have to accept that my son has decided at this time in his life to have nothing to do with me, and should he ever read this I want it made clear that I will always have an open, welcoming door and heart. What I will not accept is the toxic influence inflicted on my three daughters by their mother. My youngest daughter, Ava, lacks a voice to this point, yet she is continually subjected to neglect and father-deprivation. My girls need me and I need them.

My desire in sharing my story is to show what is happening to a loving parent who is targeted by an angry, hurt and bitter person who sees children as weapons and pawns instead of loving them enough to win over hatred of a once loved partner. I also feel compelled to expose a system of injustice that allows and even encourages the conflict to continue instead of realizing the growing body of research that shows kids need both parents.

**Note: As this manuscript goes to press, Jim H. awaits his trial and keeps me (author) informed of developments as they occur. He has never wavered in his quest to find justice for his children, especially Ava, a little girl who cannot speak for herself.*

DON

CHAPTER 31

DON

I am the father of three children: Karmen, fifteen, Gracelyn, thirteen, and Fionna who is five. Karmen and Gracelyn are my daughters from my first marriage to Penelope. My current wife Jane and I had Fionna in 2013. Jane and I have been together since early 2011; she is my love, my best friend and my rock. I really don't know how I would have gotten through these past few years without her support and love for me and for our girls. She has done more for us as a family and more for me as a partner than I can ever repay...and for that, I am eternally grateful. This story would not have a happy ending if not for Jane.

Penelope and I married on Valentine's Day of 2003, but separated in June 2010. I should have known better. Months after I had started dating Penelope, I learned that she had had a troubled youth, which included prostitution. I was shocked and angry, but eventually accepted it as it seemed such a vast contrast from who I had met and come to love: a fun, energetic, pleasant young woman who shared a lot of my interests. I thought I had hit the jackpot. We were together for a total of just over 13 years, married for 6.5... and the ensuing court battle has been going on for 8.5 years and continues today. The 'red flags' were there, but I was blind. We dated and broke up a few times because Penelope would take off with some other guy and then later come back to me. I was naïve and wanted the relationship to work, so I kept letting her back into my life. My friends, family and coworkers would tell me she was controlling and "fake", but of course, like anyone in love and looking at the world through rose-coloured glasses, I would not listen. Little did I realize how right they all were. I would learn this fact the hard way.

2010

Karmen was born to Penelope and me in July 2003, the year we got married. Gracelyn was born 20 months later. Over the years, I observed Penelope's behaviour becoming increasingly unstable. 'Accommodating and giving' gave way to 'controlling and demanding'. The fighting increased and intimacy became a thing of the past. Karmen and Gracelyn were, and are, beautiful, smart and loving little girls, but they became wary of their mother. They learned to keep out of the way and be quiet whenever the mood in the house seemed tense. I was, and continue to be, extremely close to our daughters and this bothered Penelope. She would routinely refer to me as the "good-time Dad". By the time we separated, our marriage and family dynamic had become extremely dysfunctional.

On June 3 of 2010, the trial separation began. We had been in marriage counseling multiple times by then, but Penelope said it was not helping and that she had "checked out" of our relationship. I tried everything I could think of to save our marriage, but she would have none of it, as she had secretly already started divorce proceedings. Anyway, I went to my parents' house and slept in their basement while Penelope and the two girls, who were then 6 and 4, stayed in our house. That was a big mistake; I should have never left the house.

Since my parents lived just two blocks from our marital home, it helped make this bad situation a little better. During that summer of 2010, the marital home was still my residence; I was just sleeping at my parents' home. I would go back to the house from time to time for a few reasons, mostly to see and spend time with the girls, but also to do home maintenance, check email, wash clothes, and so on. I still treated it like it was my home too. Eventually, Penelope decided that even though I was paying the mortgage and all the bills, she did not want me anywhere near our marital home. Maybe the last straw was when I asked her to please turn off the house lights before she went to work since I couldn't afford additional utilities charges; she didn't like that.

Penelope took the girls to Manitoba to see her family and during this trip, I was served with divorce papers. I had accepted that my marriage was over, but I didn't want things to turn uglier than they already had, so I proposed to Penelope that we sell the house (as it was the only real asset we shared) and split the profits, split the time with the girls 50/50 and we both go our separate ways. The tone was set right then as Penelope stated during a phone call that, "Well, you know Don (pseudonym)…the kids always go with the mother... and you're gonna pay." Those prophetic words have haunted me ever since.

On September 20, 2010, Penelope secretly filed an Emergency Protection Order (EPO) application against me while I was at work. Although there was no history or evidence of physical violence of any kind between my ex-wife and me, Penelope managed to successfully obtain the Order, granted by Justice W.D. Mann in the Provincial Court of Alberta as apparently, "yelling," as we both had come to do towards one and other, is sufficient evidence to support the proposition of domestic abuse. She falsely claimed that I was sneaking in and out of the house and that she was fearful that "I was going to blow up." I am a big guy, but I have never been in a physical fight in my entire life, but that was how she painted me, as if I was going to harm her, which of course never happened. I have the official court transcript from that hearing where Justice Mann says to my ex-wife, "I am going to grant this Order with one word of caution. Fortunately, there's not a record of physical abuse, okay? I believe, you know, his (*my*) conduct is sufficient to satisfy me that there has been family violence as defined in the legislation." Nothing could've been further from the truth, but hey, a good story seems good enough.

I received a phone call at work from a RCMP Constable asking me to come down to the local detachment after I finished my shift at work. I did and when I got there, I waited in the vestibule since it was after-hours. The Constable presented me with a copy of the EPO and I had no idea what I was looking at. I read it and distinctly remember that once I got to the part that stated all the distances I had to stay away from the marital home, my wife, her workplace, the children's school, and of course the children themselves, I looked up at the Constable and said one thing: "She's taking my kids away?!?!?" I collapsed on the floor and wailed like a baby. I felt like my heart had been ripped out of my chest and set on fire. The slow descent into this nightmare instantly became a free-fall. I didn't see my kids for a month and a half after I was served with the EPO. Little did I know that as bad as this current situation was, it was nothing compared to what was still to come.

2011 and 2012

This period of time was spent going through the process that is supposedly designed by the Family Justice System (an oxymoron if I've ever heard one) to help streamline cases. Let me tell you, it is a waste of time and more so if one of the parties has an axe to grind. The only way mediation or arbitration works is if both parties can be amicable and reasonable. If not, you will spend tons of money on lawyers and parenting coordinators, etcetera, and accomplish very little. This 'system' makes it very easy for the custodial parent to use the children as pawns to get what she or he wants. I hired and fired three different lawyers at this time, as it was a financial drain with very little progress made. Suffice it to say that all of this wasted time and money could easily be avoided if the parents can find common ground and *truly* put the needs of the children first. Sadly, that was not my experience. I was seeing my girls again, sporadically at first, and then finally after much struggle we arrived at a schedule that allowed me to spend my days off with my girls. But that was not what my ex-wife wanted. I was not going away quietly as I continued to fight to be a part of our girls' lives. She had a plan to ramp things up and this just set the stage for the next play in her game.

2013

In the couple years after I was allowed back into my children's lives, Penelope continued her attacks on my rights as a father. In my mind, she clearly wanted my role to be nothing more than a subservient figure who would do as was dictated to him, support her exclusive authority, pay the bills and merely see the girls once in a while. The problem, for her, was the relationship that I had with my girls. They knew and loved their Dad and naturally craved spending time with me. They would cry to her and question why all of this had happened, but Penelope would ignore their pleas to see more of me, instead diverting their attention and confusing the girls, telling them they weren't safe at my place. She told the girls they had "special needs" which made them feel "different," thus attempting to cement their dependence on her. While it was true that Karmen had a hearing impairment that required her to wear bilateral hearing aids and Gracelyn was diagnosed with ADHD, neither of the girls had issues that could not be managed.

Even from the early days, Penelope displayed an above average 'need' to involve the children with doctors and medications. She wore it as a badge of honour among the other school moms and seemed to be in her glory when those other moms would comment on how she was such an "amazing mother" because of how she had to deal with two kids with special needs. It is my feeling (not that I am any expert) that Penelope has some version of a disorder akin to that known as "Munchausen by Proxy".

Jane was my partner by then and my daughters loved spending time at our home. We had structure, boundaries, fun and we let them be children. With us, Karmen and Gracelyn did not need to be on-guard from one of their mother's tirades or tantrums. We always encourage(d) the girls' positive relationship with Penelope, recognizing that kids need two parents. In our case, Jane was a happy addition for all involved. It seemed, though, that Penelope was not happy that the girls enjoyed their time with us. Increasingly, she put barriers between them and us so it was harder and harder to spend time with my kids.

Penelope filed several court applications during these years, all meant to decrease or eliminate my, and Jane's, involvement in my children's lives. In fact, Penelope had made applications to the court to relocate back to Manitoba with the girls, which would make seeing my kids even more difficult and infrequent. In early 2013, we decided, in response to all the false allegations my ex continued to lodge against us, to have a home assessment done by a children's behaviour consultant, Lisa St-Laurent. Lisa came to our home several times over a one-month period for a total of 10 hours, observing the girls and their interactions with us. After the assessment was completed, Lisa wrote a report of her findings.

At the time of Lisa's home visits with us, Karmen was 10; Gracelyn 8. She used play therapy with the girls, both kids together and also independently. Lisa's subsequent report of May 7th stated that the children mentioned their mother was "controlling and aggressive." Karmen said she had occasional suicidal thoughts when she was at her mom's house. Gracelyn said her mom called her "dumb" and "stupid", comparing her to other children who were "better". Both girls said they were "scared of mom's temper." Lisa reported her professional opinion that the girls' respective behaviour reflected their home environment. When with their mother, the girls exhibited tantrums, aggression and fighting which was escalating over time. It appeared that mom's behaviour was being mirrored by the girls.

Lisa was "greatly concerned" in her report that the mother's loss of control over her children would result in further physical harm in the form of the girls' becoming depressed and engaging in self-harm. She stated that the girls were experiencing inconsistent and inappropriate parenting by their mother which was already manifesting as self-harm in Karmen and controlling, oppositionally-defiant behaviour in Gracelyn. In contrast, Lisa reported our home to have "a consistently positive moral compass representing safety, love and security".

During conversations between Lisa with Karmen as relayed in the report, my eldest daughter described hanging herself with rope from the ceiling and impaling herself on an iron fence. She detailed her plans for both. Karmen also mentioned that her mom's temper escalated her own aggression. Lisa noticed that Karmen required more stimuli than the average child of her age and demonstrated high pain-tolerance. She intentionally banged her head, punched walls, and engaged in risky behaviours. Karmen believed her sister "hates" her and was favoured by their mother. She said she did not fight with her sister at dad's home because she "feel(s) safe there".

Lisa's report then described Gracelyn as unsettled, hostile and unfocused when she first arrived at dad's from her mother's home, but would soon settle into more positive behaviour showing calm, respect and cooperation once at our place. Gracelyn was afraid of Penelope's temper toward Karmen and said the only thing her mom cared about was her (Penelope's) own cell phone. Gracelyn showed a desire to be knowledgeable about all adult subjects (e.g., *sex!)* and make her own independent decisions. My younger daughter did comment that she liked being with us because we paid her attention, played games with her and did crafts.

Both girls told Lisa that their mom "lies to get dad in trouble. Mom tells me to say things that are not true and records them". There was exact consistency, reported individually and separately, with each girl's recollection of a "choking" incident, where Karmen was apparently restrained inappropriately by Penelope. Both Karmen and Gracelyn expressed on several occasions that they would like to spend more time with me (their dad) and Jane. The report concluded that the children needed to, at the very least, spend half their time with their father and Jane.

It was at this time that Penelope was pulling out all the stops in her quest to assert total control over the girls... and me. On one of our many trips to court, she pushed hard for our family to undergo a Section 8 Parenting Assessment. What this involves is a long process of interviews of both parents by a court-appointed psychologist to determine which parent is better-suited to raise the children. Now by this point, I knew that if my ex-wife pushed hard for anything, it was for nefarious reasons. That feeling was confirmed when Penelope advocated for and even offered to pay for the entire process (despite taking every other opportunity to tell the court that she was destitute) as long as it was performed by Dr. Glenna Luxor. I had no reason to challenge Luxor as the assessor, but knew something felt 'off'. The court agreed with Penelope's choice and even said, "...well, if she (Penelope) is going to pay for it, then let's go with Ms. Luxor." The perceived bias shown was actually put into words, but I was not surprised.

I spent the summer having multiple sessions with Dr. Luxor where I described everything from my upbringing, family history and relationships, early days with Penelope, her history, our marriage and its breakdown, the children, the separation and the numerous false allegations made by Penelope. I laid it all out on the table because I felt this was the first opportunity I had had to truly tell my side of the story. Luxor listened and made notes. As I understood it, the Family Assessment would involve interviews with everyone who played a close and major role in raising the children as well as the children themselves. It turns out that Penelope only had a few sessions while her new partner was never interviewed at all. Jane was only interviewed once for a short while and both girls were only seen briefly as well. The significance of all this would not become apparent until later.

What happened next was a whirlwind that lasted seven days... the toughest seven days of my life.

It wasn't until Friday, November 22 that the report was released to the court. I was unrepresented by this point, but Penelope still had her same lawyer. We were assigned a new judge as the former one had gone on sabbatical. At the same time, Jane was due to give birth any minute to Fionna so, needless to say, this was a very stressful time. I walked into court and the new judge, Justice Hornell, proceeded to go through the Luxor report. I hoped for the best because I felt like I had finally been heard. She then read the report's last four pages which was Luxor's summary. Briefly, it stated that I was going to kill the kids, my ex-wife, my ex-wife's lawyer and then kill myself. I should have my firearms seized and my ex-wife should be given sole custody and all decision-making authority. Also, she should be able to relocate to a place of her choosing and <u>not tell me the location.</u> I was to stay away from any and all places where I might have contact with the girls and/or my ex-wife. Effectively, I was removed from my kids' lives.

The only way I would be given any access to the girls was to go through extensive therapy and then *maybe* I would get supervised visitation. Luxor had sandbagged me and had taken everything I said and twisted it around to make me look like a nut-job. I was gutted and felt like I did that night on the floor of the RCMP detachment...but a million times worse. Justice Hornell seemed genuinely perplexed because, I think, the picture of who I was as presented before her didn't seem to align with the report's claims. She said that she had never seen anything like this in her 30 years on the bench, but she hoped I would understand what she had to do. She also asked me what I had to say. In spite of how I felt, I remained calm and explained how this was all wrong and obviously (to me) had been orchestrated. The one thing I made sure to say was something like this, "My Lady, what this report has done, and now this court is about to do... is kill my oldest daughter. She already has been threatening suicide and I want to make sure it is on the court record." That was it... I had just lost my two children. Jane went into labour that night.

The next day, Fionna was born. My first picture with her has me holding her while sitting in a wheelchair because I could not walk. It honestly felt like someone had driven hot railway spikes through both my feet and my ankles were on fire. I would find out later that this was a gout attack (which I had never had before) brought on by the excruciating stress. While Jane recovered overnight in hospital, I was in agony at home. I had lost two of my kids in one day and gained another one the next day. This should have been a beautiful moment, but it was destroyed. Regardless, the following day I picked up Jane and Fionna to bring them home from the hospital. I requested my mother to help me as I was on crutches. But on the way to the hospital, my cell phone rang.

The voice on the phone said, "Mr. Cooper, my name is Chris Wellin. I am a lawyer and I don't need to solicit clients but I have been told I need to call you." Apparently, a mutual acquaintance had told him of my story. My response was simple and to the point, "Mr. Wellin, I f---ing hate lawyers... I think you guys are corrupt liars." He then said, "Well, so do I." That surprised me so I said, "Okay... then let's talk." I then spent the next 20 minutes giving him a rough breakdown of what had transpired. Mr. Wellin began exclaiming loudly how wrong this whole process had been and why. We agreed to meet the following day for a consultation in his office.

When we had all returned from the hospital on the Sunday, we went to my parents' place to introduce Fionna to my father. Jane, Fionna, and my mother went into the house ahead while I carried the bags on my crutches. Suddenly, out of the darkness two RCMP cruisers appeared and two officers stepped out. I had my suspicions about why they were there. One officer asked me who I was and what I was doing there. I explained who I was, why we were there and whose house this was. They didn't believe me so I invited them inside. I was now, I admit, more than a little pissed-off. I called everyone out to meet the officers, including Fionna... and they suddenly changed their approach as they could see I was telling the truth. The officers explained that they had been called because I was in violation of the EPO put in place when the court took away my kids. But how did the RCMP know I was at my parents' place? Well, it turns out that my parents live on a big loop in our community with their house on one side of the loop and the marital home where Penelope lived with our girls on the other side of the loop... but right beside my parents' house is a guy who goes to the same church as Penelope. He had phoned my ex-wife. I proceeded to blast the two officers for harassing me, destroying yet another 'beautiful' moment, and for being Penelope's "personal Gestapo". They backed off, apologized and left shortly after.

Monday, I went to Chris Wellin's office. While there, I got a call from my mother who told me the RCMP were outside her house. I asked what they wanted and she replied that she had not spoken to them as they were out front on the sidewalk with some weird device. Mr. Wellin decided to call the detachment and spoke to the staff sergeant to get an explanation. The sergeant explained that they were measuring the distance from the marital home to my parents' home using GPS to see if, in fact, I had violated the Protection Order which stipulated that I remain 200 meters away from the marital home. Chris asked him if that was by road or "as the crow flies" because as he put it, "I can assure you my client is not a crow!" They responded that it measured by direct line and the distance between the two properties was 185 meters, so I should turn myself in to be placed under arrest. Long story short: I went on the run for four days, leaving my wife and new baby at home alone while Mr. Wellin tried to get before Justice Hornell to explain and hopefully remedy the situation. That didn't happen until Friday.

Once Justice Hornell learned what had gone on over the past week, she was incensed. She admonished Penelope and her lawyer for "using the Order as a sword instead of a shield". While this all sounded great, at the end of it all, Justice Hornell didn't do anything other than give her a tongue-lashing. Surprise, surprise... she got away with it.

2014

The following summer, we again hired Lisa St.-Laurent to do a follow-up observation of my daughters. We had not been able to increase my parenting time with the girls despite Mr. Wellin's best efforts; the courts preferred "status quo" to "best interests". This time, Lisa came and observed us for 8 consecutive hours. It was the first whole day we had been allowed with my older girls in almost two months. By this time, Jane's and my baby, Fionna, was 8 months old. Lisa reported that both Karmen and Gracelyn seemed "regressive, stressed, and sad". Both girls wanted to spend more time with their baby sister, but said their mom was "not allowing us to visit Dad".

Karmen told Lisa things had gotten worse with her mom. Karmen said she was frustrated because she kept on telling anyone who would listen that she wanted to be with Jane and me, but it hadn't happened. She said she didn't understand why she couldn't stay at our place and sleep in her own room there. Karmen spoke of how Jane helps her with her personal hygiene; Jane helped Karmen with deodorant, her menstrual needs, laundry, and took her to buy a bra as Penelope had refused to do any of those things. My daughter disclosed that she was prevented from visiting us recently because her mom "lied" about having an appointment which conflicted with that. Karmen said her mom told her "I'm your mom and can do whatever I want."

Gracelyn told Lisa she did not remember her from the year before. Lisa was alarmed to find Gracelyn looking pale, sickly, and extremely fatigued. She did not make eye contact with Lisa even once. She said her mom had gotten baptized or "reborn" for some reason but "mom is still making bad choices." Gracelyn said the yelling had stopped at mom's house but with a sarcastic inflection in her voice, then muttered "everything is just jiffy, jiffy, jiffy". She still would not look at Lisa. Gracelyn said she "cry(ies) into my pillow" because she's frustrated. She loves her baby sister and misses her dad and the family at my house. In one conversation, Gracelyn told Lisa how she had begun to harm herself. She had taken a very fine-point pen and engraved her own arm while alone in her room at Penelope's.

Both girls also now told Lisa that they were not allowed to play outside, nor call on friends, while at their mother's house. They said being at mom's was "like being in jail." There are alarms and cameras for "security" around Penelope's house. Other comments and behaviours the girls reported to Lisa were similar to those from the previous year. Lisa reported that both girls had regressed and showed significantly more stress than was evident in 2013.

As she had in 2013, Lisa again reported our home environment as cohesive, respectful and loving. She noted that I (and Jane) "expressed overwhelming concern for his girls' futures and was more than willing to get everything in place to ensure their success by implementing appropriate support, counseling, and extracurricular activities". Even with this updated report from respected children's behaviour consultant, Ms. St.-Laurent, the Family Law courts denied me more parenting time and left my kids at the mercy of a mentally unstable, but nevertheless custodial, parent.

2015

Jane and I decided to file an application to gain more parenting time and have appropriate support implemented to help my two elder daughters. We had run out of other options. Although we had next to no money left due to ongoing legal and mental-health consultant fees, there seemed no other way to get help for my kids. Fionna was doing great, but she also missed her big sisters.

All the while, Mr. Wellin soldiered on, as he understood our situation. He was a dad himself and had single-handedly raised his son. He was also a former high-school teacher. He did a lot of background research and contacted experts to provide reviews of a so-called report by Ms. Glenna Luxor (*see also* Chapter 26: Craig), based on her psychological assessment of myself and Penelope. The report had been damning; Luxor basically accepted all Penelope's allegations about me and ignored her mental instability. My ex-wife's history of anxiety (Penelope herself also claimed to be suffering symptoms of post-traumatic stress disorder or PTSD; now called PTSS) was apparently my fault. The report was poorly written and lacked evidence to back her claims. I, on the other hand, had a valid and evidenced diagnosis of PTSD as a direct result of the legal attack Penelope had waged against me.

Chris Wellin and Jane sought out five experts in parental alienation, child development, mental health, or family dynamics. Summarized comments made by these experts are as follows. Dr. Worcester wrote that Ms. Luxor did not identify that information by the mother (Penelope) under oath was discrepant from that given the assessor; there was no documentation of reasons and rationale for the weighing of information used to form opinions; there was no comment about credibility of conflicting information given by the parents; and though Luxor commented that new information may "strengthen or level" the validity of her opinions in her report, there lacked clarification of what factors might modify her views.

The second expert, Dr. Hansmark, wrote his opinion that as a high-conflict case, assessors must temper their recommendations accordingly. This was certainly not the case with Luxor's report. Again, the contradictory information given by the mother was ignored by the assessor; Luxor failed to acknowledge the existence of the court transcript; the "Family Observation Report" by Lisa St-Laurent was omitted from Luxor's consideration; Luxor's report did not suggest that MMPI-2 RF testing scores were compared to available custody and access norms; and there was a negative spin put on the father's results such that Luxor claimed "he (i.e., I) has thought dysfunction, specifically related to persecutory and paranoid ideation". The close, loving relationships I have with my daughters were, by Luxor, labelled "enmeshment"; my emotions were interpreted as "hostile, vindictive, impulsive and in the right circumstances, violent". Overall, Dr. Hansmark summarized that the treatment of information provided to Ms. Luxor was highly selective and that she made recommendations and predictions that were not clearly supported by her test data or clinical observations.

Dr. Chase opined that Luxor's report did not list the documents she considered and failed to offer any indication of what she found influential in her opinion. She did not clarify how she used the "Quickview Social History" assessment tool. Dr. Chase also noted that this tool is not advised in cases of parental alienation. Luxor showed a "dramatic lack of transparency" by omitting the details of any collateral data collected; the report omitted Ms. St-Laurent as a collateral contact; BASC-2 scores cast doubt on the claim by Luxor that the children had been coached by their father; and there was no indication that Ms. Luxor had any training in violence risk-assessment or the use of risk-assessment tools.

Ms. St-Laurent noted the omission of her own opinion and report in the subsequent report written by Ms. Luxor; findings were extremely one-sided and appeared biased in favour of the mother. It is imperative that the assessor be unbiased; this was not the case in Luxor's report.

Finally, you (*author, Dr. Giancarlo*) reported several other important glaring omissions and misrepresentations in Ms. Luxor's report. After reading court documents, visitation and children's behavioural consultant reports, the bilateral parenting assessment, and affidavits of both parents, you wrote in your report to the court that: Ms. Luxor's report demonstrated a pervasive bias favouring the mother and her anecdotal version of the family's "high-conflict". "Though the children repeatedly state their desire to be with their father, step-mother and baby sister, and in fact, are more cooperative, calm and happy when in their Dad's care, Ms. Luxor dismisses this evidence. Her sweeping negative interpretations about Mr. Cooper (*me*) are personal extrapolations of the psychological test scores." *All data about the father was interpreted by Luxor as negative and dangerous; that about the mother was interpreted as positive and safe.*

In May of 2015, we readied ourselves to again attend court for a trial to finally decide parenting. Prior to this happening, three interesting things occurred, all during a portion of pre-trial preparation called 'Discoveries". Penelope had a new lawyer, Ms. Dyan Castel. During these sessions, each lawyer is supposed to interview everyone who will testify at the trial. First, Ms. Castel "interviewed" me during which she actually attacked my abilities as a father and questioned what I knew about my children's 'special needs'. I answered everything flawlessly and at one point I leaned over the table, looked her in the eye, and said, "I know what you're trying to do here, Dyan... and it's not gonna happen." My session ended right there.

Second, Mr. Wellin interviewed Penelope. He wanted to ask about her past history, which included prostitution, her false allegations of rape and child abuse against me, and her involvement with Glenna Luxor. Magically, once the questioning began, Penelope *pretended to vomit* into a trash can and ran from the room. She refused to return, claiming illness, so that was the end of her interview.

Finally, and most bizarre, Mr. Wellin spent three days examining Glenna Luxor. Suffice it to say it was quite an adventure listening to all the inconsistencies and 'foggy memory' that was claimed by Ms. Luxor. By the end of it all, Luxor became incredibly distressed and seemingly vexed when the things she was saying conflicted with what she had written about me in her report; that which had resulted in my children being taken away. It ended with Luxor admitting that anything she said under oath could *not* be relied upon as the truth! She then excused herself to the hallway to collect herself, and then she rushed back in, attempting to change her testimony! Of course, it was too late and the judge disallowed such a move.

My lawyer, Chris Wellin, along with Dr. Giancarlo, attended my trial hearing. The judge, Madam Justice Ernst, presided. My ex-wife, Penelope, was there as were a few of her supporters, such as Ms. Luxor, Penelope's lawyer Ms. Castel and Ms. Castel's protege (her name escapes me) who was a student-at-law. The opposition began its case by putting Ms. Luxor on the stand and basically had her read her bogus 43-page report for the court record. Castel never asked her to volunteer one bit of new information or opinion. I believe they figured their report was all that was needed. Next, Ms. Castel put Penelope on the stand where she testified that I am a bad person and she was *so* afraid of me. Oddly though, her entire testimony was about her feelings about me and how they affected her. Never once did she make any negative claims against me as a Dad; she even extolled my virtues as a father to my girls. It was very strange, but that was the end of Day One of the trial. The next day was our turn to cross-examine Ms. Luxor and Penelope.

Day Two began with Ms. Castel coming to the lectern in the courtroom where she said good morning to the judge and proceeded to burst into hysterical tears! She claimed that apparently her sister had cancer and that "...I just cannot be here right now and I need to be with her!" It was such a poor acting job that painfully obvious to me that it was staged, but here is the thing: A lawyer is an officer of the court and the court expects him or her to be truthful, so the court takes them at their word when issues come up. Mysteriously, Jane, Dr. Giancarlo, and I, had seen Ms. Castel enter the courthouse only minutes earlier, at which time she seemed jovial and well, chatting with colleagues and Security on her way up to the courtroom. Justice Ernst, nonetheless, complied with Castel's request and the hearing was shut down for the day. Let's just say that I think Castel missed that day in law school when ethics was taught. I would see another example of this acting a few months later.

Day Three began much the same as Day Two, except that Ms. Castel was absent. Instead, her protege intern acted on her behalf. Shortly after approaching the lectern, Castel's intern grabbed a nearby trash pail, hid down low behind the lectern and began to gag; it appeared *she* was vomiting (sound familiar?). Since Dr. Giancarlo was sitting in the gallery behind me, she observed that, in fact, Penelope's lawyer stand-in was *not* vomiting. This event was also witnessed by Mr. Wellin and me, who looked at each other, absolutely dumbfounded! Others in the courtroom must have also witnessed the intern's charade. Castel's intern then requested that the judge adjourn the proceedings until the following day, citing her "sudden illness" as the reason. Apparently, that apple didn't fall far from the tree. I was livid, but remained calm and silent.

Since two days of a scheduled 5-day trial had now been wasted, Judge Ernst declared that there was no point in continuing since there was insufficient time to get all arguments heard. It was obvious to me and everyone on my side of the courtroom that this entire 'dog and pony show' had been orchestrated by design to simultaneously prevent us from bringing the huge problems that we had learned in Discoveries to the court and also make sure that we could not finish the trial. You see, you have to wait a very long time to get a 5-day block of time on the court calendar. The judge recognized this and directed us to spend the remaining time we had trying to come to some parenting arrangement between Penelope and me. Of course, I knew that was impossible because if we had been able to do that before now, we wouldn't be in the court house watching the grossest obstruction and miscarriage of justice I had ever heard of.

Once we had reached an impasse, the judge gave us an interim decision based on what had happened and what she knew thus far. In short, she awarded 50/50 custody. It had taken almost three years, many sleepless nights and thousands of dollars, but I finally had my girls back! Once the words left the judge's mouth, I collapsed at the table and burst into uncontrollable tears for the second time since this nightmare began. The judge asked me why I was tearful during the proceedings to which I responded "I just miss my girls, Your Honour". She seemed quite surprised that I, painted by faulty assessments and false allegations, would be emotional about my daughters' well being. It seemed pretty clear to me that she had a preconceived bias against me, despite five expert opinions and all other evidence to the contrary. The judge granted me equal time with the girls, and I was ecstatic. I knew, however, that this mess would continue as long as Penelope was mentally unhealthy. Justice Ernst rescheduled us to finish the trial in October.

October arrived and we were fully prepared to finally complete what we had been waiting years for. The same cast of characters (except for the intern) returned to the courtroom. Ms. Castel began again, but this time she had a different approach. She informed the court that she could no longer continue with this trial as she had seen her doctor who informed her that she has "situational anxiety". Justice Ernst, visibly annoyed, asked Castel if she would be shutting down her entire legal practice due to this obviously debilitating health condition. Ms. Castel stated that wouldn't be happening... it was only *this* case that was causing her so much angst. Again, the court has to take lawyers at their word, so that was the end of our rescheduled trial. My mouth dropped open. It is my belief that Castel wanted off this file as she realized what we were going to be asking, how bad the result would be for her client and it was going to be a "loser-case" for her. She did nothing during her entire involvement other than to obstruct and delay my case and it still disgusts me. Ms. Castel still practices today. Since trial was no longer possible, the judge basically forced us into an informal trial with no transcript of proceedings and no appeal option... called a Judicial Dispute Resolution (JDR). I was against this option for exactly those reasons: no record and no appeal, but regardless, we were scheduled for January of 2016.

2016

The JDR process was pretty uneventful over all. It was a 3-day process in meeting rooms of the court house. Penelope had a new lawyer (who was referred to her by Dyan Castel... surprise?). Justice Ernst went back and forth between each of the parties and also had some sessions with both of us together in one room. Right out of the gate, the judge said, "Look...it's gonna be 50/50 custody no matter what. So let's not waste any time on rehashing the past." I liked that. Over all, it was confirmed 50/50 custody, with Penelope given decision-making authority about the girls' medical matters while I was to have authority over all things educational. Child support was calculated and that was pretty much it. The judge sent us on our way with the cautious optimism that we would be able to finally move on with our lives, but she was obviously skeptical. I knew it wouldn't work because this whole process, as screwed up and dysfunctional as it was, had not worked out well for Penelope. My ex-wife did not want me having *any* custodial rights, never mind decision-making authority. But otherwise, most of 2016 passed by with only minor skirmishes between us. The following year, however, would see Penelope return to her old ways.

2017

Up until this point, the girls had been following a week on/week off parenting regime, but as they got older, Karmen in particular absolutely detested going back to Penelope's house after spending a week with us. She had stated early on that she wanted to stay with us and, in her opinion, the week with the person who ruined her family was torture. All along, Penelope had tried to convince the girls, Glenna Luxor (with whom she succeeded), and the court that it was me who was alienating the kids against her. That was naturally the best plan for her to follow since she was causing the estrangement herself. The thing is, the girls are not dummies and children as a whole, certainly are not, in my opinion. They see what is going on, they learn, they know. So as the girls got older they formed their own opinions. Gracelyn was content to go back and forth because she didn't want to upset the apple cart of "peace' after so many years of turmoil, but Karmen had had enough.

At this point, the girls were both riding a bus to their school and one day, Karmen just decided that she was not going back to Penelope's house on that bus. Instead, she took another bus back to our house. Of course, this set off a plethora of texts from Penelope about how I was violating the court Order and not respecting her parenting time, etcetera, etcetera. The next day, Penelope waited at the school and dragged Karmen, despite her protests (in front of her friends which was incredibly embarrassing to a 14-year-old), forcing her into her truck. The next days and weeks were spent playing a game of cat and mouse between Karmen and Penelope with Karmen hiding out in various rooms and bathrooms of the school, refusing to come out until Penelope had left the school property. She would then call us to pick her up or walk to a friend's house.

By this time, it had gotten physical between my daughter and her mother and I pleaded with Penelope to stop. Her reaction was to blame me and demand that I force Karmen to go back to her house. I felt torn because of the court order, but short of putting my child in a head-lock and dragging her kicking and screaming… and I was not going to do that… she was not going to go. I asked the school for help, but the staff could only do so much. I wrote to the court in February asking for help and direction, but received none. It was now the depths of winter and Penelope was still staking out the school, trying to figure out which room Karmen was hiding in or which door she would sneak out of so as to prevent her from getting on that bus to my house. Karmen got to the point where she swore she would run through the bushes and over the hills through the deep snow to my house. This would involve a five kilometer walk along a very busy highway. Karmen's behaviour had to stop before something terrible happened to her. Eventually, Penelope gave up her daily 'stake-out" to prevent Karmen riding the bus to our house. I assumed my ex-wife would, as a result, drag me back to court to deal with this and I was right. We were scheduled for June 29.

It had been approximately 18 months since the JDR and the court wanted an update. At the June court-hearing, Penelope's new lawyer, Ms. Forman-Nittleson, started off with four lies in under 10 minutes. Apparently, I had been threatening all my kids' teachers and doctors that I would sue if any of them talked to Penelope. I had also totally turned the girls against Penelope. These were just a couple of Ms. Forman-Nittleson's claims. Unfortunately, Justice Ernst bought all of it and spent the next 20 minutes tearing a strip off me despite my evidence to the contrary. I finally got her to listen when I presented letters from the school principal stating that he was under no threat of legal action from me. My lawyer, Mr. Wellin, then reminded the judge that we had written to the court for help and direction when this whole issue around Karmen began. But now, Justice Ernst said she forgot who Karmen was and then also forgot that we had written at all. This gave me pause considering how much involvement with, and knowledge of, our family she had. Regardless, she finally agreed to speak with the children even though she had refused to do so during the JDR process. It was my belief that more than enough time, effort and money had been wasted on the 'he said/she said' that had been going on for years.

The next day, I brought Karmen in to see Justice Ernst while Penelope sat there with Gracelyn. Justice Ernst introduced herself to the girls and took each separately into a meeting room. Each conversation, one with Karmen and one with Gracelyn, was recorded, but we were not allowed a copy of the transcripts. The judge spoke to the girls for 20 and 25 minutes, respectively, and then she did something interesting. Once we (Penelope, her lawyer, Jane, the girls, my lawyer and I) were all back out in the hallway, Justice Ernst asked Jane to take both girls home. I thought that curious because if Karmen or Gracelyn had said something bad about me, there was no way the court would send them home with my wife. Jane left with the girls and the rest of us were told to go into a courtroom. When Justice Ernst entered, she had a very different tone from the day before, which had been 'fire and brimstone'. She was very quiet and subdued. She explained that she would not change anything. I was frustrated because of all that had been said to Judge Ernst over time, but my lawyer enlightened me: He felt she had heard the truth and thus did not force Karmen to go back to Penelope.

2018

This year has been an important one for our family. The older girls are doing much better. Fionna is a joy and all three girls love each other so much. Karmen has been living with us ever since January 2017 and just recently, despite Penelope's repeated attempts to vilify me and force Karmen to return to her, the court confirmed that Karmen is old enough to decide for herself, at 15 years of age, where she wants to live and the court "will not enforce the parenting of the Binding JDR Order". Oddly enough, this past September, Gracelyn also made the decision to live with us. Penelope doesn't seem to be as interested in fighting this decision. Accordingly, I am attempting to remedy the obvious imbalance in child support, as I am still struggling financially since this nightmare began almost nine years ago.

Over all, my impression of the Family Justice system is that it is broken beyond repair. Most of the people who are involved: judges, lawyers, psychologists, parenting coordinators, and the rest, are morally-corrupt, liars, manipulators, incompetent or a combination of some or all of these traits. Sadly, there are seemingly very few exceptions…. but there *are* some. I used to fall into that trap of saying things like "Dads get screwed, the court always believe the mothers" or things like that. But if you look deep enough, you will find mothers who also find themselves faced with an ex-husband similar in behaviour to my ex-wife. I am not saying the sexes are equally represented; definitely not. But I cannot say unequivocally that one sex *always* wins. The system is set up so that whichever party is either willing to lie the most, or has the most money to pay for lawyers and psychologists to lie, is the one who wins. When I hear the phrase, "...in the best interests of the child", it disgusts me. It is the biggest lie of all.

BEST INTERESTS OF THE CHILD

CHAPTER 32

BEST INTERESTS OF THE CHILD: PREVENTION AND RESOLUTION OF PARENTAL ALIENATION

The 30 stories in this book are heartbreaking, but do provide some hope for the eradication of parental alienation. Each targeted dad or mom proposed workable ideas that contributed to a model for healthy families despite separation and divorce. This model is a two-pronged approach that focuses first on *preservation of the parent-child relationship*; the second prong concerns *interventions to resolve established parental alienation*. Since this form of child abuse is often subtle in the beginning, increasing in intensity and harm over time, prevention is the best course of action. Intervention, where necessary, must occur as soon as possible after the separation of the parents. Currently, the family law system in Canada pits one parent against the other in a bid for revenge, maximum child and spousal support, and as an unwitting means of enabling one parent's mental illness, usually narcissism. Parents who were once couples remain, nonetheless, married to their children for life. It is their responsibility, duty, and awesome privilege to give their children the best tools they possibly can for a happy, productive, life. This is *real* parenting.

Preserving the Parent-Child Relationship:

When a couple decides to end their relationship, there is an inevitable emotional toll. The partnership may have fractured and finally dissolved over many years, but nevertheless, the decision to terminate the "couple identity" is extremely difficult. Mental health experts rate separation and divorce as a major cause of anxiety and depression in adults[1]. There are solemn statistics indicating that children are negatively affected by their parents' split. Physically, emotionally, and educationally, a child of divorce fares worse on average than his or her peers living in intact families[2]. But what if the parents are dysfunctional? If one or both parents is abusive or neglectful, a child may be better off without that parent, or even, in extreme cases, without both parents[3]. But good parents remain so despite their separation or divorce from the other parent. The negative effects of the parental split can be mitigated to a large degree when both parents continue to be regular, active influences in their children's lives. In some cases, children's wellbeing may improve after their parents' relationship ends, if the parental dynamic was high-conflict or otherwise dysfunctional… but the parenting was positive.

When a couple divorces, *equal parenting must be the default law.* Whether the couple relationship was high-conflict or not, children will continue to benefit most from equal time with each parent. This fact is well documented internationally, as well as in Canada[4]. If either parent, grandparent, other extended family member or other knowledgeable (about that couple's relationship-dynamic history) party suspects that the parents may be unable to co-parent effectively, that party may… no, *will…* red-flag that set of parents by reporting it to an Access Enforcement Program (AEP), to be mandated by the federal government and established by provincial or regional governments. The AEP will act as triage of that high-conflict family, assigning a long-term parenting coordinator to manage the family until all its children reach the legal age of majority.

Should the parents experience extraordinary circumstances, such as non-traditional work schedules or travel, they will negotiate, in person with the parenting coordinator as advisor and facilitator, a parenting schedule that reflects the equal-parenting mandate. For example, if one parent works regular days Monday to Friday while the other has a four-day-on, four-day-off work schedule, a meeting of both parents together with the parenting coordinator will yield a parenting plan that averages equal parenting time over any given year. The key to this proposal is a parenting coordinator who is committed (or removed and replaced) to the default equal-parenting law.

Where either parent does not cooperate with negotiations or comply with 50/50 parenting time, the parenting coordinator will prescribe mental health assessments for *each* of the parents. The assessments will be done by a registered psychologist or psychiatrist who has proven expertise in personality disorders and parental alienation. The assessment analysis will be scrutinized by the parenting coordinator who will then either assign the child(ren) to the temporary full-time custody of the mentally-healthy and cooperative parent or maintain the 50/50 parenting time schedule with provisions for enforcement and parenting supervision, for the noncompliant parent.

The triage will ensure both parents are present for their children with stable parenting, continuity and regularization of care in the long-term. When a parent is remiss in his or her responsibilities, mental-health professionals will provide the analytical tools through assessment to find out why. Where a parent is found to be mentally ill or otherwise incapable of parenting, the parenting coordinator will provide a treatment and reunification plan for that parent and his or her children.

Shared parenting will be ordered by the parenting coordinator only when default equal-parenting is not possible without undue hardship on one or both parents. Remember that equal parenting time is in the *best interests of the child.* But if one parent lives and works overseas, and this pattern was established prior to the parental split, it may be necessary that his or her children spend more than 50% of their time with the parent who still resides in the marital family home, and/or in proximity to the children's school and support network of peers and extended family. In order to have shared parenting ordered, the parent wishing to *reduce* his or her parenting time from 50% will have to provide solid evidence proving that they are not able be an equal-time parent.

Child maintenance (i.e., support) will be directly tied to access. That is, Maintenance Enforcement programs (e.g., MEP, in Alberta, Canada) will be connected to Access Enforcement programs (AEP, proposed). By so doing, there will no longer be a financial reward for a parent who convinces a family court to order him or her primary custody or day-to-day care of their children. Since a child will enjoy maximum time with *each* of his or her parents, child maintenance will be determined using a table based on the *net income difference* between the parents; the recipient will be the lower-income parent. For example, if Mom earns $100,000 while Dad earns $30,000 gross annually, then child maintenance with 50/50 parenting time will be based on a net of $70,000, paid by Mom to Dad. Each parent will be required to work full-time equivalent hours at a paid job(s). Daycare and other extraordinary costs will be paid by the same ratio as per the income of each parent. Should a parent claim inability to work due to mental illness, such as depression or anxiety, that parent will be triaged into appropriate care to become a productive wage earner.

In all cases where the parents are capable without history of abuse or neglect, the *children's right to both parents equally* shall be the overarching priority in all parenting decisions. Success in preserving the parent-child relationship will be dependent on an amended Divorce Act, which reflects and enforces equal parenting, and the child's right to both parents. Default equal parenting will be a powerful disincentive for parental alienation. Though this model cannot prevent a disgruntled parent's motivation to retaliate against or hate their former partner, it will effectively remove the current court-ordered and societally sanctioned reward system for parental alienation.

Interventions to Resolve Established Parental Alienation:

In order to resolve parental alienation, a thorough understanding of this family dysfunction is necessary. All mental health and legal professionals and educators must be able to identify at-risk children and refer their parents to the triage system (see AEP above, in *Preserving the Parent-Child Relationship*) for high-conflict families. The family law system must be restricted to its mandate, which is to apportion and dispense justice. Lawyers and judges are not mental health experts, nor do they usually have experience in the convolutions of parental alienating behaviours. All interventions must be determined and carried out by mental health professionals. Legal professionals will manage cases by writing court orders for division of property and parenting-time schedules. They will also provide enforcement orders on mental-health-expert directives where noncompliance by an alienator is a factor.

Where parental alienation has been determined, the alienator will immediately be triaged to commence assessment and treatment for their mental illness[5]. The child subjected to a parent alienator will be temporarily removed from that parent and placed into temporary primary care of the targeted parent. That child, however, will continue to have regular, but always professionally supervised, visits with the alienator during that parent's treatment. Supervision will prevent the continued brainwashing of the child against their targeted parent. At such time in future, following treatment for their mental illness, that the alienator is assessed to have become a competent parent, he or she will be reintegrated with their child for increased amounts of parenting time. Eventually, that parent may be able to earn unsupervised parenting time up to the 50/50 ratio mandated by the Divorce Act.

If the alienator is found mentally competent, but vengeful or greedy instead, the court will provide a parenting/access enforcement order *paid for by the alienator*, not the targeted parent. Real penalties, such as fines and even jail time, will be automatically imposed by law should the alienator renege on their parenting schedule, or be found noncompliant with terms of the parenting plan. For example, no parent shall discuss their legal case or show documents that in any way involve the child in its parents' dysfunction. Children subjected to the alienation campaign of their parent will *no longer* be regarded as "Mature Minors", a current legal designation in Alberta, which deems minors capable of making their own decisions regarding their care. The *mature minor* label has been the cause of countless brainwashed (PAS) children being released into the primary, even sole, custody of their dysfunctional, harmful parent. These PAS children on average are 14 years old[6]. They are making decisions that remove them from the care of their capable, productive parent with devastating consequences for life.

Legal involvement in parental alienation cases has been abysmal, almost universally, to date. The family law system in Canada actually enables and ramps up existing alienation while increasingly clogging the courts with unnecessary and harmful hearings and trials[7]. But due diligence and accountability in family law could be regulated by a third party, one that has no special interest in decisions and remedies. A system rewarded in billable hours precludes timely and effective outcomes for children and whole families.

Parental alienation can be eradicated. The 30 stories found in these pages are a devastating violation of human rights; especially, the rights of the child to a happy, healthy, and productive life. Clear, decisive and enforced laws that designate both parents as equally crucial will erase the lion's share of custody battles, including potential ones. Timely and appropriate interventions by mental health experts, where necessary, will thwart any campaign of parental alienation already in progress. For the sake of the children.

1. Rotermann, 2007.
2. McLanahan, 1994; Wallerstein, Lewis & Blakeslee, 2000.
3. Condrell, 2006.
4. Harman & Biringen, 2016; Kruk, 2013;
   Neilson, 2018; Warshak, 2010; 2014.
5. Warshak, 2010; Childress, 2015.
6. College of Physicians & Surgeons of Alberta, 2015.
7. Giancarlo & Rottmann, 2015.

Appendix: Families in this book

Participant Number	Sex of Participant	Participant's Relation to Children	Total # of Children	Ages of Female Children	Ages of Male Children
1	M	Father	2	20	16
2	M	Father	2	12	10
3	F	Paternal Grandmother	2	16	12
4	M	Paternal Grand father	2	13, 11	N/A
5	M	Father	3	12, 8	6
6	M	Father	1	N/A	8
7	M	Father	1	12	N/A
8	M	Father	2	N/A	13, 8
9	M	Father	1	15	N/A
10	M	Father	3	14, 12	10
11	M	Father	3	22	20, 16
12	M	Father	2	N/A	16, 10
13	M	Father	1	18	N/A
14	M	Father	1	17	N/A
15	F	Mother	7	16, 14, 12	23, 21, 20, 17
16	M	Father	1	8	N/A
17	F	Mother	2	21	23
18	M	Father	3	16, 12	12

19	F	Mother	5	16, 13	22, 20, 18
20	M	Father	2	N/A	7, 2
21	F	Father	1	13	N/A
22	F	Stepmother	2	3	1
23	M	Father	3	23,11	20
24	M	Father	1	N/A	13
25	M	Father	4	18, 16	20, 12
26	M	Father	3	7	9, 6
27	M	Father	3	23, 19, 17	N/A
28	M	Father	3	11, 8	9
29	M	Father	4	19, 16, 11	22
30	M	Father	3	12, 10, 1	N/A

Bibliography

Alberta Health Services (2011). Consent to Treatment/Procedure(s), Minor/Mature Minors (Document #PRR-01-03).

Alberta Human Services (May 7, 2013). Overview: An introduction to Bill 25, Children First Act. http://humanservices.alberta.ca/documents/overview-children-first-act.pdf

Alberta Justice and Solicitor General. (2018). Maintenance Enforcement Program. Retrieved from https://justice.alberta.ca/programs_services/mep/Pages/default.aspx

American Psychiatric Association. (2013). *Diagnostic and statistical manual of mental disorders (DSM-5)*. Arlington, VA: American Psychiatric Publishing.

Baker, A. (2005a). Parental alienation strategies: A qualitative study of adults who experienced parental alienation as a child. *American Journal of Forensic Psychology, 23*(4), 41-63.

Baker, A. (2005b). The long-term effects of parental alienation on adult children: A qualitative research study. *American Journal of Family Therapy, 33*(4), 289-302.

Baker, A. (2006). Patterns of parental alienation syndrome: A qualitative study of adults who were alienated from a parent as a child. *The American Journal of Family Therapy, 34*, 63-78.

Baker, A. (2007). *Adult children of parental alienation syndrome: Breaking the ties that bind.* New York: W. W. Norton.

Baker, A. (2010). Adult recall of Parental Alienation in a community sample: Prevalence and associations with psychological maltreatment. *Journal of Divorce & Remarriage, 51*(1), 16-35.

Baker, A., & Darnall, D. (2006). Behaviors and strategies employed in parental alienation: A survey of parental experiences. *Journal of Divorce & Remarriage, 45*(1/2), 97-124.

Bala, N. (2011, July). Parental alienation & the child's voice in family proceedings. Presentation at the Nuffield Foundation, London.

Bala, N. (2012, February). Parental alienation, contact problems and the family justice system. Presentation at Australian Institute of Family Studies, Melbourne, Australia.

Bala, N., & Bailey, N. (2004). Enforcement of access and alienation of children: Conflict reduction strategies and legal responses. *Canadian Family Law Quarterly, 23,* 1-61.

Bala, N., et al. (2003). Shared Parenting in Canada: Increasing Use But Continued Controversy. *Family Court Review, 55*(4), 513-530.

Bala, N., Fidler, B.J., Goldberg, D., & Houston, C. (2007). Alienated children and parental separation: Legal responses in Canada's family courts. *Queen's Law Journal, 3333,* 79-138.

Bala, N., Hunt, S., & McCarney, C. (2010). Parental Alienation: Canadian Court cases 1989-2008. *Family Court Review, 48*(1), 164-179.

Baris, M.A., Coates, C.A., Duvall, B.B., Garrity, C.B., Johnston, E.T., & LaCrosse, R.R. (2000). *Working With High-Conflict Families of Divorce: A Guide for Professionals.* Northvale, NJ: Jason Aronson Publishers.

Bernet, W. (2010). *Parental Alienation: A new diagnosis for DSM-5 and ICD-11.* Springfield, IL: Charles C. Thomas.

Bernet, W. (September, 2010). *Parental Alienation: A new diagnosis for DSM-5 and ICD-11.* EFCAP Conference Power-point presentation: Basel, Switzerland.

Birmbaum, R., & Bala, N. (2010). Towards a differentiation of high conflict families: An analysis of social science and Canadian case law. *Family Court Review, 48*(3), 403-416.

Blankenhorn, D. (1995). *Fatherless America: Confronting our most urgent social problem.* New York: Basic Books, Harper Collins.

Bow, J.N., Gould, J.W., & Flens, J.R. (2009). Examining parental alienation in child custody cases: A survey of mental health and legal professionals. *American Journal of Family Therapy, 37*(2), 127-145.

Bowlby, J. (1969). *Attachment.* New York: Basic Books.

Braver, S.L., & O'Connell, D. (1998). *Divorced dads: Shattering the myths.* New York: Jeremy P. Tarcher, Putnam.

Bricklin, B., & Elliot, G. (2006). Psychological test-assisted detection of parental alienation syndrome. In R.A. Gardner, S.R. Sauber, & D. Lorandos (Eds.), *The international handbook of parental alienation syndrome: Conceptual, clinical and legal considerations* (pp. 264-275). Springfield, IL: Charles C. Thomas.

Brown, G.A. (2013). *Ideology and dysfunction in family law: How courts disenfranchise fathers.* Calgary, CAN: Canadian Constitution Foundation and the Frontier Centre for Public Policy.

Bruch, C. (2001). Parental alienation syndrome and parental alienation: Getting it wrong in child custody cases. *Family Law Quarterly, 35,* 527-552.

Burrill, J. (2006). Descriptive statistics of the mild, moderate, and severe characteristics of parental alienation. In R.A. Gardner, S.R. Sauber, & D. Lorandos (Eds.), *The international handbook of parental alienation syndrome: Conceptual, clinical and legal considerations* (pp. 49-55). Springfield, IL: Charles C. Thomson.

Canada Divorce Act. (1985, Last amended on May 31, 2007). Retrieved May 31, 2013, from http://laws-lois.justice.gc.ca/PDF/D~3.4.pdf

Canadian Judicial Council. (2018). Canadian Judicial Council. Retrieved May 2, 2018, from https://www.cjc-ccm.gc.ca/english/eindex_en.asp

Cartwright, G.F. (1993). Expanding the parameters of parental alienation syndrome. *Journal of Family Therapy, 21*(3), 205-215.

Cartwright, G.F. (2006). Beyond the parental alienation syndrome: Reconciling the alienated child and the lost parent. In R.A. Gardner, S.R. Sauber, & D. Lorandos (Eds.), *The International Handbook of Parental Alienation Syndrome: Conceptual, Clinical, and Legal Considerations* (pp. 286-291). Springfield, IL: Charles C. Thomas.

CBS New York. (2018). Lawyer: Cops Failed To Enforce Court Order Night Before Toddler Died. Retrieved from: https://newyork.cbslocal.com/2018/04/30/mamaroneck-police-child-gabriella-maria-boyd/amp/

Central Ohio Parental Alienation (2018) Resources for Parental Alienation. Retrieved from: https://sites.google.com/site/centralohiopa/parental-alienation-resources#Parental-Alienation-Murder-News

Centre for Education on Parental Alienation. (n.d.). Retrieved June 1, 2013, from www.takeaction.org.

Children's Law Reform Act, R.S.O., 1990 ch. C 12 s. 36.

Childress, C.A. (2015). *An attachment-based model of parental alienation: Foundations*. Claremont, CA: Oaksong Press.

Childress, C.A. (2016). *The narcissistic parent: A guidebook for legal professionals working with families in high-conflict divorce*. Claremont, CA: Oaksong Press.

Cicchetti, D., Cummings, E.M., Greenberg, M.T., & Marvin, R. (1990). An organizational perspective on attachment beyond infancy: Implications for theory, measurement, and research. In Greenberg, M.T., Cicchetti, D., & Cummings, E.M. (Eds.), *Attachment in the preschool years: Theory, research and intervention* (pp. 3-50). Chicago: University of Chicago Press.

Clawar, S.S., & Rivlin, B.V. (1991). *Children held hostage: dealing with programmed and brainwashed children*. Chicago, Ill.: Section of Family Law, American Bar Association.

College of Physicians & Surgeons of Alberta. (December 2015). Consent for Minor Patients - Advice to the Profession. *The Messenger*, (220), 5.

Condrell, K. N. (2006). *The unhappy child: what every parent needs to know*. Amherst, N.Y.: Prometheus Books.

Deadbeat dad (n.d.). *Dictionary.com Unabridged*. Retrieved May 31, 2013, from http://dictionary.reference.com/browse/Deadbeat_dad

Dircksen, B. (2012). *Parental alienation is abuse: One mother's nightmare and her fight for justice*. USA: Outskirts Press.

Divorce Law in Canada, Library of Parliament. (2008, September 30, p.25). Retrieved May 31, 2013 from http://www.parl.gc.ca/content/lop/researchpublications/963-e.pdf

Drozd, L.M., & Olesen, N.W. (2004). Is it abuse, alienation, and/or estrangement? A decision tree. *Journal of Child Custody*, *1*(3), 65-106.

Drozd, L.M., & Olesen, N.W. (2010). Abuse and alienation are each real: A response to the critique of Joan Meier. *Journal of Child Custody, 7*(4), 253-265.

Dunne, J., & Hedrick, M. (1994). The parental alienation syndrome: An analysis of sixteen select cases. *Journal of Divorce & Remarriage, 21*(3/4), 21-38.

Ellis, E. (2007). A stepwise approach to evaluating children for parental alienation syndrome. *Journal of Child Custody,* 4(1/2), 55-78.

Equitable Child Maintenance & Action Society (n.d.). Retrieved June 1, 2013, from www.ecmas.org.

Everett, C.A. (2006). Family therapy for parental alienation syndrome: Understanding the interlocking pathologies. In R.A. Gardner, S.R. Sauber, & D. Lorandos (Eds.), *The international handbook of parental alienation syndrome: Conceptual, clinical and legal considerations* (pp. 228-241). Springfield, IL: Charles C. Thomas.

Family Law Act Alberta. (2003, Statutes of Alberta, Chapter F-4.5, current as of July 1, 2012). Retrieved June 1, 2013, from http://www.qp.alberta.ca/documents/Acts/F04P5.pdf

Family Law Act British Columbia. (British Columbia, Bill 16-2011, in force as of March 18, 2013). Retrieved June 1, 2013, from http://www.leg.bc.ca/39th4th/3rd_read/gov16-3.htm

Fathers 4 Justice. (n.d.). Retrieved June 1, 2013, from www.fathers-4-justice.org.

Fathers' Rights Movement, The. (February 6, 2014). *A Father's Suicide Note*. Retrieved from: https://www.facebook.com/Fathers4kids/posts/707829342580894:0

Fidler, B., & Bala, N. C. (2013). *Children who resist post-separation parental contact: a differential approach for legal and mental health professionals*. New York: Oxford University Press.

Fidler, B., Bala, N., Birnbaum, R., & Kavassalis, K. (2008). *Challenging issues in child custody disputes.* Toronto, Canada: Carswell Thomson.

Fidler, Bala, & Saini. (2005). The psychological functioning of alienated children in custody disputing families: An exploratory study. *American Journal of Forensic Psychology, 23*(3), 39-64.

Fidler, Bala & Saini. (2013) p.66 – Table 3.2 Stages of the Alienation Process adapted from Clawar & Rivlin (1991).

For the Sake of the Children: Report of the Joint Committee on Child Custody and Access. (1998). Parliament of Canada. Retrieved May 31, 2013 from http://www.parl.gc.ca/HousePublications/Publication.aspx?DocId=1031529&Language=E

Freud, A. (1966). *The ego and the mechanisms of defense.* New York: International Universities Press. (Original work published 1936).

Friedlander, S., & Walters, M.G. (2010). When a child rejects a parent: Tailoring the intervention to fit the problem. *Family Court Review, 48*, 97-110.

Garber, B.D. (2007). Conceptualizing visitation resistance and refusal in the context of parental conflict, separation, divorce. *Family Court Review, 45*(4), 588-599.

Garber, B.D. (2011). Parental alienation and the dynamics of the enmeshed dyad: Adultification, parentification and infantilization. *Family Court Review, 49*(2), 322-335.

Gardner, R. A. (1970). *The Boys and Girls Book About Divorce.* N.Y: Bantam Books.

Gardner, R. A. (1985). Recent trends in divorce and custody litigation. *Academy Forum, 29*(2), 3-7.

Gardner, R. A. (1992a). *The parental alienation syndrome: A guide for mental health and legal professionals.* Cresskill, NJ: Creative Theraputics, Inc.

Gardner, R.A. (1992b). *True and false allegations of child sexual abuse.* Cresskill, NJ: Creative Theraputics, Inc.

Gardner, R.A. (1998a). Recommendations for dealing with parents who induce a parental alienation syndrome in their children. *Journal of Divorce and Remarriage, 28,* 1-21.

Gardner, R.A. (1998b). *The parental alienation syndrome* (2 ed.). Cresskill, NJ: Creative Therapeutics Inc.

Gardner, R.A. (2001). Should courts order PAS children to visit/ reside with the alienated parent? A follow-up study. *American Journal of Forensic Psychology, 19*(3), 61-106.

Gardner, R.A. (2002). Denial of the parental alienation syndrome also harms women. *The American Journal of Family Therapy, 30,* 191-202.

Giancarlo, C., & Rottmann, K. (2015). Kids come last: The effect of family law involvement in parental alienation. *The International Journal of Interdisciplinary Social Sciences: Annual Review, 9(1),* 27-42.

Goldberg, L. (1997). A psychoanalytic look at recovered memories, therapists, cult leaders, and undue influence. *Clinical Social Work Journal, 25*(1), 71-86.

Government of Canada, Department of Justice. (2017). The Federal Child Support Guidelines: Step-by-Step. Retrieved from: http://www.justice.gc.ca/eng/rp-pr/fl-lf/child-enfant/guide/step3-etap3.html

Grant, M. (March 10, 2017). "'Vile and evil': Alberta mother who drugged, burned 9-year-old daughter gets life sentence." Retrieved from: https://www.cbc.ca/news/canada/calgary/laura-coward-sentence-amber-lucius-1.4019195

Grych, J., & Fincham, F. (1999). Marital conflict and children's adjustment: A cognitive contextual framework. *Psychological Bulletin, 108*, 267-290.

Harman, J.J., & Biringen. (2016). Parents acting badly: How institutions and societies promote the alienation of children from their loving families. Fort Collins, CO: The Colorado Parental Alienation Project, LLC.

Hoppe, C., & Kenney, L. (1994, August). A Rorschach study of the psychological characteristics of parents engaged in child custody/visitation disputes. Paper presented at the 102nd Annual Convention of the American Psychological Association, Los Angeles.

Hoyert, D.L., Kochanek, K.D., & Murphy, S.L. "Deaths: Final data for 1997." DHHS Publication no. (PHS) 99-1120. National Vital Statistics report 47, no. 19 (1999): 1-104.

Jaffe, P., Ashbourne, D., Mamo, A., & Martinson, D. (2010, June). Assessment and differential interventions for alienating allegations: Punishing parents or helping children (mp3 file). Paper presented at the Association of Family and Conciliation Courts (AFCC) 47th Annual Conference, Denver, CO. Available from http://afccnet.org/ConferencesTraining/AFCCConferences

Jenuwine, M.J., & Cohler, B.J. (1999). Major parental psychopathology and child custody. In R. Galatzer-Lary & L. Kraus (Eds), *The scientific basis of child custody decisions* (pp. 285-318). New York: Wiley.

Johnson, C.F. (2007). Muchausen syndrome by proxy (MSBP) section of Abuse and neglect of children. In RM Kliegman et al., eds., Nelson Textbook of Pediatrics, 18th ed., pp. 182–184. Philadelphia: Saunders Elsevier.

Johnston, J.R. (1993). Children of divorce who refuse visitation. *Non-residential parenting: New vistas in family living* (pp. 109-135). Newbury Park, CA: Sage Publications.

Johnston, J.R. (2003). Parental alignments and rejection: An empirical study of alienation in children of divorce. *Journal of the American Academy of Psychiatry and Law, 31*, 158-170.

Johnston, J.R. (2005). Children of divorce who reject a parent and refuse visitation: Recent research and social policy implications for the alienated child. *Family Law QUarterly, 38*, 757-775.

Johnston, J.R., & Campbell, L.E. (1988). *Impasses of divorce: The dynamics and resolution of family conflict.* New York: The Free Press.

Johnston, J.R., & Goldman, J.R. (2010). Outcomes of family counseling interventions with children who resist visitation: An addendum to Friedlander & Walters. *Family Court Review, 48*, 112-115.

Johnston, J.R., & Kelly, J.B. (2004). Rejoinder to Gardner's "Commentary on Kelly and Johnston's 'The alienated child': A reformulation of parental alienation syndrome". *Family Court Review*, 42(4), 622-628.

Johnston, J.R., Roseby, V., & Kuehnle, K. (2009). Parental alignments and alienation: Differential assessment and therapeutic interventions. In Johnston, J.R., Roseby, V., & Kuehnle, K. (Eds), *In the name of the child: A developmental approach to understanding and helping children of conflicted and violent divorce* (2 ed., pp. 361-389). New York: Springer Publishing Company.

Johnston, J.R., Walters, M.G., & Friedlander, S. (2001). Therapeutic work with alienated children and their families. *Family Court Review. Special issue: Alienated Children of Divorce, 39*, 316-333.

Johnston, J.R., Walters, M.G., & Olesen, N.W. (2005a). Clinical ratings of parenting capacity and Rorschach prtocols of custody-disputing parents: An exploratory study. *Journal of Child Custody, 2*, 159-178.

Johnston, J.R., Walters, M.G., & Olesen, N.W. (2005b). Is it alienating parenting, role reversal or child abuse? A study of children's rejection of a parent in child custody disputes. *Journal of Emotional Abuse, 5*(4), 191-218.

Johnston, J.R., Walters, M.G., & Olesen, N.W. (2005c). The psychological functioning of alienated children in custody disputing families: An exploratory study. *American Journal of Forensic Psychology*, 23(3), 39-64.

Kelly, J.R., & Johnston, J.R. (2001). The alienated child: A reformulation of parental alienation syndrome. *Family Court Review. Special Issue: Alienated children in divorce, 39*(3), 249-266.

Kernan, G.L., & Weissman. (1989). Increasing rates of depression. *Journal of the American Medical Association, 261*, 2229-35.

King, S. M. (2011). *Parental alienation: Understanding a dark truth.* Canada: Blurb.

Klayman, J., & Ha, Y. (1987). Confirmation, disconfirmation, and information in hypothesis testing. *Psychological Review, 94*, 211-228.

Kopetski, L. (1998a). Identifying cases of parental alienation syndrome; Part I. *The Colorado Lawyer, 29*(2), 65-68.

Kopetski, L. (1998b). Identifying cases of parental alienation syndrome: Part II. *The Colorado Lawyer, 29*(3), 63-66.

Kopetski, L. (2006). Commentary: Parental alienation syndrome. In R.A. Gardner, S.R. Sauber, & D. Lorandos (Eds.), *The international handbook of parental alienation syndrome: conceptual, clinical and legal considerations* (pp. 378-390). Springfield, IL: Charles C. Thomas.

Kruk, E. (1998). *The Divorcing Family: Section D. Child-parent relationships must survive divorce. Meeting #27, Vancouver.* In For the Sake of the Children. Retrieved May 31, 2013, from http://www.parl.gc.ca/HousePublications/Publication.aspx?DocId=1031529&Language=E&File=30#Children

Kruk, E. (2008). Child Custody, Access and Parental Responsibility: The search for a just and equitable standard. Father Involvement Research Alliance. Retrieved on May 31, 2013 from http://www.fira.ca/cms/documents/181/April7_Kruk.pdf

Kruk, E. (2013). *The equal parent presumption: social justice in the legal determination of parenting after divorce.* Montreal, CAN: McGill-Queen's University Press.

Kvale, S. (1996). *Interviews: An introduction to qualitative research interviewing.* Thousand Oaks, CA: Sage.

L.L. v. C.M. (2013). Family Law Ontario. CarswellOnt 3560.

Lamb, M.E. (2000). The history of research on father involvement. *Marriage and Family Review, 29*(2-3), 23-42.

Lampel, A.K. (1996). Children's alignment with parents in highly conflicted custody cases. *Family & Conciliation Courts Review, 34*(2), 229-239.

Lee, S.M., & Olesen, N.W. (2001). Assessing for alienation in child custody and access evaluations. *Family Court Review, 39*(3), 282-298.

Lowenstein, L.F. (1998). Parental alienation syndrome: A two-step approach toward a solution. *Contemporary Family Therapy, 20,* 505-520.

Lowenstein, L.F. (2005). Attempting to solve child contact disputes (Recent research). *Parental Alienation (Syndrome) - Dr. L.F. Lowenstein - Southern England Psychological Services.* Retrieved January 26, 2013, from http://www.parental-alienation.info/publications/36-atttosolchicondisrecres.htm

Lowenstein, L.F. (2006). The psychological effects and treatment of the parental alienation syndrome worldwide. *The international handbook of parental alienation syndrome: Conceptual, clinical and legal considerations* (pp. 292-301). Springfield, IL: Charles C. Thomas.

Lund, M.A. (1995). A therapist's view of parental alienation syndrome. *Family & Conciliation Courts Review, 33*(3), 308-316.

Maintenance Enforcement Act. (2000, Revised Statutes of Alberta, Chapter M-1, current as of October 1, 2011). Retrieved May 31, 2013 from http://canlii.ca/en/ab/laws/stat/rsa-2000-c-m-1/latest/rsa-2000-c-m-1.html

McLanahan, S., & Sandefur, G. (1997). *Growing up with a single parent: What hurts, what helps.* Cambridge, MA: Harvard University Press.

Millar, P. (2009). *The best interests of children: An evidence-based approach.* Toronto, CAN: University of Toronto Press.

National Association of Parental Alienation Specialists. (n.d.) *Litigating Family Law Cases with Parental Alienation on Demand Course.* Retrieved from http://nationalassociationofparentalalienation-specialists.com/

Neilson, L.C. (2018). *Parental alienation empirical analysis: Child best interests or parental rights?* Fredericton, CAN: Muriel McQueen Fergusson Centre for Family Violence Research and Vancouver The FREDA centre for research on violence against women and children.

Otis, M.R., & Warshak, R.A. (2010, June). Family Bridges: Principles, procedures and ethical considerations in reconnecting severely alienated children with their parents (mp3 file). Workshop presented at the Association of Family and Conciliation Courts (AFCC) 46th Annual Conference, Denver, CO. Available from http://www.afccnet.org/ConferencesTraining/AFCCConferences

Parental Alienation Awareness Organization. (n.d.). Retrieved June 1, 2013 from www.paawareness.org

Parliament of Canada. (1998). For the Sake of the Children: Special Joint Committee on Child Custody and Access Report. Retrieved from: http://www.parl.ca/DocumentViewer/en/36-1/SJCA/report-2

Province of Alberta. (2013). *Legal Profession Act: Revised Statutes of Alberta 2000,* L-8. Alberta Queen's Printer.

Provincial and Territorial Maintenance Enforcement Programs, Department of Justice Canada. (2013). Retrieved June 1, 2013 from http://www.justice.gc.ca/eng/fl-df/enforce-execution/provpro.html

Racusin, R., & Copans, S. (1994). Characteristics of families of children who refuse post-divorce visits. *Journal of Clinical Psychology, 50,* 792-801.

Rand, D. (1997a). The spectrum of parental alienation syndrome. Part I. *American Journal of Forensic Psychology, 15*(3), 23-52.

Rand, D. (1997b). The spectrum of parental alienation syndrome. Part II. *American Joural of Psychology, 15*(4), 39-92.

Rand, D. (2011). Parental alienation critics and the politics of science. *The American Journal of Family Therapy, 39,* 48-71.

Rand, D., & Rand, R. (2006). Factors affecting reconciliation. In R.A. Gardner, S.R. Sauber, & D. Lorandos (Eds.), *The international handbook of parental alienation syndrome: Conceptual, clinical and legal considerations* (pp. 195-208). Springfield, IL: Charles C. Thomas.

Rand, D., Rand, R., & Kopetski, L. (2005). Spectrum of parental alienation syndrome part III: The Kopetski follow-up study. *American Journal of Forensic Psychology, 23*(1), 15-43.

Rand, D. & Warshak, R. (2008). Overview of the family workshop-2.2. Unpublished manuscript.

Richardson, P. (2006). *A Kidnapped Mind: A mother's heartbreaking story of parental alienation syndrome.* Toronto, ON: Dundurn Press.

Rotermann, M. (2007). Marital breakdown and subsequent depression. *Health Reports, 18(2),* 33-44.

Royal College of Pediatrics and Child Health (October 2009; Review date: October 2012). Fabricated or Induced Illness by Carers (FII): A Practical Guide for Paediatricians.

Siegel, J., & Langford, J. (1998). MMPI-2 validity scales and suspected parental alienation syndrome. *American Journal of Forensic Psychology, 16*(4), 5-14.

Stahl, P. (1999). *Complex issues in child custody evaluation.* New York: Sage Publications.

Steinberger, C. (2006). Father? What Father? Parental alienation and its effect on children. *NYSBA Family Law Review, 38*(1), 10-24.

Stoltz, J.A.M., & Ney, T. (2002). Resistance to visitation: Rethinking parental and child alienation. *Family Court Review, 40*(2), 220-231.

Sullivan, M.J. (2004). Ethical, legal and professional practice issues involved in acting as a psychologist coordinator in child custody cases. *Family Court Review, 42*(3), 567-582.

Sullivan, M.J., & Kelly, J.B. (2001). Legal and psychological management of cases with an alienated child. *Family Court Review, 39,* 299-315.

Turkat, I.D. (1994). Child visitation interference in divorce. *Clinical Psychology Review, 14,* 737-742.

Turkat, I.D. (1999). Divorce-related malicious parent syndrome. *Journal of Family Violence, 14*, 95-97.

United Nations Convention on the Rights of the Child. (1990). Retrieved May 31, 2013, from http://www.ohchr.org/en/ProfessionalInterest/pages/crc.aspx

United Nations Convention on the Rights of the Child. (October 5, 2012, p. 8, #35). Consideration of reports submitted by States parties under article 44 of the Convention. Committee on the Rights of the Child, sixty first session. Concluding observations: Canada. Retrieved May 31, 2013, from http://www2.ohchr.org/english/bodies/crc/docs/co/CRC-C-CAN-CO-3-4_en.pdf

Vassiliou, D., & Cartwright, G. (2001). The lost parents' perspective on parental alienation syndrome. *American Journal of Family Therapy, 29*(3), 181-191.

Waldron, K.H., & Joanis, D.E. (1996). Understanding and collaboratively treating parental alienation syndrome. *American Journal of Family Law, 10*, 121-133.

Wallerstein, J.S., & Blakeslee, S. (1989). *Men, women, and children a decade after divorce*. New York: Ticknore & Fields.

Wallerstein, J.S., & Blakeslee, S. (2001). *The unexpected legacy of divorce: The 25-year landmark study*. New York: Hyperion.

Walsh, R., & Bone, M. (1997). Parental alienation syndrome: An age-old custody problem. *The Florida Bar Journal, 71*(6), 93-96.

Ward, P., & Harvey, J. (1993). Family Wars: The alienation of children. *New Hampshire Bar Journal, 34*(1), 30-40.

Warshak, R.A. (2001). Current controversies regarding parental alienation syndrome. *Journal of Forensic Psychology, 19*(3), 29-59.

Warshak, R.A. (2003). Payoffs and pitfalls of listening to children. *Family Relations, 52*(4), 373-384.

Warshak, R.A. (2006). Social science and parental alienation: Examining the disputes and the evidence. In R.A. Gardner, S.R. Sauber, & D. Lorandos (Eds.), *The International Handbook of Parental Alienation Syndrome: Conceptual, Clinical, and Legal Considerations* (pp. 352-371). Springfield, Il: Charles C. Thomas.

Warshak, R.A. (2010). Divorce poison new and updated edition: How to protect your family from bad-mouthing and brainwashing. New York, NY: HarperCollins.

Warshak, R.A. (2010). Family Bridges: Using insights from social science to reconnect parents and alienated children. *Family Court Review, 48,* 48-80.

Warshak, R.A. (2014). Social science and parenting plans for young children: A consensus report. *Physchology, Public Policy, and Law, 20(1),* 46-67.

Warshak, R. A. Family Bridges (para.1). Retrieved June 4, 2013 from http:warshak.com/services/family-bridges.html.

Weir, K. (2011). High-conflict contact disputes: Evidence of the extreme unreliability of some children's ascertainable wishes and feelings. *Family Court Review, 49,* 788-800.

Weissman, M.M., Wolk, S., Goldstein, R.B., Moreau, D., Adams, P., Greenwald, S., Klier, C.M., Ryan, N.D., Dahl, R.E., & Wichramaratne, P. (1999). Depressed Adolescents Grown Up. *Journal of the American Medical Association, 281*(18), 1707-13.

Woodall, K., & Woodall, N. (2017). *Understanding parental alienation: Learning to cope, helping to heal.* Springfield, IL: Charles C Thomas.

Acknowledgements

First and foremost, I am most grateful to **Kara Rottmann Lawrence**, my research assistant, technical writer, draft editor and support in so many other ways. Your commitment, vision and talent are... well, stellar. A huge thank you to Dr. Natasha Kutlesa for our brain-storming sessions, your advice, understanding of children and young adults, and for sharing the trails with me on our many stress-relieving outdoor adventures in the mountains. Dr. Nancy Arthur, mentor and friend, you guided me more than you know and I am humbled by your wisdom.

To all thirty dads and moms whose stories are retold in this book, on behalf of myself and families everywhere, thank you for your bravery in vulnerability. For exposing your experiences, demonstrating your steadfast commitment to your children in the face of such adversity, and patiently waiting for the publication of this book, I am forever grateful.

Drs. Edward Kruk, Jennifer Harman, and Dan McKinnon were instrumental through your professional expertise in research, with clients, students, and in your own personal lives.

George Piskor provided me with statistics about parents who have wrongfully lost their children and the children themselves, all casualties of a broken family law system. Ginger Gentile, director and creator of the soon-to-be-released documentary film, *Erasing Family*, it is an absolute pleasure to work with you toward this exciting goal. Nothing short of a major public worldview shift is needed to give children back their parents. The above people and myriad others have devoted their careers to achieving this end. Parental alienation has touched us all. Thank you for helping turn tragedy toward an eventual resolution.

David Howatt, David Kenwright, Marica Ceko, Dr. Yasmin Dean, Sophie Timmerman, Lin Harrison, and Jeri Lynne Erickson, your insights, life experiences, family values and friendship have helped shape my ideas over many years. To my children, Devon and Carmen, I am so proud of who you are and what you represent. Your dad and I, though divorced, raised you as best we could and you are a testament to the fact that equal-parenting works. Thanks also to my parents, committed in love and for life to each other and all five of their children. Finally, to my partner, Bert, your love, empathy, commitment to family and frankly, your extraordinary mental and physical strength beyond adversity, make you my guiding light.

CPSIA information can be obtained
at www.ICGtesting.com
Printed in the USA
LVHW112322220121
677273LV00002B/22

9 780228 808053